SCATTERED AND FUGITIVE THINGS

BLACK LIVES IN THE DIASPORA: PAST / PRESENT / FUTURE

BLACK LIVES IN THE DIASPORA: PAST / PRESENT / FUTURE

Black Lives in the Diaspora: Past / Present / Future is a book series that focuses on Black lives in a global diasporic context. Published in partnership with Howard University's College of Arts and Sciences and Columbia University's African American and African Diaspora Studies Department, it builds on Columbia University Press's publishing programs in history, sociology, religion, philosophy, and literature as well as African American and African Diaspora studies. The series showcases scholarship and writing that enriches our understanding of Black experiences in the past, present, and future with the goal of reaching beyond the academy to intervene in urgent national and international conversations about the experiences of people of African descent. The series anchors an exchange across two global educational institutions, both located in historical capitals of Black life and culture.

Aïssatou Mbodj-Pouye, *An Address in Paris: Emplacement, Bureaucracy, and Belonging in Hostels for West African Migrants*

Vivaldi Jean-Marie, *An Ethos of Blackness: Rastafari Cosmology, Culture, and Consciousness*

Imani D. Owens, *Turn the World Upside Down: Empire and Unruly Forms of Black Folk Culture in the U.S. and Caribbean*

Gladys L. Mitchell-Walthour, *The Politics of Survival: Black Women Social Welfare Beneficiaries in Brazil and the United States*

James V. Koch and Omari S. Swinton, *Vital and Valuable: The Relevance of HBCUs to American Life and Education*

SCATTERED AND FUGITIVE THINGS

How Black Collectors Created Archives and Remade History

LAURA E. HELTON

Columbia University Press

New York

Columbia University Press
Publishers Since 1893
New York Chichester, West Sussex
cup.columbia.edu

Library of Congress Cataloging-in-Publication Data
Names: Helton, Laura E., author.
Title: Scattered and fugitive things : how Black collectors created archives
and remade history / Laura E. Helton.
Other titles: How Black collectors created archives and remade history
Description: New York : Columbia University Press, [2023] | Series: Black lives in the
diaspora : past / present / future | Includes bibliographical references and index.
Identifiers: LCCN 2023038828 (print) | LCCN 2023038829 (ebook) |
ISBN 9780231212748 (hardback) | ISBN 9780231212755 (trade paperback) |
ISBN 9780231559546 (ebook)
Subjects: LCSH: African Americans—Archives—History. | Archives—United States—
History—20th century. | Archivists—United States—History—20th century. |
African Americans—Intellectual life—20th century. | African American intellectuals—
History—20th century. | African American book collectors—History—20th century. |
African American librarians—History—20th century. | African American historians—
History—20th century. | Libraries—Special collections—African Americans.
Classification: LCC E184.6 .H45 2023 (print) | LCC E184.6 (ebook) |
DDC 026/.3231196073—dc23/eng/20231012
LC record available at https://lccn.loc.gov/2023038828
LC ebook record available at https://lccn.loc.gov/2023038829

Cover design: Elliott S. Cairns
Cover image: Winold Reiss, "The Librarian" (1925), from "Four Portraits of Negro
Women," published in "Harlem: Mecca of the New Negro," special issue of *Survey Graphic*,
March 1925. New York Public Library Digital Collections.

In memory of Meridith, Louise, Lila, and Sophie

It has been a rare intelligence and discriminating judgment and devotion to an increasing purpose that has brought together these books and documents into one body, saving them from the inutility of scattered curios to make of them a profoundly serviceable reference source.

—*Opportunity*, 1926

CONTENTS

ILLUSTRATIONS

ACKNOWLEDGMENTS

This book is about the social life of archives. Each chapter opens not with a bibliophile alone in a library but with an exuberant scene of collaboration or convergence. So, too, has the making of this book—which began nearly twenty years ago—grown out of conversations and communities for which I am deeply grateful.

Every historian owes a debt to archivists, curators, and librarians, but my debts are perhaps more than most, given that this book draws heavily on material not only *in* but also *of* archives: the records of how these remarkable collections came to be. For sharing their expertise and knowledge of institutional histories—or for facilitating access to unprocessed materials—I am especially grateful to Beverly Cook, Joellen ElBashir, Diana Lachatanere, Thai Jones, Megan Mizak, Clifford L. Muse Jr., Tal Nadan, Dana Chandler, and the late Michael Flug. To research this book, I spent time at a more than dozen archives, and I thank the dedicated staff at each one: the Moorland-Spingarn Research Center at Howard University; Vivian G. Harsh Research Collection of Afro-American History and Literature at the Chicago Public Library; Schomburg Center for Research in Black Culture at the New York Public Library; Hampton University Archives; Roanoke Public Library; Tuskegee University Archives; Yale University's Beinecke Rare Book and Manuscript Library; Columbia University's Rare Book and Manuscript Library; Syracuse University's Special Collections Research Center; National Archives for Black Women's History at the Mary McLeod Bethune Council House; Fisk University's Special Collections and Archives; Atlanta University's Archives Research Center at the Robert W. Woodruff Library; and the institutional archives of the New York Public Library, Astor, Lenox and Tilden Foundations. In Roanoke, I am grateful to retired librarian Carla Lewis, and to

Dr. Curtis C. Reeves Jr., Virginia Young Reeves-Schexnider, and Alvin J. Schexnider for sharing their memories of Virginia Young Lee.

At the Schomburg Center in particular, I have been privileged not only to conduct research but also to collaborate over many years with Alice Adamczyk, Angeline Beljour, Cheryl Beredo, Barrye Brown, Rhonda Evans, Steven G. Fullwood, Allison Hughes, Tammi Lawson, Maira Liriano, Christine McKay, Miranda Mims, A. J. Muhammad, and Matthew Murphy—each of whom carries on the legacy of the early twentieth century's Black bibliophiles and collectors. This book took shape in our conversations as much as in any set of manuscripts. I owe special thanks to Diana Lachatanere and Mary Yearwood, who have shared their stories of the Schomburg Center's history, while also urging me to keep looking for elusive pieces of that history. I am grateful to the Home to Harlem team for allowing me to join them in a search for the Schomburg seed library: it has been thrilling to do detective work alongside you.

The idea for this book came into focus when I worked as an archivist of social movements. At the Tamiment Library, which houses the history of American radicalism and trade unionism, I learned that every social movement has its resident documentarian or archivist. As a field archivist in Mississippi, I surveyed civil rights records across the state in the early 2000s, when the still-fraught anniversaries of civil rights landmarks served as daily reminders that archives are always urgent sites of contestation in the present. Those professional experiences shaped my desire to write about the politics of historical recovery, and I thank my colleagues in New York and Mississippi, especially Gail Malmgreen, Diane DeCesare Ross, Clarence Hunter, Minnie Watson, Elaine Owens, Alma Fisher, and Alix Ross. Peter J. Wosh introduced me to archival studies and provided unparalleled support early on.

I began writing elements of this book first in the library and information studies program at Rutgers and then in the PhD program in history at New York University (NYU). At Rutgers, Marija Dalbello introduced me to the field of book history, while Meredith McGill's New Media Literacies Working Group provided a richly undisciplined space for discussion. At NYU, I was profoundly lucky to work with Michele Mitchell, Nikhil Pal Singh, and Elizabeth McHenry, who modeled exacting inquiry in African American history and allowed me to work across the disciplines of history and literary studies. I am also deeply grateful to the mentorship and generosity of Jennifer L. Morgan, who led the Working Group on Slavery and Freedom, and to Lisa Gitelman, Jack Tchen, Michael Gomez, Martha Hodes, Andrew Needham, and Maria Montoya. The insights of those in Nikhil's dissertation group—Thulani Davis, Justin Leroy, Stuart Schrader, Brittany Carter,

Carmen Phillips, and Sam Ng—still shape my thinking. Dylan Yeats has been an inspiration and co-conspirator from the beginning. Mairin Odle has provided every kind of support imaginable—from sharp-witted readings to babysitting. The quartet of Samantha Seeley, Shauna Sweeney, Max Mishler, and Justin Leroy showed me what the combination of intellectual fearlessness and friendship could produce.

At the Carter G. Woodson Center for African and African-American Studies at the University of Virginia, I spent two glorious predoctoral years engaged in collective writing and thinking. I am grateful to Deborah E. McDowell for her intrepid leadership and to the other fellows for their comradeship and close readings, especially Nicole Burrowes, LaTaSha Levy, Celeste Day Moore, Ellen Tani, David Morton, Ava Purkiss, Kwame Otu, and Taneisha Means. I am also grateful to Krystal Appiah, Ethelene Whitmire, and Maurice Wallace, who served as seminar critics and provided game-changing feedback on early chapters-in-progress. A postdoctoral fellowship from the Center for Humanities and Information (CHI) at Pennsylvania State University provided two years of additional support, and I thank Anatoly Detwyler, Bonnie Mak, Sara Grossman, Autumn Womack, John Russell, Shirley Moody-Turner, Samuel Frederick, Michele Kennerly, and Eric Hayot for the rigor of their interdisciplinary engagements. CHI also supported a manuscript workshop, and I thank Lisa Gitelman for pointing me in the right direction as I figured out how to turn many years of research into something resembling a book.

My initial research on Dorothy Porter Wesley was made possible by a Bibliographical Society of America (BSA)–Mercantile Library Fellowship in North American Bibliography in 2012. More recently, I am grateful to Erin McGuirl for the work she has done at the BSA to honor Porter's legacy as a bibliographer. My research on Virginia Lee at the Roanoke Public Library was supported by a Summer Stipend from the National Endowment for the Humanities (NEH). As I began to complete the manuscript, I was fortunate to be in residence at the Schomburg Center for Research in Black Culture in 2019–2020 as an NEH/Mellon fellow in the Scholars-in-Residence Program. My thanks to Brent Hayes Edwards, who stewards the program with such intellectual generosity, and to my fellow scholars—Neil Clarke, Jennifer DeClue, Tobi Haslett, Jarvis McInnis, Selena Doss, Tashima Thomas, Jaime Coan, and Maya Harakawa—who convened vibrant weekly discussions and kept them going on Zoom in the early months of COVID. I am also grateful for the very skilled research assistance of Naomi Lorrain.

At the University of Delaware (UD), I am a member of a community dedicated to the study of material culture. I express boundless thanks to Sarah

Wasserman for being a mentor and friend extraordinaire, and to Curtis Small, Jesse Erickson, Martin Brückner, Julie McGee, Carol Rudisell, and Derrick Spires for the many rich collaborations we have undertaken. I appreciate the unflagging support of my chairs in English and History, John Ernest and Alison Parker, and the warm welcome I received from colleagues in both departments as well as in Africana Studies. I am especially indebted to the mentorship of Emily Davis, Ed Larkin, Cheryl Hicks, Julian Yates, Gabrielle Foreman, Tim Spaulding, and Stephanie Kerschbaum. My fellow assistant professors—especially Keerthi Potluri, Ben Stanley, Davy Knittle, Kisha Porcher, Dael Norwood, and Tiffany Barber—made difficult years so much better. Several graduate students at UD have served as research assistants for this project; I thank Darbyshire Witek, Petra Clark, Jessica Thelen, and Demetra McBrayer for their careful work. Doctoral students Monet Lewis-Timmons and Melissa Benbow arrived at UD just a year after I did, and I am sure I have learned as much from them as they have from me. I am grateful to the entire staff of Morris Library and especially Megan Gaffney, who went to heroic lengths to secure access to research materials during closures in 2020–2021. UD supported the research for this book through a College of Arts and Sciences Faculty Fellowship, a General University Research award, the Charlotte and Herman Glotzer Award for Scholarship on the Study of Ideas, and a manuscript workshop facilitated by the English department. The Center for Material Culture Studies, the English department, and the College of Arts and Sciences also provided a subvention to support publication of this book; my thanks to Associate Dean Wendy Bellion and Interim Dean Debra Hess-Norris for being such champions of the humanities.

Beyond any one program or university, it has been a gift to have sustained conversations with the amazing group of scholars and curators who share my interests in the legacy of Black bibliophiles and librarians. We have convened at conferences, shared archive stories, and launched projects together—and I look forward to continuing to learn from Melanie Chambliss, Rafia Zafar, Jean-Christophe Cloutier, Vanessa Valdés, Derrick Spires, DeLisa Minor Harris, Barrye Brown, Cheryl Beredo, Jeremy Braddock, Ellen Gruber Garvey, Jacqueline Goldsby, Meredith McGill, Elizabeth McHenry, Margarita Castromán Soto, Frances Negrón-Muntaner, Kinohi Nishikawa, and Dorothy Berry. Barbara D. Savage and I have long had a mutual interest in the intellectual history of women at Howard University, so I deeply appreciate that she agreed to read the manuscript of this book and provided sage guidance to help me complete it. Brent Hayes Edwards has read versions of this project at every stage of its making—from the seminar room of the Center for Cultural Analysis at Rutgers to the scholars' center at the Schomburg Center—and he has my profoundest thanks for more than a decade of sharing ideas. I am also honored to have learned from the late Pellom McDaniels III and the late Cheryl A. Wall. All of us who work in these fields miss them and owe them so much.

For opportunities to present work in progress from this book, I thank David Squires at the University of Louisiana at Lafayette; John Pollack at the University of Pennsylvania's Material Texts Seminar; Lisa Forrest and the Card Catalog Series at Hamilton College; Karla Nielsen at Columbia University's Book History Seminar; Carla Peterson and the Women Writing Women's Lives Seminar at the City University of New York; and Adrienne Davis at Washington University in St. Louis's Law, Identity, and Culture Initiative.

Some elements of the introduction are adapted from an essay that first appeared in *Against a Sharp White Background: Infrastructures of African American Print* (2019), edited by Jonathan Senchyne and Brigitte Fielder and published by the University of Wisconsin Press. I am grateful for permission to reprint portions of chapter 1 that first appeared as "Schomburg's Library and the Price of Black History" in *African American Review* 54, nos. 1–2 (Spring/Summer 2021), published by Johns Hopkins University Press and St. Louis University. I am likewise grateful to reprint portions of chapter 4, which originally appeared as "On Decimals, Catalogs, and Racial Imaginaries of Reading" in *PMLA* 134, no. 1 (January 2019), published by the Modern Language Association.

At Columbia University Press (CUP), Philip Leventhal has been a sharp and patient editor, and this book is better for his insight. The Black Lives in the Diaspora Series—a joint project between CUP and Howard University—is an appropriate home for this book, which draws on material from archives at both universities. I am grateful to the series editors and to the two anonymous readers for CUP whose incisive reports helped me to refine the arguments of this book. My thanks also to Monique Laban, Kathryn Jorge, Cathy Hannabach, Melanie Petcoff, and Ben Kolstad for steering this project through production.

Writing a book is often solitary, but it has not been lonely thanks to the company of Lee Houck and Kip Rathke, Lassie Krishnaswamy and Erica Gilles, Helena Miller and Dara Raspberry, Kate Atkins and Ali Kronley, Janet Paskin and Jen Friedman, Angela Stuesse and Tutu Alicante, Jennifer Miller and Clare Dolan, the Cartwright-Frazee family, Megan Pruiett, and porches and backyards full of State College and West Philly neighbors. Nicole Burrowes and Paula Austin have been friends, writing partners, sounding boards, and sources of much-needed late-night laughter and commiseration for many years.

My parents, Linda and George Helton, continually invent new ways to be generous and kind-hearted. They were my first teachers, and they are still. I also owe warm thanks to Hilary and Rachel Cohen and to the late Michael Cohen, who never waned in his enthusiasm for talking about collections and who gifted me a copy of Alberto Manguel's *The Library at Night* at an opportune moment.

Amy Cohen is simultaneously the most adventurous and the most sensible person I know. Every day I am amazed and profoundly grateful for her company, ideas, and love—whether in Brooklyn or Berlin, Mississippi or Philadelphia. A fierce activist, she has made our family one in which organizing and writing somehow fit together. Although my slow work on this project has tried her patience, she has always cleared space for it. Our older daughter, Hazel, likes to say that she has written *many* books in the time it has taken me to complete one; the happiest moments I have spent writing were those when she was working alongside me. Zinnia, our younger daughter, taught me about dragons, and the happiest moments I have spent *not* writing were the ones reading stories with her. (My thanks, too, to the pandemic poodle Molly, who fiercely guarded the box of microfilm in my office and took me on many slow walks.)

I write in memory of four book women. At kitchen tables, on road trips, and in the margins of the books we shared, my sister Meridith taught me about the history of labor, civil rights, and radicalism. Although she never knew it, I followed in her footsteps when I chose to study history. My grandmother Louise was the first bibliophile I knew; her small house was a sanctuary of books. My other grandmother, Lila, worked as a school librarian and liked to tell people that my research had "something to do with the 900s" (a wry Dewey decimal reference). Finally, I was privileged to know Sophie Degan—for whom poetry meant survival—in the final two decades of her life. I give thanks for what each of these women gave to the world.

SCATTERED AND FUGITIVE THINGS

INTRODUCTION

Value, Order, Risk: Experiments in Black Archiving

What makes a collector collect? . . . For me books are friends. They are people.

—Charles Blockson, "Black Giants in Bindings"

"Dear Friend and Confrère": In 1937, the poet and novelist Claude McKay wrote to a group of fellow authors, inviting them to help launch a "democratic association of Negro writers." He proposed forming an organization that would honor "our writers of the past" while fostering the ambitions of a new generation.[1] In fellowship, he argued, they could experiment with the creative possibilities of "group culture"—expressions of Black life forged through ties to a global African diaspora and a long "struggle for existence" in the Americas.[2] As McKay searched for the right words to convey this vision of collectivity, his mind wandered to the archive created by his friend Arturo (Arthur) Schomburg. Harlem's famous bibliophile, and McKay's longtime interlocutor, Schomburg had spent a lifetime gathering "scattered and fugitive things" to make a collection, "from all parts of the world," of "books and documents dealing with the Negro."[3] This collection took shape first in Schomburg's home and then at the 135th Street branch of the New York Public Library (figure 0.1). Like many writers of the New Negro movement, McKay had relied on Schomburg's collection in practical ways, borrowing books or asking the "Sherlock Holmes of Negro History" to look things up for him.[4] In this letter, however, he turned to Schomburg's collection not as a source but as a prototype.

FIGURE 0.1 Readers in the Schomburg Collection at the 135th Street Branch Library in Harlem, 1930s. Arthur A. Schomburg is visible at the curator's desk (*far back right*). Photographer unknown.

Source: New York Public Library Archives, New York Public Library Digital Collections. Copyright New York Public Library.

"We think," he mused, "that it is possible to establish through intellectual fellowship something like a living counterpart of the unparalleled Schomburg Collection of Negro books."[5]

"A living counterpart of the unparalleled Schomburg Collection of Negro books." Why would McKay reach for this simile, intimating that a group of people could be "something like" a gathering of texts? The surprising premise that appears in McKay's letter—that people might organize themselves along the lines of a library or archive—evokes the unexpected ways that paper collections served as vital sites of Black intellectual and social life: not simply storehouses of the past, but experiments—in imagination, curation, and study—that also shaped the present. For McKay and others, Schomburg's archive was both a repository and a possibility. As a physical space, it was a magnet for Harlem's readers and was "extensively used" by those who convened to draw on its resources.[6] But it was equally an object of theorization and imagination. Contemporary commentators called the collection "hallowed ground" and saw in its size and complexity an ever-evolving representation of global Black history and culture.[7] At the time of McKay's epistle, Schomburg's collection had brought together more than thirteen thousand items in at least eight languages: books, pamphlets, letters, poems, sermons, minutes, addresses, and documents by "well-known and little-known persons" alike. In an era that often treated blackness as unlettered and absent from history, the effect of this abundance was "strange magic," McKay wrote.[8] The possibility of Black archives captivated the imaginations of bibliophile, poet, and public alike.

Following McKay, this book explores the significance of archives to Black social and intellectual history between 1910 and 1950—a period when generations of Black memory work coalesced into a frenetic moment of institution-building. In the great libraries of the North, in small repositories in the South, and across the campuses of Black colleges and universities, there arose an inaugural and enduring network of collections dedicated to documenting the history of Black life. Schomburg and a cohort of other bibliophiles, scrapbook makers, and librarians took up a long-standing appeal by Black thinkers to "devote more time to finding out the true history of the race, and [to] collecting in some museum the relics that mark its progress."[9] They salvaged records, opened their collections to readers, and cast preservation as a political act. The institutions they created have supported over a century of inquiry. Indeed, in the United States, most repositories still used today to study Black life and history have roots in this one remarkable period. As important as that legacy is, the origin of these archives—and what they meant to those who built them—is a story in and of itself.[10] *Scattered and Fugitive Things* tells that story.

This book continues a project begun in 1983, when Howard University's Moorland-Spingarn Research Center—one of the most important collections devoted to the study of Black life—hosted a groundbreaking convening called "Black Bibliophiles and Collectors: A National Symposium." Inspired by Elinor Des Verney Sinnette and W. Paul Coates, both members of the Moorland-Spingarn staff, the symposium explored the "lives, careers, and contributions of black bibliophiles to American society."[11] The resulting volume of essays, *Black Bibliophiles and Collectors: Preservers of Black History*, was the first to survey this field as a whole, augmenting studies that focused on the biographies of individual collectors. In their introduction, Sinnette, Coates, and fellow curator Thomas C. Battle called their work "a beginning—an effort that must be reflected upon, absorbed, and vigorously pursued anew."[12] *Scattered and Fugitive Things* revives this call to study Black bibliophiles and the collections they built. Conjoining African American and archival studies, this book chronicles six of the collectors who founded the field of Black archives. It illuminates the intellectual stakes and gendered politics of acquisition, arrangement, and classification—the labors that made Black archives possible. It also underscores the social life of collecting by reflecting on the communities that used and defended these collections. And finally, it unpacks the critical inquiry at the heart of collecting: What should a Black archive comprise?

The existence of these collections at the beginning of the twentieth century was hard won. They took shape at a moment when there was "no national interest in Negro books," when scholarly and popular accounts cast doubt on the idea of Black history, and when the very act of reading could require the exercise of fugitivity.[13] Schomburg, for example, grew up in Puerto Rico under Spanish colonial rule, when it was considered seditious to read the works of his favorite revolutionary poet, Rafael Serra. He recalled reading Serra "under darkness" as a boy in the late 1880s.[14] He migrated to the United States in the 1890s and came of age just as the country's first state archives emerged at the turn of the century to enshrine Confederate memory in Southern capitals.[15] As an adult, he honed his collecting habit during the nadir, when the United States policed its color line with such ferocity that eight million African American readers could not enter their hometown libraries.[16] These forms of suppression gave rise, Schomburg argued, to a collecting imperative forged by empire and exclusion: "we find the Negro," he proclaimed, compelled by "the *very pressure of the present* to become the most enthusiastic antiquarian of them all."[17] With each acquisition—including a copy of the once-banned Serra that he had read furtively in his youth—Schomburg rebuked prohibitions on Black knowledge. Against the pressure of negation, he and his generation of collectors defiantly created archives.

Defiantly, but also exuberantly: if Black archiving in the New Negro era was a form of protest, it was equally a site of invention and pleasure. "Schomburg has a penchant for books, rare books," the *Negro World* reported admiringly in 1922, "and if he should suddenly die with his overcoat on, it will be found that the pockets will contain catalogues from London, Leipsic, Italy, England and the U.S.A., all marked up by this old bookworm at the places where there is any reference to the African or Negro."[18] This vignette captures both the zeal of Schomburg's "penchant" and the community's esteem for his obsessive venture. From cabinets stuffed with ephemera, to library stacks crowded with tomes, Schomburg and other Black collectors created abundance where others saw absence. By the 1930s, their collecting pursuits had produced a stunning plenitude of texts—not only of books but also of "pamphlets, posters, prints, autographs, mezzotints, manuscripts, newspaper clippings" and more.[19] The scale and scope of their work sparked new experiments in ordering Black knowledge. Collections became vibrant spaces of intellectual life: places where Black thinkers invented taxonomies, created study groups, and reshaped racial imaginaries. As McKay's simile makes clear, then, the early twentieth century's founding generation of Black collectors did more than simply bequeath to future scholars a storehouse of research materials. As a practice of abundance, archiving was alive in the Black present, a site of intellectual risk and political possibility.

ASSEMBLING A TRADITION FROM SCATTERED AND FUGITIVE THINGS

Black history can be found everywhere, and many types of archives document blackness. In the United States, these include government repositories, such as the Library of Congress, which counts among its voluminous collections of Black culture and politics the Freedmen's Bureau records and the papers of Booker T. Washington, Mary Church Terrell, and Ralph Ellison. Archives relevant to the study of Black history also include New England historical societies, where abolitionists deposited antislavery collections in the nineteenth century, and Ivy League libraries, which have amassed important Black literary collections since the mid-twentieth century. Paradoxically, sizeable holdings dwell, too, at places that once explicitly barred Black readers, such as southern repositories that preserve plantation and court papers created by white recordkeepers—who could not imagine African Americans as history's students or subjects. Such sources have unwittingly become indispensable to the writing of Black history, if read carefully and critically. A study of collections *about* African Americans cannot overlook any of these sites, where Black history belatedly came into focus. This book examines a different set of repositories, however: those imagined *by and for* Black communities. These are Black archives—not simply archives of blackness—and they emerged in a specific constellation of early twentieth-century spaces: branch libraries in African American neighborhoods (figure 0.2); special collections on historically Black college or university (HBCU) campuses; and the homes of Black bibliophiles.[20]

In these spaces, collecting was intimately bound up with the possibilities of Black being—a relationship that none of the other types of archives had principally in mind. When he established the James Weldon Johnson Memorial Collection of Black literary papers at Yale, for example, Carl Van Vechten imagined it as an opportunity for *white* students to encounter Black genius.[21] By contrast, Schomburg linked his archive-building explicitly to the art of "thinking black." For Schomburg and his mentor, the journalist John Edward Bruce,

FIGURE 0.2 Readers on the round center seat of the Browsing Room at the George Cleveland Hall Branch Library in Chicago, circa 1930s. Vivian Harsh is visible in the background under the archway. Photographer unknown.

Source: George Cleveland Hall Branch Archives, Vivian G. Harsh Research Collection of Afro-American History and Literature, Carter G. Woodson Regional Library, Chicago Public Library.

"to think black" meant to measure one's place in the world not in terms of individual striving but rather as part of a broader story of cultural achievement and struggles for justice across diaspora.[22] A mode of thought rather than an ideological prescription, "thinking black" traversed time as well as space. Racial pride, Schomburg suggested, required both "thinking more collectively" and "more retrospectively"—an idea captured in the most famous line he penned: "The American Negro must remake his past in order to make his future."[23] These words contain a temporal imperative, exhorting readers to look back at "group tradition," thick with evidence of courage and creativity, as the foundation of a reimagined future. They also hint at a method—not for building monuments but for imagining. Rather than presuming that the past simply exists as a set of facts to be gathered, the imperative casts it as something continuously *remade*. Schomburg understood tradition as the product of intellect and invention, crafted through experiments in arranging fragmentary traces of the past.

Contemporary theorists of Black history have continued to cultivate this idea. As David Scott argues, tradition is a "contentious dramatic narrative"— or in poet Kevin Young's words, "what you seek, and then seek to keep."[24] The sites featured in this book—the parlors of Black bibliophiles (chapters 1 and 2), reading rooms of HBCUs (chapter 4), and branch libraries for Black readers (chapters 3, 5, and 6)—made this seeking their everyday work: the collective and contested art of inventing a Black tradition. The pan-Africanist historian John Henrik Clarke, who spent much of his youth in the 1930s hanging out with friends at the Schomburg Collection, wrote, "We were young people *trying to find a definition* of African people in history."[25] Schomburg's library, which Clarke considered "an extension of my home," was the right kind of place for that search because collecting, like collectivity itself, is an act of sense-making. Libraries and archives order the known world, but they also invite an "attempt to remake inherited orders" in pursuit of new ways to know and imagine.[26] In other words, collections help redefine the very things, and people, they assemble. The métier of collecting—that it creates an affiliation between distinct objects but remains actively unfinished—suited the contentious urgency of "trying to find a definition" of the Black past as the upheavals of war, mass migration, and escalating racial violence unsettled the present.

Four decades in the making, Schomburg's collection emerged from what a friend of the scrapbook maker L. S. Alexander Gumby called the "scattered and fugitive things" of Black history.[27] Echoing that language, Schomburg used the words "buried" and "fragmentary" to describe many of the materials he collected.[28] Scattered, fragmentary, fugitive, and buried: the things of a Black archive could prove elusive—dispersed in diaspora, suppressed by prohibitions on Black literacy, or harbored in secrecy. Schomburg doggedly pursued these elusive objects to create something new. From the Renaissance poems of Juan Latino to the fiery abolitionist appeal of David Walker, he pieced together what he called a "true story of race vicissitude, struggle and accomplishment."[29] Schomburg relished *acquisition*—locating one of the few extant copies of Latino's verse or a longed-for edition of Phillis Wheatley's poems—but he also understood the power of *assembly*. Schomburg imagined that his books, once summoned to his shelves, symbolized "black men and women who stood shoulder to shoulder." A sixteenth-century tome by an African in Europe joined an underground pamphlet by a nineteenth-century Black radical in America, and in that conjunction, his library manifested a vision of Black history as a global tradition of "courage and zeal," constellated across centuries and oceans.[30] This bringing together of scattered and fugitive things exercised a powerful hold on contemporary Black thought, as McKay's letter suggests. It evinced the idea of Black life as a deep reserve of traditions that could be not only recovered but also animated in new ways for the present.

The making of Black archives was thus an experiment in defining blackness—or rather, a series of experiments, for there existed no consensus about what belonged in a Black archive. Although friends described Schomburg as a "walking encyclopedia of knowledge on the Negro," his collection was not encyclopedic.[31] It was speculative and strategic. Schomburg's collection contained many types of objects—art, curios, and "coins galore"—but it conspicuously excluded others.[32] He gathered folklore and slave narratives, for example, but only in published form, remaining aloof from the era's prolific efforts to gather "unwritten history," such as Zora Neale Hurston's field recordings or interviews of the formerly enslaved by the Federal Writers' Project.[33] He expressed only passing interest in collecting music and paid little attention to contemporary genres, such as the blues, which Daphne A. Brooks has called the "sonic and cultural memory of the Black masses."[34] As these exclusions suggest, collectors made contested choices about what objects to gather and how to arrange them. They experimented with what "thinking black" in the archive might produce, weighing the question of *which* records of the past would bear value for the present. These curatorial practices are important, if often-overlooked, sites of Black thought. Rare books or ordinary ephemera; literary manuscripts or ticket stubs; the nation-state or the diaspora: collectors' decisions determined which stories would persist in the archival spaces of Black memory.[35]

In proudly bringing together scattered and fugitive things, Black collectors rebuked the forced dispersal of African people in the past and the ongoing conditions that frequently required Black knowledge to operate invisibly. Collecting brings objects into relation and gives them order. It does not, however, make them into a coherent whole. A collection invites juxtapositions and kinships among its components that can unsettle as well as unify.[36] In the practice of Black bibliophilia, this extensibility held open the creative possibilities of scattering and fugitivity—the ability to shift directions and to subvert—while refusing their authority over the story that blackness could tell.[37] It is worth remembering, too, that a singular Black archive never existed. Collections documenting Black life materialized across a broad geography of scattered locations, structured by the needs and tastes of particular communities—including some where Black reading remained under threat. At each site, what idea of blackness would a particular constellation of objects propose? Who might be drawn together to create or use that collection? These questions animate the inquiries of *Scattered and Fugitive Things*, which argues that the generative and unruly practice of archiving became central to Black intellectual and social life in the early twentieth century.

The intellectual work of Black collectors was both tactile and social. They assembled files and scrapbooks, but they also assembled people, turning their collections into gathering spaces for the study of Black ideas. Indeed, there is a kinship between *collecting* as a set of material experiments—judgments about what belongs together and why—and *collectivity* as the social practice of "becoming-together," of finding the contours of a shared commitment.[38] Despite their etymological resemblance, however, the terms *collecting* and *collectivity* are rarely theorized together, perhaps because narratives about collecting tend to privilege either the lone, eccentric bibliophile or the imperial state as primary architects of the world's libraries and archives.[39] This bifurcated approach, which depicts collecting as the exercise of either solitary devotion or bureaucratic power, obscures the fact that collections of any kind are files of social relations and affinities.[40] An emphasis on "becoming-together" instead centers the reflexive work of asking what holds a group of people, or things, together across difference. In African American history, collecting was not the cloistered pastime of a secluded bibliophile in "the company of his books."[41] Rather, a network of Black bibliophiles, scrapbook makers, curators, and librarians operated in conversation with each other and understood their work as a "social necessity."[42] They made collections that both theorized and cultivated collectivity. From Schomburg's famous library in New York to the smallest assemblage in the Jim Crow South, each of their collections was imagined and inhabited by readers, fought for and protected by communities, and embedded in social movements.

"LET IT BE REMEMBERED": ROOTS OF THE TWENTIETH CENTURY'S BLACK ARCHIVAL TURN

When people asked Schomburg why he obsessively collected "anything good of the race," he often said that when he was a boy in Puerto Rico, a teacher told him, "The Negro has no history"—a negation he then spent a lifetime disproving, object by object.[43] Schomburg's teacher voiced a devastating but familiar refrain, for the idea of Black subjects as neither agents nor authors of history had long fortified Atlantic systems of colonialism, enslavement, and subjugation. In the face of that exile from history, generations of Black thinkers before Schomburg called for defiant acts of remembering, whether in the lines of Frances E. W. Harper's poetry or in the writings of historian William C. Nell, who operated an abolitionist library for community use.[44] The foundations of African American archiving lie in the reading rooms, like Nell's, that began in the 1830s. Members of antebellum Black literary societies built small collections of texts on colonization, slavery, and abolition, often housed in churches or storefronts, which the Howard University curator Dorothy B. Porter called the "earliest depositories of Afro-Americana."[45] The Philadelphia Library Company of Colored Persons, for example, began with an appeal for books in an abolitionist newspaper, and by 1838, it held six hundred volumes.[46] Amplifying that call, delegates to the 1853 Colored National Convention issued a declaration for the "safe keeping" of "all laws and historical records and biographies of colored people," as well as for the creation of "a Library, with a Reading Room and Museum."[47]

These antebellum collections proved ephemeral, but after the Civil War, the seeds of permanent collections on Black life and history began to take root.[48] Newly established colleges for freed people, including Livingstone College in North Carolina and the Hampton Institute in Virginia, made sure their fledgling libraries documented the "progress of the race."[49] That emphasis slowly grew into holdings that would anchor a sprawling twentieth-century network of "Negro collections" at HBCUs. Outside of formal institutions, as Reconstruction descended into the nadir, a network of self-taught historians recognized the urgency of documenting race history at a moment when "we are being so unfairly criticized by public statements, [and] so inhumanely treated by mob law."[50] In Philadelphia, which Porter called "a hotbed for black collectors," a group that included the scrapbook makers William Henry Dorsey and Joseph W. H. Cathcart, as well as the bibliophiles William Carl Bolivar and Robert Mara Adger, founded the American Negro Historical Society.[51] "Enthusiastic antiquarians," as Schomburg might have called them, they amassed personal collections that later fed the holdings of Howard, Atlanta, and Cheney Universities.[52] As the century came to a close, Victoria Earle Matthews reiterated the need for a "systematic effort" to preserve the records "produced by us," while visitors to the 1900 Exposition Universelle in Paris got a glimpse of Black archives to come.[53] There, the American Negro Exhibition featured a small gallery of artifacts, newspapers, and photographs, as well a "Library of Colored Authors" assembled by bibliophile Daniel Alexander Payne Murray (figure 0.3). W. E. B. Du Bois marveled at the "unique and striking" display of texts in Paris, which pulled together the nineteenth century's scattered but vibrant traditions of Black collecting.[54]

The collection assembled in 1900 for the American Negro Exhibit was as temporary as its antebellum antecedents, but it presaged a remarkable "archival turn" in Black life after the turn of the century, launching a period Brent Hayes Edwards has described as "compulsively documentary."[55] The rise of the New Negro movement, along with expanding public library systems and college-level curricula, made the time ripe to turn long-simmering archival aspirations into

FIGURE 0.3 Exposition des Nègres d'Amerique (American Negro Exhibition) at the Exposition Universelle, Paris, 1900. Photographer unknown.

Source: W. E. B. Du Bois Papers, Department of Special Collections and University Archives, University of Massachusetts Amherst Libraries.

durable institutions. A growing number of bibliophiles and newly trained librarians answered the nineteenth century's call to collect with such fervency that the writer Arna Bontemps called them "hungry bloodhounds."[56] They amassed books and pamphlets, preserved the papers of their heroes, and created public spaces for research. They did so within a hostile information landscape, when Black scholars could not access southern archives, when major reference works did not index Black-authored periodicals, and when a branch library could ban works on "the emancipated Negro."[57] In this environment, the heightened stakes of archiving were clear, and seemingly every iteration of New Negro politics by the 1910s had collecting in its sights, from the conservative uplift ideology of Booker T. Washington to the pan-African nationalism of Marcus Garvey. Washington launched a Department of Records and Research at the Tuskegee Institute, where the sociologist Monroe Work built a massive filing system of newspaper clippings on Black life, supplying data for his annual *Negro Year Book*.[58] Garvey surrounded himself with bibliophiles, and the pages of his organizational newspaper, *Negro World*, featured a stream of articles celebrating the pursuits of Garveyite bookworms like Schomburg.[59]

The roll call of collecting projects launched in the 1910s is both formidable and still imprinted on today's research landscape. In 1911, Schomburg and Bruce cofounded the Negro Society for Historical Research, whose holdings became the nucleus of the New York Public Library's Schomburg Collection. In 1914, Jesse Moorland donated his extensive library of texts on Black history to Howard University, inaugurating what is now the Moorland-Spingarn Research Center. Sociologist Kelly Miller seized on Moorland's donation to call for a National Negro Library and Museum—an idea that prophesied the opening of the National Museum of African American History and Culture. In 1915, Henry Proctor Slaughter organized a Negro Book Collectors Exchange, and although that organization proved short lived, he later seeded a major research collection at Atlanta University.[60] The same year, Carter G. Woodson founded the Association for the Study of Negro Life and History, attending to "the long-neglected work of saving the records of the Negro race," while in Harlem, George Young opened a bookstore known as the Mecca of Literature and History Pertaining to the Negro. Young's shop, which specialized in rare books and manuscripts, fed the collections of other bibliophiles and libraries.[61] Together, these initiatives broadcast a message: that the scattered and fugitive things of Black history "are all *wanted*"—from church manuals to celebratory programs to ovations. "Let it be remembered," declared Howard University when it welcomed Moorland's collection, "that almost everything will be valuable for historical purposes a hundred years hence."[62]

In 1926, crowded by the books overtaking his family's home, Schomburg sold his collection, sending it to Harlem to expand a newly-formed Department of Negro Literature and History at the 135th Street Branch Library—the first department of its kind in a public library in the United States. A few years later, Woodson deposited manuscripts known as the "Negro Papers" at the Library of Congress.[63] Inspired by Schomburg's collection and by Woodson's exhortations to save the records of the race, an emerging cohort of Black women librarians began building collections "by and about the Negro" at branch libraries across the South and in all the major receiving cities of the Great Migration.[64] Meanwhile, at Fisk, Howard, Hampton, and other Black colleges, a monumental effort to grow and organize their "Negro collections" unfolded in the 1930s, fed by New Deal funding to index and catalog America's documentary heritage.[65] In this interwar period, the work of creating public spaces to house Black archives accelerated quickly, so that by the time McKay wrote his letter to friends and confrères in 1937, he did not have to explain his reference to the "Schomburg Collection of Negro books," which was famous beyond Harlem and emulated in libraries north, west, and south.[66] The idea of a Black archive as a facet of community life had taken told of the century.

THE INTELLECTUAL WORK OF BOOKWORMS AND LADY CURATORS

Early twentieth-century collections were crowded with paper but also included other types of objects, from the pen of Frederick Douglass to a piece of wood from the last arriving slave ship in North America.[67] This unruly mix of material resided together in what their builders called "Negro Collections" or "New Negro Libraries."[68] Not until the 1970s did major repositories, including Moorland-Spingarn and the Schomburg Center for Research in Black Culture, split their holdings according to format, establishing separate departments for manuscripts, books, artifacts, and institutional archives. Before then, Black bibliophiles and librarians managed eclectic holdings and experimented with terminology to describe them. At Howard, Porter wondered whether her collection was a "literary museum" or an "informational bureau."[69] In Chicago, librarian Vivian Harsh called her assemblage a "special collection," while in New York, curator L. D. Reddick proposed the term "cultural center."[70] In the Jim Crow South, Virginia Lee did not give her collection any name at all, perhaps fearing it would attract attention from white officials suspicious of Black history's liberatory potential.

Reflecting this unsettled nomenclature, in 1913, Schomburg asked a friend, with some insecurity, if his books, art, and papers merited designation as a "library."[71] By the 1930s, however, when these objects had come under the care of Harlem's librarians, he confidently referred to his collection as "this archives."[72] The term "archives" connotes both place and authority: the storage of records and the power to name them as valuable. In adopting that term, Schomburg captured a chronological shift, from aspirational visions of the safekeeping of Black records in the nineteenth century, to a network of enduring spaces and institutions for these materials in the twentieth.

As such experiments with terminology suggest, bibliophiles and librarians created Black archives at a moment when the nation's information infrastructure was still in formation—and hostile to Black subjects. Woodson amassed manuscripts on Black life (and struggled to find funders to support the endeavor) before the National Archives existed. At Howard, when librarians began to organize the books Moorland donated in 1914, they found that "no library in the country has a classification suitable for our purpose," because existing information systems failed to account for the capaciousness of Black subject matter (figure 0.4).[73] Schomburg opened his parlor to readers in New York at a time when no public library in the country had a collection like his. For African Americans in the South, meanwhile, churches, homes, and storefronts *had* to stand in for public libraries, which were usually restricted to white patrons. In this racially segregated and unsettled information landscape, Black communities built their own institutions and systems, and in the process defined what a Black archive, library, or collection could be. In other words, the early twentieth century was an era of definitional possibility, when the boundary was porous between public repository and private parlor, or between a literary museum and special collection. *Scattered and Fugitive Things* asks what practices of acquisition and arrangement meant in this moment to Black intellectuals, who had a vexed relationship with prevailing recordkeeping institutions but imagined radical possibilities for remaking them.

To capture this porousness, I use "collector" as an umbrella term to name a motely group of bibliophiles, scrapbook makers, librarians, and historians—and "collecting" to capture the array of labors they undertook to amass Africana materials.[74] More specifically, I adopt Schomburg's use of the word "archives" to name the sensibility at the core of their work: a desire to preserve a distinct collection of paper records—books, images, ephemera, manuscripts—and maintain them in perpetuity for public use. With this lexicon, I am in conversation not only with Schomburg's 1930s vocabulary, but also with scholars and archivists today, for whom archives is an elastic term—sometimes narrow in

FIGURE 0.4 Jesse E. Moorland in his home library, circa 1900. Photographer unknown.

Source: Jesse E. Moorland Papers, box 126–80, folder 1390, Manuscript Division, Moorland-Spingarn Research Center, Howard University, Washington, DC.

meaning (i.e., papers or records) and sometimes metaphoric (anything relating to memory and evidence). Many scholars now invoke "the archive" as an expansive concept to account for what can or cannot be said about the past, pointing to the ways archives can be embodied or imagined—a lyric, gesture, or story—as well as material.[75] This metaphoric move is useful for understanding the work of African American collectors who dreamed of archives that did not yet exist in any physical location, and which many commentators dismissed as impossible.[76] It has also opened space for archival theory within Black Studies, a field that attends closely to how African diasporic people have by necessity made archives that dwell in unwritten and imaginative forms.[77] At the same time, a metaphorical archive (singular) can float free of the people, especially women, who have created and maintained archives (plural).[78] In this book, then, I focus on "actually existing archives" and their builders, while also drawing on a rich body of archival thinking in Black Studies.[79]

I also generally avoid the popular term *counterarchive* to describe the collecting projects discussed in this book. To be sure, Black archives often operated explicitly in opposition to recordkeeping systems that disparaged or obscured Black stories. Schomburg, for example, imagined his collection in resistant terms as "powder with which to fight our enemies."[80] However, as Thavolia Glymph has noted, the prefix *counter* can position Black projects as primarily oriented toward "contesting racism," obscuring the richness of their internal "intellectual world."[81] It can also overemphasize the distinction between orthodox and oppositional approaches and belie the heterogeneity of each. As the stories in *Scattered and Fugitive Things* demonstrate, Black collectors proved expert at using *and* destabilizing dominant information practices. They worked within municipal repositories and federal programs, subverted those same institutions, and created autonomous information structures—often simultaneously. Black critique thus cuts across a complex matrix of liberation and suppression that marks the history of archives. In bestowing value on Black records and creating expansive catalogs to enumerate them, collectors aspired to grant to the materials they gathered the authoritative aura of archives, without qualification. They wanted not simply to rebut the power of dominant archival institutions but also to appropriate that power, creating "for proud black[s] and astonished white[s]" alike places where Black forms of knowledge held sway.[82]

While blurring certain distinctions among the terms library, archive, and collection—demarcations that are more pronounced to information professionals today than a century ago—I attend closely to the mechanics of each collector's specialty. I describe how a bibliophile navigated the antiquarian market for manuscripts, how a scrapbook maker chose the right bindings, and how a librarian classified her books.[83] To write about these practices, I turn to sources that often hide in plain sight: records *of*, as well as *in*, archives—or what Antoinette Burton has called "the backstage of archives."[84] The collectors featured in this book profoundly shaped knowledge structures, but most did not pen treatises or memoirs about their work. Except for Schomburg's famous essay of 1925, "The Negro Digs Up His Past," and the writings of Porter, who chronicled the world of Black bibliophiles, most collectors wrote in genres that often escape notice as *writing* at all, such as bibliographies, catalogs, and classification schema. Several of the figures I sketch—especially two women who served as public librarians, Vivian Harsh and Virginia Lee—left behind files that include little correspondence, scant prose, and no diaries. Their work is not absent from the archive, however. Rather, as Kathy Peiss has argued about the records of librarianship, it is "abundant and unrecognized."[85] Mimeographed lists, files of clippings, headings in a card file: once essential conduits to Black knowledge, all have receded from everyday use, and they have been largely ignored, until recently, as sources for writing intellectual history. Bureaucratic in tone and covert in viewpoint, such paperwork seemingly reveals little about the risks or radicality of the work undertaken by those known as lady curators or bookworms.

Recapturing the urgency of cast-off sources yields important insights for the study of Black life and letters. *Scattered and Fugitive Things* draws attention, for example, to the central place of information practices in the twentieth century's Black intellectual tradition. From Du Bois as a bibliographer to Audre Lorde as a librarian, a striking number of writers famous for their poetry or prose also engaged in significant ways with the less-heralded work of collecting, cataloging, and classification.[86] One could make a list that would soon grow long. Nella Larsen, Anne Spencer, and Arna Bontemps were librarians. Alain Locke wrote a study guide for the American Library Association. Robert Hayden inventoried manuscripts. Horace Cayton made card catalogs. Langston Hughes alphabetized files for Woodson. Hubert Harrison obsessively compiled scrapbooks, as did Alice Dunbar-Nelson. Zora Neale Hurston and Eric Walrond published essays about Schomburg's collection. Mary Church Terrell, James Weldon Johnson, and Harold Jackman each helped to launch new archives.[87] The list could go on. When we start to look for these practices, it becomes clear that Black writers exercised a deep and widespread commitment to creating the files, lists, and places for study that should have existed but did not.[88] Simply put, they understood the exigency of creating access to ideas. That the work of prominent men like Locke and Du Bois becomes a footnote to their oeuvre precisely at the moment it most resembles that of librarians points to the gendered slant of intellectual history—a field that has paid too little attention to the figures, so often women, who built the twentieth century's repositories and filing systems.[89]

Another aspect of Black thought that comes into clearer focus when attending to the unheralded paperwork of collecting and classification is the prominence of women in creating the infrastructure for what became Black Studies (figure 0.5). Broadly speaking, the gendered framework of intellectual history is often not simply an erasure of women thinkers; rather, it is an eclipse of certain *types* of labor, like librarianship or scrapbooking, that are associated with women's domestic work, even if performed by men and women alike.[90] Institutions founded at the end of the nineteenth century, such as the American Negro Academy, recognized the cultural authority of autodidact bookmen like Schomburg. As the fields of history, literature, and librarianship grew more distinct in the twentieth century, however, a rigid hierarchy emerged between the

FIGURE 0.5 Staff of the George Cleveland Hall Branch Library, 1930s. Vivian Harsh is in the second row, second from the left. Photographer unknown.

Source: George Cleveland Hall Branch Archives, Vivian G. Harsh Research Collection of Afro-American History and Literature, Carter G. Woodson Regional Library, Chicago Public Library.

"intellectual" work of scholars, the "vernacular" work of amateur collectors, and the "technical" work of information professionals—at the very moment women came to dominate library service. Challenging this cleavage, *Scattered and Fugitive Things* centers figures who turned underappreciated modes of labor into radical experiments in Black intellectual production. Many of these collectors and catalogers enacted the Black feminist insistence on understanding praxis as a "source of theory" and defied expectations for the proper comportment of gender and sexuality within Black intellectual circles.[91] They also acted in excess of certain prevailing ideas about the acceptable subjects of Black scholarship—whether it was Porter surreptitiously collecting music when her supervisors wanted her to collect only books, or Gumby enfolding queer and bohemian subcultures into the intricate designs of his Negro History scrapbooks. At times, they hid from public view the risks they took, but they filled their collections with experimental possibilities for the future.

UNFINISHED ABUNDANCE: ON THE PRINCIPLES OF BLACK ARCHIVING

Attending to this profusion of collecting practices requires an expanded critical lexicon. Although the keywords absence and silence have framed much of archival theory in recent years, this book takes up the question of archival *abundance*. To be sure, a term synonymous with plenitude may seem discordant with the archival lament that has, for good reason, preoccupied the field of Black Studies.[92] *All* archives hold just a "sliver of a sliver" of the human record, but for the African diaspora, that sliver has often been reduced even further—to a shadow.[93] The violent rupture of the Middle Passage, forced separations of families, and legal prohibitions on Black literacy produced an archive of North American slavery written almost entirely by enslavers. Texts by enslaved writers, from the verse of Phillis Wheatley to the corpus of slave narratives, stood as rare exceptions coveted by Schomburg and his friends as the incunabula of Black authorship.[94] The words of free Black activists and thinkers in the antebellum North, printed in ephemeral formats, faced long odds against preservation and in some cases were systematically destroyed by Southern whites.[95] During slavery, and in the violent aftermath of Reconstruction that ultimately fueled a mass exodus from the South, keeping a personal archive was a luxury not often afforded to fugitives or migrants.[96] The weight of these cumulative erasures has fueled a powerful body of contemporary theory that grapples with how to study Black history in light of all "that will never be recovered," as Saidiya Hartman writes.[97]

Collectors would never fill these yawning gaps or redress the violence that seared the archival record of Black life in the Americas. Yet they also engaged deeply with what Anjali Arondekar calls the "archival poetics of ordinary surplus."[98] In the face of "what slavery took away," Schomburg and his contemporaries in the early twentieth century produced scenes of excess: crowded displays of charts and photographs at the American Negro Exhibit, a vast filing system for data at Tuskegee, and piles of books and manuscripts pushing Schomburg out of his house (figure 0.6).[99] From the modest set of a hundred books collected by the Negro Society for Historical Research in 1911, to the unprecedented 150,000 documents deposited at Fisk University in 1948, Black repositories quickened the pace of their collecting. By mid-century, many had run out of storage space—even before the paperwork explosion of the modern office accelerated the linear feet of material acquired each year. Newspaper holdings filled stacks to capacity,

Scholarship and Other Distinctions

WINS KEY

YOUNGEST PH.D.

HARRISON FERRELL

A WARD SOUTHERN MAIDEN DEGREE AT WESTERN RESERVE

GIRL HONORED FOR WORK IN JOURNALISM

ALTON YOUTH HIGHLY HONORED AT U. OF C.

NEGRO STUDENTS GET DEGREES AT N. Y. UNIVERSITY

Two Women, Four Men Get B. Com. Sc. Degree From School of Commerce

Award Magazine Post To Musician

Pastor Offered Professorship

Dr. William Y. Bell May Go to Gammon Theological Seminary

FIGURE 0.6 File of clippings on "Education—1928" created by Monroe Work's Department of Records and Research at the Tuskegee Institute, which annually published *The Negro Year Book*. These files eventually became the Tuskegee Institute News Clippings File on microfilm.

Source: Box 116.001, Education Newspaper Clippings, 1928, Tuskegee University Archives, Tuskegee University.

while proliferating manuscript acquisitions sat in annexes. A backlog began to grow. Keeping up was an "almost hopeless task," one curator reported.[100] While scholars have created a rich vein of work that grapples with the silences of Black archives, particularly in the study of slavery, *Scattered and Fugitive Things* asks what intellectual traditions arise from the deluge of records Black thinkers conjured in the twentieth century.[101] Absence may have produced Black thinkers' drive to acquire—a rage born of history's denial—but the marrow of their everyday intellectual practice engaged problems of scale and scope, classification, and taste—all of which revel in the idea of blackness as "too much to know" rather than too little.[102]

Following Jacqueline Goldsby's call to periodize the study of Black archives, *Scattered and Fugitive Things* takes seriously the methods and preoccupations of twentieth-century collectors who grappled with both surplus and scarcity.[103] When he exhibited his collection in the marble galleries of the New York Public Library in 1925, Schomburg confidently proclaimed, "Here is the evidence," suggesting that the scourge of anti-blackness would wither in the face of incontrovertible evidence documenting Black artistry, genius, and courage.[104] Skeptical of the liberatory potential of archives, today's scholars would rightly point out the "shadow library of absences" that haunts such evidence.[105] However, the work of the era's bibliophiles and librarians was more complex, and more radical, than their exultant rhetoric implied. Keenly aware of the imperative *and* the impossibility of their work, they lived the questions scholars pose now about the limits of archives. They reckoned with the perverse irony that descendants of the enslaved had to purchase traces of their history from the market. They mourned objects lost to wealthier bidders; they also refused to acquire items they did not want in a Black archive.[106] At times, they produced so much abundance it became chaotic or went uncataloged—thus producing new kinds of silences. In recounting such challenges, this book treats abundance not simply as the opposite of absence but as its own complex ground of Black intellectual work. Although Schomburg once suggested that archiving might redress the "broken bridge" of slavery, collecting does not substitute wholeness for history's dispossession.[107] As the ongoing, experimental practice of assembling scattered and fugitive things, collecting iterates the always *unfinished* work of finding a tradition.

These twentieth-century bibliophiles and librarians presumed that blackness in archives, as outside them, was plentiful and unruly, and they theorized Black life through contested practices of selection and arrangement. Their practices took shape around what could be defined as a core set of three principles in Black archiving—all of which emerged from the possibilities of abundance.[108] First, they valued records of Black knowledge. Bibliophiles of the early twentieth century had to invent the very idea of a Black archive and see abundance where others saw absence. At the heart of that process sat the act of valuation, whether bestowing scraps of everyday life with gilded care—as did Gumby in his finely crafted scrapbooks of Negro History—or regarding as "priceless desiderata" the cheap, ten-cent texts cast aside by antiquarian bookdealers—as did Schomburg when he plied the bookshops of Manhattan and Brooklyn.[109] Through the intellectual praxis of appraisal and speculation, their collecting work challenged the devaluation of the Black past and present in American print culture. Encompassed in this principle, too, was the premise that these valued items needed proper spaces where they would be exhibited and preserved. Thus, the twentieth century's Black bibliophiles became institution-builders, committed to securing the future of the collections they built.

The makers of Black archives also exercised a second principle: to order—and when necessary, disorder—Black knowledge. This second principle springs from the first, because the work of appraisal presumes that Black texts warrant complex and capacious enumeration. Dislodging blackness from information structures that treated it more as a "problem" than a possibility, collectors plumbed the intricacies of the Black past and present. Fundamental to Black archiving, then, was a commitment to remix the question of what a Black archive might comprise and how it should be arranged. Through experiments in selection, arrangement, and classification, collectors unsettled the category of blackness and created new orders of possibility from the scattered but abundant records of Black life—whether in the wayward classification system Porter invented at Howard University, or in L. D. Reddick's contention that the mundane, irate, and irreverent records of "lesser known characters" belonged in a Black archive alongside the "famous names." These experiments in order and disorder illuminated what Reddick described as the "breadth, variety and sparkle" of Black history—and what Porter called the "the scope and tempo of Negro life."[110]

Both of these commitments underline a third, and perhaps the most fundamental, principle: to take risks, at once physical and intellectual, to provide access to Black ideas. Challenging laws of segregation or sedition that treated Black knowledge as dangerous to racialized hierarchies of power, bibliophiles had to protect the right for their collections to exist.[111] They embraced a radical politics of access to make their materials available to the readers and thinkers who needed them. Paradoxically, that commitment to render Black history useable often required furtiveness. As each chapter in *Scattered and Fugitive Things* shows, building archives entailed a tension between visibility and fugitivity, as efforts to value and reclassify Black materials—and to create spaces for their use—sometimes hinged upon acts of defiance. In Roanoke, Lee had to hide books on Black history, taking them underground, to preserve them—a practice seemingly at odds with the role of a public librarian. At Howard, Porter had to contravene prevailing information systems, and gendered expectations about intellectual authority, just to catalog Black books. Both women perfected the art of seeming to comply with the rules of librarianship without always doing so.[112] Black archiving, then, draws on strategies endemic to Black freedom struggles: fugitivity, dissemblance, and the underground.[113]

These principles gave rise to two ongoing legacies that have transformed Black public culture. Social rather than solitary, Black archiving generated a set of public spaces that valued a community's records and centered Black readers. From Gumby's Harlem studio to a branch library on Chicago's South Side, Black archives drew people into experiments in collectivity as they convened to read, inquire, and ask new questions of the world.[114] In Chicago, for example, where political opposition to Black books was less overt than in the South but persistent nonetheless, Harsh cultivated the space and resources to sustain an autonomous, often-unruly, tradition of Black study. The other, related legacy that emerges from these principles is the imbrication of archive-building and social movements—such as when the Schomburg Collection became a hub for anticolonial thought in the World War II period. By preserving the Black past, while also serving as dynamic institutions that evolve with the needs of a community, these collections have kindled a Black radical intellectual tradition that is abiding but iterative. *Scattered and Fugitive Things* highlights this radical legacy, as the makers of archives turned experiments in value, order, and access into sites for Black imagination and activism.

OVERVIEW: FROM NEW NEGRO LIBRARIES TO THE "NEGRO INFORMATION EXPLOSION"

This book charts a transformative period that opens with the New Negro movement, was remade by the Great Migration and the Great Depression, and reaches to the early years of the postwar civil rights movement. Across these decades, as Black collectors built archives in the United States, the country's information infrastructure changed around them. The second half of the nineteenth century had seen the debut of the nation's major research libraries—seeded by the "book madness" of Anglo-American elites—and the emergence of small, ethnic historical societies for Jewish, Irish, and Black history.[115] In the opening decades of the twentieth century, Carnegie-funded libraries for cities, towns, and college campuses transformed access to print collections of all kinds, and that infrastructure expanded again in the New Deal of the 1930s with an infusion of funding for library construction and documentary projects. Black bibliophiles and librarians leveraged these evolving resources to create spaces for Africana collections—sometimes seeking inclusion in a "great house" of literature to confer status on Black lives and letters, and other times working in the autonomous tradition of Black self-education.[116] Across its six chapters, *Scattered and Fugitive Things* roughly follows this chronology, from Schomburg's founding of the Negro Society for Historical Research in 1911 to the entanglements of Porter and Reddick in federal recordkeeping projects of the 1940s.

The six collectors chronicled in this book reflect the diverse trajectories of diasporic thinkers in the United States. Schomburg (1874–1938) spent his childhood in San Juan and the Virgin Islands before embarking for New York in 1891. Born in Maryland, the scrapbook maker Alexander Gumby (1885–1961) moved north at the turn of the century and became a fixture of Harlem's working-class gay underground. Vivian Harsh (1890–1960), the daughter of formerly enslaved parents who migrated to Chicago, ran a library on the city's South Side, epicenter of the Great Migration. Hampton Institute alumna Virginia Lee (1906–1992) stayed in the South, working within—and secretly against—the limits of Jim Crow restrictions on Black literacy. Librarian Dorothy Porter (1905–1995), raised among the northern Black elite, became a central character in the Howard University intellectual scene. Historian L. D. Reddick (1910–1995) graduated from Fisk, came to New York by way of Chicago and New Orleans, and then joined the southern civil rights movement. Despite the different geographies each traversed, they formed a loose network of bibliographically minded Black intellectuals, both self-taught and formally educated: Gumby knew Schomburg, who crossed paths with Lee and mentored Porter, who in turn corresponded with Harsh and Reddick. Along with other collectors and curators in this network, they worked out practices for appraising, arranging, and providing access to Black materials—long before the academy or the field of librarianship caught up.

Each chapter centers one of these collectors to examine how the principles of Black archiving materialized. But the story does not end with their individual pursuits. While collectors engaged in one type of experiment on their bookshelves—choosing what things to place together and how to arrange them—other experiments unfolded among the people gathered in the spaces they cultivated for their collections. Thus, another plotline appearing in this book is the social history of Black archives, which served as hubs for thinkers both heralded and unknown. Every chapter widens to bring into view the communities or collectives associated with each collector, from the cohort of Black nationalist bookworms who helped Schomburg build his archive in the 1910s, to the study group that turned Harsh's Chicago branch library into a site of Midwestern pan-Africanism in the 1940s. *Scattered and Fugitive Things* concerns not only the making *of* Black archives, then, but also acts of making *in* them. It illuminates the urgency of archive-building to Black politics and aesthetic movements in this period, while also expanding the field of Black intellectual history to include the readers, newspaper clippers, and amateur archivists who embodied what Schomburg called "enthusiastic antiquarians."[117]

The first chapter, "Thinking Black, Collecting Black," considers the radical act of imagination at the center of Schomburg's collecting practice. Arguably the most iconic Black bibliophile in American and African diasporic history, Schomburg is often associated in popular memory with the Harlem Renaissance, which coincided with the 1926 sale of his collection to the New York Public Library. Chapter 1, however, looks to the years *before* the Renaissance, when Schomburg developed an archival method for "thinking black." In 1895, Victoria Earle Matthews called for collecting Black texts in a speech titled "The Value of Race Literature." After the turn of the century, Schomburg put this idea of *valuing* into practice—but did so with a coterie of Black nationalist bookmen rather than with the clubwomen in Matthews's audience. Together, Schomburg and his interlocutors scoured antiquarian markets for rare finds and slowly pieced together ideas for what a Black archive might afford as the repository of a "treasured past."[118] They also experimented with ways to create a public archive, beyond the walls of their parlors, well before Schomburg became famous for the sale of his collection. Drawing on Achille Mbembe's theorization of archives as an "instituting imaginary," this chapter argues that Schomburg and his friends engaged in the dual work of invention and institution-building at a moment when the field of Negro History was "not only unpopular but practically unrecognized."[119]

Chapter 2, "A 'History of the Negro in Scrapbooks,'" turns from the rare books and heroic figures favored by Schomburg to Alexander Gumby's scrapbooks of ephemera, which recorded more elusive forms of blackness. A butler, waiter, postal clerk, and aspiring bookdealer, Gumby had a short period of renown from 1925 to 1930, when he hosted salons in his Harlem studio. Although Gumby, like Schomburg, prized rare tomes, only his ephemera collection survived—a paradoxical illustration of how archives emerge through entwined occasions of loss and acquisition. Gumby called himself a "vandal history maker" to describe his strategy of dismantling and salvaging texts to reassemble in his "History of the Negro in Scrapbooks."[120] That characterization applies not only to his material practices but also to his social practices. In his collection and in his studio,

Gumby experimented with what (and who) might *not* fit in other versions of Negro History, valuing what José Esteban Muñoz calls queer modes of history found in "innuendo, gossip, fleeting moments, and performances."[121] He gathered an eclectic, irreverent, and interracial ensemble of salon goers, most of whom never made it into later accounts of the Harlem Renaissance scene. Gumby carefully documented their encounters in his exquisitely crafted volumes, however. In ephemera, then, he captured fleeting forms of history and being, remixing what future a Black archive might herald.

From the late 1920s to 1940s, Black collections moved from domestic interiors to public and university libraries. That shift coincided with both the Great Migration and the entry of Black women into the ranks of professional librarians, a group exhorted by Alain Locke's *The New Negro* to "scatter" across the country and establish libraries "wherever none exist."[122] Chapter 3, "Defiant Libraries: Virginia Lee and the Secrets Kept by Good Bookladies," tells the story of one of these women, a librarian at the "colored branch" of the Roanoke Public Library in southwest Virginia. In a Jim Crow city that violently policed Black presence in public space, Lee and the women she organized in the Fauset Reading Club had to fight for Black access to information. They did so with tactics both visible and underground—raising the question Jennifer Nash has posed about Black women's often-furtive intellectual work: "How do you trace what manifests itself as secrecy?"[123] By partially reconstructing the small library "by and about the Negro" that Lee assembled, chapter 3 reimagines the popular but elusive story of what happened when she defied orders from city officials to cease collecting. That Lee had to fight for a few hundred books—that such a modest compilation was deemed a threat—underscores the risk-taking inherent in making Black archives. As this chapter argues, a theory of Black collecting must look not only to the most renowned repositories but also to diminutive collections preserved through the creative subterfuge of women who rarely appear in intellectual histories.

Chapter 4, "Unauthorized Inquiries: Dorothy Porter's Wayward Classifications," turns to another form of risk. It traces the tenure of Dorothy B. Porter (later Wesley) as curator of Howard University's "Negro Collection," known as the Moorland Foundation. Although the collection was named for bibliophile Jesse Moorland, it was Porter who made it useable by merging Howard's scattered Africana collections and creating tools to access them. Knowing that most students would arrive at Howard, as she had, with only a cursory exposure to Black history, Porter ensured that they would find in her collection the capaciousness of the African diaspora.[124] To do so, she approached Black information as a site of abundance where other catalogers and curators had seen it as deficient. Drawing on Patricia J. Williams's evocation of "magic in the ordering of things," chapter 4 shows how Porter turned the seemingly technocratic card catalog into a site where readers encountered the full scope of Black thought.[125] In the 1930s and 1940s, she challenged national information regimes that diminished the complexity of Black subject matter, while simultaneously using federal resources to expand access to Howard's collection. The intellectual risks she took broadened the questions readers near and far could ask of a Black archive, placing Howard at the center of an HBCU library network that fed the emergence of Black Studies. In designing wayward classifications, Porter activated the aspirational quality of Black collections: the promise of reordering the world.

Chapter 5 explores what the curation of scattered and fugitive things made possible in Black public life. "A Space for Black Study" dwells on the South Side of Chicago, where Vivian G. Harsh inaugurated a Special Negro Collection at the George Cleveland Hall Branch Library in 1932. For the next two decades, she built an institution that valued the community's records. The *Chicago Defender* would later eulogize her as a "historian who never wrote."[126] Although that characterization overlooks her authorship of many kinds of documents, I take the misnomer as a counterintuitive inspiration to trace the wide range of thinkers who gathered around her collection and contributed to Chicago's Black intellectual history even though they, like Harsh, were not "writers." As Cheryl Clarke has argued, collecting is an act of study: it puts a field of inquiry into practice.[127] Drawing on that argument, and on Fred Moten and Stefano Harney's theorization of "black study" as intellectual work that is dissident and collective, chapter 5 explores the little-known story of the DuSable History Club, which forged an enduring space of pan-Africanist study at the Hall Branch.[128] Focusing on archives as places for the assembly of people as well as things, this chapter measures the impact of Black collections not by their most famous names or rarest holdings, but by the everyday acts of intellectual convergence they made possible.

A thread tracing Black radicalism and archiving runs through these chapters, starting with the Caribbean anti-imperialism that molded Schomburg's politics and culminating with the story of how Reddick turned Schomburg's collection into a site for World War II–era activism. As the United States waged war for democracy abroad, Reddick stood in the vanguard of African Americans who called for radical change at home and an end to colonial power in Asia and Africa. Reddick's organizing strategy took shape, in part, through an archival initiative. Chapter 6, "Mobilizing Manuscripts," explores his nationwide appeal for Black Americans to author "their own history of the war" by saving their wartime letters and sending them to the Schomburg Collection. Penned by rank-and-file soldiers, these collected letters upended ideas about archival value, combining declarations of protest with the quotidian pleasures of everyday Black life. Inculcating the imperative to archive as an act of movement-building, Reddick summoned materials the nation-state did not want recorded, including missives highlighting the hypocrisy of a segregated military. Suspicious of the U.S. government's fidelity to democratic forms of recordkeeping, Reddick sought to position the Schomburg Collection as a globally oriented institution promoting racial democracy—a vision that collided with local officials' diminutive expectations for a branch library's ambitions.[129] Although short-lived, Reddick's archival experiment embodied the ethos of Schomburg's oft-quoted line that "the American Negro must remake his past in order to make his future": Black archives, then and now, occasioned radical reimaginings of the present and future.[130]

Scattered and Fugitive Things closes on the cusp of profound changes for Black collections, as Cold War geopolitics unleashed competing pressures and opportunities. The State Department and United Nations dispatched African American librarians to build collections in newly independent African nations, for example, while repression of dissent at home foreclosed the kind of radical archival vision Reddick had proposed. In the 1950s, Yale University opened the James Weldon Johnson Memorial Collection, making it a premier destination for research on Black letters, and Columbia University acquired Gumby's scrapbook collection. Their forays into the field prophesied what Porter called the "Negro information explosion" of the 1960s, when libraries everywhere rushed to catch up with the work of Black bibliophiles and curators.[131] Existing repositories that once did not have "any Negro books at all" now competed for their acquisition, while the nascent discipline of Black Studies—fomented by waves of student protests—gave rise to a host of new projects: "Information Centers, Afro-American Museums, Black Cultural Centers and . . . Conferences on the Negro," as Porter listed them.[132] Tools built by the founding generation of Black special collections fed this surging demand, through facsimiles of their catalogs, reprints of books from their shelves, and microfilm editions of their manuscripts and clippings.[133] Porter, one of the first Black women to earn a graduate degree in librarianship, was also one of the last founders to retire. Bridging generations, she mentored the next cohort of curators and collectors. The epilogue considers Porter's legacy and asks how the ethics and economics of Black archives have shifted since the "Negro information explosion" she witnessed.

The scale and speed of such changes since 1950 can obscure the risks and experimentation that forged Black archives in the early twentieth century. *Scattered and Fugitive Things* returns our attention to that fraught but generative period of possibility, from Schomburg's speculative ventures in his parlor library in the early 1910s, to Reddick's embattled departure from the Schomburg Collection in 1948. The transformative three decades between those moments witnessed the institutionalization of Black archives in the United States: from the emergence of major research collections—including the Schomburg Center, the Moorland-Spingarn Research Center, and the Harsh Collection—to the establishment of dozens of smaller, community-based archives. A founding generation of collectors took the idea that one could excavate and assemble a Black tradition and made it a presumption, no longer a proposition that had to be proven. They took risks to create spaces where that tradition would be debated, protected, and kept in motion through ongoing forms of imagination and inquiry. Later curators would propose other ideas for what belonged in these repositories, but the founding vision for Black archiving has endured. These six collectors and their interlocutors left behind not only an abundance of books and papers but also a model of intellectual practice—one that refuses to see Black history constrained or threatened and that, out of this refusal, makes something new.

CHAPTER ONE

THINKING BLACK, COLLECTING BLACK

Schomburg's Desiderata and the Radical World of Black Bibliophiles

Old Schomburg is digging away as usual.

—John Edward Bruce, 1914

In 1912, Arthur Schomburg was unpacking his library—again. For many years, he had collected books, pamphlets, papers, and curios that documented Black life: verses of early poets in North America, tales of Caribbean revolutionaries, African travel narratives, histories of ancient Egypt, antislavery pamphlets, a few manuscripts, and even "coins galore."[1] Of these objects, books especially had filled his apartment. "I have an innate love for such books which have within its covers anything good of the race," he told a friend.[2] In loving such texts, Schomburg followed in the footsteps of earlier Black thinkers who held aloft the memory of literary and political heroes like Benjamin Banneker, Phillis Wheatley, or Toussaint Louverture. But Schomburg was not content to pen odes to these heroes. Part of an emerging cohort of Black bibliophiles at the turn of the century, he wanted their words and pictures, on paper and *in* his library. "To have and to Hold," he declared.[3] He spent twelve years searching for a single engraving of Banneker's visage.[4] He obtained the handwritten military commands of Louverture on letterhead stamped *Egalité, Liberté*.[5] He wanted *every* edition of Wheatley's poems. Once he acquired them, he held fast. "No parting glances," he responded when a dealer offered "100 plunks" for his autographed copy of "the sable poetess."[6] Having filled three bookcases with these and other cherished things, Schomburg began to ponder his collection's future.

At nearly forty years of age, Schomburg had made many migrations both geographic and cultural. Born in San Juan and baptized Arturo, he spent parts of his childhood in the Virgin Islands before moving in 1891 to New York City, where he adopted the name Arthur. In New York, he committed himself first to the anti-imperialist clubs of Puerto Rican and Cuban exiles and then to the Black nationalist ranks of the Loyal Sons of Africa (figure 1.1).[7] He made a series of smaller migrations within the city as well, from the Lower East Side to midtown's San Juan Hill, and then to Harlem.[8] His most recent sojourn was north from 115th Street, where he had lodged with Ramon Rothschild, an old comrade from Puerto Rico and a member of his masonic lodge.[9] Now living in an apartment at 63 West 140th Street with his new wife, Elizabeth Green, Schomburg was the only Puerto Rican in the building of African Americans and West Indians.[10]

FIGURE 1.1 Schomburg with friends, August 7, 1910, likely in Yonkers, New York. From the left: Joseph Stephens, Dr. C. P. McClendon, John Edward Bruce, and A. A. Schomburg. Bruce founded several organizations in which Schomburg participated, including the Loyal Sons of Africa and the Men's Sunday Club. Photograph by Davis Photographers.

Source: Arthur Alfonso Schomburg Photograph Collection, Photographs and Prints Division, Schomburg Center for Research in Black Culture, New York Public Library Digital Collections.

He was also the only resident, among porters, elevator operators, dressmakers, and domestic workers, listed in the census as a "bookkeeper."[11] That designation was a misnomer, for Schomburg worked as a clerk in the mailroom of a bank, but it was more apt than the census taker may have realized, for Schomburg was indeed a keeper of books.[12] With each of his migrations, those books had moved, too. "I encounter much trouble when moving from one place to another this treasured lot," he reported.[13] The collection had grown heavy and large, and items sometimes got lost during moves. "I fear [I] have reached the limit," he wrote in a moment of weariness.[14]

More than a century hence, we know that Schomburg had not reached his limit. His "treasured lot" kept growing until it seeded a collection at the New York Public Library that still bears his name—one of the largest in the world then and now. In 1912, however, few collections resembled his—none in public institutions—and Schomburg harbored uncertainty about its future. Publicly, he made a name for himself as "an indefatigable searcher"; privately, he worried about how to sustain his bibliographic tendencies.[15] Although he never truly considered abandoning his book-buying habits—"the Negro is ever my subject," he declared—he began to experiment with other modes of gathering and distributing these objects of "imperishable memory."[16] He joined forces with the Black nationalist journalist John Edward Bruce to form the Negro Society for Historical Research (NSHR), and together they dreamed of creating a "circulating library" composed of the society's books and papers.[17] He and Bruce also contributed to the Negro Library Association's effort to secure a building for the "proper housing of materials," and they signed on to an idea to establish a "centre of Negro art and literature" at Saint Mark's M. E. Church.[18] Briefly, Schomburg even contemplated a sideline as a dealer of rare books to fill shelves other than his own.[19] None of these efforts materialized exactly as he hoped, but they led Schomburg to imagine potential readers and publics for his collection.

To publicize his holdings, Schomburg ordered a typewriter from Chicago and began preparing a list that he called both "my book index" and "my catalogue."[20] One version of this catalog, typed around 1914, is the only known inventory of Schomburg's library created during his lifetime. Titled "Library of Arthur A. Schomburg: Collection of books on the Negro race, slavery, emancipation, West Indies, South America, and Africa," it enumerates eight hundred books, ephemera, manuscripts, and art objects, revealing what was in the "treasured lot" Schomburg struggled to move.[21] More broadly, it captures the social world of his collection: how all his migrations, both cultural and spatial, met on his bookcases.[22] In the famous reverie of Walter Benjamin, the act of unpacking a library evokes the "bliss of the collector," who relives the thrill of each book's acquisition.[23] For Schomburg, such memories would often have been collective, linked to friends, comrades, and their joint expeditions. One of the books in Schomburg's catalog, for example—Teofílo Domínguez's *Figuras y Figuritas*, a portrait of Afro-Cuban separatists—was given to him by José D. Rodriguez, a cigar maker in New York, as a token of "affection and consideration" (figure 1.2).[24] A collection of manuscript sermons, also on the list, resulted from a "pilgrimage" with his friend John W. Cromwell to recover the papers of pan-Africanist theologian Alexander Crummell. Each page was "a memento of their rescue," Schomburg wrote.[25]

As the provenance of these two items suggests, Schomburg's collection grew out of the worlds of Black migration and organizing in the 1890s through the 1910s. In those decades, Schomburg was an organization man: secretary of *Las Dos Antillas*, "librarian" of Saint Benedict's Lyceum, cofounder of the NSHR, member of the American Negro Academy, and Grand Master in the Prince

FIGURE 1.2 *Figuras y Figuritas: Esayos Biográficos* by Teofílo Domínguez (1899), inscribed in 1910 from José D. Rodriguez to "Amigo A. Schumburg." Rodriguez uses the spelling of Schomburg's last name as it was often written in the 1890s, when Schomburg joined other Puerto Rican and Cuban expatriates in the revolutionary movement against Spanish imperialism.

Source: Manuscripts, Archives and Rare Books Division, Schomburg Center for Research in Black Culture, New York Public Library.

Hall Masons.[26] In each of these groups, Schomburg served as recordkeeper and, through these associations, he began to exhibit his materials; the first public display of objects from his library likely took place on July 4, 1912, at a community celebration held by the NSHR, where he "rejoiced at the many exhibits we had before our people."[27] He found in these groups friends who belonged to what the Philadelphia newspaperman William Carl Bolivar called DOFOB—Damned Old Fools on Books.[28] They journeyed with one another to bookshops and corresponded about their latest finds. The artifacts that remain of their ventures—letters, inscriptions in their books, and the 1914 catalog of Schomburg's library—document a social history of Black collecting. Together, these "damned old fools" engaged in the intellectual work of imagining what a "Collection of books on the Negro race" could and should contain.

In this circle, Schomburg also explored the concept of collectivity, engaging in a method he and Bruce each called the practice of "thinking black."[29] Subverting the narrow, stifling ways that the United States codified racial segregation, this method looked elsewhere—in both time and space—to harness the power of "thinking black" in diasporic and global terms. Schomburg saw the stakes of his project as at once mapping the contours of an explicitly Black modernity—embodied in objects like the earliest books printed in Africa, paintings by Black Renaissance artists, or the proceedings of free Black institutions in the Americas—and rethinking the writing of history more broadly. Through what he called the "dust of digging," Schomburg promised not only to situate Black actors at foundational moments of western civilization but also to position the African continent as a pivot of world history.[30] The past, he argued, revealed ways of thinking about blackness and solidarity that rebuked the stranglehold of imperialism and anti-blackness on the present. Thus, for Schomburg, the antiquarian was a crucial and modern figure of Black struggle. To build a library was to help build a movement.

In 1926, at the height of the New Negro Renaissance, Schomburg sold his collection to the New York Public Library. That move—from Schomburg's parlor to a "great house" of literature—marked the final time he packed or unpacked his library.[31] The widely-heralded sale made him the African diaspora's most famous collector. But what we now call the "Schomburg Collection," named for a single individual, came about through "adventures in mutuality."[32] In acts of acquisition, revaluation, categorization, and display, Schomburg and his friends engaged in both collecting and archive-building. Terms that are related but not synonymous, collecting invokes assembly (which can be whimsical as well as systematic, ephemeral as well as permanent), whereas archive-building implies infrastructure (anticipating future use).[33] It is the entwined nature of these acts that makes archives, in the words of Achille Mbembe, an "instituting imaginary."[34] In their decisions about what to acquire, and in their pilgrimages to rescue manuscripts, Schomburg and his collaborators imagined: they invented the concept of "Negroana" when it was a "forgotten field."[35] In their efforts to organize and exhibit their assemblages, they instituted: they created structures for public use. This dual work of imagination and institutionalization characterized Schomburg's project between 1910 and 1926, a period when, in concert with others, he made a future for Black collecting.

SEDITIOUS READINGS: REFRAMING THE MARKET

Before embarking for New York in 1891, Schomburg belonged to a literary world in San Juan where he learned the pleasures—and the power—of print. He worked in the employ of José González Font, who operated a *librería* that printed Puerto Rican nationalist literature.[36] Beyond the print shop, Schomburg participated in San Juan's vibrant youth clubs, competing daily to create and solve *entretenimientos* printed in the local newspaper. These word games often bore shared literary and political references. Hidden in an acrostic might be the "Cuban cry for freedom," for example, while the puzzles Schomburg crafted included references to Sophocles and the Italian poet Ugo Foscolo.[37] By his own account, however, Schomburg and other Afro-Puerto Ricans were racial outsiders in this jocular scene, whose white members were quick to "point with more pride to the achievements of their white ancestors, than the blacks seemed able to do of their[s]."[38] Moreover, Schomburg found that his avid reading habits ran afoul of Spanish censorship laws, which especially targeted Black writers critical of Spain.[39] He had to take risks to read *Ecos del Alma*, a book of poems by the radical Afro-Cuban independence leader Rafael Serra. "I first read it under darkness—when a boy 15 years at home," he remembered, "I say darkness because it was seditious to have possession of anything printed against the Spanish government."[40] As a result, when Schomburg came to the United States at age seventeen, he already knew two forms of literary exile: the exclusion of blackness from Puerto Rican patrimony, and the banning of anti-imperialist texts by colonial forces.

At some point in the 1890s, Schomburg became not just a reader but also a collector, vowing to gather "whatever is meritorious pertaining to the history and development of the Negro" (figure 1.3).[41] He already grasped the stakes of assembling a library, because he knew that the mere possession of records

FIGURE 1.3 Arturo Schomburg, circa 1896. Photographer unknown.

Source: Arthur Alfonso Schomburg Photograph Collection, Photographs and Prints Division, Schomburg Center for Research in Black Culture, New York Public Library Digital Collections.

could constitute rebellion—and from the colonial point of view, sedition. His budding determination to collect found encouragement in New York's community of Cuban and Puerto Rican expatriates, who devoted "intense energies" to preserving the texts prohibited by Spain.[42] Schomburg was not alone in the city—his mother joined him, as did his San Juan comrade Rothschild—but his circle widened as he joined New York's revolutionary organizations. Already an apprentice in the paper trades, Schomburg gravitated to recordkeeping duties in these groups, serving as secretary of the political club *Las Dos Antillas*. Although this political network disintegrated by 1898, its traces remained in Schomburg's early collection. He preserved the minute book of *Las Dos Antillas*, for example, and his copy of *Historia de la insurrección de Lares* held a newspaper clipping about the death of independence icon Ramón Emeterio Betances.[43] His volume of Serra's essays bore the inscription of an Afro-Cuban émigré who signed, "A mi amigo," and in revolutionary poet Pachín Marín's *Romances*, Schomburg included a note recounting the times he had heard this "*poeta de corazón*" read his work.[44] Such works of Cuban and Puerto Rican radicalism inaugurated his library.[45]

Schomburg also learned to keep records in Prince Hall Freemasonry, one of the oldest Black fraternal movements. In 1892 he joined *El Sol de Cuba*, a Spanish-speaking lodge that served as a refuge for Caribbean independence activists in New York.[46] After 1898, when the United States intervened in Cuba and splintered the independence movement, Schomburg and Rothschild rebuilt *El Sol de Cuba* as a bilingual and then an anglophone lodge. As he ascended through the masonic offices, Schomburg not only maintained and translated the group's documents, but also built ties to African American antiquarians.[47] By 1908, for example, he knew Prince Hall historian Harry A. Williamson, a member of the Carthaginian Lodge who created a Masonic library and museum containing "works by Negro writers on Craft matters."[48] It was also through masonry that Schomburg likely met his mentor John Edward Bruce, known as "Bruce Grit," who had a sizeable library, shared Schomburg's love of poetry, and had written extensively on Black history. Their social circles began to overlap by 1902, and Bruce soon connected Schomburg to the Men's Sunday Club at the A. M. E. Zion Church, a forum for "self-trained intellectuals," many of whom became founding members of the NSHR—the collective that most indelibly shaped Schomburg's collecting.[49]

Through Bruce, Schomburg found a network of book-collecting friends that included the Reverend Charles D. Martin in New York; John W. Cromwell, Daniel Alexander Payne Murray, and Alain Locke in Washington, DC; and W. C. Bolivar in Philadelphia (figure 1.4). This group, like the Puerto Rican and Cuban expatriates who welcomed him to New York a decade earlier, initiated Schomburg into a rich lineage of activism. Bolivar and Cromwell, for example, had ties to nineteenth-century literary societies and the colored conventions movement, which had kindled Black archival desires to gather "historical records and biographies of the Colored People."[50] In the company of such men, Schomburg's collecting impulse became habitude. Their correspondence bears witness to the pleasures they took in collecting, as well as to the challenges they confronted.

A NEGRO'S LIBRARY.

A bibliography of the Library of William C. Bolivar, of Philadelphia, Penna., has been recently issued. It contains 32 pages of books, printed tracts, magazine articles, reports, addresses, etc. "Americana, Negroana, manuscripts, autograph letters, Lincolnian, rare phamplets, travels, Africana, etc." Mr. Bolivar possesses many rare books relating to the Negro race. While there are many Negroes who have far larger libraries, there are few private persons who possess more rare volumes on the race than Mr. Bolivar who for half a century or more has been gathering together this excellent collection. Mr. Bolivar is a natural book hunter and has not only found many rare books for himself but supplied many to others throughout the country. Among the rare books in his library are the bound minutes of the anti-slavery conventions of 1831-2-3-4-5-6. 19 volumes of the African Repository, original certificate of ordination of Rev. Walter Proctor, signed by Bishop Richard Allen; Abbe Gregoire's "Inquiry," Phillis Wheatley's Poems, first edition 1773. Rainsford's Hayti, 1805; Address of Russell Parrott, 1814; of Prince Saunders, 1815; First Edition of John G. Whittier's Poems, Life of Gustavus Vassa; Ignatius Sancha, 1788; History of Colored Schools of New York, 1830; First Negro Magazine, the Moral Reform Journal, 1837; 2 bound volumes Anglo African Magazine, 1859; Christopher Rush's History [illegible] A. M. E. Zion Church, 1836; Ed[illegible]d's History of West Indies, 1864; [illegible] biography of Jarina Lee, David [illegible]r's Appeal, etc.

FIGURE 1.4 Scrapbook page with silhouettes of Daniel Murray, W. C. Bolivar, and Schomburg created in 1913 at the National Emancipation Exposition in Washington, DC. Also pasted on the page is a clipping titled "A Negro's Library" announcing the publication of a catalog of Bolivar's library and calling him a "natural book hunter."

Source: Arthur A. Schomburg Papers, Manuscripts, Archives and Rare Books Division, Schomburg Center for Research in Black Culture, New York Public Library.

"With my morning mail came the Royal Almanack of Haiti," Schomburg wrote to Cromwell, describing "the feeling of pleasure that comes over me . . . to have a memento from Sans Souci 1850."[51] When Bolivar found a copy of *The History of the British Colonies in the West Indies* with "fine engravings, bound in sheep," he told Murray he would proudly "write to Schomburg before the day goes by."[52] Because they all faced a central obstacle—"how difficult it is to obtain and find the buried facts, historical and fragmentary where Negroes are primarily concerned," in Schomburg's words—they shared their knowledge of where to search for these "buried facts."[53] When Schomburg took a break from his mailroom job to "hunt among the old bookshops" of Lower Manhattan, he returned to his office and typed up his finds: "At 42 Broadway I was told that they had quite a large variety of pamphlets re Slavery," he wrote Bruce after one jaunt. His friends offered suggestions in return.[54]

In New York, Schomburg's closest book-hunting companion was Martin, a native of Saint Kitts and minister at the Moravian Church near Schomburg's Harlem apartment. They often ventured to antiquarian shops together, such as on a day in 1913 when they took the subway to Brooklyn and "made a frontal attack" on secondhand bookstores.[55] At other times, Schomburg and Martin made their rounds separately, hoping to win bragging rights over the other. In *Negro World*, the newspaper of Marcus Garvey's Universal Negro Improvement Association (UNIA), one of their mutual friends recounted this jaunty competition:

> There isn't a reputable second hand book store in this city where [Martin] and Schomburg are not known. Sometimes one of these book ferrets get[s] a tip from a dealer about some rare item which one or the other has been looking for. Whichever of them receives the tip responds to the call. About a half hour or so [later], the other one quite accidentally drops in and . . . they ramble around the shop a few minutes together to find something new (except the latest item which is not mentioned). Finally, one of them, usually Schomburg, remembers an appointment at 6 or 7 p. m. and bids Doctor [Martin] good bye. Doctor then takes possession of his item, chucks it in his bag and flits homeward.[56]

After these machinations, the two friends would reunite, only to discover each had outsmarted the other, as the article in *Negro World* comically narrates: "Schomburg comes up to Harlem with a book under his arm and calls on Martin to see what he has new. Martin springs the 'item,' Schomburg springs an older edition on the parson and they both laugh. Somebody had given Schomburg the tip also."

A Black intellectual practice took shape in these excursions and correspondence. The book-hunting rambles of Schomburg and his friends entailed the question of desire—or in bookmen's terms, *desiderata*. Without checklists of Black writing to consult, and without pricing guides specific to the Black antiquarian book trade, they devised their own criteria for what to buy and how to theorize value—a mutable category of aspiration and appraisal.[57] In collectivity, Schomburg and his interlocutors worked out the scope of their desiderata: an imagination of what should have pride of place in a Black collection. They learned from each other what objects to acquire, as when Schomburg told Cromwell he was "indebted" for his recommendation of a book on Reconstruction.[58] They discussed fugitive items their libraries lacked. Echoing his youthful reading of revolutionary literature banned by imperial Spain, for example, the adult Schomburg went in search of David Walker's elusive *Appeal*, the fiery antislavery manifesto that Southern enslavers had desperately tried to suppress.[59] Schomburg and his friends also traded items according to their own tastes and wants. Bolivar secured a copy of William Douglass's *Annals of the First African Church* in "a trade with Miss Caps," referring to a fellow Philadelphian who "preferred a Dunbar to a Douglass"; he offered, in turn, to trade that Douglass to Schomburg for "something equally as scarce."[60] In other moments, they found the points at which their sensibilities diverged. "The list you sent is not over attractive," Bolivar reported after Schomburg shared some possible leads.[61] Together they weighed the question of which artifacts of the past held value for the present.

Appraisal sat at the very center of this collecting project. The letters of Schomburg and his friends discuss not only what to acquire, but also, in great detail, what things cost. Schomburg once asked Locke to go to a bookshop in Washington, climb up the ladder to the high shelves, and find the price for three volumes of the *Anti-Slavery Record*.[62] He boasted on one occasion of acquiring a Fante language dictionary for a dollar, while lamenting on another day that "my pocket was not equal to my mind."[63] The racial paradoxes of the antiquarian book trade put pressure on Black bibliophiles as buyers. Schomburg and his comrades valued Black texts, contravening popular and scholarly accounts that framed blackness as barren of historical worth. Yet most Black bibliophiles, lacking significant personal wealth, could not afford prices that matched their valuations. Ironically, then, their ability to collect depended on the market's devaluation of "Negro material."[64] Years before, the Black scrapbook maker William Henry Dorsey wrote that "colored people were too poor to become collectors in one sense of the word."[65] Schomburg, too, used the word "poor": "I have just gathered for my poor collection," he told Locke, "an autograph copy of Phillis Wheatley."[66] He exulted at his feat of having "purloined" a Wheatley because it was one of the few objects of Black authorship that white collectors coveted as well—and when Schomburg faced wealthy competitors for such items, he nearly always got outbid.[67] Dorsey thus captured the predicament Black bibliophiles faced. If they could not be "collectors in one sense"—able to proffer fantastic prices at auction—they would have to create fugitive strategies for navigating the market.

In 1916, Schomburg wrote to Locke about an upcoming auction of a "Splendid Collection of Publications on Slavery" from the library of the late Joseph Bryan.[68] He had his eye on a copy of Morgan Godwyn's 1680 *The Negro's and Indians Advocate*, and in his letter about this rare object, he offered several reflections on the price of Black history:

> Saturday I visited the Anderson's galleries and had a view of the rarities—By the way who is this Bryan to have gathered so interesting a lot of Negro's books in Richmond Va? I have a few bids on the rare items but I am afraid the collectors are up in arms—Now is the time to buy antislavery items the prices are cheap—dirt cheap. I paid 30c for 2 volumes that belonged to Phillis Wheatley's collection only inscribed "Sept 24 1774" But my holograph letter of Toussaint L'ouverture I consider a very priceless desiderata—I will keep you posted on the Bryan sale—I have a bid of 7.00 on the Godwin [sic] item printed in [1680] one of the [rarest] and choicest Negro [items] in existence. Mr. Harper a collector has a perfect copy for which he charges the sum of 100.00 So that my chances for putting my hands on Godwin is very doubtful.[69]

In the affective undertow of this letter, Schomburg moves between regret for the prohibitive cost of some items, bafflement at the "dirt cheap" price of others, and his sense that some objects (such as Louverture's holograph letter) could not be measured by any price. A shrewd buyer, Schomburg knew to temper his emotions with stealth, taking advantage of the market's indifference when he could—for if wealthier bidders got "up in arms," he stood little chance at securing his desiderata. Schomburg repeatedly lost bids on Banneker's eighteenth-century almanacs, for example, to a white millionaire who collected early Americana.[70] In one near miss, a Banneker sold for four dollars before Schomburg could act. "It goes without saying I would have given $20.00," he despaired, willing to spend a week's wages on this single artifact.[71] Although he planned to proffer seven dollars for Godwyn at the Bryan auction, he felt his chances were "doubtful." Such doubt marks the melancholia that sometimes crept into Schomburg's letters, especially when he knew his competitors might be the very institutions that devalued Black life. "You will be surprised to know," he once remarked to Cromwell, "that

Libraries of the South who deny the Negroes admittance have a large amount of his literature."[72]

On the day of the Bryan sale, Schomburg entered the auction gallery at odds with a market that did not account for Black collectors' theories of value. In tools of the antiquarian book trade, such as *American Book-Prices Current*, one could occasionally track the going price of a Black-authored text, like Wheatley's poems, when the appetite of Schomburg's cohort dovetailed with the market. A worn first-edition sold for three dollars in 1911, for example, while a copy treated by a famous bookbinder sold for thirty-five in 1920.[73] Most works of Black authorship, however, traded below the threshold of three dollars that would merit an entry in *Book-Prices Current*. Auctioneers often bundled items predicted to fetch less than that amount; in the Bryan sale, for instance, works by William Wells Brown, Edward Blyden, and Frederick Douglass were packaged in lots described as "5 pamphlets" or "of various sizes and bindings."[74] Since the yearly recap of auctions omitted the names of individual authors sold in these lots, their presence became invisible in the field of bibliography.[75] Those specializing in Black materials thus had to make their own assessments, as when the bookstore owner George Young remarked that copies of Douglass's autobiographies were "worth their weight in gold."[76] His appraisal had little to do with the rare book trade's valuation, for Douglass's *Life and Times* did not garner a single entry in *Book-Prices Current* between 1900 and 1926, and his *Narrative* appeared but once, for four-and-a-half dollars. (The warrant for Douglass's arrest, meanwhile, sold for eight times that amount.)[77] The discrepancy between the market's indifference to Black texts and the way Black bibliophiles spoke of their treasures—"priceless desiderata," "worth their weight in gold"—underscores Antoinette Burton's argument that archives are lodged within "varying economies of desire."[78]

Despite his pessimism, Schomburg won the item he coveted, paying five and a quarter for Godwyn's *The Negro's and Indians Advocate*. As it turned out, other buyers at the auction paid more attention to a set of genealogical books about Long Island, also on sale, than to Bryan's "Splendid Collection of Publications on Slavery."[79] Thus facing little competition, Schomburg netted twenty items from the sale—"pretty good for a novice," he told Locke—but it was the Godwyn he most admired.[80] Just as Schomburg's youthful reading of revolutionary poetry had defied Spanish restrictions on literacy, his purchase of the Godwyn rebuked its previous ownership in remarkable fashion—although he seemed unaware of the book's curious provenance. "Who is this Bryan to have gathered so interesting a lot of Negro's books?" he asked Locke. The answer, had he known, would have left Schomburg either unsettled or triumphant. A founder of the Virginia Historical Society from a family of enslavers, Joseph Bryan was a Lost Cause partisan who helped populate the South with Confederate monuments and actively opposed Black suffrage.[81] Schomburg rejoiced in winning his bid on *The Negro's and Indians Advocate*, but he may not have fully apprehended the extent to which his acquisition radically reframed this object. Godwyn's proto-abolitionist text moved from the bookshelves of a white supremacist bibliophile who saw slavery as "beneficent in practice," to the collection of Schomburg, who once doxologized slavery's insurrectionists, naming Denmark Vesey, Nat Turner, and John Brown as the figures he worshipped alongside God.[82]

Schomburg's quest for Godwyn's "ethical wonder," or for the Wheatleys and Bannekers of Black literature, might seem, at first glance, to epitomize the New Negro movement's turn away from slavery's legacy.[83] After all, the most coveted items in Schomburg's circle were often artifacts that promised to transcend enslavement (Wheatley) or anticipate its end (Godwyn). In fact, however, Schomburg did not "turn away from the memories of the slave past," as Booker T. Washington once advocated.[84] He actively acquired works on the global history of slavery, and he had four large scrapbooks, titled "Negro Problems," on slavery's aftermath.[85] In these two areas, his collection mirrored what American print culture already circulated as blackness. In U.S. repositories, the idea of blackness as a problem or peculiarity—with slavery as the "peculiar institution" and the "Negro Problem" as its effect—accounted for a tidal wave of text and was so overdetermined in prevailing knowledge structures that many libraries shelved *anything* Black under the call numbers for either slavery or the Negro Question.[86] Schomburg and his comrades navigated a marketplace in which most "Negro" materials concerned subjugation or degradation. Perversely, that market could turn even a Wheatley into an example of Black death; the white bookdealer Charles Heartman once offered to sell Schomburg a copy of Wheatley's poems, "bound in negro skin," for thirty-five dollars.[87] Schomburg's forays into auction galleries to secure Wheatleys or Godwyns thus redressed the "uneven densities" of archives: the way recordkeeping "thickens" around certain subjects and leaves scant trace of others.[88]

Schomburg gave such breathless attention to the "rarities," then, because the practice of searching for them, whether or not he won the bid, insisted on seeing blackness otherwise. Just as in his youth he had read the Black radical texts prohibited by Spain, he now surfaced veins of Black knowledge that the market had suppressed. His book-hunting excursions were exercises in both imagination and valuation: jaunty competitions with bibliophile friends to nab elusive objects, but also recalibrations of what the market typically sold as "Negro." Each acquisition, extracted from this market and recontextualized in his library, joined—as

Schomburg said after procuring Brown's *Narrative of a Fugitive Slave*—the " 'innumerable caravan' of those who sleep in my book case the sleep of the just and the rewarded of immortality."[89] In the hands of Black bibliophiles, texts conjured possibilities the market could not foresee. "I picked up Livingstone's 'Black Jamaica' paper cover for five cents," Schomburg wrote to Cromwell, "and there is a mass of facts for Negroes to peruse carefully." Here, the five cents paid for the book, its exchange value, belied its potential use as a "mass of facts" covertly residing in a pamphlet the market had practically discarded. As the market turned away, Black bibliophiles assembled equipment for struggle—or "powder with which to fight our enemies," as Schomburg proclaimed.[90] Speaking of his acquisitions in terms of potential energy, Schomburg imagined the books on his shelves as the "sleep of the just," and the Black library as a site of anticipated justice.

INSTITUTION BUILDING: MAKING THE NEGRO "EVER MY SUBJECT"

With a nose for "odd editions, lost clues and overlooked" items, as well as his fine-tuned ability to subvert the market, Schomburg gained notoriety for his "Pinkertonian virtuosity" in hunting for books.[91] Acquisition was a means, however, rather than an end. Never content to simply keep "the company of his books," Schomburg spent the 1910s, in concert with his bibliophile friends, experimenting with ways to institutionalize their collections and make them available for "Negroes to peruse carefully."[92] They opened their parlors to visitors, launched several different bookish organizations, staged exhibitions, and searched for a place to house their accumulated material. After cofounding the NSHR in 1911, Schomburg started to publicize his collection in earnest. He purchased a new typewriter and began "cataloguing" his holdings.[93] He imagined various audiences for what he called the "cat. of my odds and ends dealing with the Negro."[94] He might use the list to facilitate exhibitions of his collection—"probably in school rooms," he thought—or to advertise his skill as a collector, because he was "thinking seriously to open a store in the negro north."[95] Would the list be useful "if published," he wondered?[96] As he tentatively envisioned a public horizon for his "odds and ends," Schomburg sent his provisional catalog to friends and asked them to assess his collection.[97] While the letters between bibliophiles narrated adventures in acquisition—highlighting the practical challenges they faced in valuing individual items—the circulation of book lists engaged the question of what a "Negro collection" as a whole should comprise. Catalogs announced the existence of collections to a wider circle of readers and facilitated comparative discussions of a Black bibliographic imagination.

In 1913, Bolivar traveled from Philadelphia to visit Schomburg. "My inspection of your matchless collection was too cursory to know its full meaning," he wrote afterward, but "I do know that you have things beyond that of any other lot."[98] To continue this process of inspection, the two began trading lists by mail (figure 1.5). They would have seen in each other's catalogs much that was familiar. Of the 810 items on Schomburg's list, close to half matched Bolivar's items either in title or author (both collected Sutton Griggs and Henry Highland Garnet, for example, but Schomburg had more Griggs, and Bolivar more Garnet).[99] Many of their shared interests—in Black authors, Africa, antislavery, and the

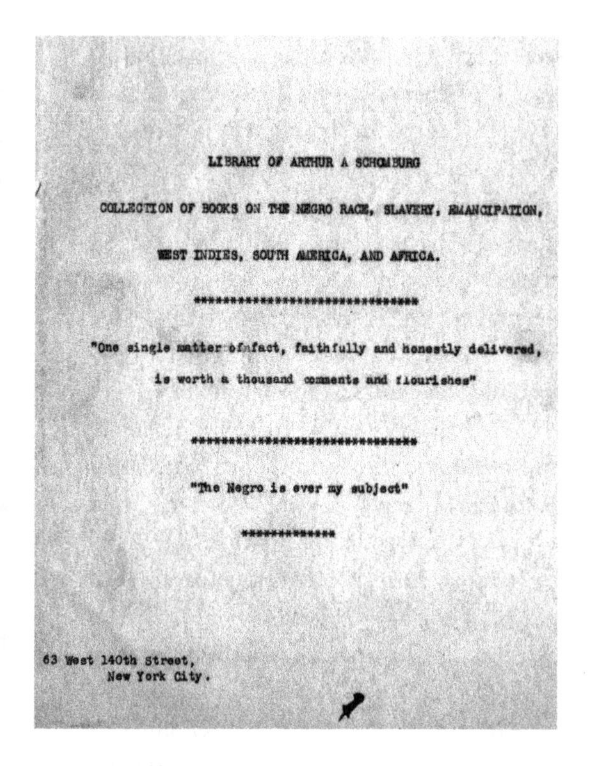

LIBRARY OF ARTHUR A SCHOMBURG

COLLECTION OF BOOKS ON THE NEGRO RACE, SLAVERY, EMANCIPATION, WEST INDIES, SOUTH AMERICA, AND AFRICA.

****

"One single matter of fact, faithfully and honestly delivered, is worth a thousand comments and flourishes"

****

"The Negro is ever my subject"

****

63 West 140th Street,
New York City.

(N)
Negro writers

LIBRARY
OF
WILLIAM C. BOLIVAR
PHILADELPHIA, PENNSYLVANIA

Together with Printed Tracts, Magazines, Articles, Reports, Addresses and Miscellaneous Not Enumerated.

Americana, Negroana, Manuscripts, Autograph Letters, Lincolniana, Rare Phamphlets, Travels, Africana, Etc.

Member American Negro Historical Society, Philadelphia; Corresponding Member Negro Society For Historical Research, Yonkers, N.Y.; Co-Editor "Murray's Colored Encyclopaedia;" Twenty-Two Years Writing Philadelphia History Under The Pen Name Of "Pencil Pusher," "Philadelphia Tribune;" Director Of Department Of Negro History, Downingtown Industrial and Agricultural School.

PHILADELPHIA
1914

FIGURE 1.5 Catalogs of two bibliophiles and friends: "Library of Arthur A. Schomburg Collection of Books on the Negro Race, Slavery, Emancipation, West Indies, South America, and Africa," circa 1914, and *Library of William C. Bolivar* (1914).

Source: Schomburg: Robert Park Papers, John Hope and Aurelia E. Franklin Library, Special Collections, Fisk University; Bolivar: *Library of William C. Bolivar* (Philadelphia: Watson, 1914).

church—mirrored other collecting projects of the period, such as the library of "colored authors" created by Daniel Murray for the Paris exposition in 1900 and the bibliographies on Africa compiled by Monroe Work at Tuskegee. To a certain extent, then, Schomburg and Bolivar used each other's catalogs as checklists, or delectuses, to learn of additions that would fit into well-established areas of Black inquiry. "Did you find in my list Mungo Park's travels?" Bolivar asked, referring to *Travels in the Interior of Africa*, which Schomburg had not yet acquired.[100] Bolivar, in turn, spotted on Schomburg's list Luis Emilio's *A Brave Black Regiment* and wished for one of his own.[101] Schomburg would ultimately follow Bolivar's lead in several collecting areas. Bolivar was ahead, for example, in acquiring proceedings of the colored conventions movement; Schomburg, who arrived in the United States in that movement's twilight years, learned of its significance from comrades like Bolivar and Cromwell, who had cross-generational ties to convention-goers. Schomburg soon caught up, however, boasting of owning the records of seven conventions.[102]

Comparison thus led to convergence and duplication, cementing a consensus about what might form the core of a "Negro collection." It also exposed the frictions between their visions, however. Although Schomburg's list bore an epigraph that suggested a singular category—"the Negro is ever my subject"—both he and Bolivar recognized "the Negro" as composite and conditional. Each had strategic areas of specialization evident in the halves of their catalogs that did *not* overlap. The stakes of collecting became most clear at these moments where they defined "Negroana" differently, underscoring the heterogenous political, geographic, and religious possibilities for imagining racial collectivity.[103] Bolivar concentrated on Americana, especially works on the antislavery movement and Black organizational life in the United States. That meant collecting more ephemera of Black Philadelphia—constitutions of the Pennsylvania State Equal Rights League and the Banneker Institute, for example—but also more "Lincolniana" and even white Southern nostalgia literature. By contrast, half of the works exclusive to Schomburg's list would have been called Africana rather than Americana. He owned three times as many books on Africa, as well as significant holdings on British abolition; writings by European Black authors; titles on Haiti, Cuba, Puerto Rico, Surinam, Dutch Guiana, and Jamaica; and global histories of religion, empire, science, and exploration. Upon studying Schomburg's list, Bolivar recognized this difference in their desiderata and kept an eye out for works that belonged on Schomburg's shelves rather than in his own library (figure 1.6). In 1914, he sent Schomburg a "finely bound book in re Africa," which he found at McGirr's State House Book Shop in Philadelphia. "This item," he wrote, "will not be lonely in your Africana."[104]

FIGURE 1.6 William Carl Bolivar, known as "The Pencil Pusher," in his home library, circa 1910. Photographer unknown.

Source: Arthur Alfonso Schomburg Photograph Collection, Photographs and Prints Division, Schomburg Center for Research in Black Culture, New York Public Library.

For Schomburg and Bolivar, cataloging activated a field of inquiry. In composing, comparing, and updating their lists, they found a productive workspace for exploring the coordinates of blackness as a subject. Schomburg gestured to these generative possibilities of list-making in another epigraph to his catalog: "One single matter of fact, faithfully and honestly delivered, is worth a thousand comments and flourishes." The epigraph comes from a seemingly unlikely source—Edmund Gibson's preface to *Britannia*, a sixteenth-century chronicle of British geography—but Schomburg likely drew this reference from a subsequent text that quoted it, Thomas Southey's 1827 *Chronological History of the West Indies*.[105] Southey remarked upon the challenge of writing an archipelagic history of the West Indies, where each island was shaped by its own topographies, languages, and imperial laws. His remedy leveraged the "unpretending form" of a list—an inventory of West Indian events in which meaning emerged through constellated fragments rather than a single narrative.[106] In choosing this epigraph for his own list, Schomburg embraced the "unpretending form" of a catalog to explore the integrity of "the Negro" as a field of study. Without a "thousand comments and flourishes," Schomburg's list hinted at lines of possible inquiry across difference.[107]

In Schomburg's catalog, for example, an account of the revolt of enslaved captives aboard the ship *La Amistad* sits adjacent to Blyden's *The Negro in Ancient History*; the Puerto Rican poet Salvador Brau's "Mi Campo Santo"; a biography of the prophet Muhammad; and two books on Haitian independence. Also situated nearby on the list are works on the Barotse Kingdom, emancipation in the West Indies, churches in Philadelphia, and Black participation in the American Revolution. In these entries, Schomburg moves bibliographically across language and continents, from ancient history to the present, while underlining Haiti as a marrow of his catalog. Elsewhere, his list includes thematic outliers—a lone work on Obeah and one on voodoo—that do not have enough company to coalesce into a clear collecting line but represent as-yet-unrealized possibilities about where the edge of collectivity might dwell. Schomburg's list poses the question, without fully answering it, of how these eight hundred objects constellate. It is at once intellectually ambitious and unfinished.[108] The quality of unfinishedness operates in tandem with the other epigraph on Schomburg's title page, "The Negro is ever my subject," which professes continuation. Although only one version of each bibliophile's catalog has survived, in practice, Schomburg and Bolivar kept cataloging, inking in additions, and typing new lists as their collections grew.[109] The catalog is an invitation, then, to the future.

That implied future attracted offerings from friends and other "finders." Although the radical orator Hubert H. Harrison described Schomburg's collecting strategy as "compact, systematic and well-ordered," it also reflected the disorder of sociality.[110] Schomburg's collection was never his alone. He obtained Robert Jones's *Fifty Years in the Lombard Street Church*, for example, as a gift from Jones's daughter Julia. "Don't forget to send a card," Bolivar wrote Schomburg afterward, urging him to "keep all finders in [a] good mood."[111] From London, Dusé Mohamed Ali mailed a copy of *In the Land of the Pharaohs*, signed "Bismillah!" David Fulton inscribed his account of the 1898 white supremacist coup in North Carolina to "Mr. Arthur A. Schomburg" with an explanation: "This little volume Hanover is the outpouring of a heart full of love for the people of my race."[112] Schomburg's catalog, then, did not just manifest his own bibliographic imagination but also reflected how others imagined his library and desired to be included in it. Long before Schomburg's collection made its way to a public institution, such gifts anticipated an archival future. James Bertram Clarke, a Spanish teacher in Brooklyn and a writer for *The Crisis*, gave Schomburg a biography of abolitionist Gerrit Smith with the prescient note, "To Arthur Schomburg, with the deepest appreciation of the work he is doing for colored posterity."[113]

Schomburg, too, pondered his collection's posterity, and in collaboration with his band of bibliophiles began to institutionalize his collecting practice. In 1911, he cofounded the NSHR with fellow masons Bruce and Fulton, artist William Ernest Braxton, musician W. Wesley Weekes, and a network of corresponding members from the Americas, Europe, and Africa. Among its first initiatives, the NSHR created the "nucleus of a Negro library," drawn largely from Schomburg and Bruce's holdings, and displayed these "archives and mementoes" to those attending its events at the Yonkers home of John and Florence Bruce.[114] Schomburg envisioned "a remarkable gallery" of items that "the Congressional Library would *like* to have."[115] Indeed, the NSHR aspired to show that an organization founded by a group of largely self-taught Black intellectuals could accrue cultural wealth rivaling any venerable institution. The organization circulated a brief list of its holdings in the press and proudly announced new acquisitions: a "true story written by a Negro of the Denmark Vesey insurrection," for example, or "a very rare book" on Crispus Attucks.[116] "We are constantly receiving accessions," Bruce told Locke, who was a corresponding member. Counting "Schomburg's collection Dr. Martin's and my own humble assortment" as part of the organization's library, Bruce boasted that by 1914, the NSHR held five thousand items. "We have we think a fair collection," he wrote, "of books and pamphlets, mss and letters, foreign and domestic, modern and ancient."[117]

When the NSHR launched in 1911, an active network of Black archives and libraries did not yet exist. Although some historically Black colleges or universities (HBCUs) had collected African American materials for half a century, their holdings remained modest and little known beyond campus. It would be another three years before Jesse Moorland donated his prized library to Howard University, and another twenty years before that collection (or any at an HBCU) had a fulltime curator. No public library in the country had yet established a research collection on Black life, nor had Carter G. Woodson established the Association for the Study of Negro Life and History. At its founding, then, the NSHR stood as the twentieth century's most ambitious attempt to give organizational structure to Black collecting practices. Its members felt an urgent, restless need not only to make resources available to readers but also to combat the "inutility of scattered curios" by providing a secure home for Black records.[118] A catalyst for that sense of urgency was the uncertain fate of the collection of Alexander Crummell, the revered Liberian nationalist and founder of the American Negro Academy. After Crummell's death in 1898, his papers and extensive personal library passed to his wife, Jennie Morris Crummell, and then to his protégé, Walter B. Hayson.[119] By 1912, Hayson's widow planned to sell the book collection, but the fledgling NSHR, short on funds, could not buy it unless "on the installment plan," Bruce lamented. Bruce tried to broker a sale to Howard University, and when that possibility fell through, he railed with characteristic astringence against "rich Negroes" who "do not seem to have foresight enough to see the advantage to them and the race which such an investment offers."[120]

"Some day," Bruce wrote after that disappointment, "a good angel will flap his wings and a roll of $10000 in $20 bills will drop out." Then he would have the funds for acquisition and a "permanent home" for the NSHR, "where the public could have access to its wonderful collection of rare historical Africana."[121] In the meantime, the NSHR continued a tradition of Black bibliophiles' parlors serving as public libraries. Teacher Laura E. Wilkes toured the homes of Martin, Schomburg, and Bruce to see the NSHR's collection, and Alice Dunbar-Nelson pored over their holdings to prepare an anthology of Black oratory.[122] Among the items each saw were Crummell's sermons and letters—the one part of his collection the NSHR had obtained. Julia Hayson gifted these manuscripts, which had been stored in a hayloft, and Schomburg recounted a sacred "pilgrimage" to recover them for the NSHR's "collection of Historical mss."[123] Soon after, Dunbar-Nelson selected one sermon, "The Black Woman of the South," for her volume *Masterpieces of Negro Eloquence*, thanking the NSHR for "lending priceless books and manuscripts."[124] Crummell's papers, and indeed most of NSHR's joint holdings, resided in Schomburg's apartment on West 140th Street. As a result, Schomburg's personal collection and the organization's became entangled in the public imagination.[125] In 1912, for example, the *A. M. E. Church Review* published a list of books and manuscripts in the NSHR's collection; two years later, the *African Times and Orient Review* printed the exact same list but attributed it solely to Schomburg.[126] That misidentification anticipated the way Schomburg's individual story came to stand in for the social history of Black archiving in the early twentieth century. Although he spent the 1910s collectively building an institution, by the 1920s, Schomburg's name alone would grace Harlem Renaissance marquees as the maker of a "Famous Library."

"WILL BE PRESERVED IN THIS ARCHIVES": BLACK HISTORY'S FUTURE

As plans for the NSHR's permanent space idled, Schomburg's home library increasingly took on the group's collectively imagined functions as a place of research, display, and congregation. One NSHR member recalled "Biblical, Social and Political" arguments taking place at the 115th Street apartment Schomburg shared with his old friend Ramon Rothschild, and Hubert Harrison stopped by whenever he needed the collection, which he called "better than mine."[127] Indeed, Schomburg cultivated a bookish scene in his home. Relishing his reputation as an "antiquarian and bookworm," he probably delighted in a 1912 newspaper article that described his next apartment, on 140th Street, as a "den" where one would "find a man busily delving among the ruins of Meroe or Egypt."[128] He made known to friends and strangers that his library was open for visitors to "peep at the books."[129] "I have fixed up things," he wrote to Locke, "and the library has a few easy chairs so that you can drop in and feel at home."[130] Locke and many others took him up on that invitation—not only in Harlem, but also on Kosciuszko Street in Brooklyn after Schomburg and his family made the last of their moves. He hosted an ever-growing number of readers and guests, among them W. E. B. Du Bois, J. E. Kwegyir Aggrey, Marcus Garvey, Carter G. Woodson, William Ferris, Arthur Spingarn, Elsie Clews Parsons, and the Liberian missionary Alexander Camphor.[131]

One of the most famous visits to Schomburg's library took place in 1922, when the writers Eric Walrond and Zora Neale Hurston journeyed to Brooklyn and wrote for the UNIA's *Negro World* about their time on "hallowed ground": "A visit to Arthur Schomburg's library! It is easy to appreciate why writers and artists, poets and anthologists, of both races, flock to the unpretentious little dusty-brown house of Kosciusko [sic] Street. Not only is it famous for its golden treasures, but the man, the mighty human spirit behind it, is the most precious, the most interesting curio of them all."[132] As they crossed the threshold into Schomburg's home, Walrond and Hurston found themselves in "a sitting room that exudes a classic odor." At a moment when many commentators deemed blackness a problem in the present and an absence from the past, Schomburg had carefully transformed the sitting room of his "unpretentious little dusty-brown house" into a "classic" library that was both symbol and sensorium—one that brought to life the museum of historical icons imagined decades earlier in William J. Wilson's "Afric-American Picture Gallery."[133] "On the walls are a mezzotint of St. George, a water color drawing of a Negro drum-major in Queen Anne's army, a sylph-like sketch of an Ethiopian princess, prints and pictures, paintings and daguerreotypes," Walrond recounted. His description foretold Elizabeth Alexander's theorization of the living room as a sacred space "where we see black imagination made visual."[134] Indeed, Schomburg prized the ocular as well as textual effects of his archive, with the images on his walls complementing what Hurston called the "marvelous collection" on "his extensive shelves."[135]

By the time Walrond and Hurston arrived at Schomburg's home, he had spent a decade trying to recreate in public settings this parlor gallery and reading room. Beginning in 1915, the bookmen in Schomburg's circle collaborated with a network of Black women writers and teachers to make a home for Black archives in New York. Schomburg, Bruce, and Martin joined an effort, chaired by Maude G. Hall, to establish a "Library of Negro Literature" at Saint Mark's M. E. Church.[136] A few years later, this same group contributed to an exhibition in Brooklyn of art, manuscripts, and books (many of them Schomburg's) in collaboration with the short-lived Negro Library Association, which hoped to secure a building for the "Proper Housing of Materials."[137] Although both efforts stalled, they marked a notable convergence between traditions of Black collecting: the church-based social libraries of the nineteenth century; exhortations by Black clubwomen to establish archives; and the largely masculine milieu of Black nationalist historical societies.[138] By 1921, this convergence moved uptown, where librarians Ernestine Rose, Catherine Latimer, and Regina Andrews were turning the 135th Street Branch Library into a hub for Black cultural and political life.[139] Located down the street from UNIA headquarters, the library drew in Garveyites like Harrison, as well as the bookmen of the NSHR and the women who had powered the Negro Library Association. Joining Schomburg to organize two "Negro Arts Exhibits" at the branch were the Negro Library Association's Maude Hall, Elizabeth Frazier, and Emily Downing, as well as NSHR founders Schomburg, Martin, Braxton, and Bruce—each of whom loaned items for display.[140] Years of experimentation in Black collecting began to institutionalize on 135th Street.

In 1924, as Schomburg drew closer to the 135th Street library, his longtime friend and mentor Bruce died. Together, he and Bruce had dreamed of a repository for the NSHR's holdings. The "good angel" Bruce hoped would "flap his wings" and deliver the requisite funds never appeared, however, and Bruce's death left Schomburg with even more books filling his house.[141] If in 1912 Schomburg had wondered whether he could manage his "treasured lot," a decade later, he reckoned with a collection that had tripled in size, with paper spilling from his living room to dining room, stacked in piles on the piano, and trailing down to the basement.[142] As someone told Elizabeth Schomburg, the collection was "pushing you out of the house."[143] This crowding intensified questions about the collection's institutional future. If the NSHR, the Negro Library Association, or Saint Mark's Church could not secure a permanent repository, where would it go? An auction house approached Schomburg about a potential sale, while Kelly Miller urged him to give the collection to Howard University.[144] Schomburg weighed these possibilities. He had watched Bolivar's collection sold at auction and "hate[d] to see it dismantled."[145] He once declined to sell a rare book on the Haitian Revolution to the Library of Congress because it "should be among the archive of some Negro institution."[146] His friend Aggrey, a West African educator, wanted the collection for Achimota College in Ghana, but Schomburg preferred that it "remain at home."[147] Thus, even after the demise of the NSHR, Schomburg held fast to his comrades' vision to create a Black repository in New York City.

Left with pieces of the NSHR's joint holdings, Schomburg intensified his dedication to creating a public collection. He chaired a citizens' committee at the 135th Street library to establish a Department of Negro Literature and History for non-circulating books, papers, and art.[148] In March 1925, an appeal to help gather these materials appeared in the special issue of *Survey Graphic*, edited by Locke, that also carried Schomburg's manifesto, "The Negro Digs Up His Past."[149] Many people answered the call to seed this new reference collection, including all of the NSHR's founders. Charles Martin and the widowed Florence Bruce donated items, as did Harrison and the bookstore owner George Young.[150] The largest acquisition by far, however, arrived in 1926 when the National Urban League brokered a deal, funded by the Carnegie Corporation, for the New York Public Library to purchase Schomburg's entire collection and install it at 135th Street. Bruce's quip proved prescient: the ten thousand dollars he wished from an angel was the precise sum that ultimately gave Schomburg's collection a permanent home. Behind the scenes, Urban League officials expressed ambivalence, for they had hoped Carnegie would fund an independent repository rather than giving ownership to the New York Public Library, which was hardly a "Negro institution."[151] Publicly, however, the sale attracted instant and widespread acclaim. "The Schomburg Negro Library Sold for $10,000," proclaimed the *Washington Eagle*; "Famous Library of Arthur A. Schomburg Purchased for $10,000," announced the *Philadelphia Tribune*.[152]

As these ovations suggest, the collection's price captured the public imagination. Schomburg surely understood why. Aware of the imbrication of cultural authority and finance, he leveraged the sale of his "poor collection" to grant it institutional value. Ten thousand dollars may have been what Arna Bontemps called a "token price"—"one-fifth of its real value," averred J. A. Rogers, and "cheap" even at twice that amount, said the *Negro World*—but to Schomburg, the desire to be paid for the collection was symbolic as well as pragmatic:[153]

> Some of those books are actually priceless, and cost a great deal of money. Others, not so rare, cost less. But the whole amount hardly gives me back the money I spent to get them. My time, labor, etc., go free, and I give them

> gladly. . . . I would have gladly given the books outright had I not felt, in a way it would have been unfair to the public, for, as a gift they might not have been deeply appreciated as they are by having cost something. Those who know what they cost, naturally feel there must be some real value attached to them.[154]

Schomburg knew that the collection would have research use, but he also knew that even for those who never ventured to the reading room, the *idea* that a Black library bore value mattered. The sale publicly confronted the charge that Black books—and, by proxy, the lives they chronicled—had no value. For decades, he and his fellow bibliophiles had negotiated over modest prices for individual items, from five cents to five dollars, in service of a proposition crystallized by the sale: that the sum of those transactions—and the labor of years of fugitive engagement with a hostile or indifferent market—would command respect for Black history.[155]

Arriving in Harlem in 1926, Schomburg's collection seemed perfectly aligned with Harlem Renaissance rhetoric that predicated cultural revival on the reimagining of a golden past. Jubilant press accounts of the sale touted the crown jewels of Schomburg's collection, such as its oldest book, printed in 1550, and his hallowed manuscripts of Crummell and Louverture.[156] The value of Schomburg's collection arose, however, not from the singular rarity of any one item, but from the fact that each existed in kinship with 4,600 others.[157] A collection's meaning emerges in assembly. That is why, when Walrond and Hurston visited Schomburg's library, he had insisted they experience its abundance, presenting them with a profusion of objects they described as both "marvelous" and "unsettling."[158] Indeed, Schomburg often called his collection "astonishing" or "startling."[159] He drew attention to the abundance of Black history, even where, to some people, it seemed surprising: in early modern Latin, in eighteenth-century poetry, or at the North Pole. In creating an "innumerable caravan" of Black radical texts, like Walker's *Appeal*, he also traced Atlantic history as a preponderance of what Michel-Rolph Trouillot would later call "unthinkable" histories, accumulating titles that, when brought into proximity, serialized Black revolt: *la révolution, les troubles, las insurrecciones, les noirs révoltés, les noirs insurgés, los rebeldes.*[160] In defiance of the suppression that had made it necessary for him to read Rafael Serra in secret, or the dismissal of Wheatley as an isolated curiosity, or the suggestion that slave insurrections were uncommon, the practice of assembling abundance insisted that Black expression could be neither destroyed nor diminished.

When Schomburg packed his books and papers for the last time, in 104 crates bound for the New York Public Library, he fulfilled his prophesy of 1912, that someday "the public will compel the libraries to have rooms devoted solely to Negro themes."[161] Dorothy Porter's observation, that Black bibliophiles had turned their parlors into public libraries, now became literal: no longer a private set of bookshelves on West 140th or Kosciuszko Street, Schomburg's library transformed into the "world famous Schomburg collection."[162] Indeed, the "Negro Division" at the 135th Street Branch Library eventually became known simply as the "Schomburg Collection."[163] Although named for an individual, the collection in fact preserved a sprawling set of bequeathals both material and intellectual. Wheatley had a small library of her own, a few volumes of which Schomburg bought, more than a century later, for a tiny sum. Crummell bequeathed his papers to the Hayson family, which in turn gave the sermons to the NSHR. Cromwell passed his family's knowledge of the conventions movement to Schomburg, who then collected its proceedings. Bruce left his books, papers, and Nigerian art works to his wife, Florence Bruce, who entrusted some to Schomburg and others to the 135th Street branch. The library thus manifested Schomburg's idea of Black history as an inheritance—"material upon which we can base our future"—that grew out of entwined and collective labors of remaking the past.[164]

In the public reading room, that inheritance would be subject to ongoing invention. Even after the sale, Schomburg added voraciously to the collection, knowing that it remained unfinished: "ever my subject."[165] As he did so, his lexicon for describing the collection's habitus shifted, from "my chambers" to "this archives."[166] That lexical shift signified the collection's institutional future as both a place of storage and a site of public imagination. Schomburg could assure a giver that her materials "will be preserved," and readers or visitors who climbed to the third floor of the library would find a space librarians cultivated with the specific aims to "inspire art students," "give information to everyone," and "arouse race consciousness."[167] These aims—to inspire, inform, and arouse—presumed that the collection, itself the product of many collectivities, would give rise to other forms of collective imagination. "The final destination of the archive is . . . in the story that it makes possible," Mbembe writes.[168] What forms that imagination would take—in art, erudition, or politics—the bibliophile and librarians could not predict, but cross-generational Black preservation practices would make these forms possible. The "instituting imaginary" of Schomburg and his comrades tendered space for Black archival futures.

CHAPTER TWO

A "HISTORY OF THE NEGRO IN SCRAPBOOKS"

The Gumby Book Studio's Ephemeral Assemblies

To Mr. Scrapbook, all the best,

—Ethel Waters, 1936

While the Schomburg Collection took shape at the 135th Street Branch Library, five blocks away another Harlem archival scene was in full swing: a site known not only for its books in "expensive printing" but also for a "vandal" history made of disappearing things—ephemera.[1] "How many things people trample under their feet that should be put in their heads," scribbled L. S. Alexander Gumby in his notes, paraphrasing a nineteenth-century manual on scrapbooking.[2] Gumby salvaged the things that might be trampled or trashed—ticket stubs, newsprint, calling cards—and pasted them into what he called a "History of the Negro in Scrapbooks."[3] He was a fan of boxing, vaudeville, and musical revues, an ardent admirer of pugilists and performers. One of the city's many flaneurs, he wore "fancy clothes" and "pale yellow kid gloves" as he moved between uptown and downtown, a member of the audience at Harlem's Lafayette Theater one night, a party goer in Greenwich Village's not-so-underground gay "atmosphere" the next.[4] He saved the gleanings from these outings and carefully placed each one in an exquisitely handcrafted scrapbook, made of brown paper and eleven by fifteen inches in size (figure 2.1). His souvenirs mingled with those sent by friends and idols, from the letters of once-aspiring little-known artists to the autographs of stars like Ethel Waters, who affectionately called him "Mr. Scrapbook." For Gumby, these were

FIGURE 2.1 L. S. Alexander Gumby in the Gumby Book Studio with friends Ted and Vincent, circa 1930. Gumby's "History of the Negro in Scrapbooks" collection is visible on the shelves behind the trio. Photographer unknown.

Source: "Gumby's Autobiography" scrapbook, Vol. 3, Series III: Scrapbooks, L. S. Alexander Gumby Collection of Negroiana, Rare Book and Manuscript Library, Columbia University.

the history makers—"every famous Negro and many not so famous"—and he was their archivist.[5]

Born in 1885, Gumby grew up in a world flooded by texts and images made possible by cheap paper technology.[6] Encompassing broadsides, pages of the penny press, and "gawdy throw-abouts," ephemera's abundance paradoxically encouraged both discard and reuse.[7] Although not meant to linger, ephemera was ripe for salvage, whether pasted on walls for decoration or cut into something functional, like a sewing pattern. One type of reuse sought to capture the documentary value of ephemera as a record of fleeting events, and scrapbooks enjoyed wide popularity as a method to corral information—in newspapers or programs, for example—that might otherwise disappear.[8] For African American readers, scrapbooks offered political possibility as well. By allowing creators to cut apart and rearrange ephemera, scrapbooking facilitated critical reproaches to the racist caricatures that saturated the era's mainstream print culture.[9] As the

Black radical thinker and scrapbooker Hubert H. Harrison argued, white newspapers "feature our criminals in bold head-lines," while relegating "our substantial men" to the smallest print, the "agate type division."[10] Gumby, too, recoiled from the stock characters depicting blackness in popular periodicals, which he taxonomized as the servant, charity seeker, pimp, and buffoon.[11] In the face of that hostile print, scrapbooking offered the opportunity to remix. Disassembly became Black knowledge production. Bits of "agate type" in the white press, if salvaged and assembled, could be transformed into a compendium of Black achievement.[12] Akin to Arthur Schomburg's ten-thousand-dollar library composed of thirty-cent books, Gumby's scrapbooks took fragments of blackness salvaged from what other people might "trample under their feet" and remixed them to create grandeur.

Gumby carefully prepared each scrapbook for perusal. He cut leaves of craft paper and strengthened their edges with dark *passe-partout* tape, adding trimmings to bestow "glamor" to each page.[13] In one album, he tucked a silk playbill from the Ziegfeld Follies into a pocket labeled "Please handle with the greatest of care," a note that invited readers to remove and unfold the silk, and by exercising care, to revel in Black history's fineness.[14] By treating every scrap with the same reverence as a prized first edition, he signaled that it belonged in a History of the Negro—even if other versions of that history thought otherwise. Indeed, Gumby's scrapbooks captured a different frequency of Black history than did the rare books that made Schomburg famous. Gumby, too, was an antiquarian when he had the means. He eagerly purchased Frederick Douglass letters, antislavery almanacs, and, from Schomburg, an edition of Phillis Wheatley's poems.[15] But the tilt of his collection was contemporary, recording the pulse of history-in-the-making. "Not only does Mr. Gumby seek the great things that [have] been done," the *New York News* reported, "but also the seeds of things that will be great in the future."[16] Gumby's scrapbooks reverberated with this tension between two forms of time: the "been done" and the "will be great." To record both, in ever-shifting relation to one another, Gumby engaged in what he called "vandal" strategies.[17] He rummaged, salvaged, and took things apart. To put them back together—to create an archive—required material improvisation, an approach that understood blackness as a set of ensembles, poses, and scenes still in formation.[18]

Drawing friends and followers into that method, Gumby turned scrapbook making into an exuberant collective sport.[19] A Southerner who migrated to New York at the turn of the century and pieced together jobs as a butler, porter, waiter, and postal clerk, he enjoyed a small degree of fame between 1925 and 1931 for the salons he hosted in his Fifth Avenue flat in Harlem.[20] Gathered in the Gumby Book Studio, as he called it, an eclectic coterie of visitors found themselves inside a meticulously constructed reading room—a mélange of archive, gallery, and Prohibition-era lounge—where the scrapbooks enjoyed central billing. Those who joined the "Gumby Group" were not denizens of Negro academies and lodges, as were those in Schomburg's milieu. Gumby's sphere was queer, co-ed, and interracial. Equally enthused by high art and low art, these salongoers did not gather for racial uplift.[21] His consorts were, on average, younger than Schomburg's set and newer to New York, with scrappier employment and bohemian desires. They formed organizations—such as the Southern Utopia Fraternity and the Art Students' Club—that were aspirational, occasionally mysterious, and often more temporary than even the ephemeral paper scraps that recorded their activities. When friends brought offerings to Gumby's scrapbooks, he carefully pasted them onto pages that recorded the era's experimental collectivities, thus interleaving the metanarratives of Negro History with what José Esteban Muñoz describes as queer modes of history in "innuendo, gossip, fleeting moments, and performances."[22] He turned his vandal method into an archive that used ephemera to record irreverent ensembles of race and sexuality.

Although Gumby salvaged the fragile flotsam of Black ephemeral life, his collection was itself ephemeral, held together with paste and subject to the vagaries of his health and finances. Like Schomburg, Gumby had public ambitions for his collecting project, but while Schomburg's library went public at the right time and place—secured at a venerable city establishment in the 1920s, when institutional money flowed to the Harlem Renaissance—Gumby's collection barely endured the 1930s. During the Great Depression, his studio closed, Gumby fell ill, and parts of his collection were destroyed, consigned to the "shadow archive" of African American culture.[23] Those losses, however, ushered in other archival acts. Gumby's friends rallied to save the collection, forming a temporary collective to protect the scrapbooks. Meanwhile, Gumby turned his hospitalization into another set of scrapbook pages that documented the liminal, homosocial world of sanitariums where men spent time convalescing, and where disease and desire comingled.[24] Archives take shape through such entwined moments of erasure and invention. They disintegrate, get remade, and give rise to new forms of sociality—without necessarily producing permanent files.[25] Gumby's ephemeral methods, then, dramatized the ambivalent tempos of New Negro identity: a vanguardism that eschewed the past, a contravening impulse toward historical recuperation, and fleeting collectivities that resisted preservation. His archive, made from disappearing things and then almost disappearing itself, captured these queer refusals and longings to belong to history.

COLLECTING AND COLLECTIVITY: THE SOCIAL LIFE OF THE GUMBY BOOK STUDIO

A "delicate child," Gumby began scrapbooking in his youth, when he lived with his grandmother in a small town on Maryland's Eastern Shore.[26] At the turn of the century, he and his sister used a discarded paperhanger's book to save poems printed in the newspaper and clippings of the latest headlines, including President McKinley's assassination in 1901. Leaving home shortly thereafter, Gumby briefly enrolled at Delaware State College before embarking for Philadelphia. Around 1906, with his suitcase of clippings in tow, he landed in New York, where he discovered "more freedom of action than I had ever known." Soon a "New Yorker in spirit and principle," he frequented vaudeville houses as well as serious theater, and "frolicked to gratify every caper of a youth alone in a big city."[27] His circuit of friends revolved around the Cheatham brothers, Charles and Henry, sons of a Black political family from North Carolina. They helped him collect ephemera, as did Charles's brother-in-law, the vaudeville star Leigh Whipper.[28] While working as a butler in the wealthy Riverdale enclave (figure 2.2), Gumby met Charles W. Newman, the son of a prominent white manufacturer.[29] Newman became what Gumby publicly called a "staunch friend," while privately calling him "the loved one."[30] By the 1920s, Gumby had taken up residence in Harlem, first on West 132nd Street and then at 2144 Fifth Avenue. With his own salary as a postal clerk and the financial support of Newman, who became a Wall Street broker, Gumby expanded his living space and launched the Gumby Book Studio in 1925 as a place to "entertain my Wall Street friend" and to "master the art of making scrapbooks."[31]

"Soon other friends formed the habit of visiting the Studio," Gumby recalled, "and they in turn brought their friends who brought their friends, regardless of race or color... The Studio became a rendezvous for intellectuals, musicians, and artists."[32] As the writer Arthur Davis remembered it, Gumby's studio welcomed a "broader social mixture" than other Harlem Renaissance salons.[33] Operating at the lower frequencies of the Renaissance—away from the gilded crowd at A'Lelia Walker's Dark Tower or the marquee performances of blackness at the Cotton Club—Gumby organized weekly, invitation-only parties for a crowd of aspiring and unfamous artists known as the Gumby Group. Less often, he played host to large events that drew famous attendees, as when Edward Perry threw a stag party for his friend and former lover Countee Cullen.[34] On such occasions, the *Amsterdam News* reported, one would find at the Gumby Book Studio "as cosmopolitan a crowd as New York affords," full of well-known figures from uptown

FIGURE 2.2 Photograph of L. S. Alexander Gumby, circa 1910, when he was working as a butler for the Burghard Steiner family in Riverdale; across the street lived the family of Charles Newman, who became Gumby's lover and patron. Photographer unknown.

Source: "Gumby's Autobiography" scrapbook, Vol. 5, Series III: Scrapbooks, L. S. Alexander Gumby Collection of Negroiana, Rare Book and Manuscript Library, Columbia University.

and downtown: poets Maxwell Bodenheim and Langston Hughes; artist Aaron Douglas; actress Rose McClendon; musician Paul Robeson; writers Alain Locke and Wallace Thurman; and cartoonist Haile Hendrix, among others.[35] Most of the studio's guests, however, were minor characters in the era's major plotlines—including Perry, who briefly appeared in *Porgy and Bess*, and Henri Wessel, a Cotton Club dancer.[36] Along with Richard Bruce Nugent, Perry was part of the studio's conspicuously queer milieu, composed of men who held afterhours gatherings at a time when public gay venues (such as the nearby Hobby Horse) were frequently raided by police.[37]

At the center of these overlapping scenes presided the muse known as the "Great God Gumby," who made the studio a place where the tactile experiments of collecting met the social experiments of bohemian collectivity. "You really didn't know Harlem till you knew Gumby," the columnist Floyd G. Snelson Jr. wrote, "the tall figure lying back on a divan in an exotic dressing-gown, nursing along the imagination of his guests till the air was full of philosophy, esthetics and love" (figure 2.3).[38] Not just Gumby, but the scrapbooks, too, drew people in. The Book Studio was one of Harlem's most consciously constructed spaces signifying New Negrodom, a "miniature museum" decorated with scrapbooks, paintings, and books.[39] When visitors arrived, Gumby made sure they felt immersed in "a veritable shrine to Negro greatness"; as his friend Theodore Hernandez wrote, anyone who entered "receives an indelible impression of true

FIGURE 2.3 Detail from "Gumby's Autobiography" scrapbook depicting a party scene inside the Gumby Book Studio, circa 1930. Gumby is seated in a floral jacket at right (back to camera). Photographer unknown.

Source: Series III: Scrapbooks, L. S. Alexander Gumby Collection of Negroiana, Rare Book and Manuscript Library, Columbia University.

Negro attainment."[40] Gumby's authority to command visitors grew along with his collection. "I remember spending hours poring over your marvelous scrapbooks," Hernandez recalled.[41] Gumby even invited the boxing champion Jack Johnson to stop by, telling him that he would be "amazed" by the collection.[42] Indeed, Gumby imagined his collection as a "far-reaching" attraction, "with each one of its volumes so fine and selective in its makeup that no other collection could even hope to equal it."[43] Designed for display, the scrapbooks appear in nearly all extant photographs of Gumby's studio: filling shelves along the walls; open and in presentation to visitors; or lending a bookish backdrop to an interracial, mixed-gender crowd of salon goers.

Gumby evoked scrapbooking's pleasures—"There is nothing more interesting than going through a bundle of old newspapers looking for clippings," he wrote—and he invited others into his practice.[44] Although Gumby called the salon goers his "Muses," they were also fellow collectors, helping him build the collection.[45] Schomburg presented Gumby with an item for his "Breaking Bonds" volume on the history of slavery and freedom.[46] Gladys Flynn, a stenographer for the NAACP (the National Association for the Advancement of Colored People), brought him carbon copies from the office.[47] Whipper, on tour in London, promised to send "a bunch of junk."[48] Gumby paid tribute to these contributors by keeping their canceled envelopes or noting their initials next to items he pasted into the albums. The letters C.E.C., for example, memorialize the contributions of his friend Charles E. Cheatham, who gave Gumby artifacts of public success—his father's stint as one of Reconstruction's last Black politicians—and of personal taste—his own devoted fandom of the vaudeville star Bert Williams.[49] The presence of these initials recalls Katherine Ott's argument that scrapbooks subtly shift our attention from ephemera's content to the associational life of its compilers.[50] As traces of everyday life, mass-produced ephemera harbors an ironically intimate quality, recording the "serial passage" of paper from "body to body" through the punch of a ticket or the circulation of a calling card.[51] Gumby's collection, then, was neither personal papers nor organizational records, but something in between—an attempt to represent what one visitor to his studio called the "scattered and fugitive things" of Black cultural life.[52]

In the studio, a "young clique of enthusiasts" gathered to share writerly experiments and make a place for themselves in the frenetically inventive Harlem scene of the late 1920s.[53] Among the conveners were Nell Occomy, a teacher and poet; "sweet Teddy Hernandez," a journalist; Leontha Wright, an actress from Georgia; and Constance Grayson, a young playwright.[54] Not just admirers of the studio's scrapbook collection, these unfamous creators also became *subjects* of the scrapbooks. As the journalist Aubrey Bowser wrote, Gumby "has a full set of clippings about every famous Negro and many not so famous. If you visit Gumby's studio you may be surprised when he pulls an enormous ledger-sized book from a shelf and informs you that it is devoted to you and your doings."[55] Indeed, in a series of pages labeled "Negro Intellectuals Rendezvous," Gumby recreated what might have been a typical evening with the Gumby Group.[56] Photographs of Hernandez and Grayson face each other as if in conversation. Between them appears a poem by the Jamaican-Irish salon goer Ferdinand Levy, while the autographs of studio regulars Louis González, G. San Novarro Songer, and John A. Jenkins encircle the page.[57] To their left, a drawing of Hernandez hides a cache of letters exchanged among the group—a gesture toward a salon's intimacies that would be lost if these documents were properly housed in folders and filed under individual names. By pasting the Gumby Group's ephemera into a "far-reaching" History of the Negro, Gumby made the argument that Black history takes shape as much through these fleeting gatherings as through the more enduring storylines documented in his albums on Frederick Douglass or the NAACP.

Gumby declared that the Book Studio gave rise to "the first unpremeditated interracial movement in Harlem."[58] His vanguardist claim may be tenuous, but the studio did welcome types of knowledge and sociality unheralded elsewhere. Declaring his "Negro Intellectuals Rendezvous" free of "social and academic snobbery," Gumby made clear that in his studio a Black thinker "would not be expected" to produce works of a "strenuously Negroid" sort.[59] What did it mean to curate a space dedicated to the History of the Negro, while asserting that what transpired inside it need not be "strenuously Negroid"? Anticipating Stephen Best's interest in art that refuses "conceptions of blackness as authenticity, tradition, and legitimacy," Gumby cultivated irreverent forms of Black artistry.[60] Much of the work shared in the studio was decidedly out of vogue, such as Willie Branch's rendition of the English operetta *Zurika the Gypsy Maid*.[61] Few of the poets in his orbit got reprinted in Harlem Renaissance anthologies, and the studio failed to manifest the trove of "Negro Arts and Letters" that cemented the legacy of other literary networks, such as those later enshrined in the James Weldon Johnson Memorial Collection at Yale.[62] Johnson himself excluded the Gumby Group from his documentary work *Black Manhattan*, despite the fact that the story of Gumby's white millionaire patron mimicked Johnson's fictional plot in *Autobiography of an Ex-Colored Man*, reprinted in 1927.[63] The Gumby Book Studio traversed the color line, and as was also true in Johnson's novel, its lack of fidelity to racial categories dovetailed with queer forms of sexuality.[64] Left out of texts and archives that would define the Renaissance period, Gumby longed for his own form of print circulation.

In 1929, the Gumby Group moved to transform its social and intellectual scene into a new print public through the creation of a journal, *Gumby's Book Studio Quarterly* (figure 2.4). In an unpublished preface written by Hernandez, the *Quarterly* introduced itself as an extension of the "untrammeled discussion" among Gumby's friends who congregated in the Studio:

> The QUARTERLY is an outgrowth of Gumby's Book Studio which houses the modest but significant collection of L. S. Alexander Gumby, who, in addition to his efforts of securing and preserving items and documents pertaining to

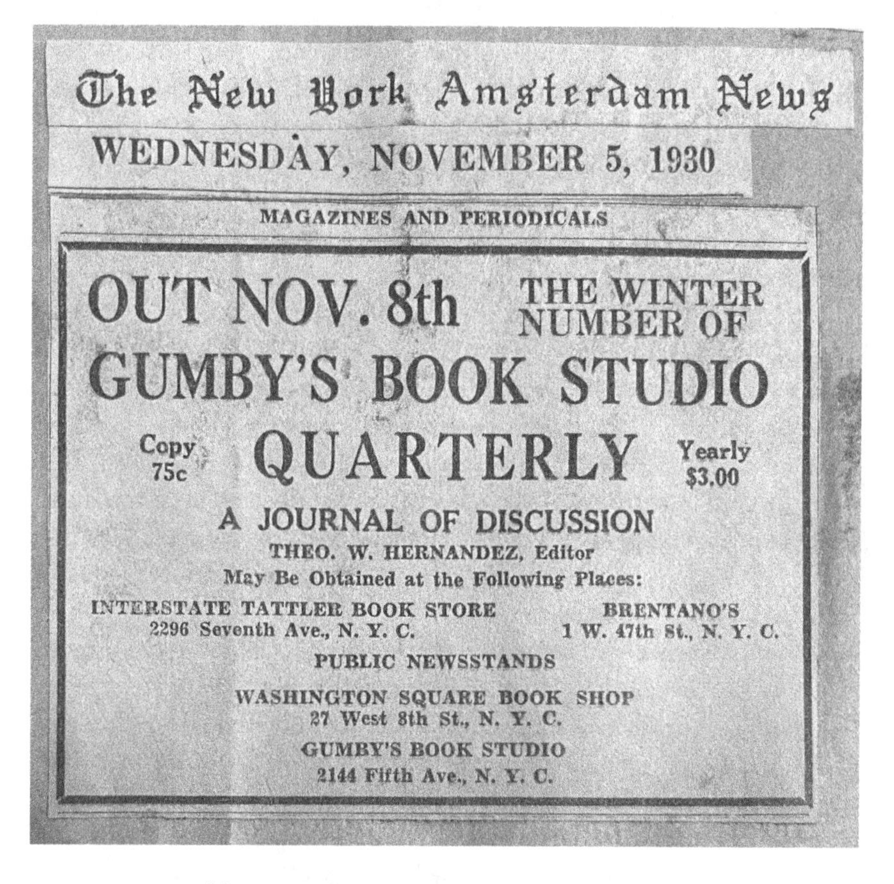

The New York Amsterdam News
WEDNESDAY, NOVEMBER 5, 1930

MAGAZINES AND PERIODICALS

OUT NOV. 8th THE WINTER NUMBER OF
GUMBY'S BOOK STUDIO
Copy 75c QUARTERLY Yearly $3.00
A JOURNAL OF DISCUSSION
THEO. W. HERNANDEZ, Editor
May Be Obtained at the Following Places:
INTERSTATE TATTLER BOOK STORE
2296 Seventh Ave., N. Y. C.
BRENTANO'S
1 W. 47th St., N. Y. C.
PUBLIC NEWSSTANDS
WASHINGTON SQUARE BOOK SHOP
27 West 8th St., N. Y. C.
GUMBY'S BOOK STUDIO
2144 Fifth Ave., N. Y. C.

FIGURE 2.4 Detail from L. S. Alexander Gumby's "Gumby Book Studio" scrapbook. Advertisement printed in the *New York Amsterdam News* for the *Gumby Book Studio Quarterly*, November 5, 1930. The advertisement promises the *Quarterly* will be available on November 8, but it never appeared.

Source: Series III: Scrapbooks, L. S. Alexander Gumby Collection of Negroiana, Rare Book and Manuscript Library, Columbia University.

> Negro History and Letters, for some years has been engaged in compiling a most unique scrapbook collection. . . . From time to time the Studio is the meeting place of poets, artists, musicians, writers and laymen who come together under the quickening influence of literary and musical recitals, art exhibitions and for the purpose of research and, above all, discussion. . . . [T]here has grown up such a spirit of unity and accord that it is possible to speak of the Gumby Studio Group. . . . Primarily it was the realization of the greater good to be achieved, if it were possible to enable larger numbers to share with this nascent group the beneficent effect of free and untrammeled discussion, that inspired the conception and publication of the QUARTERLY.[65]

A friend warned that "the launching and publication of a magazine" was a "terribly uncertain, hazardous thing," but for Gumby, it represented the logical culmination of his years of collecting both scraps and people.[66] He owned copies of Wallace Thurman's fledgling journals—*Harlem: A Forum of Negro Life* and *Fire!*, which grew out of a gathering at Aaron Douglas's apartment—and he likely knew of the magazines started by "conclaves" of Black artists in other places, including *Saturday Evening Quill* from Boston, *Black Opals* from Philadelphia, *Black Bard* from Alabama, and a relaunched edition of *Stylus* at Howard.[67] A magazine of its own would shore up the credentials of the Gumby Group within this literary orbit. Indeed, the *Amsterdam News* predicted that "the Quarterly will do for this group of writers what The Quill has done for a similar group in Boston, that is, serve as a medium for the expression of their efforts, as well as mold them into a forceful body which must be considered when the literary life of New York is mentioned."[68] As a collectivity formed in—and archived by—Gumby's collection, the "nascent group" drawn to the Book Studio now sought to extend its reach.

Featuring experimental fiction, sentimental poetry, and social commentary by writers both established and unknown, the *Quarterly* enacted the blend of "philosophy, esthetics, and love" that characterized the studio's social scene.[69] It was to include Schomburg's review of the African origins of the tango, Hernandez's science fiction tale depicting Christianity as a cosmic lab experiment gone awry, and Nugent's imagined romance about Simon of Cyrene (the North African biblical figure who carried the cross).[70] Although eleven of the fifteen writers for the first issue were Black, the *Quarterly* declared itself "not . . . a racial magazine."[71] To a certain degree, that declaration signaled the inclusion of "writers of all races," but more so it positioned the *Quarterly* as "anti-everything"—the term Nugent used to describe Gumby.[72] Billed as "a medium of discussion available to all shades of thought and opinion," the *Quarterly* rejected the parameters of other Black-edited magazines, refusing the mantle of literary vanguardism, social reform, or propaganda.[73] To underline that point, George Schuyler would set the tone of the issue with his opening piece, a satirical romp titled "A Plea for Intolerance," and other entries lampooned reigning power brokers of Black culture. T. Thomas Fortune Fletcher's story, for example, spoofed a professor of "Negro culture" who indifferently waxed poetic as a lynch mob raged nearby, while a review by the film critic Sydney Sanders critiqued Hollywood's depiction of Black characters as "singing in the kitchen, singing in the jail, singing in church."[74] A literary version of Gumby's "vandal history," the *Quarterly* intended to irreverently cut apart and cut across representations of blackness.

CLIPPING AS BLACK INTELLECTUAL PRACTICE

Calling himself a "vandal history maker," Gumby constructed his "History of the Negro in Scrapbooks" by dismantling, salvaging, and improvising.[75] With scissors he purchased at Woolworth's, he cut things apart, and with a homemade paste of flour and water, he turned that destruction into new forms.[76] Between cutting and pasting, however, stood decisions about who, what, and how. As Gumby's piles of clippings and throwaways grew larger, how would he arrange them? His process of ordering and classifying unfolded across several decades. In those decades, his circumstances and companions changed. He was a salon host in Harlem one year, a convalescent on Brother Island the next. He lost the coveted job of postal worker, returned briefly to domestic service in Newman's house, and waited tables at Columbia University. He gathered with old friends, kept going to the theater, longed for love. His scrapbooking practice was entwined with each of these scenarios. Indeed, the eclecticism Gumby cultivated in his salons and in the *Book Studio Quarterly* also took shape in his scrapbooks, leading to themes and categories as untidy as his own desires and itineraries. That unruliness is less visible today, in his collection now preserved at Columbia, because the library cataloged it narrowly, assigning subject headings only to those parts of his collection easily legible as "Negroiana."[77] But the story of Gumby's experimental praxis points to the multifarious fancies that have always shaped Black archives.

Narrating his earliest experiments in organizing the contents of his "bureau-drawers . . . jammed with clippings," Gumby wrote: "Without experience in the arranging of such a vast amount of miscellaneous material, I naturally made a botch of it in my first efforts."[78] He amended his attempts to "classify the material into groups" before conceding that "it would all have to be done over."[79] Early in his collecting practice, Gumby pasted his "Negro" items into a single volume, and when they grew abundant, he divided that volume into subjects and chapters. "I arranged the clippings chronologically that were not too badly damaged by their repeated remountings," he remembered, but soon this one Negro volume was "bulging . . . whereupon I broke the chapters up into separate books. Thus began my Negro Scrapbook collection."[80] This sequence of improvisations underscores the tactile and intellectual labors required to define the "Negro" as a subject of inquiry. Individual clippings and sometimes entire pages needed testing in a variety of combinations. Changes in a storyline, or the sudden fame of a minor character, might require recalibrating the collection's focus. Gumby might change his mind about what items belonged together, or he might find new material to interfile among what he had already assembled. To accommodate this flux, Gumby adopted the "looseleaf method," a binding that could be taken apart and put back together. He thus staked the future of his collection on perpetual expansion and rearrangement.[81]

Such experimentation became necessary as Gumby's collection grew from a few "odds and ends" toward an ongoing, multivolume "History of the Negro."[82] That expansion took him far beyond the bounds of conventional scrapbooking. To be sure, Black intellectuals had made albums documenting their lives and interests since at least the 1850s. Frederick Douglass and his sons kept scrapbooks, as did educators Sarah Mapps Douglass and Ada H. Hinton; Ida B. Wells-Barnett and her husband; Alice Dunbar-Nelson and her sister; James Weldon Johnson and his wife Grace Nail Johnson.[83] Only a few documentarians, however, scaled clipping to the epic proportions that Gumby dreamed of. Among them was William Henry Dorsey, whose four hundred scrapbooks—many devoted to Negro History—resided in his parlor museum in Philadelphia. Between the 1880s and 1900s, Dorsey welcomed visitors to see and use his collection, which also included books, African artifacts, and "engravings by eminent Negroes."[84] Gumby may or may not have encountered Dorsey in Philadelphia, but he followed in his footsteps. He also answered the call of journalist Gertrude Mossell, who in 1886 heralded clippings as "unwritten history" with "value to us as a people."[85] Echoing Mossell, Gumby wrote, "There are so many surprising and startling historical events . . . relating to the American Negro that are not recorded in the Standard Histories," with "only newspaper, magazines, and unpublished letters that record them."[86] That ephemerality characterized much of Black print culture—especially for the topics that most interested Gumby, from art and boxing to youth and aspiration.

Unlike his predecessors, Gumby cut and pasted in an era when scrapbooks were growing obsolete as a mode of information management. With the rise of "industrialized memory work," libraries and clipping bureaus took over the work of saving and sorting bits of newspaper.[87] Spurred by the invention of filing cabinets in the 1890s, clipping files became a standard feature of institutional libraries, a place for storing "miscellaneous odds and ends that . . . before the days of the Clipping File were as wanderers with no suitable abiding place."[88] Librarians at the Hampton Institute launched a system for classifying clippings that a subsequent commentator called "one of the earliest large-scale, systematic ventures in day-to-day Black documentation."[89] At the Tuskegee Institute, Monroe Work maintained thousands of clipping files that supplied data for the annual *Negro Year Book*, first issued in 1912.[90] At the 135th Street Branch Library near Gumby's studio, Catherine Latimer began a vertical file in 1924.[91] With the invention of such tools, the need for personal information retrieval systems declined. Scrapbooks remained popular primarily for memorabilia and poetry, two forms "closely associated with women and more vulnerable to derision."[92] Gumby nonetheless embraced this discarded way of archiving and its gendered obsolescence. Although always a wage laborer, Gumby cultivated his reputation as a bohemian, an identity associated with unmanly decadence and resistant to industrialized productivity.[93] Likewise, he wielded scrapbooking's inefficiencies—its attention to improvisation and aesthetic detail—to obliquely record insurgent formations of race and sexuality.

One could not quickly pull from Gumby's collection concise data on Black achievements, as one could at Tuskegee or in Latimer's files.[94] Rather, Gumby's scrapbooks required the slow perusal of oversized volumes filled with information at once too abundant and too fleeting to be indexed in a clipping file. As if "by means of a magic camera," his friend Hernandez wrote, Gumby captured "traces of social forces" and "details which might otherwise have been forever lost."[95] In his "Negro in Drama" scrapbook, for example, pages on the short-lived Broadway play *Scarlet Sister Mary* detoured from theater history to a sidebar on queer Harlem. Alongside the play's program, Gumby pasted in a letter from the literary critic Sam Steward. It described not only the "colossal fiasco" of Ethel Barrymore's blackface performance, but also (apropos of nothing related to the play) Steward's visit to Gumby's studio—an evening he described elsewhere as full of "bathtub gin, a game of truth, and assorted homosexual carryings-on."[96] This detail is *in* Gumby's "Negro in Drama" but not quite *of* it: he neither hides nor highlights this extraneous bit of queer information. Abundance thus makes space for allusive forms of evidence that fall outside or between the categories formally named in his scrapbook's titles. Made for browsing rather than searching—anticipating the gaze of the flaneur as much as the researcher—Gumby's purposefully, queerly anachronistic method of archiving harbored such unindexed storylines, tuned to Negro History's other frequencies.[97]

By the late 1920s, Gumby's collection contained at least seventy volumes. Among them were scrapbooks devoted to Africa, slavery, Haiti, Liberia, art, politics, music, pugilism, and drama as well as biographical volumes on Jack Johnson, W. E. B. Du Bois, Frederick Douglass, and Booker T. Washington.[98] In the 1930s and 1940s, when he updated the collection, Gumby expanded many of these categories; his attention to boxing, for example, stretched to fifteen scrapbooks, including a nine-volume set on Joe Louis alone. When he donated his collection to Columbia University in 1950, the "History of the Negro in Scrapbooks" had grown to more than a hundred volumes, including six he called "Gumby's Autobiography." But that was not all. His collection always contained scrapbooks outside of the series on Negro History. Categorized as "Personal," these included volumes on the "Prince of Wales," "Art—The Pictures of Christ," "Charles Ginsburg's Flight," "Gentile Persecutions of the Jews," and "Broadway Classics."[99] Some of these personal albums have not survived, but others—those devoted to Frank Sinatra, the actor Jimmy Stewart, and Gumby's cat Toby—remain in the collection today. Seemingly out of sync with the theme of Negro History, the topics of these wayward albums do not appear among the subject headings Columbia librarians later chose for the collection. For his part, however, Gumby seemed to take pleasure in disrupting the categories he had improvised.

The scope of Gumby's collection suggests a Negro History on less certain ground than Schomburg's brand of "thinking black."[100] Although Schomburg stated that he had always collected with a singular ambition—to "awaken the spirit of loyalty to the race"—Gumby made no such claim.[101] His collecting impulse, he said, began in a meandering way, with a left-behind book of wallpaper samples, some poems, and the coverage of McKinley's assassination. The queerness of that route into Negro History highlights what goes unremarked in Schomburg's origin story and in those of other famous bibliophiles who seeded major research collections on "the Negro." Each one, whether they said so or not, pursued sidelights. Dorsey kept a scrapbook about ancient relics, buried cities, and meteorites, for example, and Jesse Moorland devoted a part of his collection to works on felines.[102] Phil B. Brooks's library, which went to Hampton in 1924, included not only books "by Negro authors and about the Negro" but also sections on sports, dogs, and magic, which led librarians to call his collection not only "remarkable" but also "bewildering."[103] By lavishing care on his "truant" volumes (as literary critic Gene Andrew Jarrett might call them), Gumby made visible what was true in every "Negro collection": that blackness wanders beyond the headings found in a catalog.[104]

Reveling in ephemera's unruly abundance, Gumby tested ideas of blackness by following subjects as they moved between the categories and geographies of his scrapbooks.[105] Gumby's "Greenwich Village" scrapbook was not officially part of his History of the Negro series, for example, but it focused to a great extent on the downtown presence of Black artists, such as composer Theodore Upshur, and on cultural traffic between the Village and Harlem. On one set of pages, vocalist C. Carroll Clark, known as the Warbling Othello, appears in a pencil sketch drawn by the white downtown cartoonist Haile Hendrix (figure 2.5). That image sits opposite two other items: an autographed, smoke-filled photograph of the artist Nicholas Pisarro; and a pocket labeled "Recipe" that contains Hendrix's scrawled instructions for making a half-gallon of punch from shaved oranges and "equal parts water & alcohol."[106] The scene evokes a party in Greenwich Village, but it constellates with a second event documented in the History of the Negro series. This same trio of Clark, Hendrix, and Pisarro recurs in the guest book

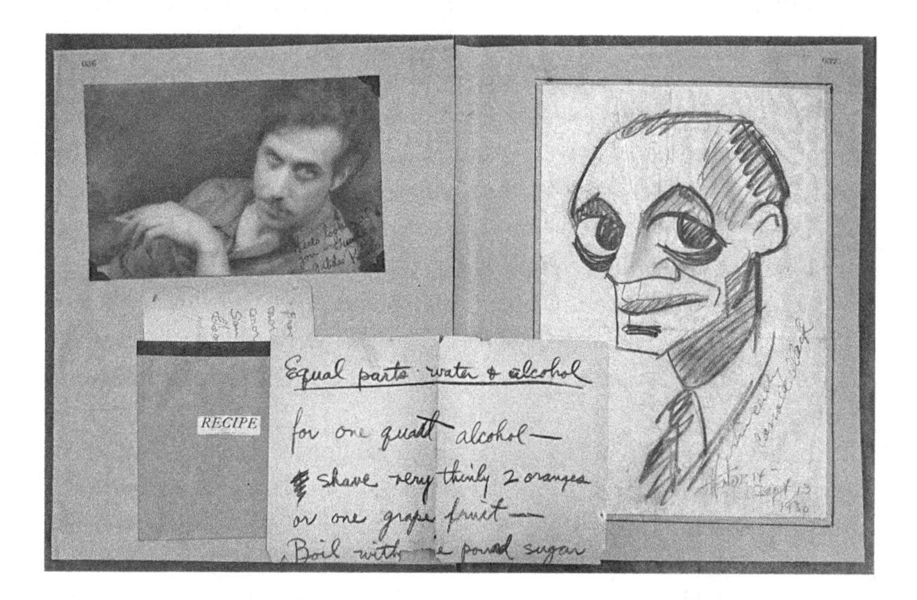

FIGURE 2.5 Page from L. S. Alexander Gumby's "Greenwich Village" scrapbook. Photograph of Nicholas Pisarro autographed and signed "Here's looking at you-Gumby!" Sketch of C. Carroll Clark by Haile Hendrix. Pocket labeled "recipe" contains Hendrix's instructions for making a punch with "Equal parts water & alcohol," circa 1930.

Source: Series III: Scrapbooks, L. S. Alexander Gumby Collection of Negroiana, Rare Book and Manuscript Library, Columbia University.

for the Gumby Book Studio, in attendance at the uptown stag affair that Perry hosted for Cullen.[107] Such echoes repeat across the collection as Gumby's Harlem salongoers show up in downtown scenes and vice versa.[108] Gumby thus followed blackness in transit between different sites of collectivity, queering the boundaries of race and history writing. He mapped a Harlem-Village circuit enfolding complex stories of interraciality, beyond tales of white pleasure-seekers in Jazz-Age Harlem.[109]

A "thousand ways of dressing, moving around, and imagining" gave to the city a kinetic restlessness, which Gumby captured by layering ephemeral forms extracted from circulation.[110] Through collage techniques, Gumby explored contrasting ways of being Black in the cityscape—in vogue or out of vogue, on stage or off. On one page, for example, he selected two contrasting images of actor Leigh Whipper: one posed as a vaudeville "funny maker" in grinning blackface; the other, out of costume, reposed on a porch swing.[111] In this particularly elaborate layout, both images, and an autograph of the songsmith Porter Grainger, overlay sheet music for Whipper and Grainger's song "There Ain't No Fool Like an Old Fool." While the blackface portrait evokes minstrel stereotypes, Gumby's composition as a whole takes seriously the work of Black lyricists and comedians-turned-entrepreneurs. "It's great to be crazy and *know it*," Whipper said; Gumby's layout—with one pose outlandish and the other cool—attests to this knowing.[112] Perhaps Gumby lavished such care on this scene because he knew that the comedic, foolish stage persona that launched Whipper's career (and enabled him to bankroll other Black artists) stood at the precipice of disappearance. Gumby dwelled on the complexity of a version of blackness seemingly of little use to the contemporary, one that might even "estrange a collective present."[113] His layout makes conspicuous the scrapbook's core function of "preserving impermanence."[114] Indeed, Gumby's design choices underscore the fact that collecting does not capture a static subject. Rather, it engages with that subject's transformations.

As Nugent observed, Gumby had an "amazing ability to garner every little news item about anything that he happened to fancy."[115] He was particularly adept at leveraging ephemera's form—its reliance, José Esteban Muñoz argues, on "traces, glimmers, residues, and specks of things"—to evoke "minoritarian" scenes.[116] By creating flaps, folds, and pockets in his scrapbooks, he gave refuge to traces of Black life that went unclassified elsewhere. At the 135th Street library, Latimer saved articles on many of the same subjects Gumby chronicled. Each dedicated a scrapbook to the 1930 play *Green Pastures*, for example, and to its acclaimed all-Black cast. Gumby's treatment of the subject, however, veered off stage to the afterhours spaces that animated Black creativity.[117] In his "Autographs" album, a photograph of the play's choir director, Evelyn "Hot Shot" Burwell, lifts back to reveal a hidden cluster of ephemera that takes us to Sally Lou's Club in Harlem, a spot where Burwell, Gumby, and others gathered for birthdays and meals under the watchful eye of a cross-dressing host, Mr. Jarahal?, who signed her name with a question mark and called Gumby "the great scrapbook man."[118] Sally Lou's is documented but briefly, in a handful of throwaways behind Burwell's portrait. Such reclusiveness on the page mirrors the ephemerality of this group, convening for a season before moving on to other experiments.[119] Although they arc across more than a century, then, Gumby's scrapbooks accept the short-lived, queer collectivity as one strain of Black history.

In Gumby's studio and scrapbooks alike, he thus cultivated what Shane Vogel describes as "social and literary places where lines of sexual and racial identifications might be frustrated."[120] Guided by "anything he happened to fancy," Gumby developed a Black archival practice committed to the continuous improvisation of history's categories. Did that commitment embody Gumby's self-proclaimed identity as an "individualist" or his declaration, akin to his friend Schuyler's brand of Black contrarianism, that he was "not permeated by any race pride"?[121] Did it reflect Gumby's day-to-day life in social networks of same-sex desire and bohemianism that already affronted the rules of respectability policing the color line?[122] Or, perhaps, was it Gumby's rebuke—on paper—of the constricting norms of race and sexuality that made him cautious about which Greenwich Village spots he could haunt as a Black flaneur and limited what he could say about his "staunch friendship" with Newman?[123] Gumby's collages refuse answers to these questions. Sometimes, Gumby suggested, only an "autograph or picture holds the [incident] and records its full history."[124] His scrapbook pages, which provide few captions to explain this "full history," only hint at these storylines, inviting speculation—but also opacity—as a mode of reading Black history. Gumby's collection lingers in the unindexed pleasures of following blackness through the "small narratives" of ephemeral solidarities.[125]

EPHEMERAL ARCHIVES: A FAILURE, A PARTY, A FLOOD

"When will the Gumby crowd bring out that long-threatened quarterly?" an impatient reader asked.[126] The answer turned out to be never, for *The Gumby Book Studio Quarterly* failed to circulate. At the moment Schomburg set off for Fisk University as a visiting curator, Gumby's collection—and his collective—verged on disintegration.[127] In the winter of 1930, just before the journal's release, the Gumby Book Studio closed, and his friends "grieved and wondered."[128] A series of calamities had befallen Gumby: he lost his job at the post office, joining "the army of unemployed," while Newman, his lover and patron, lost a fortune in the stock market crash that marked the beginning of the Great Depression.[129] Gumby found himself without money for the studio's rent or the printer's bill for the *Quarterly*. He sold off rare books to generate funds, but his financial improvisations proved insufficient. After he lost his studio and home, he placed the scrapbooks in storage, visiting them daily while worrying over their fate.[130] Under strain, Gumby's health declined, and he was treated for tuberculosis at Riverside Hospital and another city sanitarium, where he remained for four years. His long-held dream of producing a magazine collapsed. "I failed," Gumby lamented.[131] The studio's moment of splendor had passed, as had the hope of amplifying its collective aspirations through print circulation. Although other experimental periodicals of New Negro literary culture found their way to archives—"crystalliz[ing] their fleeting beauty into the permanency of the historical record," a librarian wrote—the *Quarterly* was so ephemeral that no one ever possessed a finished copy.[132]

Soon the public life of Gumby's enterprise shifted from long-awaited magazine to rallying cry: save the scrapbooks! As Gumby's hospitalization continued, the storage facility threatened to sell his possessions, including the scrapbooks, for unpaid rent.[133] Frantic but improbable proposals ensued. Schomburg suggested forming a company and selling shares to raise funds. Another friend thought the Guggenheim Museum might buy the collection. Coworkers from the post office prodded the Urban League—which had brokered the sale of Schomburg's library—to find "some rich man" to save Gumby's treasures.[134] Perhaps if the request had come before the Depression, a buyer would have emerged for Gumby's collection. It is also possible, however, that Gumby's scraps—which documented the everyday and the experimental, scandals as well as successes—never would have garnered the same institutional financing as Schomburg's collection, for not every Black archive fits the image of a ten-thousand-dollar library.[135] That did not mean, to be sure, that Gumby's ephemera went unvalued. In another demonstration of the scrapbooks' collective life, dozens of New Yorkers sponsored an Arts Ball, attended by four hundred people, to raise money for the storage bill (figure 2.6). The *Amsterdam News* reported that Gumby was "to be aided by the group of artists who used to make his studio . . . a rendezvous."[136] Those who gathered in the Studio—Cullen, Nugent, Schuyler, Schomburg, Perry, Occomy, Upshur, Grayson, and Hendrix—along with subjects of his scrapbooks—among them Rose McClendon, Langston Hughes, Harold Jackman,

FIGURE 2.6 Flyer and tickets for an "Arts Ball" to benefit L. S. Alexander Gumby and his collection, November 18, 1931, pasted in the "Gumby Book Studio" scrapbook.

Source: Series III: Scrapbooks, L. S. Alexander Gumby Collection of Negroiana, Rare Book and Manuscript Library, Columbia University.

Paul Robeson, Leigh Whipper, and Zora Neale Hurston—came together as a temporary committee of organizers.

In a circular letter (itself a piece of ephemera) the committee alerted the public: "Mr. Gumby is seriously ill. The world is about to lose him and his Collection which is scattered here and there." It issued a plea to aid Gumby and "save an invaluable collection."[137] Gumby's archive, which served as the backdrop of many gatherings and the recorder of scores more, now compelled the making of yet another collective to ensure its preservation. "'Get together for Gumby!' That is the current song of the artists and writers of Harlem and the Village," cried the *Pittsburgh Courier*.[138] It was a moment of archival mobilization among the "Harlem and Village Intellectuals," as Gumby called them, who rallied to save from destruction the collection that had so often brought them together.[139] The scrapbooks took shape within the world of Gumby's Book Studio, and it was that same social life that ultimately saved them from disappearance. The Arts Ball reflected an urgent sense that a collection lost or salvaged had meaning not just for the future's past—in the specter of some later historian using the records—but also for "imagining other ways to live in the present."[140] Gumby's exuberant archiving had documented the New Negro Renaissance while also helping to make it.[141] The subsequent effort to save his archive registered widespread investment, among the communities he cut and pasted, in keeping this record of their frenetic, ephemeral experiments.

At a time of economic straits, the Arts Ball prevented the collection's imminent dispersal. But that triumph proved temporary, too. As Gumby's illness lingered, funds for maintaining the scrapbooks again grew scarce. Through a friend of a friend, Gumby negotiated a "gentlemen's agreement" with a stranger in Brooklyn, who agreed to store the collection in his basement in exchange for some of Gumby's first editions, which had more market value than his ephemera.[142] As Gumby convalesced, the scrapbooks sat in this underground storage, far from Harlem. Although one journalist mistakenly took Gumby for dead after his long absence from the scene, he recovered after four years of confinement.[143] Upon leaving the sanitarium in 1934, Gumby went immediately to the "farthest end of Brooklyn" to inspect his collection.[144] Any scrapbooker knew the vulnerability of their volumes to light, dust, the "lack of tenacity in the paste," and, above all, water.[145] When Gumby climbed down to the "cellar where the collection was stored (I should say scattered)," he found telltale signs of flooding, and upon opening his trunks with dismay, discovered many of his scrapbooks reduced to paper-mud and mildew.[146] Devasted, yet grateful for what remained, Gumby removed the scrapbooks he could carry to his rented room in Harlem. He began saving money to transport and salvage the rest.[147]

When reunited with the surviving volumes in 1936, Gumby found that much of his History of the Negro series had escaped damage, and he set about to rebuild the collection.[148] He added to his scrapbooks on pugilism and drama, while creating new ones on Paul Robeson and the Italian invasion of Ethiopia. He also expanded his "Autobiography" albums to document his years of treatment for tuberculosis. Surprisingly, these pages on illness and convalescence had much in common with the socially raucous volumes he devoted to Greenwich Village and the Gumby Book Studio. In Gumby's lifetime, men diagnosed with a "tubercular personality" were understood as creative but languid, strong in sexual appetite but too weak to fulfill the masculine duties of manual labor or heterosexual marriage. For Black men specifically, the diagnosis insinuated an incapacity to manage modern life.[149] In his sanitarium scrapbooks, however, as in his other albums, Gumby subverted constrictions of race and gender not by presenting counterimages of respectable masculinity, but by refusing the power of these categories to compel correct behavior. In a rebuke to images of tubercular patients as passive and alone, Gumby documented in a scrapbook on Riverside Hospital, under the headline "They're All Glamorous," an interracial, homosocial world of close friendships and literary experiments among patients, including love sonnets for fellow "cure chasers."[150] Queering both desire and disease, Gumby thus continued his vandal method, remixing expectations about history's proper subjects.

Although he rebuilt his scrapbook collection, Gumby could not recreate his social world of the Renaissance years. He maintained friendships from the Gumby Book Studio's heyday, but he now lived in a series of furnished rooms and hotels, some of ill repute, where he could not host large gatherings.[151] "I have no where to display [the scrapbooks] in the proper atmosphere," Gumby lamented, "where people genuinely interested may come and browse."[152] Meanwhile, many of his interlocutors had faced their own setbacks and drifted away from Harlem. From the *Quarterly* group, Constance Grayson was sidelined by chronic illness, John Jenkins passed away, Nell Occomy moved to Boston, and Ferdinand Levy sailed for Britain. Another friend, mourning the "passing of the 'Gumby Group,'" longed for "that world I once knew."[153] Gumby, too, felt keenly the loss of the Book Studio's world, but he could not uphold it. Even if Gumby's collection barely survived the Depression—an example of the often-imperiled state of Black history—it ultimately proved more enduring than many of the groups it recorded. Gertrude Mossell's vision, that a scrapbook might capture a future race leader on the rise, found its opposite in Gumby's project, for his scrapbooks preserved shards of ambitions poised not at the threshold of greatness, as hoped in 1930, but at the edge of dispersal. While archives promise "temporal endurance," Gumby's collection posed the question of how to archive collectivities that "come together and fall apart."[154]

In a self-consciously transformative era of migrations, debuts, and manifestoes, Gumby's scrapbooks were imbued with a tension between history-making and impermanence. As Farah Jasmine Griffin has suggested, the Gumby Book Studio and its entourage belonged to a Harlem "constantly writing, documenting, preserving itself—as if it knows it is temporary."[155] Gumby's collection facilitated that frenetic self-documentation through archival acts that captured Black collectivity in motion. "Scrapbook[s] are not Histories," Gumby wrote, but rather "sketches," or compositions in their preliminary stage.[156] To be sure, no collection is ever complete, especially one made from ephemera—the scraps always "piled up," clippers knew—but Gumby aestheticized that incompleteness.[157] He left conspicuously blank spaces throughout his scrapbooks, labeled "wanted" or "reserved," to mark the absence of desired flourishes. Such strategies made visible the negative space and unlabeled qualities of history-in-the-making. Gumby tried to explain that approach to Arthur Fauset, who wanted to exhibit the scrapbooks for Negro Achievement Week in 1928. "I am afraid you would not be able to show this collection to its best advantage," Gumby wrote to Fauset, "for each volume is yet in the making."[158] That equivocation contrasts with Schomburg's confident declaration, "Here is the evidence," upon the exhibition of his own treasures.[159] While Schomburg wanted to show, indisputably, that the Negro had a history, Gumby's scrapbooks sketched the unfinishedness of that history.

Gumby launched his scrapbooking in 1901 with an event, the assassination of a president, destined to be historic the moment it occurred. Ultimately, however, he developed a method more attuned to the outskirts of such moments. Even his albums devoted to famous figures depict history's celebrities from the perspective of the onlookers and supporting cast who saved their ticket stubs, carbon copies, and programs. The collection thus preserved stories of the era's gleaners and conveners—not only Gumby but also his friend Charles Cheatham, whose initials appear next to items he donated; John A. Jenkins, whose brief career in the "literati" brought him to Gumby's studio; and many others who aspired to be part of the New Negro world (figure 2.7). Nearly a century later, few would know to search for their names, but they survive in collage, pasted into the scene then and now. So, too, survives a record of the studio's queer sociability, which lingers in scrawled references to Gumby as "a miniature God whose company is desirable," or as one "with whom it is a pleasure to have a poem."[160] Although Gumby gave conventionally monumental titles to his scrapbooks—Haiti or Harlem, for example—he smuggled into their pages minute and transgressive forms of aspiration and affilitation.[161]

How could that vandal method be institutionalized? It took Gumby a long time to imagine his collection in a formal repository. When Dorothy Porter wrote from Howard University in 1949 asking him to donate his scrapbooks, he demurred. He was "unknown in Washington," he told her, and because his "friends of all races and creeds that have such deep interest in the collection are centered in New York City," the scrapbooks should stay there.[162] Porter promised

FIGURE 2.7 Detail from L. S. Alexander Gumby's "Williams and Walker" scrapbook. Photograph of and clipping about entertainer George Walker, with Gumby's note that these items were given to him by John Taylor.

Source: Series III: Scrapbooks, L. S. Alexander Gumby Collection of Negroiana, Rare Book and Manuscript Library, Columbia University.

that the collection's "great historical value" would earn proper recognition at Howard and that his material would find company with the Black clippings, theater bills, and portraits she, too, had gathered.[163] For Gumby, however, history was made from the intimacies of place and people, so he promised instead to give the scrapbooks to Columbia, up the hill from his room at the Revella Hotel.[164]

(The prestige of the Ivy League likely appealed, too, perhaps assuaging whatever hurt Gumby might have felt about his exclusion from Yale's Harlem Renaissance archive.) At first, Gumby proposed keeping the collection until his death, but Columbia coveted the "mine of data" in the scrapbooks and worried about their fate in his makeshift living quarters.[165] In a counterproposal, Gumby suggested setting up a desk at the library where he could receive visitors and continue working on the volumes.[166] He wanted his collection to remain at the center of a rendezvous. Columbia briefly accommodated that request but did not "feel that Mr. Gumby should be encouraged to give up his whole life" to the collection.[167] The scrapbooks already *were* Gumby's life, however, and for a period, his archival acts had been part of Harlem's life, too.

Gumby could imagine the scrapbooks' future for "serious historical research," but his ambivalence evoked other reasons for collecting, ones that had little to do with a future historian's arrival.[168] What might an archive look like if its negative spaces—its blanks, absences, or desired material—could be on display? If friendships could be cataloged? If creators kept rearranging and inventing even after their materials entered a repository?[169] Gumby's collecting methods tested those questions. In the churn of Harlem in the Renaissance period, scrapbooking became a form of collective autodocumentary that linked the enduring to the ephemeral, the famous to the fleeting. In this interplay—between a documentary impulse toward preservation and the temporary quality of the subjects documented—ephemera aptly compiled a story of Black history in the texture of everyday improvisations, made from things taken apart and reimagined. For Gumby, scissors in hand, a vandal method was both the necessity and the pleasure of Black historical craft.

CHAPTER THREE

DEFIANT LIBRARIES

Virginia Lee and the Secrets Kept by Good Bookladies

The Negro runs great risks—of being arrested or worse—in the exercise of his right to use the library.

—Eliza Atkins Gleason, 1941

In April 1920, in the southwest Virginia city of Roanoke, eight hundred people registered to use an imagined library. They inserted themselves into a law that did not intend to include them. The state of Virginia had recently passed a statute authorizing the establishment of public libraries, and although it did not mention segregation directly, Black residents understood how the law would unfold: Roanoke would make plans for one library—a white library.[1] Despite iconic images depicting Jim Crow in twos—two separate water fountains, two entrances, two schools—Black Roanokers knew that it also took shape through absence, for the true goal of segregation laws was to banish Black citizens from public space. If that goal was not wholly attainable in physical conduits—roadways, bridges, depots—it was more fully realized in Progressive-era social projects to build public schools, libraries, parks, and playing fields. Roanoke established its first white high school in 1899, for example, but waited twenty-five years to provide one for African Americans.[2] When the city's new Library Association announced plans for a library, then, Black townspeople knew what was afoot. They immediately formed a "Colored Branch Library Movement," led by teacher Lucy Addison and ministers A. L. James and L. L. Downing and mobilized by Black Roanoke's informal political network of churches, garden clubs, and civic leagues.[3] They raised money for books and staged an "advanced registration" in which hundreds of adults and children presented themselves as patrons with the "desire and intention" to use a "colored library."[4] They acted *as if* they were the law's intended citizenry. They asked for library cards in a city that could not imagine them as readers.

The gambit worked. Faced with the demand to "meet the needs of colored citizens," Roanoke had to pay for its commitment to white supremacy, allocating funds for not one but two libraries.[5] It joined a growing number of Southern cities where, as historian L. D. Reddick remarked, "Negro branches have been set up mainly to keep Negroes out of 'white' libraries."[6] The Gainsboro Library in Roanoke opened on December 14, 1921. It was among the first branch libraries for Black readers in the South. Over the next two decades, nearly a hundred more of these "colored branches" opened, each housing a small collection at once unremarkable and, at a moment when at least seven million African Americans still lacked library access, exceptionally rare.[7] In Roanoke and elsewhere across the South, these libraries served Black communities remade by the Great Migration as much as storied meccas North and West (figure 3.1). Drawn by the possibilities of "anyplace but here," millions of African Americans made their way out of the South, but an almost equal share moved within the region, bringing rural transplants, students, workers, and soldiers into towns and cities.[8] Branch libraries followed these migrations, setting up shop in Black business and cultural districts crowded by legal and extralegal forms of segregation.

Sweet Auburn in Atlanta; Gainsboro in Roanoke; and Louisville's Harlem in Kentucky: in each of these neighborhoods, on streets reminiscent of "the Stroll" in Chicago, Black organizational life clustered in shops, pool halls, professional storefronts, newspaper offices, mortuaries, after-hours clubs, cafés, and YMCAs. In the past, some of these establishments had doubled as reading rooms, but as their numbers grew, Black residents pressed city officials into negotiations over public library access. Indeed, most of the Black branch libraries in the South had a backstory similar to Roanoke's. They grew out of organizing efforts in which the entrepreneurs who built what Davarian Baldwin dubs the "nighttime Stroll" of leisure businesses joined with the doctors, teachers, and ministers of the "daytime" Stroll to wage battle for public services in their neighborhoods.[9] As places not only to find books, but also to hold meetings and classes—regardless of denomination, gender, or class—branch libraries became key sites of communication and convergence for the heterogeneous Black publics of these remade metropolises.[10]

Poets and protestors alike knew the policing of the "nighttime Stroll," watched over, in Langston Hughes's words, by "Detectives from the vice squad / with

FIGURE 3.1 "The Librarian," drawing by Winold Reiss, 1925.

Source: From "Four Portraits of Negro Women," originally published in Harlem: Mecca of the New Negro, special issue of *Survey Graphic*, March 1925. New York Public Library Digital Collections.

weary sadistic eyes."[11] But surveillance shadowed daytime establishments, too. In libraries, that policing took shape through struggles over what Black readers should read. As Hazel Carby has argued, in branch libraries, Black middle-class women schooled their working-class counterparts on "proper diversion," disseminating "wholesome reading materials" in "highly Negro" communities.[12] White library administrators, in turn, exercised control over Black librarians' work, including what books they could acquire.[13] Some colored branches were stocked with discards, and many had no card catalog or reference collection, which were accessible only to whites at the main branch.[14] Across the South, library systems practiced idiosyncratic forms of censorship, such that a reader might find books on the "emancipated Negro" missing from one collection and works on race relations excluded elsewhere. Texts deemed "too radical" were banned nearly everywhere, and Black authorship might be off limits, too.[15] In 1943, a soldier stationed in Alabama, hungry to find the works of Zora Neale Hurston, lamented this absence: "The next day after finishing 'Dust Tracks—' I went to the library in search of anything else of hers. Not a thing could I find. However, the library was not only barren of Hurston books; it was barren of books by most of the well known Negro writers. This seems to be a strange lack—a library for Negroes conspicuously lacking in books by Negroes."[16] Well into the 1940s, custodians of public libraries restricted access to Black print. Even as more Southern African Americans gained entry to libraries, then, few of their branches resembled the "laboratory of Negro literature" that Catherine Latimer built at the Schomburg Collection in Harlem.[17]

Inside a handful of these branches, however, a cohort of Black women amassed African American literature, created clipping files on local people, mounted exhibits on race history, and led reading groups that gave "special study" to "the life of the Negro."[18] Virginia Lee in Roanoke; Annie McPheeters in Atlanta; Mollie Huston Lee in Raleigh; Marian Hadley in Nashville; and Martha Sebastian in Greensboro: among the first professionally trained Black librarians, these women created a remarkable set of small archives of Black life. Although New York boasted the first Negro Collection in a public library, and Chicago the second, there were smaller, *unnamed* collections at Black-serving branch libraries across the country.[19] Few would host iconic scenes like the great modernist poet Robert Hayden sitting among Arthur Schomburg's books to pen "Middle Passage." Nor did they benefit from the receipt of large collections from famous bibliophiles, as did their university counterparts—Jesse Moorland's library at Howard University, Henry Slaughter's papers at Atlanta University, and Phil Broome Brooks's collection at the Hampton Institute. Instead, librarians at colored branches built their collections clipping by clipping, book by book, and they did so against forbidding circumstances, treading cautiously within the confines of white municipal bureaucracy.[20] "Considering that my library is small, I am rather proud of the Negro collection," Mollie Lee wrote from Raleigh.[21] At a moment when civic space depicted Black history as absence, these collections gave it presence and form.

In Roanoke, Virginia Young Lee built one of the smallest of these archives. At first glance, her work as a branch librarian mirrored that of other information workers to the North and West. But her four decades at the Gainsboro Library, starting in 1928, were shaped by the history of policing Black literacy, and thus, unbeknownst to her supervisors, her librarianship harbored a fugitive side. Through a set of clandestine practices, Lee continuously fought restrictions on Black materials and Black readers. Her story illustrates how Southern branch libraries put recordkeeping at the center of Black public life, even under threat of erasure or destruction. The underground strategies compelled by this threat make it difficult to reconstruct some of Lee's practices. Pieced together from fragments that hint at the hidden parts of her work, however, the story told in this chapter explores how Lee undertook these battles. Small collections like Lee's—at once secret and public, replicable and rare—are key to any theory of Black archives, which must encompass not only the iconic collections in New York, Washington, or Chicago but also the proliferation of sites that prioritized local access to Black texts, even when it was perilous to do so. Such collections underscore the risks—and the radicality—of Black archive-building. "Good bookladies," as they sometimes called themselves, proved to be good at keeping secrets, too.[22]

A COLORED BRANCH LIBRARY MOVEMENT

When the Gainsboro Library opened in 1921, it followed a model established by the Louisville Free Public Library's Colored Department, where Thomas Fountain Blue and Rachel Harris advocated for every branch to become "a real center of education; a real place of culture."[23] Because no library education programs were open to African Americans in the South, Louisville dispatched one of its own staff to train Ella Bowden, Gainsboro's first librarian.[24] Bowden established the branch as an "intellectual headquarters," and for three decades, it was the only public place where Black residents in Roanoke could check out a book.[25] Located in the ground-floor storefront of the Odd Fellows lodge, the library sat within blocks of the neighborhood's major congregations and the busy Black commercial strip on Henry Street. Community organizations gifted the library subscriptions to several "leading Negro papers" and adorned it with a portrait of Booker T. Washington and a bust of Madame C. J. Walker. The branch's twenty-two hundred borrowers had access to the *Journal of Negro History*, James Weldon Johnson's *Book of American Negro Poetry*, work by Paul Laurence Dunbar, Washington's *Up from Slavery*, Charles Chesnutt's *House Behind the Cedars* (which would later be filmed in Roanoke by Oscar Michaux), and Jessie Fauset's *There Is Confusion*, among other titles. Surrounded by these words and images, library patrons observed one of the first Negro History Weeks.[26] "I am sure that our Negro collection will rapidly increase," remarked Harriet M. Miles, Gainsboro's next librarian, "as there are more and more demands" for it.[27]

When the Gainsboro Library celebrated its first anniversary in 1922, Virginia Dare Young, a sixteen-year-old student at the Harrison School, gave a speech to mark the occasion.[28] Her talk was a premonition, for she would later, under her married name Virginia Lee, become Gainsboro's longest-serving librarian (figure 3.2). Born in a coal camp in West Virginia, Lee was the daughter of a miner who moved his family in the 1910s back to Roanoke, where he managed a pool hall.[29] Lee's parents did not attend high school, and just a few years earlier, she, too, would have been unable to do so, for it was not until 1924 that Roanoke offered an accredited Black high school program.[30] Without the Gainsboro branch, Lee would have had limited access to books as well, because local schools for Black students did not then have libraries.[31] It may have been in the Gainsboro Library, in fact, that Lee discovered the work of Jessie Fauset, who became her hero. The existence of Gainsboro's high school and hard-won library shaped Lee's ability, after graduation, to enroll two hundred miles away at the Hampton Institute. There, she encountered the Huntington Memorial Library, an "impressive" building on a "beautiful campus," designed to produce awe in anyone who walked through its doors (figure 3.3).[32] Hampton's librarians

FIGURE 3.2 Virginia Young Lee (*right*) and her mother, Lula B. Young, in their home on Harrison Avenue in Roanoke, Virginia, circa 1930. Photographer unknown.

Source: Courtesy of Dr. Curtis C. Reeves, Jr. and Virginia Young Reeves-Schexnider.

FIGURE 3.3 Exterior (*top*) and interior (*bottom*) views of the Collis P. Huntington Memorial Library at Hampton University, 1911.

Source: The 42nd Annual Catalogue of the Hampton Normal and Agricultural Institute for 1911 (issued by The Hampton Normal and Agricultural Institute, Hampton, Virginia).

described the "silent, sub-conscious influence of its beauty and order on a youth with no previous sense of such things."[33] Lee immersed herself in the Huntington's George Peabody collection of three thousand volumes on Black history, where Black knowledge was both abundant and respected. Having watched her community in Roanoke fight for reading space, she learned at Hampton what the full possibilities of such a space might be.[34]

In the library, Lee joined a world of Black letters that extended beyond campus. She enrolled in the new Hampton Library School, the first academic program for Black librarians in the South, and worked as an assistant in the Peabody Collection of books "by and about the Negro." Down the hall, in the Leonora Herron Room for pleasure reading, the community's Library Forum convened to discuss books—an example of how Hampton's collection, and indeed most HBCU libraries, doubled as public facilities, distributing literature to local readers who could not otherwise access it.[35] In the 1920s, this network of colleges began to craft a national agenda for Black librarianship. Hampton and Fisk each hosted a national conference—the first in 1927 and the second in 1930—that connected librarians in Washington, DC, New York, and Nashville to smaller cities like Roanoke. For Lee, who was soon to be one of just eight Black public library workers in the entire state of Virginia, these conferences must have been formative.[36] She would have met Ernestine Rose, who brought the Schomburg Collection to the 135th Street Branch Library in Harlem; Thomas Blue, who organized the Colored Department at the Louisville Free Public Library; E. C. Williams, head librarian at Howard; and other newcomers, like Mollie Dunlap, who would later conduct the first survey of Black special collections in the United States.[37] Among the topics discussed at the first conference was the need for updated bibliographies on Black literature—a call answered by Hampton in 1928 with a list titled "Historical Books About the Negro Race."[38]

Lee might have returned to Roanoke with such a list in hand. She became Gainsboro's librarian in 1928 and set to work activating the literary network she experienced at Hampton.[39] She established the Jessie Fauset Reading Club in honor of the writer whose work had proven popular at the branch.[40] The club's members, including teachers, cooks, beauty operators, nurses, and the wives of railyard workers, put into action Pauline Hopkins's exhortation to women to serve as public thinkers and study "all phases of the race" (figure 3.4).[41] They met twice a month to discuss books, such as *The New Negro*, as well as current events and the "world situation."[42] The proliferation of Black literary societies in the 1920s is often associated with Harlem Renaissance writers like Fauset, but as the club's agenda makes clear, reading groups across the country—even in a small metropolis—saw themselves as part of an international Black cultural scene.[43] In 1930, for example, the Fauset Club devoted six months of study to "the Negro" and six months to "travel abroad."[44] Often led by teachers, its meetings offered intergenerational education in a city where many Black adults grew up without a high school open to them.[45] Members brought texts to share, drawn from clippings about "things that are not recorded in books"; one evening, Electer Allred,

FIGURE 3.4 Patrons of the Gainsboro Library in Roanoke, Virginia, including members of the Jessie Fauset Reading Club, 1939. Photograph by Lambert Martin.

Source: "Gainsboro Library Fills Need," *Roanoke World-News*, March 13, 1939. Courtesy of the Gainsboro Library Archives and Lee Enterprises for the *Roanoke Times*.

the wife of a laborer, presented an article on soprano Dorothy Maynor.[46] Lee described such occasions as conjoining "intellectual and aesthetic pleasure." The Fauset Club, she argued, facilitated "association and contact" between readers who did not necessarily belong to the same congregation or class position, thus creating a space where "their different interests harmonize."[47]

In this paean to the Fauset Club, Lee evoked Progressive-era rhetoric about the public library's ability to assimilate democracy's unruly subjects—a portrait as calculated as it was romanticized.[48] As Lee well knew, many cities resisted municipal services for Black residents precisely because they understood the power of infrastructure to "constitute political subjects, and generate social aspirations."[49] Indeed, within a decade of its founding, the Fauset Club had grown into more than a reading group, becoming a political force in Roanoke. Club members not only honored Fauset's writing, but also emulated her work as an organizer of Black culture. That shift became most visible in the late 1930s, as the Gainsboro branch grew increasingly crowded in its small storefront. Physical conditions had deteriorated, shelves overflowed, and the Fauset Club had to convene after hours because the library had no meeting room. Moreover, Lee recalled that she "had to serve in water whenever there was a heavy rain," and one morning she encountered a rat in the flood waters.[50] To get the collection out of water, Lee mobilized the Fauset Club. The Great Depression had ushered in a decade of Black voter organization in Virginia, while also spawning programs to fund bridges, armories, libraries, and other public works.[51] These two streams converged when Roanoke's municipal bond elections created an opening for Black Roanoke to test its power at the ballot box. In 1937, when the city proposed a bond initiative to construct a new central library—once again excluding Black readers—the Fauset Reading Club sprang into action.[52] They became not only book reviewers and newspaper clippers but also political operatives.

Fauset Club members formed a coalition with local Black voter leagues, the NAACP, the Ideal Garden Club, the YMCA and YWCA, and the Women's Auxiliary to the Association of Colored Railway Trainmen. Over the four years it took the city to pass a bond initiative for library construction, this coalition made it known that "their people were organized" and would turn out to vote—*if* the ballot made provision for a new and larger Gainsboro branch.[53] Meanwhile, Lee sent word to her professional network of Black librarians, who advised the campaign from afar. A telegram came from the Hampton Library School with specifications for "definite needs": a building with two reading rooms, extended hours, space for club meetings, and increased community control of branch operations.[54] Seemingly technical, the list was also aspirational, sketching an imagined future for Black public life in Roanoke, with institutional power and space to assemble.[55] After the "Negro delegation" confronted City Council in 1940, the city finally agreed to amend its bond proposal, designating $20,000 for a "colored branch" out of the $170,000 earmarked for library construction.[56] After this agreement, the bond passed in November 1940, representing one of Black Roanoke's first political victories.[57] When construction on the new branch began, Fauset Club members continued their organizing efforts, canvassing the neighborhood for donations to furnish the building. Their gifts to the new library included a subscription to *The Crisis*, a flag and staff, a revolving globe, a table lamp, a filing cabinet, and three portraits of local heroes: the Reverend L. L. Downing and teachers Lucy Addison and Ella F. Dean.[58]

On May 10, 1942, the new Gainsboro Library opened with fanfare, feted by a large crowd gathered at First Baptist Church. The mayor and City Council brought "expressions from the city suitable for the occasion," and after the festivities, the crowd walked downhill to the new building, passing near the Black-owned drugstore and the YMCA, which now occupied the storefront vacated by the library.[59] Lee no doubt relished the opportunity to show off the expanded reading areas as well as the lecture room where the Fauset Club would meet. To the *Roanoke Tribune*, the city's new Black-owned weekly, she delivered newspaper copy chronicling every detail of the opening. Perhaps she imagined that the story would dominate the front page, attesting to five years of door-to-door campaigns and scores of donations from those stretching their Depression-era budgets to support a community institution. In her text, Lee noted that it was not only the widely credited businessman C. C. Williams who led the campaign, but also the Black women of Roanoke, and especially Fauset Club members, who "labored zealously" behind the scene.[60] Lee did not make visible her own role as an organizer, however, staying true to the public persona she had cultivated as a writer of poetry and pageants, teacher of the Golden Rule Bible Class, and garden club host—not as a political figure.[61] Circumspect and strict, she hewed to the propriety required of a Black woman employed by the city—exercising what Eliza Atkins Gleason, in *The Southern Negro and the Public Library*, described as the "excessive restraint which the branch librarian is usually compelled to exercise."[62] Lee embodied this restraint, but as she repeatedly discovered, it did not always protect her or her library.

BLACK COLLECTING UNDER SURVEILLANCE

When Lee's much-anticipated issue of the *Roanoke Tribune* appeared, her story about the library opening was not alone above the fold. The celebratory account, headlined "Twenty Thousand Dollar Library Opening," was flanked by a story far more ominous: "City 'Cop' Shoots to See Innocent Negro Lad Run" (figure 3.5). The day after the library's opening, at the very corner where it stood, a white Roanoke police officer had fired "like a thunder bolt from the clear sky" at a group

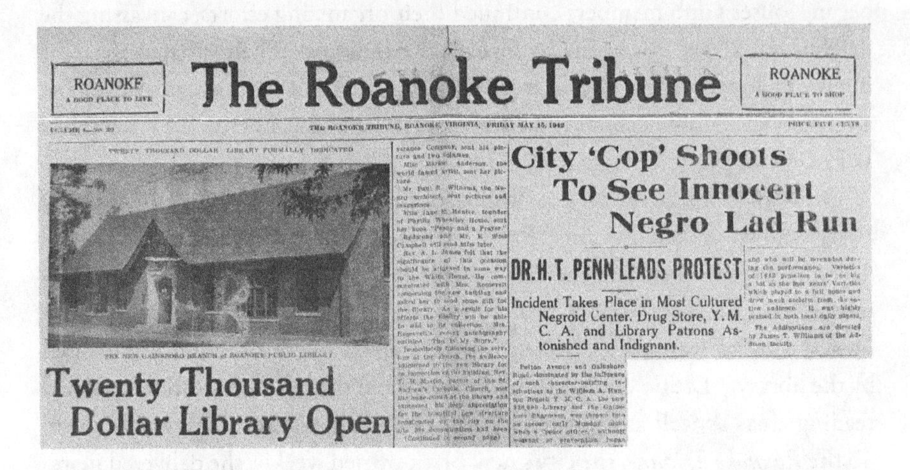
ROANOKE

The Roanoke Tribune

ROANOKE

A GOOD PLACE TO SHOP

City 'Cop' Shoots To See Innocent Negro Lad Run

DR. H. T. PENN LEADS PROTEST

Incident Takes Place in Most Cultured Negroid Center. Drug Store, Y. M. C. A. and Library Patrons Astonished and Indignant.

Twenty Thousand Dollar Library Open

FIGURE 3.5 Front page of the *Roanoke Tribune,* May 15, 1942, with contrasting headlines: "Twenty Thousand Dollar Library Open" and "City 'Cop' Shoots to See Innocent Negro Lad Run," May 15, 1942.

Source: Courtesy of the Gainsboro Library Archives and the *Roanoke Tribune.*

of Black high school students leaving a gathering at the YMCA.[63] Injuring no one but terrorizing everyone, state violence intruded upon, and mocked, the site of Roanoke's Black "civic advancement," touted only the night before in the library's opening ceremonies. On Sunday, the city had dispatched emissaries to applaud Black achievement, but on Monday, its officers made clear the limits of such recognition—a stark reminder of Elizabeth Alexander's argument that "African Americans have always existed in a countercitizen relationship to the law."[64] With these inverse gestures—a welcome and a warning—Roanoke made sure that Black residents remained outside the fold of municipal belonging.

The pairing of these headlines captured the audacity of Black respectability in public space and the threat posed by Black literacy specifically. Indeed, the *Tribune*'s coverage zeroed in on the fact that the shooting occurred near the library, with the subheadline "Incident Takes Place in Most Cultured Negroid Center. Drug Store, Y. M. C. A. and Library Patrons Astonished and Indignant":

> Patton Avenue and Gainsboro Road, dominated by the influence of such character-building institutions as the William A. Hunton Branch Y. M. C. A., the new $20,000 Library and the Gainsboro Pharmacy, was thrown into an uproar early Monday night when a "peace officer," without warrant or provocation, began shooting to stop Alphonso Edwards. . . . Edwards was only pranking

> on the corner when the coppers drove up . . . The [t]hing was done so suddenly the crowds were temporarily dazed. Some ladies were passing on their way to the Library. When the shooting occurred they ran into the building nervous wrecks.[65]

The place and timing of the shooting—at Roanoke's Black civic hub, just after it had drawn a crowd to celebrate the new library—suggest that the police made a point to demonstrate their power over whatever cultural capital Black residents possessed.[66] For the Lee family, the incident must have felt personal. Virginia Lee likely was inside the library when witnesses "ran into the building nervous wrecks." Her husband, YMCA secretary L. A. Lee, had filed suit against the Roanoke police for excessive force a few years earlier; this time, such violence had targeted the youth in his responsibility.[67] Both Lees advocated for the community to respect its young people. On this evening, however, no young person, even one in a YMCA program that promised a "higher experience of living," was safe from an officer, "strutting like a fighting cock," who shot "just to see the boy run."[68] Nor could the library "ladies"—teachers, domestic workers, and the wives of railroad men—inhabit the street without being perceived as transgressors. The incident captured what Richard Wright once termed the "ethics" of Jim Crow: a regime that policed Black presence in public space even when that presence was utterly ordinary—teenagers "pranking," ladies "passing."[69] As the shooting made clear, no amount of respectability or learning could alter those ethics.

The intersection where the library stood—the "Most Cultured Negroid Center"—represented the possibility of Black autonomy and class mobility. It was supposed to be a place where Black women could walk as "ladies," where Black youth could own the corner, and where Black readers could be, in Lee's words, "entertainers of their own soul."[70] In a landscape of white violence, however, a Black library posed a threat, as it seemingly always and everywhere had: during the race riot of 1921 in Tulsa, Oklahoma, among the structures whites burned down was the colored branch library.[71] In Roanoke, the police shooting continued a pattern of limiting Black use of public space—especially uses perceived as symbolically or physically encroaching on white territory. Not long before Lee moved to Roanoke as a child, white rioters attacked African Americans in the streets, targeting in particular those who had spoken out against white supremacy; one woman told the newspaper that any Black person entering white space should be shot.[72] Even within Roanoke's "segregation districts" (outlawed in 1917 but informally operative for decades), the city criminalized how Black residents used public space in ordinary ways. In 1938, for example, police went to Henry Street, the main Black thoroughfare, and fired tear gas at revelers celebrating boxer Joe Louis's victory over Max Schmeling.[73] The shooting near the library thus repeated a pattern in Roanoke, where landmarks of Black success and moments of triumph affronted white control.

If the shooting warned of the limits of Black civic institutions, it was a lesson Lee had already learned. She saw the library as a space of Black inheritance—an idea she carried since her Hampton days—but she also knew she could not fully enact that vision in her hometown. Her position as a city employee mattered to residents like the Dudley family, who by 1939 had read everything available at Gainsboro and relied on Lee to secure more books for them (figure 3.6).[74] Because African American readers had no direct access to the larger holdings of the whites-only central building, the Dudleys needed Lee to make interlibrary loan requests in order to borrow books from the main library. She advocated for years to improve that access, but in the meantime, her relationship to library administrators rested on fragile ground.[75] For the first two decades of Lee's tenure, African Americans had no shared governance of the library system. In theory, a Citizens' Advisory Committee represented Gainsboro's interests, but city officials made it clear that the committee had "no official powers" and no "jurisdiction in the matter of the selection of books." The committee's desire to subscribe to *The Crisis*, for example, had to go to the main library for approval.[76]

FIGURE 3.6 Virginia Lee, librarian of the Gainsboro Library (*right*), with Dr. Edward R. and Theresa Dudley and their children, described as "probably the most widely read family in Roanoke," 1939. Photograph by Lambert Martin.

Source: "Gainsboro Library Fills Need," *Roanoke World-News*, March 13, 1939. Courtesy of the Gainsboro Library Archives and Lee Enterprises for the *Roanoke Times*.

The Library Board, for its part, referred to white staff members by title—as Head of the Juvenile, Reference, or Catalog Department—while calling Lee "the Colored Librarian."[77] As that naming suggests, administrators paid close attention not simply to how Lee performed her job but also to how she behaved as a Black woman. To maintain a public space of Black reading in Roanoke courted surveillance.

Nevertheless, Lee quietly pursued what became her signal achievement: a collection of works "by and about the Negro." She argued that "in order to get somewhere, one must know that he has come from somewhere," and she gathered materials that conjured that "somewhere."[78] Her desire to collect might have been fueled by her time in the Peabody Collection at Hampton, or by the talks she heard at Fisk, which became a "mecca for librarians" in 1930 when it hosted a Negro Library Conference.[79] In Fisk's new library, which featured Aaron Douglas's murals on Black life and an "alluring Negro collection room," Lee would have heard Monroe Work, the Tuskegee bibliographer, give a talk on "Using a Collection of Materials on the Negro."[80] She would have met Schomburg, who was then serving as visiting curator at Fisk, and Ernestine Rose, who might have talked to her about how the 135th Street branch in Harlem built its Division of Negro Literature and History.[81] Lee never had the budget or authority that her colleagues at these other institutions enjoyed. Nor did she have the kind of mobility that allowed Schomburg to travel in pursuit of rare books. Despite those obstacles, she built a modest African American collection for Gainsboro, one item at a time, mirroring projects that took shape in public libraries across the country—each an instance of the collective aspiration to make Black archives. That aspiration took root as fiercely in places like Roanoke as it did in New York or Tuskegee. In small branch libraries of the South, however, archival desires had to operate under different strategies.

With no city funds to grow a specialized collection, Lee sought out Sara Brown, principal of the Gilmer School, and Reverend James of First Baptist Church to help her solicit materials from "outstanding Negro leaders" who might give a "memento of historical significance to be placed in our library."[82] The trio's letter-writing campaign brought in donations from educator Charlotte Hawkins Brown, who sent *The Correct Thing to Do*; social worker Jane E. Hunter, who gifted a copy of *Nickel and a Prayer*; businessman C. C. Spaulding, president of North Carolina Mutual Life Insurance, who offered two volumes; scientist George Washington Carver, who donated his biography and some pamphlets; composer W. C. Handy, who supplied sheet music; contralto Marian Anderson and architect Paul R. Williams, each of whom sent their photographs.[83] Lee also approached elderly residents of Roanoke and asked them to donate "books and other materials they had."[84] She knew who might have such materials because both in and out of the library, she served as a community recordkeeper, not only a collector of well-known authors, but also a "resident obituary writer," a clipper of newspapers, and a chronicler of local happenings in *The Church News*.[85] In summoning a collection of "Negro leaders" from afar, while also assembling a clipping file on local clubs, schools, and events, Lee refused the prevailing logic of a city that saw Black achievement as a transgression.

By 1942, Lee's collection likely held a few hundred volumes. Among them were the following (in chronological order):

Monroe Work, *Negro Year Book*
James Weldon Johnson, *Along This Way*
Benjamin Brawley, *A Short History of the American Negro*
Eva Jessye, *My Spirituals*
Melville Herskovits, *The American Negro*
Countee Cullen, *The Black Christ and Other Poems*
Robert Moton, *What the Negro Thinks*
J. H. Harmon Jr., Arnett G. Lindsay, and Carter G. Woodson, *The Negro as a Business Man*
Edwin Henderson, *The Negro in Sports*
Louise Venable Kennedy, *The Negro Peasant Turns Cityward*
Carter G. Woodson, *The Rural Negro*
Sadie Daniel, *Women Builders*
Edwin Embree, *Brown America: The Story of a New Race*
Langston Hughes, *The Dream Keeper and Other Poems*
Zora Neale Hurston, *Jonah's Gourd Vine*
Hildegarde Hoyt Swift, *The Railroad to Freedom*
George R. Arthur, *Life on the Negro Frontier*
J. A. Rogers, *100 Amazing Facts About the Negro*
Marion Cuthbert, *Juliette Derricotte*
Willis Richardson and May Miller, *Negro History in Thirteen Plays*
Carter G. Woodson, *The African Background Outlined*
Harvey L. Baxter, *Sonnet for the Ethiopians and Other Poems*
Benjamin Brawley, *Paul Laurence Dunbar*
John and Alan Lomax, *Negro Folk Songs as Sung by Lead Belly*
Maud Cuney-Hare, *Negro Musicians and their Music*
Fitzhugh Lee Styles, *Negroes and the Law*
Claude McKay, *A Long Way from Home*
William Grant Still, *Twelve Negro Spirituals*

Benjamin Mays, *The Negro's God as Reflected in His Literature*
W. E. B. Du Bois, *Black Folk Then and Now*
Ira DeA. Reid, *In a Minor Key: Negro Youth in Story and Fact*
Charles S. Johnson, *Growing Up in the Black Belt*
Sterling Brown, Arthur P. Davis, and Ulysses S. Lee, *Negro Caravan*[86]

As this list suggests, in Lee's collection, one would encounter no rare tomes of Haitian history, as one would find in the Schomburg Collection; no files that teased the edges of Black propriety, as did Alexander Gumby's scrapbooks of queer life; no incendiary literature of the past, such as David Walker's *Appeal*, which Lee's contemporary Vivian Harsh would procure in Chicago. Such works would have been impossible for Lee to acquire, even if she could find or afford them, because each of her books had to pass inspection at the main branch. As a whole, however, the collection assembled forms of Black aspiration, tradition, and autonomy that exceeded Roanoke's mechanisms of control. Enacting her own call to "serve the life of the community," Lee built a collection that connected strands of Black life in Roanoke to currents beyond it: *The Negro as a Business Man* at the height of Roanoke's Black business boom; stories of Black women educators at a moment when they were fighting for equal pay in Virginia; compositions by Black musicians in a town where no occasion passed without a performance by the Addisonians or the Norfolk and Western chorus; studies of migration in a town that had lost and gained migrants; volumes of the famed Harlem poets to keep company with Roanoke's celebrated but lone New Negro bard, Harvey Baxter; and, finally, Zora Neale Hurston for readers who, like the frustrated soldier in Alabama, simply wanted to keep reading.

Lee did not mark these titles with special bookplates, as her colleagues did in Harlem and Chicago, or designate a "Negro history" room, as did Fisk.[87] In fact, she rarely described these acquisitions as a "collection" at all.[88] Lee may have felt the assemblage was too modest to deserve the moniker, or perhaps, in a city where facilities were white unless specifically marked "colored," she declined to put these books in a separate category, opting to show bibliographically that "Negroes are an integral part of our society."[89] Although she did not label the special collection as such, she purposefully drew attention to its presence through displays on "forgotten accomplishments" in Black history.[90] Such presentations doubled as a form of classification. If Lee wanted to make known the full range of her collection, from Black business to poetry, she could not rely on the Dewey Decimal Classification, which confined most books on Black subjects to shelves on slavery or the "Negro Question." Nor could she undo these classifications, as did her colleagues at academic libraries, because cataloging decisions in Roanoke took place at the main branch.[91] To bring blackness into view, then, she designed exhibitions and advertised them within the community. In 1932, Lee inserted into *The Church News*—the city's only circulating Black publication at that time—the following announcement: "The Gainsboro Branch Library has on display a number of outstanding books by and about Negroes that are proving quite popular. . . . Are you interested in the progress of our people? If so, keep informed by reading the books that are being released from time to time on the Negro. The Library may have the exact book that you wish. Inquire and see."[92] *The Library may have the exact book you wish:* In a city that so often deemed civic property off limits to Black aspiration, these displays recognized blackness in public space and kindled the desires of Black readers.

However modest in scope, these displays tested the limits of what the city would authorize, highlighting a shadow history of library suppression in Roanoke that circulates in popular memory but is only partially documented in city records.[93] Nearly as soon as she became branch librarian in 1928, Lee recounted, she received warnings about what the Gainsboro Library should *not* do. When she designed exhibitions on Black accomplishments, city officials told her to "slow the pace"—or, in another version of the story, "not to put those books out."[94] In the segregationist structure of Roanoke, the branch library existed as a convenience for whites, a mechanism for keeping Black readers out of the main library.[95] Unlike the 135th Street Branch Library, which publicly described its mission to "stimulate race consciousness and encourage race pride," Roanoke officials did not intend their colored branch to be a space of racial consciousness.[96] Lee and her collaborators, however, regarded the library on their own expansive terms, beyond those ascribed by the city. "People considered it their second home," one Roanoke resident remarked, because it was the place where "the Negro could find some of the things pertaining to him."[97] Thus, when the new Gainsboro Library building opened in 1942, community members defiantly gifted it a museum case—a rebuke to the city's aversion to Black tableaus.[98] Echoing that determination, Lee would continue to make public space for Black knowledge, even if warned against it.

BASEMENT EXILE: BLACK ARCHIVES UNDERGROUND

Soon after the new library building's opening, the city again rebuked Lee, and her collection seems to have faced the threat of destruction. This is the moment at which Lee's story is most famous but least documented. According to a well-known anecdote in Roanoke, at some point in the 1940s city officials, possibly City Council members but probably the library director, once more warned Lee against collecting and displaying Black literary and historical materials. This time, Lee was told not just to "slow the pace," but to remove "offending books from the library's shelves."[99] Moreover, she learned that she might lose her job if she did not comply with this demand to dismantle the collection.[100] In the act that has made Lee a local legend, however, she responded by *appearing* to comply with the order without actually doing so. She moved the "offending books" to the library's basement, where she hid and provided secret access to them.[101] "When a patron wanted something," recalled her successor, Carla Pullen Lewis, who heard the story from Lee, "she'd go and get it and bring it up to them."[102] This story captures a rare moment when Lee strayed beyond the boundaries of proper professional comportment. She knew that to protect the collection entailed risk, but "if it was going to cost me my job, that is the way it would have to be," she argued. "I wasn't going to stop. I said blacks needed accurate and precise information on their history."[103]

As with the police shooting at its corner, once again the Gainsboro branch became an unlikely scene of crisis: a seemingly undemonstrative library where neither the collection, its curator, nor its patrons could exist in peace; where a walk to the library was a precarious passage through streets prone to outbursts of racist terror; and where a careful city employee—one who in her public writings recommended innocuous titles, such as the frontier romance *The Lieutenant's Ladies*—acted subversively.[104] To save the collection, Lee took it underground. At this moment, Lee's career in the public library might have resembled her father's job in a Prohibition-era pool hall more than she ever would have expected. She transposed everything she learned at Hampton—about the grandness of a Black collection and the need to give it space—and enacted it secretly. Under threat, Lee exercised a bibliographic strategy of dissemblance, calling on Black women's use of concealment and privacy to shield themselves from violence.[105] Seemingly antagonistic to the philosophy of public librarianship, this move to obscure the books from view is a reminder that hidden collections sit at the center of any information landscape. That principle holds true in the general sense of Peter Galison's argument that the universe of secret data dwarfs "the open world . . . lodged in our libraries" as well as in another, more specific context. Black communities, so often the target of surveillance, have made their archives unreadable when necessary—enacting what poet Kevin Young calls the "hiding tradition" in African American life.[106]

In Lee's brief telling of the story decades later, and in talk that still circulates around town, many details remain aloof. For example, what provoked the ire of city officials at that particular moment? How did they learn of Lee's collecting practices, and which materials did they target? Did officials tell her to "get rid of the black history collection altogether," as some accounts suggest?[107] It may have been the city's library director who threatened Lee's collection, but the Library Board's records from this period are unavailable. If City Council members pressured Lee, they did not commit that threat to their minutes. Roanoke took great pains to stay out of the headlines of "race relations" in the South, and Council members often went into closed-door executive sessions to discuss issues pertaining to race—a refusal to make their conversations part of the city's official archive.[108] Lee, too, would have avoided leaving a detailed paper trail, for it might have incriminated her and others by showing how long she kept the books in their "basement exile," how many books she hid, and who gained secret access.[109] Decades later, Lee's portrait now hangs in the Gainsboro Library—alongside those of Madame C. J. Walker and local educator Lucy Addison—and Roanokers celebrate her for the act of subterfuge that ultimately saved the collection. She has become Roanoke's proud contribution to a long history of Black undergrounds, from the Underground Railroad to *Invisible Man*.[110] The details of that heroism are still something of a mystery, however. As Jennifer Nash asks, capturing a central methodological and ethical dilemma in writing about Black women's often-furtive means of survival, "How do you trace what manifests itself as secrecy?"[111]

Perhaps city officials grew alarmed by Lee's attempt in 1942 to visibly mark a "Negro History" area in the library—an effort that, unlike her previous work, drew regional media attention. Three months after the new Gainsboro Library building opened, Lee received a significant addition to the collection: a donation of about two dozen Black history books from A. E. Lichtman, the white owner of a regional chain of Black performance venues.[112] Near the inner hinge of each of these books, Lee wrote, "Donation of A. E. Lichtman." Of the ten books that remain traceable via that notation, most were published by the Association for the Study of Negro Life and History, including Lorenzo Greene's *The Negro Wage Earner*, Kelly Miller's *The Everlasting Stain*, W. E. B. Du Bois's *The Negro*, and seven titles by Carter G. Woodson, from *Negro Makers of History* to *African Myths Together with Proverbs*.[113] A camera operator arrived to document the occasion, and the *Norfolk Journal and Guide* twice ran a picture and brief story with the headline "Lichtman Theatre Gives Books." The published photograph featured Lee standing alongside Emmett P. Nabors Jr., manager of the Virginian Theatre, who presented the books on behalf of Lichtman. These books, the story announced, would sit in "a section of the library to be called 'The Lichtman Shelf on Negro History.' "[114]

Lee already possessed several of Woodson's books, so it may seem puzzling why these additions would have suddenly triggered the city's wrath. One possible explanation is that the appearance of "The Lichtman Shelf on Negro History" coincided with a crescendo of statewide civil rights activity that reached southwest Virginia in 1942 and involved Lichtman, Nabors, and the Fauset Reading Club—thus drawing the Gainsboro Library unwittingly into the fray. Although the state had long served as a testing ground for civil rights litigation—on bus and train segregation; on equal pay for teachers; and on public library access—few of these cases touched Roanoke, which sat closer to the mountains of West Virginia than to the capital city of Richmond.[115] By contrast, the NAACP's high-profile, statewide organizing drive in the early 1940s swept up Roanoke and no doubt alarmed the city's white leadership. A life member of the NAACP, Lichtman donated to its Virginia movement the same year he gifted books to Gainsboro.[116] Justina Spencer, a Fauset Club leader, chaired the local NAACP campaign along with Nabors, the theater manager photographed giving books to Lee.[117] A fixture of Black society in Roanoke, Nabors worshipped at Lee's church and served on the board of the YMCA across the street from the library. With Lee's husband, Nabors had filed suit against the Roanoke police several years earlier.[118] In this context, perhaps, Lee's plan to label a shelf for "Negro History" and name it for one of the civil rights movement's white patrons ran afoul of Roanoke's racial conservatism. Lee had carefully avoided attention in the past, but with newspaper coverage now highlighting her library's ties to NAACP activists, she may have crossed one of the lines Black Roanokers were warned not to cross.

Whether or not Lichtman's donation triggered the city's threat, the fact that *any* part of Lee's collection would invite censorship should catch our attention, because it was not an assemblage anyone outside Roanoke would have called subversive. Compared with larger or finer collections elsewhere, Lee's acquisitions were modest. Indeed, others might have seen the materials she had gathered as utterly replaceable, and thus not worth risking one's job. That the Gainsboro collection ended up in basement exile, then, underscores the stakes of collecting for Black communities and white officials alike. To Lee, these books—and her collecting project more generally—were essential to defend. "It was an effort I absolutely refused to deviate from," she insisted.[119] Lee's adamance, and the small collection's struggle to exist, epitomized the urgency and radicality of recordkeeping in Black public life. "I wanted to keep our children mindful," Lee argued, that "we have had leaders in our race that are . . . worthy of being honored, looked up to."[120] Echoing the tenets of Woodson and the Negro History movement, Lee drew a direct line between a history "worthy of being honored" and Roanoke's present. In a room where portraits of local leaders Lucy Addison and Ella Dean hung near a "shelf on Negro history," readers could perhaps imagine *themselves* as "Negro Makers of History." Such a vision upended the rules of social order that governed the library. No longer just a place of "proper diversion," the library hinted at forms of political and social disorder.

As a municipal institution, the Gainsboro Library seemed to operate within a sanctioned public sphere, but in fact, even those Black archives lodged within dominant structures had to contend with the mutable and hazardous racial boundaries of civic membership. White residents complained to City Council about Black trespass onto white territory, yet officers policed Black presence even on purportedly "colored" streets. Library officials established "colored libraries," and then objected to Black collections in them. These fickle contradictions undercut the ability of Black citizens to hold steady ground in the public sphere—and when exiled from civic belonging, public desires can shift quickly into counterpublic imperatives.[121] In attempting to control the circulation of Black books at Gainsboro, Roanoke officials broke their unwritten compact with Lee, who had tried to comply with the requirements of public service under Jim Crow. In response, the "Colored Librarian" began to stray from expectations that her library would quell Black unruliness. Her strategies thus moved between uplift and fugitivity. As Lara Langer Cohen has argued, going underground is both an "effect of subjugation"—necessitated by prohibitions—and an "act of refusal"—a voluntary migration to a world that defines itself on its own defiant terms.[122] When infrastructure is commandeered by a counterpublic, it arcs toward futures not imagined by state planners.[123] The moment Lee took the Negro History books to the basement, they became the property not of the "Roanoke Public Library," as stamped on their title pages, but of a liberatory Black knowledge tradition that eluded capture or control.

Below ground, Lee turned the library's order into subversion, while above ground she maintained its rule. Black branch librarians carefully adhered to protocols of racial respectability and insisted their patrons do the same. They did so to protect the counterpublic practices they enacted *within* public infrastructure—for the act of preserving, displaying, and defending Black knowledge remained radical.[124] Lee demanded decorum inside the library, going so far as to require children to wash their hands before handling books.[125] In a city where the white establishment imagined the colored library as a "solution" to Black crime and disorder, Lee's rules might seem like little more than mechanisms of control.[126] Yet a bifurcated view of American libraries—either celebrating them as spaces of democratic possibility or critiquing them as sites of social control—does not account for the complexity of Lee's work. Her legacy in Roanoke remains twofold, embedded in stories about her defense of the collection *and* her decrees about its proper use. These twinned anecdotes, though seemingly at odds, represent the same ethos. Lee's radicality grew out of her propriety. The same reverence toward books that caused her to reprimand young readers also underlined her determination to save the books from threats of destruction, because in Roanoke, even a collection that was a paean to respectability struck white officials as dangerous. Unbeknownst to these officials, however, patrons might have washed their hands upstairs to use a secret library downstairs.

After moving her collection to the basement, Lee waited out the threat, "determined but patient," until she could bring the books upstairs and return them to public space.[127] By 1947, a Gainsboro resident (her husband at the time, L. A. Lee) had joined the Library Board to represent users of the "colored branch."[128] That same year, she felt comfortable enough with the collection's safety to print a Negro History Week reading list of "Adult Books By and About Negroes" held by the branch.[129] In the early 1950s, the Roanoke Public Library system desegregated, and Lee kept collecting, adding a thousand or more books to the collection, from *Annie Allen* to *I Am A Black Woman*.[130] Until her retirement, she said little on record about the opposition she faced early in her career, and she kept quiet about the act of fugitivity that had preserved the collection. Finally, in 1970, just as she was leaving the city's payroll, she revealed the story to the *Roanoke Times*.[131] In 1982, when the community decided to officially name the collection the Virginia Y. Lee Afro-American History Collection, Lee made another intervention (figure 3.7).[132] During her speech at the naming ceremony, which was recorded, she alluded only vaguely to the resistance she had faced from city officials. But later, deciding that something more should be said, she doubled back, turned the reel-to-reel recorder back on, and added the story of the collection's basement exile.[133] Since then, this story—of the city's attack on the collection, and Lee's defense of it—has become ubiquitous in local histories.

Why, at the moment of her public commemoration, did Lee insist on recording this story? By this time, she had survived the city's threat to her collection, and even garnered citywide recognition, only to witness a different form of erasure. For three decades, from 1955 to 1984, urban renewal in Roanoke dismantled first one Black neighborhood and then another. If in the Progressive era the city attempted to exclude Black citizens from civic architecture, in the era of desegregation, it bulldozed the spaces Black communities had built for themselves in response to that exclusion. Roanoke had imagined a long future for Jim Crow and built its urban geography accordingly; when that future crumbled, the city began to tear down Black real estate.[134] In waves of "repeated dispossession," the Roanoke Redevelopment and Housing Authority cleared Black

FIGURE 3.7 Room dedicated to the Virginia Y. Lee Afro-American History Collection, Gainsboro Library, Roanoke, Virginia. Photograph by Laura E. Helton.

Source: Gainsboro Library, Roanoke Public Library.

homes and businesses to make way for a new interstate, convention center, and bottling plant.[135] The city's bulldozers soon reached the Gainsboro neighborhood, encroaching on the commercial and cultural corridor of Henry Street, where Lee's father once managed a pool hall. By the time Lee committed to tape the story of her secret collection, the library building stood as one of Gainsboro's few remaining structures amidst the ruins of Jim Crow's furious demise. With its patrons scattered, the library soon faced repeated calls to shut its doors.

Confronted with uncertainty about whether the public space she created would last into the future, Lee made sure her story survived, not as a triumphalist record of racial achievement, but as a counterpublic tale of survival. She easily could have lost her battle of subterfuge with the City of Roanoke in the 1940s. That loss would have consigned her collection to the realm of "shadow books" lost or destroyed, and she knew, as Kevin Young writes, that the lost book "is the book that blackness writes every day."[136] She also understood that the struggle to preserve spaces of Black knowledge did not end with her victory in 1942, or with the arrival of racial integration a decade later. The hard-won Gainsboro Library—as well as the institutions that surrounded it—did not exist simply to wait for the legal dismantling of the color line. Lee's collection represented an investment in Black life and autonomy, and the struggle for that autonomy continued long after desegregation.[137] In the face of ongoing calls to close the Gainsboro Library after urban renewal, then, Lee may have wanted the naming ceremony to mark not just her years of public service, but also her critical praxis: the idea that even in the smallest, most diminutive spaces, and even under conditions of erasure, a community has a history worth taking risks to save. Although it left no paper trail, her basement library stoked an ongoing tradition of counterpublic archiving. That tradition carried over to the work of Lee's successors, who maintained bulging clipping files on urban renewal—and activism against it—even as the city destroyed the library's surroundings.

Neither Lee's clandestine collecting practices, nor the work of her successors, yielded an iconic archive. In Roanoke, the story of her basement library has taken on larger-than-life dimensions, but the Gainsboro Library itself is not one of the national research sites that feed the field of African American Studies. The small brick building on Patton Avenue still serves the readers it always has: local students and teachers; lay readers; and researchers who study southwest Virginia. Indeed, few of the collections built inside colored branch libraries in the 1920s and 1930s, with the exception of Atlanta, ever grew enough in size or stature to join the postwar pantheon of Black research institutes. Their importance has receded from view in part because of their modest content—consisting largely of clippings, church bulletins, photograph albums, and twentieth-century books—and in part because reprinting initiatives in the 1960s and 1970s duplicated their holdings in a belated push to fill mainstream repositories with Black literature.[138] Lee's collection nevertheless sits at the center of a history of Black archives. It represents the proliferation of small collections—projects of both respectability and risk at the height of segregation—that made space for Black literature, and protected it, inside of civic systems that imagined the library otherwise. These diminutive sets of books and clippings were at once foundational and fugitive. They shaped Black public life upstairs and, when necessary, underground.

CHAPTER FOUR

UNAUTHORIZED INQUIRIES

Dorothy Porter's Wayward Catalog

Although there is rich and varied material by and about Negroes, it is so widely scattered in homes, in bookshops, in great reference libraries where it is a small part of the whole, and in private collections that it is comparatively unknown to most white people and to a large proportion of Negroes themselves.

—*The Crisis*, 1925

The telephone rang and mail arrived, addressed to "Negro Collection, Howard University, District of Columbia." Each call or letter presented Dorothy B. Porter, the curator in charge, with a question (figure 4.1). A clubwoman from Virginia asked for a list of outstanding men and women "who have contributed most to the Negro race."[1] A film company in California asked for information on Black soldiers in the nineteenth-century Mexican Expedition.[2] A Fisk graduate, living in Indiana, asked after "great Negro women in all fields."[3] A "young race man," imprisoned in New York, asked how he could obtain "books with which to begin my study of Negro history."[4] A graduate student in Michigan asked if any American games were African in origin.[5] Black teachers wrote from around the country: from New Jersey, a request for histories of "the Negro in Reconstruction"; from New Orleans, an inquiry about Afro-French Creole dialect; and from a school just down the street, a question about the origins of the Urban League movement.[6] Hundreds and soon thousands of such questions found their way to Howard University in the 1930s and 1940s—sometimes sent directly to Porter, and sometimes forwarded by those

FIGURE 4.1 Dorothy B. Porter in 1951. Photograph by Carl Van Vechten.

Source: Carl Van Vechten Papers Relating to African American Arts and Letters, Beinecke Rare Book and Manuscript Library, Yale University. Copyright ©Van Vechten Trust.

who did not have answers but suspected she would. Each reference request, whether transmitted by telephone or post, had its own horizon, with an imagined future taking shape as a syllabus, script, or campaign. Together, however, these individual imaginaries coalesced into a collective query: What could a Black archive yield?

The archive in question, called the Moorland Foundation to honor bibliophile Jesse E. Moorland, did not begin with these letter writers or callers in mind. Rather, its founders imagined the collection as primarily designed for students at Howard, the "capstone of Negro education," later called "The Mecca." Since its 1867 founding, the university had amassed Black history and literature. Significant early holdings included scrapbooks on John Brown, the Civil War, and the Freedmen's Bureau, compiled by the Philadelphian Joseph W. H. Cathcart, and sixteen hundred antislavery narratives and manuscripts donated by abolitionist Lewis Tappan. In 1914, Moorland, a minister and YMCA secretary, gave to his alma mater three thousand "books, pictures, statuary etc., on the 'Negro and Slavery' "—an acquisition so significant it inspired calls to brand it the National Negro Library and Museum.[7] Moorland declared that "our young people who have the scholarly instinct should have the privilege of a complete reference library on the subject."[8] After Porter arrived in 1930, she opened a reading room to house Moorland's collection and assist students in using it.[9] The room also served as a research space where the District's school teachers planned Negro History Week events and where Howard's faculty—including E. Franklin Frazier, Charles Wesley, John Hope Franklin, and Howard Thurman—prepared their speeches and books. With Porter at the helm, the collection's public soon extended beyond the local readers Moorland had anticipated. As Porter made the collection's resources more widely known, queries began to arrive from elsewhere and everywhere: a "constant demand," she reported, not just from researchers on campus but also from faraway letter writers who came to see Howard's resources as an archive of their own.[10]

These queries, and the desires for knowledge they harbored, found their way to Howard because few other repositories could answer—or even fathom—the questions the letters posed. Most libraries in the United States did not explicitly collect Black information, a disregard that echoed the negation young Arturo Schomburg heard in the 1880s: *The Negro has no history*.[11] Even those institutions that deliberately preserved Black material, including the Library of Congress and most historically Black colleges and universities (HBCUs), often lacked systems to locate what they had.[12] Such was the case at Howard in the years before Porter arrived. Moorland expected his library to be "catalogued and placed in an appropriate alcove or room," but the difficulties of classifying such specialized objects resulted in much of it remaining "boxed up . . . and unused."[13] HBCU libraries valued Black archival material and gave it harbor—the Hampton Institute had spent three decades building its Peabody Collection, for example—but they could not always devote time or staff to organizing it.[14] Worried about the fate of the items he donated, Moorland urged Howard to hire a librarian dedicated to the university's neglected accruals. When Porter took on this new role, Howard became the first HBCU with a full-time curator for Africana materials.[15] While concerned with readying the collection for students and faculty, Porter also grasped her inaugural responsibility within this broader network of collections and readers. She would become a curator not just of Howard's holdings, but of Black materials everywhere.

Twenty-five years old and just out of library school when she accepted this assignment, Porter would grow the collection over four decades, acquiring texts by "every way except stealing."[16] In the beginning, however, she had to find what was already there. "I had to teach myself black history," she recalled. "Then I went around the library and pulled out every relevant book I could find—the history of slavery, black poets—for the collection."[17] Porter looked for objects that "lay unknown in the basement" or among "odds and ends on the shelves in Founders Library."[18] Unlike Virginia Lee in Roanoke, Porter did not have to create a collection from scratch or defend her right to acquire Black materials. Her challenge, by contrast, was to turn the "splendidly inspired and inevitably uncoordinated" work of earlier bibliophiles into something useable. While Lee had to hide her collection *in* the basement to protect it, at Howard and other HBCUs, the most urgent work often entailed retrieving long-dormant texts *from* the basement.[19] Porter's search produced a dizzying array of items, including hundreds of sources Moorland had added in the years since his initial donation. "I found a number of pamphlets and books tied together which you had sent here in 1919," she wrote him. "I also found some specimens of brightly colored butterflies, beetles, along with some native objects which may have been sent to the university from Africa or which you may have given."[20] If she never figured out what to do with the butterflies, Porter could proudly report, after a two-year search, "I know every book that is here."[21] Moorland advised that such a mass of texts would "require careful organization," and indeed, Porter's next imperative was to bring order to this reclaimed collection.[22]

As Black collections moved out of the parlors of Schomburg or Moorland and into institutional spaces such as the New York Public Library or Howard, they became accessible to broader publics.[23] As "crossroads for authors and leaders and ordinary men" alike, these new research collections had to accommodate the manifold queries of the crowd.[24] No longer governed by the idiosyncratic arrangements of individual bibliophiles, they passed into the hands of librarians like Porter, who were trained to catalog, classify, and declutter a world encumbered by "too much to know."[25] Yet the prevailing information taxonomies used in librarianship faltered in the face of Black print culture. Porter and her colleagues inherited systems that treated blackness not as the site of too much to know, but rather of too little. The authority lists used by catalogers to standardize data excluded many Black authors, while subject headings and classification schemes omitted or misfiled Black topics. "No library in the country has a classification suitable for our purpose," Porter's predecessors remarked when they tried to classify Moorland's collection in the 1910s.[26] That lament still held true when Porter arrived on the scene. As her colleagues elsewhere waged battle over physical access to Black books, Porter confronted the dilemma of intellectual access: how to help people find Black print when so little of it had been adequately enumerated. "I believe that materials on the Negro are to be found in every University and public library, in every historical society and in every county and state library in this country," she declared.[27] She set out to make new systems for locating such materials, her ambitions surging across this scattered, and sometimes submerged, Black archive.

Porter first had to reenvision Black information as a site of abundance—finding it where others thought it absent—and then design tools to manage that abundance. To do so, she invented wayward classifications.[28] She dismantled the rules she learned in library school and, contravening official prohibitions, remade them to capaciously taxonomize blackness. She renumbered Dewey decimals; filled her card catalog with unauthorized subject headings; and, looking beyond Howard, proposed a national Black catalog linking well-known collections of Africana to the unexpected places where Black texts might be hidden.[29] With this codifying impulse, she modeled a new way to see Black collections. She looked for blackness "out of place"—whether mis-shelved or straying beyond its prescribed subjects—and designed a classification system in which that fugitive material could belong.[30] This insistence that "materials on the Negro" were everywhere, and that they warranted complex delineation, was more radical than the steadfastly diminutive Porter let on. She faced persistent opposition for challenging the limits placed on Black inquiry. Epitomizing David Scott's argument that archive-building is "at once conserving *and* a condition of criticism, revision, and change," Porter imagined the seemingly technocratic card catalog as a place where people could access the full scope of Black thought.[31] As evidenced in her correspondence with readers, Porter's effort to enlarge and enumerate the intricacies of blackness as a category of knowledge fueled a broader imagination of what stories might dwell in a Black archive.

DISORDERLY DECIMALS: ORGANIZING BLACK KNOWLEDGE

As Porter sorted through Moorland's books, she extended a tradition of wayward classifications at Black institutions, from W. E. B. Du Bois's turn-of-the-century bibliographies at Atlanta University to Tuskegee's filing systems for clippings.

An earlier cohort of bibliophiles—Du Bois, Daniel Murray, Monroe Work, and Schomburg among them—had recovered and enumerated a lineage of Black texts.[32] In the late 1920s and 1930s, Porter and her colleagues—part of a wave of African American women professionally trained as librarians—built on the countercataloging practices of these bookmen. Porter's entry into the world of collecting captures this blending of traditions. She did not learn Black history in the "predominantly white environment" of her New Jersey high school. But she "was always a bibliomaniac," she recalled, "because my father insisted on buying books when I wanted money for skates."[33] She traveled south for college, studying first at Miner Normal School and then at Howard. There she met librarian E. C. Williams, who gathered Porter and a dozen other students on Wednesday nights to study Black literature.[34] After enrolling in library school in New York, she worked as an assistant in Schomburg's collection. She recalled that her first conversation with him "lasted all day . . . examining copies of the books he so dearly loved."[35] To identify materials for her thesis on pre-1835 Black writers, she visited the private library of white bibliophile and National Association for the Advancement of Colored People (NAACP) activist Arthur Spingarn.[36] Upon her return to Howard, she developed close friendships with Carter G. Woodson, who encouraged her to collect Black abolitionist texts, and with Henry Proctor Slaughter, a local printer and bibliophile who nurtured her with meals as well as books.[37]

Porter saw Howard's Negro Collection as "a monument to the ideals, labor and farsighted intelligence" of these mentors and others who built the Black bibliographic tradition.[38] She sought to honor those ideals as she ordered the books in the Moorland Foundation. She soon found, however, that library classification systems were incompatible with the intellectual traditions passed down to her. In the early twentieth century, the prevailing system of arrangement for libraries was the Dewey Decimal Classification, a late-nineteenth-century scheme developed by Melvil Dewey in which "the infinity of the universe can be contained within the infinite combination of ten digits."[39] On the left side of Dewey's decimal point were ten disciplinary classes—100 for Philosophy, 200 for Religion, 800 for Literature, and so on—each of which could be subdivided. On the right side, a trail of up to eight figures led into an array of narrower concepts. Books on women's intellect, for example, could be found by beginning with the number 300 for the Social Sciences, continuing to 376 for Education of Women, and finally arriving at 376.4 for "Mental capacity of women."[40] Dewey deployed a cadre of specialists to organize his system for each discipline, freeing individual librarians—at a moment when small public libraries were proliferating—from having to independently classify books on topics ranging from the branches of chemistry to the periodization of British literature. Dewey prized this efficiency, arguing, "No one person is learned enough to class wisely books on all subjects and sciences; but botanists can assign all botanic subjects to the right number, mathematicians all mathematical topics, and thus the Index will in time become as accurate as the best scholarship of the day can make it."[41]

Dewey's universe was peculiarly—if predictably—proportioned. An influential information technology of its time, the Dewey classification sorted the globe into racial, cultural, and religious hierarchies. Dewey's philology class, for example, divided the linguistic world into nine areas: Comparative, English, German, French, Italian, Spanish, Latin, Greek, and *Other*. The Religion class similarly reserved just one subdivision for all non-Christian faiths.[42] Not surprisingly, then, blackness occupied a marginalized place within this system. Dewey's 1927 index, which Porter consulted, listed these subjects under "Negro": Vocal music—Negro minstrelsy and plantation songs; Slavery; Education of special classes; Negro troops in the U.S. Civil War; the Thirteenth and Fourteenth Amendments; Household personnel; Race ethnology; Mental characteristics as influenced by race; and Suffrage. Libraries typically placed any work that did not fit into one of these areas at 325.26, a number in Political Science (320) under Colonies and Migration (325) for works on "Emigrants of a special country or race" (325.2). An editorial note explained that "in United States 325.2 will relate almost wholly to specific nationalities . . . e.g. 325.26 Negro question."[43] As a result of this system, nearly every text relating to African American life and history—aside from those on slavery, suffrage, minstrelsy, education, or domestic labor—landed in a section of the library reserved for works about people foreign to the nation.[44] Thus, even when African American readers had access to repositories (and in much of the South, they did not), they often failed to find what they sought.[45]

Porter recalled struggling with this classification, which rendered the American Negro as enslaved or, when not enslaved, an immigrant: "in the Dewey Decimal System, they had one number—326—that meant slavery, and they had one other number—325, as I recall it—that meant colonization. So [in] all the libraries—many of the white libraries, which I visited later—every book, [even] a book of poems by James Weldon Johnson, who everybody knew was a black poet, went under 325."[46] Calling this approach "illogical," Porter lodged a protest with the editor of Dewey's classification, headquartered at the Library of Congress. "I remember visiting Miss Dorcas Fellows, the editor of the Dewey Decimal Class[ification] Scheme," she recalled, but "I could not convince Miss Fellows that histories of the Negro belonged in 973 and the poetry of James Weldon Johnson should be placed in 811.5."[47] Although Dewey's system aspired to organize knowledge by discipline rather than theme, in practice, librarians shelved at 325.26 anything Black, regardless of genre or field, including E. C. L.

Adams's *Congaree Sketches* (folklore), Johnson's *Autobiography of an Ex-Colored Man* (fiction), Benjamin Brawley's *The Negro in Literature and Art* (criticism), and *The Speeches of Booker T. Washington* (oratory). The eclectic works of the polymath Du Bois frequently ended up here, too, including *Black Reconstruction*, *The Souls of Black Folk*, and *Black Folk Then and Now*.[48] As such, each title was made an unwitting answer to the "Negro Question," a term often synonymous with the "Negro Problem." To Du Bois's famous and poignant query—"How does it feel to be a problem?"—his books might have answered that it felt like sitting on a shelf at 325.26.[49]

If Dewey's system crowded wide-ranging works not on slavery into a single category, it simultaneously underdeveloped 326, the class for works that *were* on slavery, limiting it to one figure after the decimal point. A fifth of Howard's Negro Collection concerned slavery, including sixteen hundred titles donated by abolitionist Lewis Tappan, but there were just five Dewey categories to sort them out.[50] At Hampton, cataloger Sarah Line echoed Porter's frustration with this constriction, calling for more minute subdivisions for works on slavery.[51] The lack of detail at 326 stood in stark contrast to the fastidiousness elsewhere in Dewey's system, which assigned intricate, six-digit class numbers to subjects such as Daughters of the Confederacy (369.175) and the placement of hat racks in libraries (022.921). Such treatment was not necessarily meant to mark the category of slavery as small (for, surely, more books existed on slavery than on hat racks), but in epistemological and practical terms, it signaled that the subject required little analysis. To counter that judgment, Porter and her colleagues needed a more complex classification for Black subject matter. Dewey prohibited independent changes to his system, however: "Whenever you use our exact numbers," he instructed, "use also our exact and universal meanings for them."[52] While instructing librarians to await official revisions, Dewey's editors often dismissed their requests for change as "clamorous," "frantic" and not "worth their cost."[53] "Only gravest reasons," they warned, "justify changing numbers."[54] Many librarians defied these warnings and made adaptations to suit their holdings, but Dewey's edict kept most of these alternative systems out of circulation—as Porter would soon learn.

Dewey's prohibitions presumed that classification tools were functional rather than philosophical.[55] Such a posture belies the fact that any enumeration orders the universe according to underlying hierarchies; in a library, "a certain vision of the world is imposed upon the reader through its categories."[56] From the separation of profane from sacred texts in Islamic libraries of the Middle Ages, to the display of "Books by Negro Authors" at the 1900 Paris Exposition, classification reflects authorized points of entry into the known world.[57] To be sure, acts of reading can rebuke the authority of classification, because imagination often defies what Walter Benjamin called the "mild boredom of order."[58] As Sharifa Rhodes-Pitts suggests, readers might find a mysterious "order within the library" that is "unfathomable and inaccessible from any catalog system."[59] Yet, although no catalog controls how a reader makes her way through a text, it can determine whether a reader *finds* that text. This power to frame the imagination compelled Porter, and her colleagues at other Black institutions, to quietly dismantle Dewey's decimals. They understood what was at stake in systems that made ideas inaccessible. In one of her notebooks, Porter copied the words of Librarian of Congress Archibald MacLeish, who wrote in 1941: "Keepers of books, keepers of print and paper on the shelves, librarians are keepers also of the records of the human spirit. . . . The keepers, whether they so wish or not, cannot be neutral."[60] Activating MacLeish's words, curators of Black collections rejected Dewey's argument that classification was merely functional, and they resolved to revise his taxonomy.

By 1940, American libraries held at least two dozen special collections "by and about the Negro," all of which were located at Black colleges or in Black neighborhoods, and primarily staffed by Black women.[61] Nearly half of these women refused to use 325.26 for *any* book, rejecting the professional habits that had long misfiled blackness.[62] They understood blackness not as a subcategory of sociology but as a constellation of subjects, expressions, and ideas encompassing the entirety of the printed record. As a result, they made their collections speak across taxonomy's universe—which was the theory, if not the practice, of Dewey's classification. In dismantling the 325.26 class, librarians undid the stifling singularity of the "Negro Question" as a container for blackness and insisted that Dewey's system follow its own logic. Porter moved Booker T. Washington's *Selected Speeches*, which some libraries placed at 325.26, to the Dewey class for American oratory—thus anticipating Alberto Manguel's call to "*rescue* the book from the category to which it has been condemned."[63] She moved Du Bois's books to history and literature. "Why not take the whole Dewey Decimal System," Porter asked, "and put a book by James Weldon Johnson, the poet, underneath the number for poetry?"[64] At the 135th Street Branch Library in Harlem, librarian Catherine Latimer and cataloger Kathleen Hill likewise removed books on Africa from the class for travel, where catalogers often placed them, and shifted them to ethnology or history.[65]

The keepers of Black books kept rearranging. While refusing the "Negro Question" as a catchall category, Porter and her colleagues also reframed what that question signaled when authors did, in fact, pose it. They relocated books by Edwin R. Embree, who authored a liberal "Manifesto on the Negro

Question," from 325.26, under "Emigrants," to 323, the class for "Internal relations with groups and individuals."[66] By shifting one digit, they argued that race was entwined with class, family relations, political struggle, notions of equality, rights of petition, and laws of citizenship *within* a state or society—all concepts available at 323 but not at 325.[67] Echoing long-standing debates among African American thinkers about colonization, this epistemological move declared that if blackness troubled the nation, it did so from the position of citizen or exile, rather than as presumed foreigner.[68] Admittedly, this maneuver disallowed the possibility of thinking productively about blackness alongside questions of global migration or statelessness, but it also refused to view blackness as homogenous. By finding a niche for works on race relations inside the United States, catalogers stressed the particularity of blackness outside it, underlining the need to attend more carefully to works on African descended people in the Caribbean, South America, and Europe. Porter, for example, spent the 1940s enumerating Afro-Braziliana, and later collected African street literature printed in pamphlet form—"things other people hadn't even thought about" in the United States, as the pan-Africanist John Henrik Clarke remarked.[69]

Forging an even more radical approach to classification than her colleagues, Porter both mapped new territory in Dewey and changed its coordinates. At 326—Slavery, Serfdom, and Emancipation—Porter turned Dewey's ten categories into a hundred. Borrowing some class divisions from the Library of Congress's competing arrangement and inventing other categories herself, she opened specific locations for psychological aspects of slavery, Mohammadism and slavery, fugitive slave laws, colonization debates, and insurrections.[70] Under Religion, Porter authored expansions dedicated to the Free Masons and to the A. M. E. church.[71] Her most audacious moves, however, took place in History and Sociology. Operating wholly outside of approved cataloging protocol, she did not simply move books within Dewey's taxonomy, but rewrote what the decimals themselves signified. While Dewey organized American history—the 970s—largely around wars and presidents, Porter reimagined it through the lens of Black experience: 973.7, which Dewey called "War of secession," Porter retitled "The Negro during the Civil War"; 973.81, Andrew Johnson's presidency, was replaced by "Emancipation"; 973.83, Rutherford Hayes, became "Ku Klux Klan"; 973.84, James Garfield, yielded to "Education of freedmen"; and 973.85, Grover Cleveland, turned into "Slavery pensions."[72] Scanning the 900s, a reader in the Moorland Foundation would find a chronology in which nineteenth-century American political history turned on the question of Black freedom. On Porter's shelves, that struggle—for emancipation, education, compensation, and safety from violence—was the engine of historical change.

Porter thus infused library practice with a democratic impulse to open the catalog to other ways of organizing and knowing, drawn from her close study of the collection and her immersion in Black intellectual history (figure 4.2).[73] She used what Patricia J. Saunders has called "magic in the ordering of things" to insist on the heterogeneity of blackness.[74] For example, she reconstructed and expanded 323—"Internal relations with groups and individuals"—which Dewey subdivided by nationality, to make it exclusively descriptive of "the race problem" within the United States, inventing additional numbers for subjects like intraracial class distinctions.[75] She thus transformed a hierarchy of comparative nationalisms, the animating logic of Dewey's 323, into a singular, infranational aperture on the specific conditions of blackness in North America. While Porter interiorized the geospatial lens at 323, elsewhere she fractured it. She created a special class, M9—a nomenclature with no correspondence anywhere in Dewey—to classify works encompassing the history of Black subjects "in Africa and America and elsewhere," such as William Ferris's *The African Abroad*. That form of diasporic sense-making ran afoul of Dewey's nationalist division of knowledge,

FIGURE 4.2 Card catalog room, Moorland-Spingarn Research Center, Howard University. Dorothy B. Porter created a separate catalog for Howard's "Negro Collection" in the early 1930s. Photograph by Laura E. Helton.

Source: Moorland-Spingarn Research Center, Howard University, Washington, DC.

but it fully inhabited the idea that the catalog is always a space of overlapping orders.[76] Porter could not change the official Dewey classification, but inside the Moorland Foundation, she served as its unauthorized guest editor. Anticipating what David Palumbo-Liu would later describe as a minoritarian imperative to "intervene in and appropriate" the universal, Porter revealed the fictions of Dewey's universalism.[77]

Having "recatalogued every book on the American Negro in our collection," Porter told Moorland in 1933 that "other Negro schools are waiting to see what we have done."[78] She planned to share her classification, but as was often the case when Porter tried to disseminate her work, she encountered resistance. A leading reference publisher told her that no audience existed for her indexes of Black poetry and periodicals—which resulted in neither index appearing in print.[79] Likewise, Porter's request to reproduce her modified Dewey system drew sharp warnings. The American Library Association cautioned that she might face charges of copyright infringement.[80] Dewey's editor told her that mimeographing her scheme "would be entirely out of the question unless we had approved it in detail" because sharing such work "would quickly result in destroying all standardization."[81] That Porter's emendation elicited such rebukes underscored the disruption posed by blackness to the library's order. Porter and those in her network circumvented this prohibition, however, with acts of subterfuge. Gertrude Franklin, a Schomburg Collection cataloger, traveled to Washington, copied Porter's classification, and used that bootleg copy to revise cataloging practices in New York.[82] Naomi Rushing, Porter's colleague at Howard, reprinted the classification in her master's thesis.[83] When Porter published the *Catalogue of the Moorland Foundation* in 1939, using Works Progress Administration (WPA) funds, she embedded her custom Dewey numbers in it, risking censure to "aid libraries in the classification of the same title[s]."[84] Immediately after publication, a librarian at Dillard University wrote to Porter to "voice the sentiment of many of the smaller Negro colleges" in expressing gratitude.[85]

Although Porter found a way to surreptitiously share her classification system, her radicality in doing so went unremarked for most of her career, in part because of gendered presumptions about the nature of intellectual work, and sometimes by Porter's own design. Like Virginia Lee, Porter did not disclose the professional risks she had taken until years after the fact. As part of the first generation of Black women with professional library training, Porter expanded access to the stores of Black knowledge created by the bibliophile activists who mentored her.[86] But she would not get the same academic recognition as those from whom she learned her craft—men elected to the American Negro Academy whether self-taught or PhDs. Porter was firmly situated in a long-standing, gendered pattern of recognition within curatorial organizations. In the American Negro Historical Society, for example, men positioned themselves as experts in acquisitions and interpretation while regarding women as caretakers of their collections.[87] In the library profession, a number of men served as administrators—E. C. Williams (1916–1929) and Walter G. Daniel (1935–1946) at Howard, Wallace Van Jackson at Virginia Union (1927–1941), L. D. Reddick at the Schomburg Collection (1939–1948), and Arna Bontemps at Fisk (1943–1965)—but "trained library work" had become a largely female field. Even those who took on the directorial positions once reserved for men, such as Jean Blackwell Hutson at the Schomburg Collection, might find themselves described, as Hutson was, as a "lady curator."[88]

These lady curators dismantled prevailing information systems that constricted the capacious scope of blackness, and they got away with it by strategically exploiting the gendered erasure of their intellectual labors. Librarianship and archiving take shape through the invention and maintenance of tools that make ideas accessible to others. These tools do not broadcast the scholarly authority required for their making. In articles and press releases about the Moorland Foundation's resources, for example, Porter's name was often absent.[89] When she penned university publications, authorial credit often went to the institution.[90] Porter herself titled her bibliographies "initial working tools," a hesitant naming that belied their significance.[91] She did not adopt the moniker "collector," despite the fact that during her tenure she acquired tens of thousands of items for the Moorland Foundation.[92] At times, she purposefully hid her role in shaping the archival record. Aware that an administrator did not want her to collect music, Porter once did so secretly: "I would buy something like Samuel Coleridge Taylor's 'Imaginary Ballet'—which was music—and list it along with books [in my reports]," she recalled.[93] Porter knew she was more than a "mere tabulator" but did not always correct perceptions to the contrary.[94] She adopted these diminutive strategies to circumvent resistance from "male colleagues who believed a woman 'had no business' " engaging in intellectual endeavors.[95] Such tactics gave her cover to operate more boldly than she might otherwise have been allowed to do.

BLACK ACCESS: CREATING A NETWORK

Being a curator on a Black campus engendered a responsibility, Porter argued, to "sustain a very definite ratio to the scope and tempo of Negro life."[96] Not every HBCU library with Africana holdings handled them the same way, however.

Atlanta University did not "segregate [its] books on the Negro"; by contrast, the collection Porter curated existed apart from the university's other library materials, both physically and analytically.[97] The Moorland Foundation had its own card catalog and reading room, where the call number for each book carried the prefix M.[98] That sequestration as a special collection descended in part from the legacy of racial segregation's spatial and epistemological rules, in which the presence of blackness was marked and its absence went unmarked. Under Jim Crow, there were libraries and *colored* libraries; the Library of Congress Subject Headings named Inventors and *Negro* Inventors.[99] At the same time, the Moorland Foundation also represented a nationalist ideal articulated by Schomburg that such collections would kindle "racial patriotism."[100] Porter stoked that autonomous tradition even as she fought the exclusion of Black knowledge from national information protocols. She used her location in Washington to intervene in federal knowledge structures, transmitting Black bibliographic records to the National Union Catalog and advising the War Department about "Books on Negroes" for soldiers.[101] At no point, however, did Porter assume that Black information practices should simply correct existing infrastructures. Searching for modes of enumeration that were creative as well as corrective, she anticipated Elizabeth Alexander's question: "How do we create a world in which our vision makes sense?"[102]

Inside the Moorland Foundation, intervention gave way to invention. Its separation from the rest of the library gave Porter space to experiment, enabling her radical revision of classification protocols. Rather than look for tight passageways through an ill-fitting taxonomy, Porter approached blackness as a expansive field of inquiry in its own right. She could take the class 323—which Dewey divided by country, such as the "struggle of nationalities in Austria 323.1436"—and wholly renumber it for "the race problem" in the United States because she had no books on Austria, or many of the other topics that required space in another collection.[103] That independence allowed her to develop expertise in a field, Black bibliography, that most scholars had overlooked. It also made possible a meticulousness not previously granted to Black materials. For a pamphlet that elsewhere might be grouped with other ephemera broadly labeled "Negro," Porter individually mapped the subjects it discussed, from Babylon to the Baptist Church.[104] Indeed, early in her tenure, Porter disbound fourteen hundred pamphlets on slavery that had been bound together and classified in aggregates. In taking them apart to catalog individually, Porter expanded the known universe of Black authorship, identifying items such as a rare 1810 pamphlet protesting slavery by the African American minister Daniel Coker.[105] She thus mapped blackness as a subject with hundreds of points of entry rather than two.

Porter undertook this work not only with the decimals that determined a book's physical location, but also with the subject headings that governed intellectual access. Porter cooperated with Frances Yocom at Fisk and Latimer at the Schomburg Collection to remake these headings and coin "unauthorized" vocabularies for Black texts. To name topics absent in the Library of Congress Subject Headings, or LCSH, they inserted in the catalog terms such as Passing, Pan-Africanism, and the Blues, and they elevated subheadings like "Insurrections" to the status of "access terms" (figure 4.3).[106] Porter and her colleagues also cataloged "analytically," in library parlance, to surface subplots of blackness within a text. Then as now, libraries depended on centralized bibliographic services provided by the Library of Congress, where federal catalogers chose a maximum of three headings to capture a book's central plot.[107] Such brevity meant that minor forms of blackness in a text did not rise to the surface of the catalog. Charles Samuel Braden's *These Also Believe*, for example, had a chapter on the

FIGURE 4.3 "Slave insurrections" as subject heading in the card catalog of Howard University's Moorland Foundation. Dorothy B. Porter created this "unauthorized" heading in the 1930s, when it did not appear in standard cataloging tools. Photograph by Laura E. Helton.

Source: Moorland-Spingarn Research Center, Howard University, Washington, DC.

African American spiritual leader Father Divine, but bore just one subject on its official catalog card: "Sects—U.S." To draw such a book into the corpus of Black print, so that a reader would find it in a search on Black religion, Porter typed a new term, "Father Divine," in red ink at the top of the card she purchased for Braden's book. She then filed the emended card in the Moorland catalog under "F."[108] Moreover, Porter once again pursued these strategies to more radical ends than her colleagues elsewhere did. For LCSH terms like "Negro artists" and "Negro inventors," Porter removed the racial qualifier, changing them to "Artists" and "Inventors."[109] She created an intellectual world in which art or invention might be a priori Black.

A reader who entered the Moorland Foundation thus encountered a reimagined universalism, where blackness was authorial rather than exceptional. Such filing strategies reflected Porter's keen grasp of the politics of access: her understanding that Black material faced exile from the catalog while Black readers faced exile from research spaces. She daily navigated the convoluted Jim Crow landscape of collections around Washington, DC. The Library of Congress had no racial restrictions on who could use its reading rooms, but at least one Black researcher in the 1930s recalled having to "sneak candy bars" inside because he could not use its dining facilities.[110] University repositories employed contradicting arrangements, with Catholic University sending its white students to use the Moorland Foundation but refusing to reciprocate for Howard's students.[111] Porter's husband James, a painter and art professor, attempted to use reference materials in the Public Library's Art Division—unsegregated in theory—only to be harassed by staff and watched by a policeman.[112] Porter likewise understood how context and categorization could hide a text—another form of denied access even when the doors of a library were open. She knew, for example, that the American Antiquarian Society, though it did not catalog material as "Negro," possessed a treasury of relevant documents, including the rare newspaper *Rights of All*.[113] She also had learned that Harvard's vast holdings on slavery, as Bontemps noted, lived in its *business* library.[114] These she called, fully leveraging the term's freighted doubled meaning, "fugitive materials."[115]

In short, Porter recognized the difference between a Black archive, which she built at Howard, and an archive of blackness, which increasingly resided outside Black institutions. What had surprised Schomburg in 1912—that white institutions amassed significant holdings on Black history—became commonplace in the decade after the Harlem Renaissance. As one bookdealer noted, "The larger white colleges and universities . . . have realized the unusual brilliance of the history of the Negro," resulting in "broad demand" for material hitherto overlooked.[116] New centers of gravity emerged at places with largely white readerships. Adding to earlier acquisitions, the Library of Congress acquired Booker T. Washington's papers, and it held rare books, such as the poems of Afro-Brazilian Domingos Caldas Barbosa, that no HBCU or Black institution possessed.[117] The Library of Congress lacked adequate descriptive tools for these holdings, however, which is why it often forwarded reference inquiries to Porter. Yale, too, joined the quest for Black manuscripts when Carl Van Vechten founded the James Weldon Johnson Memorial Collection in 1941. As Porter knew, Black materials often entered such repositories as strangers. "I sincerely hope," she wrote to Van Vechten, "that your gift of materials will serve a useful purpose at Yale University, which perhaps has very little material on the Negro."[118] Confirming her suspicion, Van Vechten replied, "I am planting my material in virgin soil."[119] Yale did not own complete runs of *Opportunity* and *The Crisis*, magazines that even the tiniest of Black libraries, such as Virginia Lee's Gainsboro branch, had always collected. "We ought to have had complete sets," the Yale librarian wrote to Porter sheepishly, "but it is particularly important we have them now."[120]

Faced with the capacity of white institutions to buy large swaths of Black history—Duke and the University of North Carolina (UNC) were "swallowing up all the Negro books from the old timers," one of her colleagues remarked—Porter emphasized intellectual as well as physical ownership.[121] If she could not compete with Duke for acquisitions, or undo how other libraries cataloged Black print, or abolish the segregation that kept Howard's students out of neighboring repositories, she would make Howard a national portal linking scattered and fugitive objects. She requested sixty thousand dollars in WPA funding to catalog hidden materials, first in her own collection and then elsewhere. She deployed relief workers to inventory manuscripts, index clippings, and prepare *A Catalogue of Books in the Moorland Foundation*.[122] Such tasks were part of a surge of bibliographic work in the 1930s, some fueled by the WPA, such as regional union catalogs, and some ongoing, such as the Library of Congress's survey of American manuscripts in Europe (led by Black archivist Ruth Anna Fisher).[123] Porter and other Black intellectuals leveraged this bibliographic fever to fund long-dreamed-of projects. Roscoe Lewis and Mentor A. Howe published a catalog of Hampton's Negro Collection under the auspices of the Federal Writers' Project, for example.[124] At Woodson's urging, the Historical Records Survey tallied Black manuscripts in New York and Detroit, while in Chicago, sociologist Horace Cayton launched the Afro-American Analytic Union Catalog, an access point for Black print in the city's libraries.[125]

If Cayton focused on the depth of one city's holdings, Porter aimed for breadth. Blocks from the federal Capitol, she proposed a Black counterpart to the National Union Catalog. In the bureaucratic lexicon of the WPA, she called it "Project A: A Union of Books By and About the Negro." The most ambitious of Porter's WPA-era initiatives, Project A aimed to transform Howard into the center of a network, where one could search across scattered bibliographic aspirations. Porter's colleague Kelly Miller once envisioned moving federal records about African Americans *to* Howard's campus, but Project A represented a different, nonproprietary form of collecting.[126] The ten institutions piloting the project in 1938 included those that had amassed Black writing for decades, such as Fisk, Hampton, and the Library of Congress; a network of small Black academic libraries, such as Prairie View and St. Augustine's College; and public libraries in Black Southern communities, such as Houston, Texas.[127] Project A revealed the comparative heterogeneity of these collections, and thus of blackness itself.[128] It also illuminated traces of blackness in predominantly white spaces—such as Drew University—and highlighted unexpected caches, such as the Cleveland Public Library's African language holdings.[129] Just as she had reconvened Moorland's fragmented library, Porter now summoned Black data to her catalog. Each library mailed paper sheets or card boxes to Howard, and a team of WPA workers, led by Ethel Williams and Margaret Hunton, copied them to create a file of thirty thousand records—"the largest card record of publications by and about the Negro ever made available in one place."[130]

Perhaps the largest, but only the beginning of what Porter dreamed: "There are so many thousand things I would like to do, but the days are too short," she wrote.[131] The onset of World War II soon turned federal funding away from the WPA's cultural projects. As a result, Porter could not expand Project A to involve other sites, including the Schomburg Collection, which had withdrawn from the pilot after Schomburg's death in 1938—cutting short the tantalizing possibility of the country's two largest Black archives joining forces.[132] In a different vein, Porter had also planned to incorporate Duke and North Carolina, which had created their own bibliography of "materials relating to the Negro."[133] Her desire to include these two white Southern universities underscored the entwined ethics of intellectual and physical access. Porter recognized the irony of Black information headquartered at a place where Black data could exist more easily than Black people. She knew that while UNC's regional catalog held records from four local Black colleges, none of UNC's classrooms would admit their students.[134] Porter wrote to ask whether Black students could use materials *at* Duke and UNC or only via the proxy of interlibrary loan.[135] Her skepticism echoed Du Bois's wry observation, decades earlier, that though his own books were shelved at the Atlanta Public Library, he could not go inside to read them.[136] Of the dozens of union catalogs created in the 1930s, only two—Porter's at Howard and Cayton's in Chicago—resided in libraries where Black readers would not have to wonder if they were allowed to enter, or, like Du Bois, be met with stares that asked "what business we had there."[137] Porter's move to create a union catalog at Howard reflected the imperative that bibliography must serve Black materials *and* readers.

UNBINDING BLACK INQUIRY

More than three thousand readers a year came to the Moorland Room, and as they moved among the books that lined its walls, they would see Du Bois's *Black Reconstruction* shelved with works of history and find James Weldon Johnson with poetry, thanks to Porter's rearrangements of the Dewey classification (figure 4.4). By the end of the 1930s, they could peruse indexes to biographies, poetry, music, and manuscripts and use the union catalog as a portal to texts in

FIGURE 4.4 Dorothy B. Porter with a student in the Moorland Foundation reading room, with a portrait of Jesse Moorland visible above the fireplace, circa 1950s. Photographer unknown.

Source: Courtesy of the Moorland-Spingarn Research Center, Howard University Archives, Howard University, Washington, DC.

eleven repositories.[138] These resources served not only those who came in person but also those who sent questions from afar. Letters and calls came to Porter's office from "high school students and Ph.D. candidates . . . from libraries, book dealers, editors, housewives and writers," who posed every size and kind of question about the African diaspora: on nationalism, Haitian poetry, West African languages, police brutality, enslaved grandparents, and all-Black towns.[139] Some of these letter writers may have been among the African Americans barred from Southern libraries. Or, at a moment when the print life of even the most famous Black writings proved brief, perhaps their searches elsewhere proved fruitless. Or maybe they turned to Porter because their questions had elicited the refrain young Schomburg heard in the 1880s: *The Negro has no history*. Whatever their motivation, these correspondents and telephone callers became part of the public Porter served. Indeed, she had two desks: one, with a typewriter, for composing letters; and a second one for helping faculty and students who appeared at the reference desk. "Hopping up and down from one desk to the other," she toggled between readers near and far.[140]

To serve distant readers, Porter needed methods of recall and retrieval scaled for efficiency.[141] Before the rise of institutional African American collections, bibliophiles made their parlors quasi-public spaces, and they, too, fielded epistolary inquiries from strangers. Schomburg replied to such queries by copying lengthy passages from his books, which he ordered as he pleased—by color and spine height.[142] His mode of recall was sensory. "I saw the book in a dream," he once wrote, "and it was resting on the third shelf near the right side."[143] By contrast, Porter read her collection by proxy, using cards and alphanumeric codes that routinized the practice of expertise.[144] To an ever-growing volume of reference requests, she responded not with the flowery phrasings of Schomburg's prose, but with crisp lists that purposefully bore no mark of authorial style. She produced countless such lists for her correspondents. In 1936, for example, she authored lists "of works of individual authors Dunbar, Miller, Chesnutt; of subjects like voodooism, drama, dentistry; of the history of a movement or event like insurrections, industry, art; of all the books . . . on a particular subject like slavery."[145] Although Porter ultimately became best known for singular, monumental reference tomes—her groundbreaking *Early Negro Writing* or the three-hundred-page *Afro-Braziliana*—the true scale of her work took shape through an abundance of these small bibliographies "produced upon request."[146] However unromantic to a bibliophile like Schomburg, her systematic sensibility facilitated a growing reading public for Black letters.[147]

Through such correspondence, the Moorland Foundation functioned as a national repository—notionally if not officially—for Black materials in the twentieth century.[148] After Porter arrived at Howard, an NAACP officer wrote: "Because we are getting so many requests for material about the Negro, you can imagine how happy I am . . . that at last I have a place to forward these inquiries."[149] The Schomburg Collection, too, received a high volume of reference queries—more than four thousand a year in the 1940s—but the proximity of Howard to federal agencies implicated Porter in national information infrastructures.[150] Her tools anchored what became, in effect, a relay network for Black bibliographic and archival information. In this network, the Library of Congress, the country's default library of record, diverted inquiries about African American and African diasporic subjects to Porter. It likely held the relevant materials to answer these queries, but it had not developed descriptive mechanisms to retrieve them, and thus reasoned that "it would be much simpler for her to get the information than for this Library to do so."[151] Once the letters reached Porter, sometimes from correspondents thousands of miles away, she did not instruct them to come to Washington, DC, for a rare book or manuscript. Instead, she often turned their attention back toward texts that had been close at hand, but undetected, all along. Her bibliographies identified titles readily found in local libraries, precisely the places where unalloyed use of Dewey decimals and the LCSH made Black print culture hard to see.[152] Although Dewey's editors kept Porter from sharing her taxonomy—thus preventing her from revolutionizing classification practices more generally—she nevertheless managed, through correspondence and redirection, to change how readers read.

Howard's archive became a site of collective imagination, a place where Black inquiry could thrive. By making a complete representation of the collection in catalog or index form, she could summon its scope, or its minutiae, on demand. Porter aimed to "keep the resources of the Collection in a state of readiness."[153] That effort to forecast the future perimeters of Black inquiry—the "yet unwritten," as she described it—entailed readying her catalog for an expansive imagination of what Black reading might yield.[154] Indeed, as the volume of inquiries Porter received grew, they also multiplied in character, from a handful of keywords in the 1930s—"interracial cooperation, poetry, soldiers, Douglass, Cullen, labor, music, abolitionism, biography, education"—to an astonishing range of subjects twenty years later.[155] A fragment from a single year of Porter's reference log in the 1950s, a layer of what Scott names the "archaeologies of black memory," captures this array:

> African administration; African agriculture; *West African Pilot*; Impact of western civilization on Nigeria; Bushmen paintings; Capitalism and slavery; Carter G. Woodson; Impact of Europe on Africa; Integration in Washington, D.C.;

> Ku Klux Klan; Gold Coast; Emancipation and the Haitian Revolution; Martin R. Delany; Educational programs of Freedmen's Bureau in S.C.; Carmen Jones; Economic Problems of Africa; Ethiopia; Denmark Vesey; Emancipation; Haiti; History of Negro economics; Freedmen; Faculty contributions; Integration; Civil Rights; Negro College Graduates; Negro medicine; Negro spirituals; Negro press; Negro poets; Negro progress; N.C. state conventions; American Colonization Society; Negro in fiction; Negro slavery; Negro in labor; Negro medical schools; Negro women; Racial and cultural conflicts; Sierra Leone; Leopold Senghor; Slave resistance; Union League of America; and West Indian Politics.[156]

The enlargement of collective inquiry shows "a complication of the possible pictures of the past available for remembering."[157] Porter described this shift, amid postwar Black freedom struggles brewing at home and abroad, as one in which "curiosity about Negro life has turned urgently to profounder interest in Negro cultural background and history."[158] The contours of what could be known underwent revision, a widening scope Porter's work had foreseen. She knew that Black inquiry had to be "unbound," to use Benjamin Quarles's term.[159] Her method required literal unbinding—taking apart volumes of pamphlets and cataloging each one anew—as well as figurative unbinding: allowing Black subjects to wander away from 325 or 326.

After World War II, in the wake of the WPA's collapse, Porter faced the dilemma of how to support the growing field of Negro Studies when the pace of queries threatened to overwhelm her capacity to respond. Even as she kept growing the Moorland Foundation—acquiring the coveted Arthur Spingarn collection of Black authors in 1945—she began to turn her systems-building outward. She focused not only on making Howard a hub but also on replicating her intellectual vision so that Black materials elsewhere—often extant but not identified—would be accessible without Porter as intermediary. She initiated projects to microfilm materials split between repositories, and she proposed a collaborative acquisitions strategy for Black collections.[160] She thus echoed the sentiment of her counterpart at the Schomburg Collection, curator L. D. Reddick, who argued that the most important question was not "which of the dozen-odd collections of Negro literature scattered over the country is the biggest," but rather how they might "cooperate in a system."[161] As with Porter's new Dewey scheme, however, this idea met with resistance, because Black institutions did not garner the level of federal or foundation support received by Cold War–era African Studies programs at white institutions.[162] Lacking funds for an alliance of Black collections, and unable to extend Project A, Porter would transmit her work by other means, as she had done earlier with her prohibited Dewey numbers. She taught others how to radically reimagine and reorder the scope of Black inquiry.

Porter drafted a call to action that resembled her own method: to develop an "ever-vigilant eye" for acquiring materials and to facilitate access through catalogs and lists.[163] She instructed librarians to "begin a search for unknown information on the Negro in your own town archives, in your public and university libraries and in private collections in your geographic area. Have your students index items on the Negro in your newspapers and state historical periodicals. Examine the early city directories . . . Pour over the pages."[164] Porter argued, in essence, that Black history existed everywhere, and abundantly, even where unmarked or unexpected—in the basement, in "your own town archives," and sometimes in hostile territory. In the wake of reordering the Moorland Foundation, she unleashed a vast project of cataloging blackness across collections, stretching the terrain of inquiry. Reflecting on the stakes of Black archives, Porter remarked, "it's important to our young people . . . to know how we survived."[165] For her insistence on expanding access to that record of survival, Porter had faced persistent opposition, sometimes explicit and sometimes embedded in the quiet mechanisms of bureaucracy. Thus, to Simon Gikandi's recent provocation—"Could one be a revolutionary and still love the library?"—Porter might have pointed out that to love the library, as a Black woman taxonomer in the early twentieth century, was already to be a revolutionary.[166] In finding fugitive texts, claiming them as part of a dispersed Black archive, giving them names and ordering them capaciously, Porter inaugurated a vision of blackness more expansive than what would fit in the drawers of any catalog.

CHAPTER FIVE

A SPACE FOR BLACK STUDY

The Hall Branch Library and the Historians Who Never Wrote

The George Cleveland Hall Memorial Library . . . is an external manifestation of faith in the future.

—Barefield Gordon, *The Crisis*, 1932

"Hear Mr. Carter G. Woodson speak," beckoned Ida B. Wells in August of 1915. She invited "all persons interested" to Chicago's Negro Fellowship League, where the historian would give a talk on Black history and its "bearing on problems of today."[1] Woodson had come west that summer to conduct research at the University of Chicago, but he passed his evenings among the institutions and activists of the South Side—soon to be transformed by the Great Migration. In the area that would become known as Bronzeville, he visited the reading room of Wells's migrant boarding house and convened a meeting at the Wabash YMCA to propose a new organization, the Association for the Study of Negro Life and History (ASNLH). Before returning to Washington, Woodson exhibited books and portraits of Sojourner Truth, Frederick Douglass, and other icons at the Half-Century of Negro Freedom Exposition.[2] Woodson thus tested the ASNLH's future work—to gather and popularize Black history—through Chicago's Black reading rooms, meeting halls, and exhibition spaces. Two decades later, when he returned to the South Side to celebrate the organization's twentieth anniversary, he found those three types of public space merged in a single institution: the George Cleveland Hall Branch Library, named for one of the ASNLH's founders, the physician Dr. George Hall, and presided over by one of its local vice presidents, librarian Vivian G. Harsh.[3]

The Hall Branch opened to the public on January 18, 1932, in the throes of the Great Depression (figure 5.1). No funds were available for the "usual ceremony that accompanies such events," but the residents of Chicago's South Side did not require pomp to bring them to the new library. More than a thousand people arrived on the first day. As they entered the "imposing structure" at the corner of Forty-Eighth and South Michigan, they encountered the "vaulted effect of the rotunda," surrounded by four handsome reading rooms noted for their "beautiful interior of dark English oak finish."[4] As the only full-service Chicago library in a predominantly Black neighborhood, the Hall Branch owed its existence to a legacy of Black organizing.[5] It bore the name of Hall, who had campaigned for the library, and it contained a hundred books gifted by the family of Charles

FIGURE 5.1 Opening day at the George Cleveland Hall Branch Library in Chicago, January 18, 1932. Vivian G. Harsh stands behind the circulation desk (center) with library staff members Ellyn Askins and Bessie Benson to greet new library patrons. Photograph by the *Chicago Defender*.

Source: George Cleveland Hall Branch Archives, Vivian G. Harsh Research Collection of Afro-American History and Literature, Carter G. Woodson Regional Library, Chicago Public Library.

Bentley, a Niagra movement veteran and a founder of the NAACP (National Association for the Advancement of Colored People).[6] Bentley's books formed the core of the "Special Collection of Books By and About the Negro" that Vivian Harsh began to gather as soon as she was appointed librarian—making the Hall Branch the second public library in a U.S. city to prominently feature a collection on Black life and letters.[7] Harlem came first, and others, including Los Angeles, quickly followed Chicago. Located in Black enclaves of the Great Migration's receiving cities, these sites fed Black artistry and activism in a period forged by entwined strands of Black radicalism: an internationalist Black left, a New Negro Renaissance that shifted westward, and fitful forms of cultural nationalism that kept alive the popular legacy of pan-Africanist Marcus Garvey.[8]

In an opening-day photograph of the Hall Branch that appeared with fanfare in the *Chicago Defender* and *The Crisis*, Harsh stands at the center, watching the scene with her famously "meticulous" gaze, while her colleagues Allyn Eskins and Bessie Benson issue library cards and check out books to new patrons.[9] Slightly to their left is the entrance to a reference room, where visitors would encounter the first three hundred volumes of Harsh's special collection. Facing the circulation desk stand members of the library's new public, dressed warmly for the January day: a tall figure silhouetted by a fur collar and cuffs, and to her left, a more simply-clad quartet, including one girl clutching a pair of books. Intent on their tasks, none of the librarians or patrons looks toward the camera in this opening-day image. Likewise, they have eluded the gaze of intellectual history in the decades since. The first person to check out a book that day (Charles C. Luck, a postal clerk from Texas) and to get a library card (Andrew Sims, a student) received special mention in the press, as did the literary writers who soon flocked to this South Side "intelligence center."[10] Few accounts of the Hall Branch fail to mention its influence on the poet Gwendolyn Brooks, for example, or on Richard Wright, who met his future collaborator, playwright Theodore Ward, in one of its reading rooms.[11] Most of the people who crowded into the Hall Branch, however, on opening day and in the years after, did not transform their encounters with the collection into famous works.

To be sure, the legacy of the Hall Branch can be measured by the impressive series of publications, performances, and public initiatives it incubated. In the 1940s, the branch served as research headquarters for one of the country's first citywide Black history curricula, and journalist Richard Durham used Harsh's special collection to create scripts for his radio series *Destination Freedom*. John H. Johnson, founder of *Negro Digest* and *Ebony*, received early training in Black history at the branch.[12] Richard Wright read the work of Gertrude Stein at the Hall Branch, an encounter that shaped his modernist experiments, and

Margaret Walker pursued advanced study in creative writing at Harsh's urging.[13] Indeed, countless writers credited Harsh and her collection as enabling their work, from St. Clair Drake and Horace Cayton in *Black Metropolis* to Arna Bontemps and Jack Conroy in *They Seek a City*.[14] To assess the impact of the Hall Branch collection based solely on the texts or productions it inspired, however, means defining archives primarily in terms of storage: as places that regulate access to documents and from which information is extracted. Another way to understand archives, by contrast, is as "desire settings," to use art historian Romi Crawford's phrase for urban sites that invite "myriad scenarios of learning, labor, and conviviality."[15] For those who convened at the Hall Branch, the "Special Collection of Books By and About the Negro" fed a hunger for sustained and collective inquiry. That inquiry most often unfolded in the "scattered and fugitive things" of informal knowledge production—conversations, theories, and lineages of thought that took shape at the proverbial "kitchen table" of a community's intellectual headquarters.[16]

The *Chicago Defender* once described Harsh as "the historian who never wrote," an inversion of how Audre Lorde would later describe herself as "the librarian who wrote."[17] Although not quite true—Harsh was a prolific author of book reviews and reading lists, among other genres—this characterization hints at an intellectual history of Black Chicago that goes uncited and uncataloged.[18] Like Harsh, most Chicagoans who came to the library were not "writers," but they nevertheless shaped the scene of Black ideas. Collectively, they turned the Hall Branch into a literary salon, exhibition site, and community archive. A similar dynamic unfolded at the Hall Branch's kindred sites in New York and Los Angeles. As L. D. Reddick noted in reference to the Schomburg Collection, such spaces served as "crossroads for authors and leaders and ordinary men," whose convenings often took place in the evening hours.[19] In Harlem, for example, library goers stayed until midnight to hear Paul Robeson sing.[20] The reading room of the Vernon Branch in South Central Los Angeles became an art gallery at night.[21] In Chicago, teachers met after the school day to read the latest books by African authors.[22] The Hall Branch thus served as an informal space of Black intellectual work, where people who taught, sorted mail, or styled hair by day came in the evening or on the weekend to theorize literature and history—without leaving much of a paper trail.

The record of Harsh's own thought is likewise sparse. Her personal papers did not survive, a fact that has compounded the sense that she "never wrote."[23] What remains are ephemeral traces that document the world of the library she tended: newspaper stories that mention the special collection she built; photographs that show what she pinned to bulletin boards in makeshift exhibitions; and mimeographed programs that record gatherings in the reading room. Known for her no-nonsense demeanor, Harsh likely would have preferred it this way—allowing other thinkers to crowd into her story—but the fugitivity of her story, and the necessity of studying her work through a community's scattered ephemera, underscores the point that although an archive begins with assembling paper, the "story that it makes possible" does not always end on paper.[24] Archives can be "used" in myriad ways, serving as bookish places to gather or as places to simply linger with a question. Long before the city officially designated the Harsh collection as a research site, she and her colleagues welcomed the community's "serious seekers after knowledge."[25] Black archives created public space for intellectual desire.

Following Ann Cvetkovich's argument that "the history of any archive is the history of space," this chapter recreates the visual tableaus inside the Hall Branch and listens in on the conversations it made possible.[26] At the center of this scene are the unfamous historians of the DuSable History Club, who gathered weekly at the library to use Harsh's collection. Led by curators, orators, and teachers, the club had roots in Woodson's Negro History movement. In meetings framed as "question periods," its members engaged in what Fred Moten and Stefano Harney call "black study"—intellectual work that is dissident and speculative, collective and informal.[27] Commemorating the Haitian Revolution one night and making a pilgrimage to Sojourner Truth's grave the next, the DuSable History Club fused Midwestern placemaking with pan-Africanist politics.[28] The Hall Branch, then, not only harbored resources but also occasioned collectivities. Ultimately, it gave rise to a major archive of Black Chicago, but in its first decades, this archive took shape as a community's study hall rather than as a set of files.

A SPECIAL COLLECTION AND ITS PUBLICS

Born in Chicago in 1890, Vivian Harsh belonged to an "old settler" family that had moved from Tennessee in the 1880s. For much of her life, she lived on East 44th Place, about a mile from where the Hall Branch would open. Until 1920, the Harshes were the only African American family on their block, but by 1930, Black migrants from the South became their neighbors on all sides. As the new arrivals found work as mill or coal yard workers, factory laborers, maids, porters, and cooks, Harsh continued to climb the ranks of the city's civil service system.[29] When the Chicago Public Library announced plans to build a Bronzeville branch, Harsh got the nod to become its head librarian—the first Black woman

FIGURE 5.2 Librarian Vivian G. Harsh outside of the George Cleveland Hall Branch Library, undated. Photographer unknown.

Source: George Cleveland Hall Branch Archives, Vivian G. Harsh Research Collection of Afro-American History and Literature, Carter G. Woodson Regional Library, Chicago Public Library.

in Chicago to hold such a position (figure 5.2). To open the George Cleveland Hall Branch Library, Harsh assembled a staff composed largely of Black women, most of whom, like her, had Chicago upbringings and social ties that set them apart from the new arrivals.[30] The new library sat a block from what Cayton and Drake, in their study *Black Metropolis*, described as the neighborhood's "village square," anchoring a South Side "cultural collective" that included the

Chicago Defender, the Good Shepherd Community Center, and the South Side Community Art Center—as well as the social clubs and entertainment venues of Bronzeville's "nighttime Stroll."[31] In this cultural geography, the Hall Branch served, for old and new settlers alike, as the neighborhood's archive, reading room, and study hall.

While Woodson preserved letters of the Great Migration's sojourners to deposit at the Library of Congress, Harsh prepared a space to welcome in these migrants as readers.[32] In doing so, she revived a tradition of the South Side, which had been home in the 1910s to at least half a dozen reading rooms—at the Frederick Douglass Woman's Club, the Wabash YMCA, Ida B. Wells's Negro Fellowship League, and other institutions.[33] Designed as alternatives to the pool hall, these spaces of social uplift housed small reading collections stocked with Black newspapers from around the country as well as the "best books."[34] They also facilitated political organizing, as when Wells used the Fellowship League's reading room in 1912 to hold a mass meeting defending the boxing star Jack Johnson from attacks in the white press.[35] When the Hall Branch opened in 1932, it carried on these functions of uplift, organizing, and reading—reconceived for the space of a public library. For inspiration on how to revive this tradition, Harsh traveled to Howard University's Moorland Foundation, where she likely met curator Dorothy Porter, and to New York, where she spent time with Catherine Latimer, reference librarian for the Schomburg Collection.[36] There she would have seen how a branch library could act as a "laboratory of Negro literature": a place where a bibliophile might give a lecture on Nat Turner, a literary forum might discuss Black poetry, or a civil rights leader might discuss an antilynching campaign.[37] Harsh returned to Chicago with visions of how, as Latimer argued, "[r]ace consciousness and race pride are being aroused and inspired by the preservation of these historical records."[38]

Such visions sparked suspicion among whites uneasy about the city's changing demographics. Libraries were expected to prevent crime and keep order; for some white Chicagoans, a public space centering Black knowledge seemed portentous of disorder.[39] Harsh took charge of the Hall Branch during Chicago's "tense years" of 1930 to 1932—a moment when Black protestors picketed Woolworth stores and organized antieviction marches. During a chilling incident known as the "Chicago massacre," police killed three housing activists a few blocks from the library's construction site.[40] In this atmosphere, the mayor fielded concerns from white Chicagoans that Harsh's special collection would ignite a "race riot." The city's chief librarian, Carl B. Roden, countered by downplaying the library's significance. He acknowledged that the branch would include a "small collection of books by colored authors," but he described the collection as ordinary: "When we open a Branch in a Jewish neighborhood, we install books of interest to Jews. In a bohemian neighborhood, we emphasize Bohemian books." Roden promised that "there is nothing in the Hall Branch collection of an incendiary or revolutionary character."[41] Likewise, when Roden received a request to ban from the Hall Branch Scott Nearing's leftist treatise *Black America*, which Langston Hughes described as a portrait of the "terrible realness" of caste in America, he once again countered that neither Nearing's book, nor any others at the Hall Branch, would spark a riot.[42] While Arthur Schomburg once prophesied a Black collection as "powder with which to fight our enemies," Roden assured white Chicagoans that the Hall branch special collection was nothing to fear.[43]

Contrary to Roden's benign framing of the collection as simply a "source of information," for Harsh it was a "prize possession."[44] Faced with a Depression-era library budget, she could not recreate what she had seen at Howard or the 135th Street library, and like branch librarians in the South, she did not benefit from the type of large gift or purchase that seeded those two famous collections.[45] To build her collection, then, Harsh posted "Books wanted" signs in the library and cajoled neighborhood residents to "search the house" for anything they could give.[46] A grant of five hundred dollars from the Julius Rosenwald Fund allowed her to search for older books, while a friend who owned a bookstore offered Harsh discounts on new texts.[47] Her colleagues Charlemae Rollins and Marian Hadley built a clipping and ephemera file, gathering "every scrap" they considered "invaluable as source material."[48] Harsh "loved to talk about the books that she was buying," and by 1943, she had expanded the special collection from three hundred items to two thousand.[49] Among these were some rare works—a first edition *Narrative of Sojourner Truth* and *The Ethiopian Manifesto*, published in 1829—as well as contemporary works published abroad, such as the scarce London edition of Claude McKay's *Spring in New Hampshire* and the Haitian study *Un Chant Nouveau*.[50] Items in the collection proved so popular that librarians sometimes had to restrict how long borrowers could use them, especially during Negro History Week.[51]

Harsh's special collection, which began as a small set of books, slowly transformed into a South Side archive—a place where the neighborhood could keep the notes it kept and records of the lives it lived. That transformation took place at the hands of those who used the Hall Branch, as history club meetings and literary forums became occasions for acquisition. The DuSable History Club added its "missing pages" of Chicago history to the special collection.[52] The Negro in Illinois unit of the Federal Writers' Project, which used the library as its headquarters, deposited a large cache of research files—covering everything from Emancipation Day celebrations to gambling rings—which Harsh promised to "arrange and sort."[53] When Langston Hughes appeared at the Hall Branch's Book Review and Lecture Forum to discuss his memoir *The Big Sea*, Harsh asked him to donate the typescript to the library. Hughes obliged, and *The Big Sea* became one of the first literary manuscripts in the collection, followed by Richard Wright's "Blueprint for Negro Writing" and his "Big Boy Leaves Home."[54] Horace Cayton and Elizabeth Wimp's Chicago Afro-American Analytic Union Catalog, another Works Progress Administration (WPA) project, also deposited its records at the Hall Branch. With seventy-five thousand card entries mapping Black life and history across the city's libraries, this catalog made the Hall Branch *the* place in Chicago to launch a search for Black materials.[55] Meanwhile, the core book collection kept growing through additional gifts, including items given by Sylvestre and Mabel Watkins, who wanted Chicago to one day rival the famous Schomburg Collection.[56]

In the words of *Chicago Bee* columnist George Coleman Moore, the Hall Branch became a place where "books are live things," humming with gatherings that operated in close relationship to the special collection.[57] Chief among these was the Book Review and Lecture Forum (BRLF), which Harsh inaugurated in 1933 as an opportunity for artists, writers, and neighborhood thinkers to share their work and review books. A standing-room-only crowd greeted Langston Hughes and Gwendolyn Brooks, for example, and Katherine Dunham gave an illustrated talk on the Haitian Revolution.[58] Arna Bontemps, a forum regular, reviewed Zora Neale Hurston's *Tell My Horse* and C. L. R. James's *The Black Jacobins*, while a young Margaret Walker discussed Edna St. Vincent Millay's *A Conversation at Midnight*.[59] Such occasions made the Hall Branch famous as an incubator of the Chicago Renaissance, celebrated in both popular and scholarly accounts as a shaping force in the city's literary culture. Like Harsh, however, most of the forum's longtime organizers, hosts, and reviewers were not "writers" themselves. Ethel Wickliffe and her husband were postal clerks, as were Russell Marshall and George Sanford. Harry I. Jones led the International Brotherhood of Red Caps. Ruth E. Shepard was the wife of a janitor. George Dorsey taught school, as did Etta Evans, Thelma Sims Ford, Grace McCray, and Bessie King. Pearl Pacheco was recreation director of the Rosenwald Homes, and Brunetta Mouzon was an actress and social worker.[60] Such figures may not seem like the protagonists of literary history, but together they sustained a vibrant, collective practice of literary criticism in Bronzeville.

Although the Chicago Public Library downplayed the radicality of the Hall Branch, Harsh and her collaborators welcomed the disquiet Black books provoked.[61] In one of Harsh's few surviving letters, she noted that the publication of Wright's *Black Boy* had caused "controversy as usual" and that Walter White's *A Rising Wind*, an expose of discrimination against Black soldiers, left much "unsaid, no doubt due to army censorship."[62] The BRLF put both books on its agenda in 1945.[63] The same year, Harsh invited the leftist and blacklisted writer Jack Conroy to give a talk at the library.[64] Respected by writers of Bronzeville—and well known at the library for the research he and Bontemps directed for the WPA's Negro in Illinois project—Conroy had recently been identified as a "writer for the Communist press" by the House Committee on Un-American Propaganda Activities.[65] The *Chicago Tribune* allegedly refused to print an announcement of Conroy's talk at the Hall Branch.[66] That was not the only time Harsh took the side of a banned author, however. In 1954, she warned John Oliver Killens that the Chicago Public Library had refused to endorse his book *Youngblood*, deeming it "unfair to white folks." Thus alerted, Killens defended his book to library administrators, while also making sure Harsh received a copy for the special collection.[67]

This unafraid approach extended to the reading lists Harsh created. For a forum on Wright's *Native Son* and Ira De A. Reid's *The Negro Immigrant*, for example, she printed a short but provocative list of supplemental readings that spanned Dostoyevsky's *Crime and Punishment* to James Vandercook's *Caribbee Cruise*, weaving together themes of exile, diaspora, and psychology.[68] Harsh widely circulated these book lists to invite potential readers into the collection. Unlike a card catalog, a reading list is ephemeral, printed in a fleeting format for a particular occasion or group and made to "find its users" through circulation.[69] In the United Transport Service Employees' newspaper, one of Harsh's lists pointed readers to Horace Cayton's study of the Black labor movement and a proletarian novel about workers scraping by during the Depression.[70] In the *Chicago Bee*, another list paired texts on South Africa, Russia, and India with works on racial segregation in the United States.[71] Such lists are conditional rather than prescriptive: they do not answer questions as much as suggest new directions one might take to find intellectual kinships in unexpected places. Harsh saw these lists as invitations to the collection, knowing that once people arrived, they might find expansive reasons to stay—even "for some other purpose than to take out a book."[72] Contrary to the idea that she "never wrote," Harsh likely penned hundreds of these lists, although most are not attributed to an author or have disappeared along with the cheap paper on which they appeared.[73] That disappearing act provokes questions about the social life of an archive: If Harsh herself is not fully visible in the history of a collection she built, who else is missing from depictions of Black Chicago's intellectual scene? Who took her up on the invitation to visit the library, drawn by curiosity or desire?

"LIBRARY LIVES" IN BLACK PUBLIC SPACE

When W. E. B. Du Bois gave a public address in Chicago in 1939, many Bronzeville residents, including Harsh and her colleagues, listened on the radio as he described the experience of wandering a library, where readers might begin with newspapers, "drift into the book section and . . . become acquainted with that heritage sent down from the past."[74] The possibility of such drifting guided how Harsh organized the space of the Hall Branch. She wanted readers to encounter a Black archive not only in a cabinet of files or on the shelves of the special collection, but also surrounding them in the reading room. Like the tableaus organized by Schomburg and the Negro Society for Historical Research in the 1910s, Harsh's Negro History Week displays attracted "a great deal of interest." They featured "rare old books," documents, and an issue of *The Chicago Conservator*, the city's first Black newspaper.[75] Harsh also mounted on bulletin boards recent ephemera of "The Negro in Action" and a recurring exhibition called "Original Manuscripts by Contemporary Negro Writers" (figure 5.3).[76] She obtained for these displays gifts or loans from "obliging friends": local authors and editors Robert Sengstacke Abbott, William Attaway, and Chandler Owen; as well as those who passed through Chicago, including sociologist Charles S. Johnson, poet Owen Dodson, and Du Bois, who called the Hall Branch a "very interesting library."[77] After Du Bois loaned Harsh a page of one of his speeches for the exhibit, she wrote appreciatively that it "gave inquiring persons an opportunity to see for themselves one your unpublished manuscripts written in your handwriting."[78]

The 1930s and 1940s ushered in finer and more famous collections of Black manuscripts elsewhere, including those at Yale University and the Library of Congress.[79] Unlike those institutions, however, the Hall Branch was first and foremost a space made for Black readers, and Harsh's workaday approach to collecting manuscripts—including pinning them to bulletin boards—grew out of how these readers used the space. Harsh solicited manuscripts from writers whose words were actively debated and discussed by the groups who met at the Hall Branch, and her displays showcased the value placed on their work by the South Side's readers. Among those featured in the "Original Manuscripts" exhibit, for example, Charles Johnson drew a "very good crowd" when he spoke to the BRLF.[80] Du Bois's publications appeared regularly in BRLF programs, too, and Abbott and Owen's work arrived at the branch each week, pored over by library patrons who came to read newspapers.[81] During World War II, Owen Dodson and artist Charles Sebree visited the Hall Branch when they were stationed at nearby Camp Robert Smalls.[82] A few years later, Harsh exhibited drafts of their

FIGURE 5.3 "Original Manuscripts by Contemporary Negro Writers" exhibit on bulletin board at the George Cleveland Hall Branch Library, circa 1943. Photographer unknown.

Source: George Cleveland Hall Branch Archives, Vivian G. Harsh Research Collection of Afro-American History and Literature, Carter G. Woodson Regional Library, Chicago Public Library.

poetry and art.[83] Like the books in the Special Collection, then, the manuscripts Harsh collected were "live things." In her bulletin board displays, Harsh argued that the intellectual pleasures and affective power of looking at manuscripts—which preserve a record of ideas in the making—should not belong only to credentialed scholars in a quiet reading room.

Harsh also turned the branch into a gallery for the neighborhood's many privately held collections. These included letters from actress Ethel Waters preserved by a local writer; memorabilia of thespian Ira Aldridge collected by drama instructor Owen Mortimer; art and photographs assembled by librarian Marian Hadley and artist Fannie M. Stubbs; and "rare curios from Africa" owned by activist and orator Hammurabi Robb.[84] These personal displays revealed the extent of collections from what Elizabeth Alexander would call Chicago's "black interiors."[85] By displaying them, Harsh made the library a public interior, a shared space that valued the community's records. When another library branch opened farther south, it followed Harsh's lead, displaying convention proceedings saved by Geneva Gentry Simpson and books given by Ida B. Wells to her daughter, Alfreda Duster.[86] Neither the Hall Branch nor any other Black space in Chicago was yet equipped to store such a wide range of materials on a permanent basis, so most of these manuscripts and artifacts were loans rather than gifts. But the Hall Branch's sustained attentiveness to Black collecting, both public and private, was not solely about storage and retrieval. An archival experiment in Black public space, the Hall Branch celebrated the South Side's many traditions of recordkeeping.

A public library, Harsh believed, should exist "in relation" to the struggles and strivings of the "whole community": "All effort is bent on making the library so vital a part of the community it serves that it [is] looked to and called on to participate."[87] The library's community, she felt, included those both in and beyond the reading room. She thus extended the reach of the library into congregations, union halls, social spaces, and storefronts.[88] When the Parkway Community House hosted a talk about Toussaint Louverture, Harsh set up a mobile display of "current literature relating to Haiti."[89] She spoke at meetings of the Joint Council of Dining Car Employees, printed reading lists in the Red Caps' union newspaper, and helped host an event for the National Negro Congress.[90] On occasion, she also took her book reviewing on the road, showing up at the South Parkway YWCA to discuss Bucklin Moon's novel *The Darker Brother* with a group of overnight factory workers who held social gatherings in the morning rather than at night.[91] At other times, Harsh and her colleagues created pop-up exhibits along the streets of Bronzeville.[92] One of these displays, in the shop window of the Knight-Young Shoe Store, focused on labor issues (figure 5.4).[93] These window offerings invited passers-by to the branch, where they might come for a book about boiler repair and then find themselves unexpectedly immersed in Harsh's archive-on-display, whether "Original Manuscripts by Contemporary Negro Writers" or an arrangement of photographs on race relations in the union movement.[94]

For the most part, Harsh restricted her orbit to the meeting halls and sanctuaries of daytime Bronzeville, where the Chicago Renaissance unfolded in middle-class spaces of reform, religion, and art, rather than in the realm of what Hazel Carby identifies as the era's broader renaissance, which belonged to the late-night blues women singing the desires of working-class migrants.[95] Harsh's exhibits did not acknowledge the achievements of Black Chicago's entertainers or hustlers, and some South Siders likely bristled at the studious

FIGURE 5.4 Books from the George Cleveland Hall Branch Library on display in the window of The Knight-Young Shoe Stores, Inc., 47th Street, Chicago, 1941. Photograph by Edwin Rosskam for the U.S. Farm Security Administration.

Source: Farm Security Administration/Office of War Information Photograph Collection, Prints and Photographs Division, Library of Congress, Washington, DC.

propriety she demanded of library patrons, which earned her the nickname "The Lieutenant."[96] Like one of the characters in Wright's novel *Lawd Today*, many may have passed by the library and declined to enter, muttering "not today."[97] Yet Harsh did not denigrate the public she served. The historian Timuel Black, for instance, recalled being tossed from the library by Harsh when he made fun of migrants from the South.[98] For all the ways Harsh hewed to the mores of her old settler enclave, then, she also pursued an expansive sense of bookishness.[99] Her storefront displays and union hall visits enacted a commitment to reading and research as practices open to all the neighborhood's thinkers.

Harsh's cultivation of neighborhood bookishness echoed in Langston Hughes's writings about the South Side. In a city so windy it "blows whole sheets of newspapers up and down the streets," Hughes named his favorite Bronzeville haunts in a newspaper column he titled "Things I Like About Chicago."[100] His list captures what the critic Houston Baker Jr. calls "black imagination and the resources of its public sphere."[101] It nods to landmarks of the daytime Stroll—the Parkway Community House, Woodlawn A. M. E. Church, and the *Ebony* magazine offices—and of the nighttime stroll—Pitt's Pub, Blue Dahlia, and Bon Aire, where "the patrons holler out loud." Along the way, Hughes narrates, he might stop in at a record shop to find the "best in hot jazz," or he might find himself at the Hall Branch Library, "whose Negro book collection is excellent and whose librarians are charming." Hughes may have been unusual in his attunement to both the "slow-drag chants" at Pitt's Pub and the book collection at the Hall Branch, but his cartography hints at how the daytime and nighttime strolls shaped Bronzeville's cultural scene in overlapping ways.[102] The significance of the Hall Branch was not simply its "excellent" collection, but also its familiar presence in this local landscape, where one might travel in an "ever-at-hand" jitney, ask for "piles of platters" at the record shop, inquire after something at the library, and hear the voice of Mahalia Jackson wafting from a radio.[103] The library was one in a series of neighborhood hangouts—a spot that, as Hughes's friend Bontemps remarked, indulged the desires of "those to whom reading is a pleasure."[104]

None of the city's public or academic libraries officially excluded Black readers, but as Hughes noted while staying at the University of Chicago, many were made "foreign" to Bronzeville's residents.[105] The university trained many Black intellectuals, including Cayton, Drake, Abram L. Harris, and Allison Davis, all of whom moved between Bronzeville and campus. In the university's formidable library, they would find more "Negro" items than they did at the tiny Hall Branch.[106] For most Hall Branch visitors, however, that crosstown journey was forbidding, and not just because of Hughes's complaint that to "get anywhere from anywhere" required multiple streetcar transfers.[107] The University of Chicago blocked construction of public housing and supported the use of restrictive covenants to prevent Black residents moving into its surroundings—policies decried by attendees at a mass meeting in Bronzeville, who called for a boycott of the university.[108] That history exacerbated the sense that the campus existed, in Hughes's words, "far away from the Horace Cayton—'Baby'

Bell—Etta Moten—Bigger Thomas—Gwendolyn Brooks—Joe Louis—world of Bronzeville." The "'Black Belt' is only a few blocks off," he added, but on campus "one cannot hear it. No el trains cut the quiet.... No jitneys blow their horns.... No Bigger Thomases come home to kitchenette confusions. Here in the University's sociology classes students only study about such things, but do not live them. The 'Black Metropolis' is a book in the library."[109]

In this passage, Hughes evokes Bronzeville through its icons—gangster Albert "Baby" Bell, screen star Etta Moten, and superhero Joe Lewis—and through its writers' characters, where Richard Wright's Bigger Thomas chafes at the "dry hours" of crowded kitchenette apartments depicted in Gwendolyn Brooks's *A Street in Bronzeville*.[110] He references the title of Cayton and Drake's popular book about the neighborhood to sketch the "Black Metropolis" as a place where residents lived a "makeshift dream."[111] For Hughes, Cayton, and Drake—who were participants in as well as theorists of the neighborhood—"Black Metropolis" represented the daily improvisations and struggles that shaped everyday life along Michigan Avenue or Forty-Eighth Street. In the university's classrooms, by contrast, *Black Metropolis* was simply an object—a book, Hughes argued, read by readers who "live clean, quiet, library lives" and scorn "those whose lives are shattered by the roar of the el trains and chilled by the cold water that comes out of the faucet marked HOT."[112] Like Hughes and Bronzeville's other resident scholars, Harsh maintained a steadfast but radical commitment to the possibility that "library lives" could be lived, quiet or not, by those in Bronzeville under "the roar of the el trains." They invested in the idea that *Black Metropolis* could be a book in the library *and* the world of that library's users.

These users, a study found, were not only students, but also housewives, teachers, barbers, clerks, cooks, ministers, secretaries, taxi drivers, and the unemployed.[113] Rollins confirmed this account, writing that Black readers at the Hall Branch included "every social and economic level from the successful writer, checking material for his latest book, to the kitchenette dwelling child who stays every night until nine o'clock because there's no place at home to read or do homework."[114] That the library wove together these South Side demographics reflects the multiple ways it acted as a public space: an urban site where strangers crossed paths; and, at the same time, a civic space that constellated Black organizational life. Teachers, students, and congregants from the neighborhood's various schools and churches met at the Hall Branch, as did members of voter leagues, civil rights organizations, and the teachers' union. People found their way to the Hall Branch through both the anonymity of the street and the infrastructures of belonging.[115] The *Chicago Bee* extended an invitation to join this scene: "Come on now, join the crowds. The best people. The common people. All the p-e-o-p-l-e! People who are living real, live lives—with books."[116]

FIGURE 5.5 George Cleveland Hall Branch Library, circa 1940s, with Vivian Harsh's "Special Collection of Books By and About the Negro" visible on shelves in the background. Librarian Dagmar Bell seated at desk; Arna Bontemps standing at center. Photographer unknown.

Source: George Cleveland Hall Branch Archives, Vivian G. Harsh Research Collection of Afro-American History and Literature, Carter G. Woodson Regional Library, Chicago Public Library.

When they arrived at the library, these crowds sought materials on many topics, from how to "organize a club" to "how to say good-bye in [an] African language" (figure 5.5).[117] One person asked for an astrology book "to aid him in playing the numbers," while another wondered about "the attitude of Britain to her colonial subjects in the West Indies."[118] Notably, Rollins pointed out that interest tended to cluster in the 300s, referring to the range of Dewey decimal numbers where most "books on the Negro are classed."[119] Bronzeville came to the Hall Branch, then, to study *itself*. "Imagine a black Chicago," Elizabeth Alexander writes of this period, "understanding itself as a people *seen*."[120] When Richard Wright visited the office of University of Chicago sociologist Louis Wirth, he saw with amazement that data on "the Negro community" was "pinned to the wall like a collector would pin butterflies."[121] When he went to the Hall Branch, by contrast, he encountered a reading room, not reserved for university experts, where a community posed its own questions about its past and future.[122] A family dispute led one woman to the library, for example; she "cleared up the matter" about whether she was descended from a Reconstruction-era Congressman by consulting *The Negro, Too, in American History*.[123] Young students in Madeline Morgan's class consulted the library's collection of Black biographies for their A.B.C. notebooks (A for Marian Anderson, B for Mary McLeod Bethune, and so on).[124] On Tuesday evenings, meanwhile, a small group known as the DuSable History Club gathered for "map study periods," drawn to the question of how Bronzeville intersected with Black diasporic elsewheres.[125]

THE DuSABLE HISTORY CLUB AND THE PRACTICE OF "BLACK STUDY"

Nearly as soon as it opened, the Hall Branch became a headquarters for Chicago's Negro History Week celebrations, with exhibits and reading lists that "attracted a great deal of interest."[126] Not in February alone, however: Harsh and Rollins made the library a year-round space for the study of Black history and sponsored a dozen or more history clubs for all ages.[127] For fifteen years, from around 1938 to the early 1950s, one of these groups, the DuSable History Club, met at the Hall Branch, sustaining a series of weekly, informal discussions that linked the history of the Black Midwest to global currents of pan-Africanism. Named for the Black settler Jean Baptiste Point du Sable, "Father of Chicago," the DuSable History Club began around 1934 as a "study club" of congregants from Quinn Chapel A. M. E. Church who were frustrated by Black history's "omission . . . from the press and text-books."[128] Led by Annie E. Oliver, an old settler from Tennessee who worked as a hairdresser and stylist, the club set out to learn about "culture in Africa" as well as the "Negro's part in the development of America."[129] Early meetings took place in members' homes, and then at the Wabash YMCA, until Samuel Stratton, the group's instructor, moved its gatherings to the library to make use of Harsh's special collection.[130] A teacher at DuSable High School, Stratton shared Harsh's commitment to collection-building and had created circulating libraries for classrooms when he taught in the South at schools with few books.[131] Harsh, in turn, shared Stratton's sense that history education belonged outside the formal classroom as well as in it.[132]

In 1941, Harsh and Stratton teamed up with Ethel Hilliard, a teacher and NAACP activist, and F. H. Hammurabi Robb, a soapbox speaker known as Hammurabi, to offer a program on global Black history for the DuSable History Club.[133] As the club's research director, Hammurabi delivered six lectures that spanned five centuries of African and African American history, from "history making women" to "leaders and misleaders" of Reconstruction. He closed with a question: "Why are some 400,000,000 Africans and their descendants as they are today?"[134] These talks were followed by those of Colonel John C. Robinson, an aviator who commanded the Ethiopian Air Corps against Italy's 1935 invasion.[135] At the end of the season, club members toured the Egyptian and Ethiopian collections at the University of Chicago.[136] This 1941 series presaged the expansive geography of the club's studies, and it highlights the Hall Branch's underappreciated role as a space of pan-Africanist thought in mid-century Chicago.[137] In 1945, for example, the Nigerian writer Mbonu Ojike visited the Hall Branch, and the DuSable Club joined Ojike's fledgling organization, the African Academy of Arts and Research.[138] The following year, it read A. A. Nwafor Orizu's anti-imperialist treatise *Without Bitterness*, as well as Ojike's book *My Africa*.[139] This 1946 season was led by Mae A. Chapman, who sought to understand the place of Africa "in the universal circuit of the world."[140] The club's pan-Africanist agenda encompassed discussions of current events, too, from Black soldiers' interactions with Filipinos during World War II to Nigerian independence and African labor movements.[141]

The group's leaders represented ideological crosscurrents of Black thought in Chicago. Stratton, a South Carolinian who came to Chicago after World War I, was a charter member of the Chicago Teachers Union. In the 1940s, he served as president of the left-affiliated National Negro Museum and Historical Foundation.[142] Hilliard, like Stratton, was an ASNLH member and a "voracious reader and collector of Race literature," but her brand of racial uplift did not tack left. One of Chicago's "prominent women," she was president of the women's NAACP auxiliary.[143] Chapman, by contrast, lived just briefly in Chicago. After graduating from Howard, where she studied African history with William Leo Hansberry, she trained as a Baptist theologian.[144] She nearly overlapped at Howard with Robb, who changed his name to Hammurabi in the 1930s.[145] A radical "street scholar," he led local efforts to support Ethiopia during the Italian invasion and frequented Washington Park's "open air forum," where speeches reflected Chicago's Garveyite legacy, the rise of the Moorish American Science Temple and Nation of Islam, and the influence of South Side communist organizers.[146] Hammurabi's *Defender* column blended African travelogues with anti-imperialism, and he declared that "Africa, like China, will rise up some day and slay her invaders."[147] Although the *Defender* turned against him in 1942 during a crackdown on African Americans suspected of loyalty to Japan, Hammurabi remained a respected figure at the Hall Branch.[148] He continued to serve as the DuSable History Club's director of research, bringing his street pedagogy to a space shared with school teachers.[149]

The DuSable History Club fused Hammurabi's pan-Africanism with a focus on the Black Midwest. On the eve of Independence Day in 1941, club members commemorated the Haitian Revolution, and the next day, they made a pilgrimage to Michigan to visit the burial site of Sojourner Truth.[150] Although the club planted an American flag at Truth's grave, its celebration of Haiti the night before framed this July Fourth trip as an homage to Black freedom struggles globally. Indeed, the club made visible within diasporic history the presence of local figures, such as John Jones, a Black abolitionist who campaigned against Illinois's Black laws.[151] To recover this history, the club collected "experiences and stories," asking anyone with relevant knowledge to contact the Hall Branch.[152] At one meeting, a woman shared her mother's memories of mutual aid networks in the Underground Railroad.[153] Club members also sought "historic records"—a search made urgent by the sparse commemoration of Chicago's Black founders.[154] (As Du Bois noted in a letter about DuSable, "Chicago has not been particularly proud of him."[155]) The club deposited copies of its research at the Hall Branch, which alone among Chicago's formal reading spaces served this dual focus on Black life and pan-African geography. Across the city, biographies of well-known figures, such as Dunbar, Truth, Richard Allen, and Paul Robeson, could not be found at just any public library; they sat on the shelves only at the Hall Branch, where Harsh connected these American icons to a global African pantheon, pointing readers to works on the Ghanaian intellectual J. E. Kwegyir Aggrey, the Ashanti leader Osei Tutu, and the Zulu king Shaka.[156]

In the tradition of the American Negro Academy and the Negro Society for Historical Research, the DuSable History Club understood itself as a scholarly collective for "research study."[157] Unlike these precursors, however, which limited their ranks to invited members already established in their fields, the DuSable Club widely advertised its gatherings, welcomed young people to join its roster, and was frequently led by women.[158] It also differed from the ASNLH, which staged elaborate Negro History Week celebrations featuring distinguished speakers in the pulpit or on the dais.[159] By contrast, most DuSable gatherings took shape simply as "timely and lively discussions" or "study periods."[160] In this informal, cross-generational collective, Amos Meredith, an old settler born in 1875, read alongside the young men Edison and Burghardt Dubois Smiley, who had just arrived from Mississippi. Hattie Ogletree, a stenographer, took her place alongside NAACP Youth Council member Bernida Robinson. They joined forces at the Hall Branch because it was where they could "use books on the Negro."[161] As a space, the library both assembled a lineage of Black inquiry and sustained it as an ongoing practice. One year, club members gathered for a "question period" on Drusilla Dunjee Houston's book on the Nubian Kingdom.[162]

Another year, Hammurabi, Stratton, teacher George Dorsey, and Udo Ekam, a Nigerian law student, led a series of evenings dedicated to working through John Hope Franklin's chapters on Africa in *From Slavery to Freedom*.[163] They did not engage in this research to craft a script or a novel, and the results of their study did not produce anything a scholar could cite in a direct way.

The club's gatherings mimicked other collective reading structures built around skill sharing and sociability, from literary societies to religious study to leftist discussion circles. "[N]o citizen's education," Harsh argued, "need cease simply because he no longer formally attends school," and she extended the library's hours to accommodate the club's evening study sessions.[164] The Hall Branch became an afterhours space for Negro History, where historians with other jobs convened for bookish gatherings after work. By functioning outside of the classroom, the DuSable History Club sustained an informal practice of "black study," a term Moten and Harney define, in part, as a "common intellectual practice" marked by a "dissident relation."[165] The club had its origins at Quinn Chapel—a site in the underground history of aiding fugitives from slavery—and it formed around a critical praxis: to find in history's omissions a new way to imagine Black futures.[166] From that dissident position, it launched a decades-long series of Tuesday night sessions that drew on the collection of the Hall Branch. The practice of Black study depends on access to a repository, whether a library, a collection of record albums, or a bootleg photocopy of a text passed from reader to reader.[167] Built by and for the community that used it, Harsh's collection made Black study possible, and it created convergences in Chicago's intellectual history that complicate distinctions between soapbox and library, radical and respectable, written and unwritten.[168] The teachers, postal workers, librarians, and "street scholars" who served as the Hall Branch's historians were formally educated but not embedded in the university. Few appear in histories of Black thought, and their legacy has a fugitive quality, evading recognition. A focus on the branch as a place of collecting and convening, however, brings into focus this network of intellectuals who, like Harsh, "never wrote" (figure 5.6).

When Harsh retired in 1958, more than two decades after the Hall Branch opened, Chicago's intellectual geography had shifted. Many of its borrowers moved west and south into other neighborhoods, while new Black collecting spaces opened, extending the terrain for Black study forged by the Hall Branch.[169] The DuSable History Club disbanded by the 1950s, but many who had joined its weekly "question and map study" sessions helped build other institutions, linking an earlier generation of Negro History activists to an emerging network of Black museums. Hammurabi, for example, opened the House of Knowledge, a Black nationalist bookstore and forum that housed

MONDAY, AUGUST 29, 1960 DAILY DEFENDER PAGE 9

Feature SECTION DAILY DEFENDER

The Vivian Harsh Story

Historian Who Never Wrote

By Adolph J. Slaughter

A brilliant historian who never wrote, who was an enigma to friend and foe alike, was Vivian Gordon Harsh, the first Negro woman to serve as head of a branch library in the Chicago Public Library system.

Although Miss Harsh, at 70, died Aug. 17 at Provident hospital after serving as head librarian at Hall branch, 48th st., and Michigan blvd., since its opening in 1931, a veritable heritage on both the woman, herself, and Negro Americana has been left for posterity.

NEGRO COLLECTION

In honor of the small, quiet woman who walked softly, but carried "a big stick," it would not be unlikely that a future date, the more than 2,000 books she gathered on the American Negro and placed in special collection at Hall branch might someday be called "The Harsh Collection." Similar to the Schomburg collection in New York's Harlem branch library, the collection of Miss Harsh is regarded among the finest in the country.

A small, petite woman who loves clothes as well as her books, Vivian Harsh was an innovator who brought life and purpose to Hall branch and the Negro community is served.

FAM was one of her pet projects for adults. It meant Fun At Maturity and was a club where older people could come and participate more completely in the library and the community.

For many years she led the first Great Books discussion club at Hall branch.

LECTURE FORUM

But there is no doubt that this little woman whom only her most intimate friends would dare call "tootie," will be long remembered for the Book Review and Lecture forum which lasted at Hall branch for more than 20 years."

The great names in American literature, the professions, and every walk of life came to the forum. It was a milestone for the Negro and Chicago.

Born in Chicago on 44th place, Vivian Harsh was a "blueblood." Her mother was among the first women graduates of Fisk university and was one of its outstanding alumni.

LIBRARY HER LIFE

Graduating from Wendell Phillips high school, Boston, Columbia, and Chicago universities, Vivian Harsh was nurtured in library science. It had never been a job. It was always her life.

Meticulous and a professional perfectionist, Miss Harsh developed qualities which demanded severe love and devotion or quiet rejection.

Giving always more than she demanded, this "li" arian's librarian" was a devotee of the theater, the concerts and the arts.

For 50 years she belonged to Grace Presbyterian church and was a member of the YWCA; the NAACP; the Illinois and American Library Associations and the Chicago Library club.

With more facts, figures and information about the Negro and American history, stored in her phenominal mind and memory, Vivian Harsh died, two years after retiring from the Chicago library system.

OPENING DAY of the George Cleveland Hall branch library, Jan. 16, 1932, at 48th st. and Michigan blvd., was a highpoint in the life of Miss Vivian Gordon Harsh who was appointed its first head librarian. Miss Harsh who retired from the system in 1958, is shown standing between two women, behind the desk, waiting on some of the first patrons to use the branch's facilities. The noted librarian died Wednesday Aug. 17, at Provident hospital.

NOVELIST WILLIAM ATTAWAY is shown autographing a copy of one of his books as Miss Vivian Harsh prepares to add it to the collection on the Negro she established at Hall Branch library. Attaway, now a TV script writer in New York, wrote "Blood On the Forge" and "Let Me Breathe Thunder."

The Almanac

By United Press International

Today is Monday, Aug. 29, the 242nd day of the year, with 124 more in 1960.

The moon is in its first quarter.

The morning star is Mars.

The evening stars are Jupiter, Saturn and Venus.

* * *

ON THIS DAY IN HISTORY:

In 1809, American physician poet and essayist Oliver Wendell Holmes was born.

In 1852, Brigham Young signified his approval of the practice of polygamy among Mormons.

In 1862, Belgian dramatist and poet Maurice Maeterlinck was born.

In 1901, Carrie Nation, Kansas temperance agitator, descended on a New York saloon operated by former boxing champion John L. Sullivan, armed with a hatchet.

In 1945, U. S. Marine hero Maj. Gregory Boyington was found alive in a Japanese prisoner of war camp after he had been missing for 20 months.

* * *

Thought for Today: American essayist Oliver Wendell Holmes said: Sin has many tools but a lie is the handle which fits them all."

FIGURE 5.6 "The Vivian Harsh Story," which describes Harsh as a "Historian Who Never Wrote." *Chicago Daily Defender*, August 19, 1960.

Source: Adolph J. Slaughter, "Historian Who Never Wrote," *Chicago Daily Defender*, August 29, 1960.

Margaret and Charles Burroughs's Ebony Museum of Negro History and Art.[170] Hall Branch librarian Marian Hadley played a key role in establishing that museum, now the DuSable Black History Museum and Education Center; Harsh and Stratton supported it, too. Stratton, meanwhile, went on to teach the city's first university-level courses in Black Studies. He also worked closely with the young members of the Frank London Brown Negro History Club, part of a new wave of Black history activism in the 1960s linked to direct action groups of the civil rights movement.[171]

The Frank London Brown Negro History Club deposited its exhibition materials at the Hall Branch, an acknowledgment that what began as the "Special Collection of Books By and About the Negro" continued to function as a community archive even after Harsh's departure.[172] Named for Harsh in 1970, the collection moved across the South Side to a larger space; since then, what was once a modest book collection—with a few manuscripts to display on bulletin boards and a cabinet of WPA files tucked in a corner—has grown into the primary archival repository of Chicago's Black cultural and political movements, home to the records of the Chicago Renaissance and of postwar Black activism. Quinn Chapel, which seeded the DuSable History Club, now has its records in the Harsh Collection, as do many of the writers and researchers who gathered at the Hall Branch in its first decades. Subjects documented in Harsh's file cabinet of WPA records reappeared in collections acquired later, including manuscripts on the bandmaster Walter Dyett, beauty culture businesswoman Annie Turnbo Malone, and artist William Edouard Scott. After these mid-century records came those of subsequent movements, from CORE to the Coalition of Black Trade Unionists. Through acts of cross-generational preservation—both in study and on paper—the Hall Branch gathering space became an archive of Black Chicago's transformations in the twentieth century.

Such a sprawling repository was not prophesied on the library's opening day. Rather, it grew from the space Harsh and her colleagues cultivated: a hub where divergent iterations of Black imagination and intellect found refuge. In the space of the Hall Branch, intellectual life emerged through collective processes of accumulation, exhibition, reading, and discussion. There, a neighborhood of thinkers gathered to talk politics, find the "always wanted" novels of Jessie Fauset and Richard Wright, or to learn about "map making, dress designing and mental telepathy."[173] They brought to the space of Black study the research tradition of Negro historical societies from the 1900s, the organizing work of the ASNLH, the Black nationalism of popular history-writing, and the pan-Africanism of Black politics in the 1930s and 1940s. In effect, they built a Black Studies movement in public space, outside the classroom and before any formalization of that field.[174] They were not all writers, and theirs are not the marquee names that draw researchers to the Vivian G. Harsh Research Collection today. In its earliest years, however, this collection grew as a response to the sustained desire of everyday thinkers to "use books on the Negro." Their practice of Black study endowed an archive of Black ideas.

CHAPTER SIX

MOBILIZING MANUSCRIPTS

L. D. Reddick and Black Archival Politics

> *You should need no further bidding about this. It is your duty to preserve this valuable data.*
>
> —Carter G. Woodson, 1929

War Letters Wanted: One soldier saw the notice on a bulletin board at the local YMCA. The uncle of another soldier read about it in the newspaper. A private serving in Europe heard the appeal from a friend—*Don't throw away that letter.*[1] Intrigued and compelled, those who felt called by that imperative began to send documents to the Schomburg Collection. "I understand that it is your desire to collect letters from our soldiers over seas for publication," penned a mother in Missouri, enfolding a letter from her son stationed in the South Pacific.[2] "Enclosed you will please find a letter which I would like to have included in the collection," wrote a Georgia woman in 1945.[3] A soldier who had driven trucks in Okinawa sent a brief note. "I don't know whether this will be [of] value," he worried, though he wanted "very much to help make history."[4] All felt a duty and a desire to archive—to help build a collection that would tell "a true history of the Negro in the war."[5] Some of these respondents became collectors in turn, enlisting others to join them in preserving the papers of those serving at the fighting fronts or training camps. From Texas and Virginia, Italy and Burma, bundles of documents arrived in Harlem, addressed to The Negro in World War II (figure 6.1).

FIGURE 6.1 Incoming mail addressed to "The Negro in World War II," 1946.

Source: Lawrence D. Reddick World War II Project Collection, Manuscripts, Archives and Rare Books Division, Schomburg Center for Research in Black Culture, New York Public Library.

Receiving these letters in New York was the young historian L. D. Reddick, who took the helm of the Schomburg Collection in 1939 after the unexpected death of its founder, Arthur Schomburg. Like Schomburg, Reddick had made many migrations. "I have lived and worked in Florida, Louisiana, Tennessee, Kentucky, Illinois and New York," he wrote, and in each place, "I have studied social thought among Negroes."[6] The two men crossed paths briefly at Fisk University—Reddick as a student, and Schomburg, having retired from three decades of office work, as a visiting curator.[7] They belonged to distinct generations, but like Schomburg, Reddick's historical vision was forged by political revolt: not by the surge of Caribbean radicalism in the 1890s, as was Schomburg's, but by the "revolution in Negro thought" that brewed during the economic and global crises of the 1930s.[8] Drawn toward workers' movements and the global fight against fascism, Reddick attended the first National Negro Congress the same year he composed his influential scholarly manifesto, "A New Interpretation for Negro History."[9] He forcefully challenged his fellow historians to chronicle not just the achievements of "talented Negroes," but also the "feelings and thoughts of the common folk" in a global context of race, labor, and capital.[10] At the Schomburg Collection, Reddick put this manifesto into practice. He wanted to make the collection, which was already a "perfect source for Negro thought in . . . the *written* literature," more reflective of Black radicalism's murmurings and "unorganized mass upsurges."[11]

Reddick's call for a new interpretation of Black history took on greater urgency as war enveloped the globe and exerted "decisive social pressures" on race and power across Europe, Asia, Africa, and the Americas.[12] After a decade of crushing economic inequality and ongoing anti-Black violence in the United States, the onset of World War II left African Americans asking, "Whose war is this and for what?"[13] How could the country wage war in the name of democracy abroad when it failed to enact it at home? Could a war to end fascism in Europe also vanquish imperialism in its colonies? Activists rallied around the slogan Double V, mobilizing for victory in the war *and* in the Black liberation movement.[14] Geographic upheavals had expanded the scope of demands in this "two-front attack," Reddick observed, as draftees were "pulled up from Mississippi and deposited in India" or "taken from the North and shoved into the South for the first time."[15] Wartime dissent thus intensified calls for radical change at home and appeals to end colonial rule in Africa and Asia. Sensing an inflection point, Reddick both participated in and chronicled the era's many iterations of Black radical thought, which pulsated not only through the pages of the *Pittsburgh Courier* or the *Chicago Defender*, but also through the streets. He took note, for example, of the "attitude of the fellow I talked with at the Joe Louis-Max Baer fight," who declared that "the time would come when these white S-O-Bs would have to respect a man as a man."[16] It was a moment, as Farah Jasmine Griffin has noted, when Black life seemed poised "on the verge of something new and consequential."[17]

Attuned to the "mood and temper" of this restless moment, Reddick turned the Schomburg Collection into a site of wartime activism.[18] Since the early 1920s, under librarians Catherine Latimer, Ernestine Rose, Regina Anderson Andrews, and others, the collection's home at the 135th Street Branch Library had served as a bustling community center.[19] In the 1940s, Reddick broadened the library's reach into global Black politics, drawing on the Schomburg Collection's renown to create an intellectual hub for the Black freedom struggle (figure 6.2). He invited into the reading room "leaders of the important mass movements" and "their

FIGURE 6.2 L. D. Reddick (*seated at right*) in the Schomburg Collection, circa 1940s. Photographer unknown.

Source: Photographs and Prints Division, Schomburg Center for Research in Black Culture, New York Public Library.

lowliest followers," and he hosted international forums at which Harlem thinkers met representatives of the African National Congress and the League of Coloured Peoples.[20] Beyond the reading room, he put the Schomburg Collection on the radio, broadcasting an annual tribute to heroes in the fight for racial democracy. The Honor Roll in Race Relations, as he called this tribute, became a national radio event, replayed on the BBC network, given a nod by Eleanor Roosevelt, and touted by the Office of War Information.[21] Despite these successes, Reddick's foray into archival politics ultimately proved short-lived. His desire to position the Schomburg Collection as a globally oriented institution promoting Black freedom collided with local officials' more modest expectations of a branch library, and he departed New York with an unfinished vision. During his decade at the Schomburg Collection, however, Reddick harnessed the enduring aim of Black archival practice to collect freedom dreams—not as a memorial to the past but as a catalyst to the ongoing work of remaking the world.

To build such an archive at the height of World War II, Reddick issued an appeal for Black Americans to author their "own story of the war" by sending servicemen's letters to the Schomburg Collection.[22] This appeal inculcated the imperative to archive as a participatory form of Black politics. It asked people, far from the library's doorstep, to imagine themselves as collectors—and to imagine archiving as movement building. In response, Reddick received hundreds of letters. Penned by rank-and-file soldiers, they upended ideas about archival value, combining declarations of protest with the quotidian pleasures of everyday Black life. They also subverted how the nation-state kept its records. Publicly, the United States circulated heroic portraits of Black soldiers and heralded their service as emblematic of a multiracial democracy (hence touting "an America that does not exist," quipped one commentator).[23] Internally, however, military officials questioned their fitness to serve and surveilled their dissent.[24] In military files, Reddick argued, the Black soldier was "classified as controversial."[25] Thus wary of the government's record-keeping, Reddick summoned the letters to the Schomburg Collection to document "what the Negro thinks about democracy."[26] He showed the letters to Richard Wright, who described them as a catalog of humiliations: soldiers barred from combat; restricted to segregated facilities; insulted by white officers. "A sea of despair," Wright declared after reading.[27] Reddick, for his part, saw the collection differently. The Negro serviceman was tired of being "pushed around," he wrote, and the letters captured "what he is willing, ready and able to do."[28] In this archive was the "glimpsed potentiality" of radical change.[29]

CALL AND RESPONSE: EXPERIMENTS IN MANUSCRIPT COLLECTING

Reddick assembled the war letters at a moment of archival abundance in the 1940s, when African American collections proliferated—not only appearing in new places, but also changing in kind. In the preceding decade, the New Deal's cultural wing had infused the field of "Negro Studies" with funding for documentary projects. The outbreak of war intensified this interracial attention to the study of Black life, as American organizations emphasized pluralism and national unity to repudiate Axis propaganda.[30] In this context of rising racial liberalism, the Library of Congress accelerated its collecting of Black manuscripts, while Yale University entered the field after having "no Negro books at all."[31] Black institutions embarked on an era of creative ferment and experimentation, pushing the boundaries of what a Black archive might contain. Rather than trying to amass "everything concerning the Negro," many collectors now turned to more calculated and distinctive assemblies of material, from oral histories in Oakland to Afro-Braziliana at Howard.[32] Harold Jackman named a collection of Black arts ephemera at Atlanta University after the poet Countee Cullen, while the Detroit Musicians' Association founded a collection on the history of Black song.[33] The National Council of Negro Women (NCNW) proposed a "national shrine" to house Black women's papers in Washington, DC.[34] Each of these projects tested the possibilities of collecting as a practice of racial representation and staged the question: What histories—and thus what futures—does an archive imagine?

Many collectors increasingly turned their attention to manuscripts—a project urged on by Carter G. Woodson, who for two decades had argued that "something must be done to save the records of the Negro."[35] In the early years of the Association for the Study of Negro Life and History (ASNLH), Woodson imagined preserving manuscript material as a core part of the organization's work. He knew that important collections of printed books and pamphlets were taking shape at the Tuskegee Institute, Howard University, and at what would later become the Schomburg Collection. He worried, however, about what remained outside these collections: the unpublished records, "scattered throughout the country," that people kept in attics, trunks, or basements.[36] To find and preserve these materials, Woodson launched a collecting campaign in the late 1920s. He published appeals in the Black press asking readers to "send us the historical materials bearing on the Negroes of your community" and dispatched field agents to the South to find and collect records.[37] As the *Chicago Defender* explained, "The material sought is a varied sort, old letters, diaries, family records, wills, deeds, receipts, bills of sale and the like."[38] In response to these appeals, an archive of "valuable accessions" began to accumulate at the ASNLH headquarters in Washington, DC, ranging from the papers of Whitefield McKinlay, a state senator in Reconstruction South Carolina, to the Urban League's files of Southern migrants' letters.[39] Woodson deposited these documents—totaling roughly five thousand pages—at the Library of Congress, where they became known as the "Negro papers."[40]

Woodson struggled to maintain funding for his groundbreaking collecting initiative, but other collectors, swept up by an "archival awakening" in the 1930s, soon followed his lead.[41] At Howard University, the newly appointed curator Dorothy B. Porter sought "unusual material of an archival nature," and when he arrived at the Schomburg Collection in 1939, Reddick joined her in this work.[42] A sense of urgency drove their efforts. "Negroes have kept few records," Porter lamented, and "when we finally come to appreciate the gravity of the situation it will be too late. There will be nothing left to salvage."[43] She despaired over papers discarded by families or "carried off to oblivion by the junk man."[44] Determined to forestall such losses, Porter and other curators began to pursue the records of contemporary organizations, such as the files of the National Negro Congress, and the personal papers of a wide range of living creators and activists.[45] At Howard, Porter brought in a deluge of manuscripts by the early 1950s, among them the papers of Alain Locke, musician Isabele T. Spiller, actor Leigh Whipper, physician Louis Wright, the family collection of Ida and William Hunt, and records of the Marian Anderson Citizens Committee, among others. Adding to the surge was the fact that many of the collections amassed in this period were far larger than typical deposits of a previous era. The proliferating output of the modern office crowded into mid-century archives. Locke's papers filled 120 boxes, for example, while the Rosenwald Fund records, acquired by Fisk, totaled 150,000 pages.[46] In the postwar era, Black archives experienced abundance—indeed, often too much to keep up with—as well as absence.

In the years that led to this postwar crescendo in collecting, which Jean-Christophe Cloutier characterizes as an "age of the black archive," a series of experiments asked what novel forms of racial representation might emerge through manuscripts.[47] Distinct from the acquisition of family papers or organizational records, these experiments emerged in the early 1940s as a practice of call and response. Each project used print and epistolary appeals to summon records from a sprawling network of creators, who consolidated their papers not to produce a general "Negro Collection," but to capture a specific iteration of Black politics—as uplift, revolution, or modernist vanguard. If the founding generation of Black bibliophiles had decisively shown, after decades of struggle, that Negro History could fill a library, a new crop of collectors now harnessed that confidence to build archives expressive of their own sensibility about what histories the future needed. The NCNW, for example, challenged the "masculine intellectual self-fashioning" of the Negro History movement by asking its members to launch a national Black women's archive and assemble "documents concerning themselves."[48] One member suggested that this archive should include not just papers, but also textiles, "made by skilled and loving hands," to encompass the multiple and often overlooked forms of Black women's thought.[49]

The NCNW's vision contrasted with the decidedly literary bent of the James Weldon Johnson Memorial Collection, another archival experiment of the 1940s. To build that collection, the white Harlem Renaissance chronicler Carl Van Vechten enlisted an entourage of well-known Black writers to deposit their manuscripts at Yale.[50] He aspired to assemble a "complete file of manuscripts of ALL modern Negro authors" that would materialize the idea, made famous by

Johnson himself, that "the amount and standard" of literature created by a group served as the measure of its greatness.[51] Van Vechten chose Yale, rather than a "Negro University," because he believed the Johnson collection would act as "propaganda," accrediting Black genius in the eyes of white readers.[52] Although Van Vechten positioned art as an antidote to the "race problem," his choice to place the collection at Yale fell under the specter of that problem all the same, for it reinscribed the power of a white institution to anoint the value of Black ideas, even as it refused to hire Black curators.[53] In a countervailing move, the NCNW imagined an archive that would stay within the uplift movement, accessible at the organization's headquarters. A collection built and maintained by Black women, it predicted, would inspire "Negro women coming down thru all the years" to "struggle on for a fairer life."[54]

Echoing the NCNW's vision of archiving as movement building, Reddick, too, launched a call-and-response collection. His first appeal appeared in the *Atlanta Daily World* on December 1, 1944.[55] The announcement asked readers to save letters of the war:

> The Schomburg Collection of Negro Literature of The New York Public Library is making a nation-wide appeal for letters from Negro service men and women that have been written to their friends in this country. . . . The Library seeks to collect and preserve for history the thousands of letters that have been written by Negroes in the armed forces to their wives, sweethearts, brothers, sisters and other friends in this country. These letters tell what the men have experienced in camps and on the fighting fronts, what they have seen and felt, how they have been treated and how they have treated others. Thousands of these letters are necessary so that a true history of the Negro in the war can be written.[56]

The call rippled through the Black press, running in papers across the country and amplified by columnists like Margaret Taylor Goss, who urged readers to "collect all of the letters that you have."[57] Reddick also made this appeal in speeches, telling a crowd at Bethany Baptist Church that African Americans would have to write their "own story of the war."[58] He asked for the cooperation of "all churches, Greek letter fraternities, fraternal orders, clubs, USO's, YMCA's, YWCA's, colleges, newspapers and individuals" to spread the word.[59] This appeal mirrored earlier scenes of crowdsourcing in African American collections, such as when friends sent memorabilia or ephemera to Alexander Gumby for scrapbooking, but the call to collect had never been made so broadly public. Unlike the NCNW and Van Vechten's collecting projects, Reddick's call was not rooted in the membership of one organization or literary network. He pursued material from writers who were "semi-illiterate or Ph.D., Northerner or Southerner, gradualist or revolutionary."[60] Reddick imagined that an archive, of this variety and at this scale, would capture Black demands for "real democracy"—a phrase that had long resounded in Black thought as a critique of what W. E. B. Du Bois called the "choked conscience of America."[61]

As the war churned on, battles raged globally over print culture and paperwork: book burnings; propaganda sheets; surveillance files. In the United States, the Office of War Information circulated patriotic photographs, American librarians traveled abroad to collect foreign materials that were in harm's way, and the War Department kept voluminous—if often secret—files on military activities.[62] In this documentary fervor, Black curators asked, who would "write the history of the Negro"?[63] The Schomburg Collection actively gathered what Reddick called "official records," from speeches by race leaders and reports by war correspondents to the voluminous files of "Mrs. Latimer's clippings."[64] The *unofficial* paper trail of the war eluded these records, however. Black soldiers, nurses, and other war workers wrote hundreds of thousands of letters documenting their experiences. These missives made their way not only to family and friends but also to journalists, whose wartime columns elicited responses from readers on the front lines. "Somebody ought to make a book," Langston Hughes remarked, "out of the hundreds of letters on Jim Crow which colored soldiers write to the Negro press."[65] Marjorie McKenzie and George Schuyler, both of the *Pittsburgh Courier*, agreed. Schuyler vowed to keep incoming letters "on file" and "select the best for publication."[66] Hughes suspected, however, that the War Department would never allow the publication of such a book.

That same suspicion drew Reddick to the soldiers' letters. The Schomburg Collection would tell a fugitive story, he vowed—one that state recordkeepers would not. In making that promise, Reddick echoed earlier moments of Black wartime dissent. In each U.S. war, African Americans had fought for the nation, only to face what Du Bois called an "unbending battle against the forces of hell in our own land."[67] At the close of World War I, then, when Du Bois penned his famous refrain, "We *return from fighting*. / We *return fighting*," he also asked soldiers to supply documents for the writing of a "true" history of the war.[68] He never completed that project, but his impulse resonated with another generation of Black thinkers, two decades later, equally distrustful of the nation's loyalty to its Black citizenry. The politics of archiving, Ada Ferrer has argued, turn on "conflicts between histories and their would-be tellers."[69] Reddick urged those who held the records of Black valor and Black anger to join the ranks of "would-be tellers" because other accounts of the war, he feared, would fail Black citizens, erasing or impugning their role in the nation's mobilization. "If the mythmakers should have their way," he contended, "there will be a steady stream of memoirs written by anti-Negro officers. These memoirs will be quoted for the *Congressional Record* by anti-Negro Congressmen. Textbook writers will copy from the *Congressional Record.* And then we shall have a generation growing up in the belief that Negroes are devoid of courage and that, therefore, it is of no great importance that they should not receive equal rights."[70] Such a failure of memory, Reddick warned, would subtend the persistence of segregation and subjugation, for the nation-state could disclaim those it had cast out of its archive.

Pieced together, Black soldiers' letters would answer the question, "How does it feel to be a Negro in the army?" More pointedly, Reddick noted, these letters would address what official reports would not: "how does it feel to be a Negro in a jim-crow unit of the Army of American Democracy, waging war for World Freedom, when word comes by rumor or letter or the *Pittsburgh Courier* or '*Axis Sally*' that an anti-Negro pogrom has wrecked the Negro section of Beaumont, Texas or that racial warfare is raging in the streets of Detroit?" Indeed, Reddick felt, the war letters would document the contradiction between democracy's slogans and its reality, as told by wary soldiers tasked with defending the principles of equality while serving in a military that treated them as unfit for combat roles.[71] That contradiction was part of a global crisis, Reddick argued, and African Americans—getting "tougher all the time"—would join what he called the final stage of international mobilization, a "war for freedom for all peoples."[72] Reddick's reading of the letters hinged on a masculinist understanding of struggle and valor, expressed by Black soldiers whose refusal to be "pushed around" symbolized revolutionary possibility. An archive assembled in the spirit of a "world-fight for black rights," the collection would log the experience Du Bois had described of donning, with "far-off hope" and "bitter resignation," the uniform of a country that "lies and knows it lies" by calling itself democratic.[73] Reading the letters, which did not mince words about that embodied contradiction, Reddick found it mysterious "as to how some of them got by the censor."[74]

For Reddick, whose scholarly compass pointed to the history of the "common folk," the letters bore value because they voiced their protest from a rank-and-file perspective.[75] Unlike the press clippings that filled the Schomburg Collection's wartime subject files, Reddick noted, the "letters are very intimate. They tell what was on the soldier's mind."[76] To summon these intimate missives, Reddick rallied "senders"—those who penned the letters—as well as "receivers"—those to whom they were addressed. He sometimes described senders as both "servicemen and women," including nurses and Women's Army Corps recruits, but more often, he cast the archive in masculine terms, imagining that the letters would "tell what the *men* have experienced."[77] Radical in terms of class but not gender, Reddick's collecting project could have encompassed more women if, for example, he had sought letters from war industry workers. Instead, he replicated the well-worn, gendered dynamic in archiving that imagined women as caretakers but not creators of documentary value.[78] Reddick acquired just one set of letters authored by a woman—those of Red Cross worker Lucia Straham. Yet women were the uncredited makers of the archive of war letters he assembled. Among the individuals who contributed most significantly to the collection were Fredi Washington, actress and writer for *The Pople's Voice*, and Evelyna Forney Marable, a United Service Organization (USO) worker in Utah and Oklahoma (figure 6.3). Washington and Marable each sent Reddick a sizeable share of the letters they received from servicemen—more than two hundred in total. Another large batch arrived from Prairie View College in Texas, where students in Malcolm A. Davis's literature classes—nearly all young women—collected V-mails sent by friends, cousins, and former classmates.[79]

FIGURE 6.3 Evelyna Marable, one of the women who sent letters for L. D. Reddick's World War II collection, speaking with soldiers at a USO club, 1942. Photographer unknown.

Source: Afro American Newspapers/Gado via Getty Images.

"Men seldom bare their breasts to strangers," Reddick wrote, but "they will write the truth home, if the censor lets them. They will tell a pal. And, in the case of Negroes in World War II, they would complain and appeal to the N.A.A.C.P. and the Negro Press."[80] Reddick and his intermediaries sought to transform these scattered but ubiquitous forms of Black writing into a popular project of archive-making. As Goss wrote, "Here is a way that we can help to make a contribution to the building of the history and culture of our people. Make yourself a committee of one to collect all of the letters that you have and tell others about it."[81] In the early 1940s, which saw the rise of call-and-response experiments in Black archiving, Reddick wanted to build a collection that would capture, in ways both quotidian and revolutionary, "what the Negro thinks about democracy." In response to these appeals, letters began to arrive in New York addressed to The Negro in World War II. Soldiers sent their stories to Reddick, while family members packaged letters they had received and forwarded them to the library. Each letter arrived with an idea about what belonging to a Black archive might mean. "Yes, I have somethings to contribute to the writing of my race in the Second World War," wrote a Navy messman to Reddick.[82] "If you should see fit to use this letter, I shall appreciate it for my son's encouragement," penned the mother of a soldier in the South Pacific.[83] To readers tempted to discard letters once soldiers returned home, Goss enjoined, "For goodness sakes, don't do that! Your letters that you have received from your GI can be of definite service to the Negro people."[84]

"YOURS FOR REAL DEMOCRACY": AN ARCHIVE OF WAR LETTERS

Reddick claimed to have received "thousands" of letters by 1945, but the number in the collection today is much lower.[85] Perhaps Reddick returned some letters to their senders, as requested, or perhaps he lost some along the way. Just as likely, he may have inflated the number in press accounts as a rhetorical strategy to demystify the utterly unfamiliar act of sending one's personal correspondence to a far-away archive. It was one thing to read about the Schomburg Collection in the newspaper, or to hear Reddick's voice on the radio announcing the Honor Roll in Race Relations. It was something else entirely to imagine one's own words *in* that collection, awaiting the eyes of strangers. Reddick wanted to draw "lesser known characters" into the "world famous" archive Schomburg had launched with the manuscripts of pan-African heroes like Alexander Crummell or Toussaint Louverture.[86] In this regard, Reddick's call-and-response archive differed from the James Weldon Johnson Collection, which preserved the genius of "prominent Negroes," and from the NCNW, which despite its vision of collecting the material culture of unsung makers, ultimately solicited documents primarily from professionally accomplished women.[87] To create an archive of "real democracy," Reddick would have to inspire a much wider range of people to think of the records of their lives as valuable in an archival sense—as belonging to the public history of a movement.

"Collecting personal papers is not always an easy task," Porter warned. Some people "wonder why I am interested," she remarked, or "cannot be convinced that their grandparents' papers should go into an institution for anybody to examine."[88] Likewise, Reddick understood what it meant to ask "a mother to part with the letter she has received from her son."[89] What claim did an archive have on documents initially understood as repositories of affection, gossip, or kinship? To turn letter writers and recipients into the unlikely archivists he wanted them to become, Reddick tried to recast the value of personal papers.[90] In his appeals, he framed archiving as act an of racial solidarity: a joining of forces, through paper, with "the Negro from all parts of the world."[91] Promising what Achille Mbembe has named as the archive's allure—not just "data, but a status"—he also pointed readers' attention toward the lofty company their materials would keep.[92] The "Schomburg Collection contains hundreds of letters," he wrote in his appeals. Senders could join the ranks of Frederick Douglass, Paul Laurence Dunbar, and Booker T. Washington, as well as "Negro soldiers and sailors who fought in previous wars."[93] Reddick and his intermediaries urged letter writers of the current war to take their place in this pantheon, invoking a duty to "help record Negro history."[94]

Despite that framing, letter writers did not unequivocally embrace the mantle of fame or duty. They expressed both aspiration and ambivalence about archiving their words. A recipient of the Soldier's Medal told Reddick that while he wished to help "any effort for the benefit of our race," he wanted "no further publicity."[95] Another letter writer, who witnessed the liberation of a concentration camp in Germany, cast his experiences as horrific rather than heroic, haunted by the atrocities of "Nazi dogs."[96] From Italy, Hoyt Fuller bitterly described how white officers turned a commendation ceremony for his regiment into a condescending rant about venereal disease. "I'm not sure of exactly why I'm writing you," he told Reddick skeptically, "except that I've got to tell someone."[97] That unsettled sense of needing to "tell someone" motivated many of the letter writers and recipients who forwarded their documents to the Schomburg Collection—even if they were not as certain as Reddick about joining a pantheon of Black heroes. Engaged in a war for "World Freedom," while confined to the role of mess man and ditch digger in a Jim Crow army, these writers experienced a high-stakes version of America's contradiction between "word and deed."[98] If they had little recourse to battle that contradiction on the front lines, perhaps they could join their words of resignation or refusal with the words of others—and hold open the possibility that their testimony might help deliver justice in the future. In a letter received by George Schuyler, for example, a soldier wrote, "It is clearly evident that the word 'democracy' in so far as it pertains to the Negro is a joke to military authorities," and then added: "I am sending this information to you because it must become public after the war ends."[99]

Letter writers noted, too, what they could *not* say—a form of protest by way of absence. "Even though I would like very much to discuss some of these problems," hinted one letter sent from the Pacific, "I doubt . . . if it would go through."[100] Soldiers well knew that their letters would have unwanted readers. Mail posted from military bases abroad, once received by Reddick, bore telltale marks of surveillance in redacted or punched-out words and "Passed by Army Examiner" stamps. Those stationed inside the United States more easily avoided military censors, as was evident in a set of letters given to Reddick by Schuyler (whose newspaper columns were surveilled by military commanders and filed under the heading "Negro Agitation").[101] Enlisted men wrote candidly to Schuyler about their struggles at Fort Huachuca, home to a widely celebrated Black combat division.[102] Subverting the celebratory coverage of Huachuca that appeared in military publicity and the Black press, writers stationed there instead described it as a "Negro Camp like Mississippi is a Negro state," where Black officers faced court martial simply for refusing to be called "dogs."[103] Reporting such incidents could imperil the sender.[104] Nevertheless, a lieutenant in Georgia took the risk of enclosing copies of internal intelligence reports from his base to show Schuyler how military paperwork on "subversive activities" within the ranks doubled as "anti-Negro propaganda." By sending these records to Schuyler "for your file"—a feat of countersurveillance—the writer enacted a Black archival critique of future state secrets.[105]

Reddick recognized, however, that the letters were more than just proof of Black valor or protest. "The Negro soldier did not spend 24 hours of each day thinking about [segregation]," he wrote. "Somehow, he managed to *live*."[106] Part of the revolutionary nature of this archive was that it preserved the quotidian as well as the valorous. The letters expressed boredom, flirted with their readers, and chronicled the "sights and sounds of foreign lands."[107] Embedded in the letters Reddick received, for example, were repartees like the one written by a master sergeant, stationed in France, to his sister: "Say, Gloria, How is my fiancé? Which one!?! Why Lydia of course!"[108] These "mediocre bits," as Porter called them, were "as valuable as the phenomenal."[109] In many letters, critical reflections on the war made fleeting appearances amid routine lists and thoughts of home, as in one soldier's account of life in training camp:

> *Saturday July 3*
>
> *Everything out for Inspection*
> *did not pass*
> *In ditches in afternoon . . .*
>
> *Letter from Helen + Mama*
> *answered Helen's in grass . . .*
>
> *Monday July 5*
>
> *Orientation lecture*
> *Why are we fighting*
> *yes—why?*[110]

While public debates narrowly worried about the question of Black citizenship, these letters rarely did. Instead, they recorded the dissonances of Black military service—to feel "grand fighting for this country" only to be called "lousy sailors and soldiers," or to be denied officer training because there would be nowhere for a Black officer to take his meals with white officers.[111] Running through the letters, meanwhile, were threads of survival that refused to testify to anything other than the mundane strangeness of passing the time in the midst of war: "took a long walk . . . played Ping Pong . . . wrote to Everdine and Thelma."[112]

Far from triumphalist liberal narratives of progress, then, these letters served as irreverent reports of life in a Jim Crow army. Many such reports came from the mailbox of Fredi Washington, an entertainer and columnist at *The People's Voice* who sent Reddick more than a hundred and fifty letters she received from the soldiers who read her columns—"steadily diggin' your scribe," they told her.[113] Washington's newspaper writings laced commentary on popular culture with forthright critiques of American racism, and the soldiers who addressed her did the same. At first glance, their letters appeared primarily concerned with the quest for "colored pin-up girls."[114] Hoping to decorate their barracks with pictures of "our very fine Sepia Stars," soldiers asked Washington, in every letter, to send photographs of herself and other "leading singers and dancers of our race"—a request she always granted.[115] Seemingly about leisure during the stresses of war, the letters, like Washington's journalism, documented the struggles required to engage in Black leisure at all. In between banter about Lena Horne or reviews of the 1944 documentary *The Negro Soldier*, for example, they told stories about boycotting the movies shown at army camps, such as *South of Dixie*, with its racist stereotypes and Southern nostalgia. They told stories, too, about having to build their own libraries because they couldn't access the better-stocked, whites-only reading rooms on their bases (figure 6.4).[116] To Reddick, these letters—a

FIGURE 6.4 Navy men with Negro Books display, 1940s. Official U.S. Navy Photograph.

Source: Photographs and Prints Division, Schomburg Center for Research in Black Culture, New York Public Library.

repository of protest, but in the fullness of Black life—belonged in an archive as much as the formal proclamations or sermons of Schomburg's heroes.

Those who responded to an archival call had to ask, first, if they could imagine their papers collected, and if so, to what end. What form of racial imagination would that archive activate? At Yale, Van Vechten positioned the Johnson Collection as an effort to "glorify the Negro" (a framing that caused Langston Hughes, for one, to excise salacious gossip from letters he knew might be read in New Haven).[117] In Washington, DC, the NCNW envisioned its archive as a "pageant of progress," while in New York, Reddick asked senders to imagine their letters as part of a "war for freedom" stretching into the future.[118] Wary of combatting derogatory stereotypes with narratives of "talented Negroes" who "leaped over all hurdles," Reddick saw in the angry, irreverent letters of soldiers a new horizon of revolutionary possibility for the postwar world.[119] Like Reddick, the letter writers looked to the future and prepared for another battle. "It's a democratic irony that the Negro has . . . to wonder what his score will be after fighting so valiantly," wrote one soldier, "Let's tackle it, or it's too late."[120] "Would that I could be away forever," another soldier lamented, before promising that "we shall return"—an echo of Du Bois's famous refrain from World War I, "We *return from fighting.* / We *return fighting.*"[121]

In issuing a national appeal for letters by Black soldiers and war workers, Reddick put Black ideas at the center of conversations about the war's aims and aftermath—in the words not just of leaders but also of those stationed at Ledo Road in India or at training camps in Indiana. Taking seriously "what the Negro thinks about democracy," Reddick framed the letters as urgent tools in Black political futures. Although one soldier mused that he "could write a book about this joint," most sent their letters to Reddick hoping that *he* would mobilize their words.[122] A private in South Carolina remembered reading in the *Courier* that Reddick wanted "to write a book" (despite the fact that the printed notice did not say so), as did a sergeant in Okinawa, who sent a letter "in hopes that you will be able to find space in your book."[123] Imagining their words alongside the "thousands" Reddick invoked in his press releases, senders expressed their investment in archive-building as an exercise in solidarity. "Hoping you will receive thousands of letters as per appeal," the letters began; or "I hope you can gather enough stuff . . . to help write that memorial to the guys who fell in France, Italy, Africa, [and] China."[124] When the authors or recipients of these letters forwarded them to Reddick's archive, they did so not for preservation alone.[125] Sending their papers to be archived gave their words potential energy—to animate the unanswered, radical possibilities of the question one private posed: "why are we fighting / yes—why?"[126]

HYMN TO SCHOMBURG: "THE PULSE OF THE NEGRO WORLD"

The Schomburg Collection both collated and convened a Black radical tradition. People came through "the library portals to read, to study, and above all, to talk," Reddick observed, contradicting ideas of the library as a place of quiet study. While summoning war letters, he invited audiences to the reading room to hear reports from Europe and the Pacific on "what is happening to the Negro."[127] He filled exhibition cases with original manuscripts mapping out visions for postwar freedoms, from Roosevelt's Atlantic Charter address to speeches from China, Haiti, Egypt, India, and French Equatorial Africa.[128] At war's end, he hosted an international meeting of anticolonial activists to draft demands to the United Nations, which historian Gerald Horne has called "the most significant meeting of its type held in North America before or since."[129] Marshalling this "rising wind" of wartime Black consciousness, Reddick envisioned a future for the Schomburg Collection as an ongoing hub for Black thought, accountable to solidarity struggles locally and globally.[130] New York was home to "more Negroes than any city in Africa," he argued, making it "the ideal setting for a magnificent world capital of Negro culture." The collection should build on the tradition of Schomburg and his collaborators by gathering "books, pamphlets, newspapers, paintings, sculpture and rare unpublished manuscripts from all parts of the earth," but it should also extend its reach across the diaspora, using mass media to "popularize the truths, problems and beauty of Negro life and history."[131] Reddick's vision resonated in the Black press, which called the Schomburg Collection the "pulse of the Negro world": a repertoire of politics, in the space of a Black archive.[132]

A magnificent world capital of Negro culture. "That was the dream," Reddick recalled.[133] But it was not a dream shared at library headquarters downtown. Reddick's vision made little sense to the New York Public Library, which financed the Schomburg Collection as if it were a typical branch operation serving a single neighborhood rather than the "Negro world." For years, administrators had contemplated moving the Schomburg Collection out of Harlem, shifting it to the central building for safekeeping—a proposition held off by Franklin Hopper, the circulation director who acquired Schomburg's library in 1926.[134] After Hopper's retirement, Reddick found few comrades among the library's new postwar officials, who felt the Schomburg Collection had perhaps been "overplayed."[135] They rebuffed Reddick's requests for more staff and funds to develop a comprehensive research center with global ambitions. When offered a position at Atlanta University, then, Reddick concluded that "there was nothing else to do but leave."[136] His announced departure set off a storm of public protest in which the Schomburg Collection became an object of mobilization. Nearly two decades after Harlem artists rallied to save Alexander Gumby's scrapbooks, the "Negro world" again rose up about the fate of an archive. "The colored American sorely needs a national museum," cried the *Courier*, "and this Schomburg Collection is the nearest thing to it."[137] Leftist publications echoed the rallying cry: "Maintain the Schomburg Collection!"[138] The Committee for the Negro in the Arts commenced a protest campaign, and the ASNLH sent a resolution to the mayor. Demonstrators even picketed in front of the New York Public Library after a rumor circulated that the collection would shut down (figure 6.5).[139]

Such controversy underscored the fact that Black archival visions exceeded, and often threatened, the prevailing structures that governed access to information—whether through the branch library system, federal classification protocols, or Dewey decimals. In his critiques of the War Department and his call for soldiers' letters, Reddick questioned the politics of who controlled recordkeeping. On the

PUBLIC LIBRARY PICKETED—A symbolic picket line demonstrated before the Fifth Avenue entrance of the New York Public Library last week in protest against "indifference" on the part of the city fathers and library officials in the fight to secure increased financial support for the Schomburg Collection of Negro Literature, located in the library's Harlem branch.

Pittsburgh Courier 3/27/48

FIGURE 6.5 Picketers in front of the New York Public Library protesting the resignation of L. D. Reddick, 1948. Photographer unknown.

Source: *Pittsburgh Courier*, March 27, 1948, Schomburg Center Clipping File.

cusp of Cold War surveillance that would turn Federal Bureau of Investigation files into some of the largest, if unwitting, archives of Black activism, Reddick's clashes with local library officials forecast the fitful dynamic between social justice movements and the institutions that housed their records.[140] For decades, collectors built Black libraries and archives, protected them from threats, created systems for using them, and made them into spaces for Black study. This work always involved collectors—plural—rather than bibliophiles operating in isolation, but in the 1940s, Black archive-building became more explicitly conjoined with activist and organizational agendas, from Reddick's call for war letters during the Double V campaign, to the NCNW's founding of a national archive to support its ongoing justice work. The same was true in Detroit, where the Detroit Musicians' Association created an archive of Black performance—an effort that gained momentum in the wake of race riots in 1943, when white mobs attacked the Black Bottom neighborhood, including its business and entertainment venues. The E. Azalia Hackley Collection, which opened several months after the riots in Detroit, explicitly rebuked those acts of destruction.[141]

Provisional and unstable, these projects sometimes fell short of their ambitions. The NCNW and Detroit projects moved in fits and starts, and Reddick proved to be a better convener than conservator. He resolved to turn the soldiers' letters into two books, but the sprawling project remained unfinished.[142] "Hello, my scholarly lad," one letter-sender prodded, "have you done ought on the GI letters?"[143] When he left the Schomburg Collection in 1948, Reddick "borrowed" the war letters, thinking he would finish writing his books and then return the collection to Harlem.[144] The exigencies of movement work were at odds with the protocols of preservation, however. The quickening pace of civil rights campaigns, and Reddick's restless instinct for recording them, drew him from one documentary emergency to another. He moved from the maelstrom of World War II to the ranks of Montgomery bus boycotters (whose mass meetings he carefully transcribed), and to India with Martin Luther King Jr. (whose biography he published soon after). Reddick generated an astonishing set of activist collections in the 1940s and 1950s, none formally archived until much later. The war letters thus stayed in "Doc Reddick's traveling library," coming back to the Schomburg Collection (by then renamed the Schomburg Center) fifty years later along with all he had accumulated in the meantime.[145] Reddick's archive never stayed still. Indeed, for all the successes of Schomburg's generation in institutionalizing the call to collect, Black archives were difficult to contain, at once preservationist and resistant to the structures that made such preservation possible.

This lag between the war letters' initial collection and their permanent preservation reflected the harried pace of Reddick's work but also his sense that the time of Black archives was *now*—that documents needed to be mobilized quickly rather than quietly await future researchers. Reddick's embattled departure from New York foreshadowed the coming era, when Cold War–era politics would foreclose his vision of archives as radical institutions at the center of global freedom struggles.[146] But it also entrenched an idea—perhaps *the* idea animating Black archives, big and small, in the early twentieth century—that collecting was about reimagining collectivity and feeding collective struggle. Captured in Reddick's bold but stormy tenure at the Schomburg Collection, this vision of Black archives as sites of activism has persisted. Uproar over the Schomburg Collection's fate, first registered in the 1940s, recurred as a flashpoint in the 1960s and again in the 1980s, reflecting ongoing tensions between the municipal library's understanding of the collection as its property and Reddick's evergreen argument that Black publics had to make their "own history."[147] A tradition of archive-building crystallized in these moments as a political demand: that collections borne out of Black activism belonged to—and stood in service of—the "Negro world."

The fervency of that demand distinguished Reddick's project from many of the other Black experimental collections that emerged at the same time. If measured by the immediate preservation of manuscripts, the Johnson Collection at Yale proved far more successful than Reddick's efforts, and the Library of Congress soon eclipsed most Black organizations in the acquisition of African American papers. It is hard to imagine either of these institutions, however—or the growing number of white institutions that soon joined the pursuit of Black manuscripts—as the site of street protests over the departure of a curator. Nor would they likely have inspired a hymn:

> *Hymn to Schomburg*
>
> To thee welcome to search, to read, to dream
> Of mighty kingdoms from the ancient past
> From many lands across the page of time
> Black king, black slave assemble here at last
> Our thoughts, our hopes, all glories and all tears
> Our hearts are filled; new courage routs old fears
> We've built, we've bled; our blood's mixed with the sand
> To all we've given the world, from all we've gained
> For peace, for right, forever may we stand
> This is our home—the world's our fatherland
> All this we learn, the charm of history
> Whispers onward, Schomburg, when we come to thee
> Our pride, our faith, Schomburg, salute to you[148]

Is it surprising to find a song composed in the name of an archive? Although surely written by Reddick, the precise use of this hymn is unclear.[149] As an artifact, it illuminates how the institutions inherited by scholars as places for research were, for the generation that built them, occasions for many other practices: talking, strategizing, organizing, and, perhaps, singing. Indeed, the hymn invites us to consider the significance of the early twentieth century's Black archival fervor in a different light.

To measure the significance of these repositories, scholars typically call upon iconic scenes in the reading room. We imagine a poet looking for inspiration, as did Robert Hayden when he combed the Schomburg Collection's stacks to compose his epic poem "Middle Passage" in the 1940s.[150] We imagine a historian digging for answers, as did the pan-Africanist scholar John Henrik Clarke, who came to the Schomburg Collection in the 1930s to "find a definition of African people in history."[151] Or we imagine seekers of evidence, such as Thurgood Marshall and his team of fellow lawyers, who researched their desegregation briefs in the 1950s using the libraries founded by Jesse Moorland and Schomburg.[152] Reddick's hymn, however, conjures a different idea of the archive's reach in Black life: one that emerges not only from the research value of materials *in* an archive, but also from the symbolic, political, and affective power *of* that archive. The hymn voices an archive's meaning to those who picket outside its doors, who listen to the curator's voice on the radio, or who find a notice for "Letters Wanted" on a bulletin board. Even if these protestors, listeners, and recordkeepers did not sit in the reading room, they, too, drew from its storehouse, for an archive is something imagined as well as accessed—a repository and an idea.

The hymn is at once a psalm, an anthem, and an invitation. Voiced as a choral paean to Schomburg—which could refer either to the collection's founder or to the collection itself—it invokes a "we" both in the reading room (*we come to thee*) and the diaspora beyond it (*To all we've given the world*). The hymn names the collection as a place of textual assembly—pages devoted to "black king and black slave"—and of social assembly—those who desire to "search, to read, to dream." It then invites these searchers to draw "courage" from the collection and issues a call to action—to take a stand "for right." Finally, the hymn asserts a claim to the future, anticipating that this call "Whispers onward." In this last line, the hymn celebrates the central work of Black archives: to arouse a repertoire of Black thought and offer it to the future. If Schomburg had once described his collection as "powder with which to fight our enemies," Reddick arrived in his wake ready to light that powder.[153] Drawing in readers and recordkeepers from afar, he imagined convening a Black radical tradition both past and present. Like the bibliophiles, scrapbook makers, and curators before him, he fought to preserve that tradition, and in doing so, he held open its urgent and unfinished possibilities.

EPILOGUE

It cannot be said that the work he started was finished at his passing. But it can be said that he gave to Negroes throughout America a consciousness of the importance of keeping the written record.

—Obituary for Arthur A. Schomburg, *Opportunity*, 1938

When Claude McKay penned his invitation to a Black writers' group in 1937, invoking Arthur Schomburg's library as a model of collectivity, the famed curator and his collection were close at hand. Schomburg occupied a small desk, surrounded by his books, papers, and artifacts, in a corner of the Division of Negro Literature and History on the third floor of the 135th Street Branch Library in Harlem. McKay moved with some frequency in and out of this reading room, as did many of the writers to whom he sent his invitation. Thus, when McKay suggested that these writers might create "something like a living counterpart of the unparalleled Schomburg Collection of Negro books," he was referencing a specific set of objects still associated with the daily presence of their well-known collector.[1] Schomburg died the year after McKay's epistle. His library—which came to be known officially (not just colloquially) as the Schomburg Collection—stayed in place, at once a repository of vaunted rarity housing Juan Latino's verses—among the world's scarcest tomes—and a workaday site for Harlemites to read a book or pass the time.[2] The *idea* of his archive lived on as well, in ways not always moored to the particularities of place or time.

Nearly a quarter of a century after McKay's invitation, another famous writer again invoked Schomburg's collection. Langston Hughes's 1963 essay, "My Early Days in Harlem," opens with a sequence of destinations. Upon arriving in Harlem in 1921, Hughes recalls, he stopped first at the YMCA, an iconic landing spot for "so many new, young, dark, male arrivals in Harlem." From there, he walked straight to the "Harlem Branch Library" and its "Schomburg Collection." (If Hughes noted that the YMCA was a space for "male arrivals," he gendered the library, too, describing Ernestine Rose, the head librarian, as "warm and wonderful" and Catherine Latimer, reference librarian, as a "luscious café au lait.") Hughes then crossed Lenox Avenue to the Lincoln Theater to hear some blues and, soon after, rode downtown to see Harlem on stage in *Shuffle Along*.[3] The problem with this opening sequence, however, is that it is *out* of sequence. In 1921, Schomburg's collection remained in his home in Brooklyn, a private collection not yet in Harlem. Hughes could not, then, have made the "Schomburg Collection" his first stop after depositing his belongings at the YMCA. The fact that Hughes so confidently misremembered this fact illustrates the extent to which Schomburg's archival agenda had come to seem self-evident by 1963, when Hughes penned "My Early Days in Harlem." If McKay turned a physical collection into a simile, here Hughes took an idea—Black culture as something collectable and collected—and read it backward, conjuring an archive that surely had always been there.[4]

Hughes looked back from a moment of heightened popular Black historical consciousness that was deeply indebted to Schomburg's generation of bibliophiles and Negro History activists.[5] Today, as in 1963, engagements with Black archives are vibrant, contested, and pervasive to a degree that, like Hughes, we may misremember the tentativeness of the era when these institutions emerged with just a few shelves of books, in an information landscape hostile to Black thought. In the early twentieth century, Black archives took shape as experiments in collecting and collectivity—and like most experiments, they left behind tales of deferral as well as triumph. Schomburg, who spent his first years in New York organizing against empire, and who imagined his books and papers as discursive weaponry, died suddenly in 1938 and did not live to see the revolutionary future he conjured on his bookshelves. Likewise, although Alexander Gumby secured the safety of his often-imperiled collection by donating it to Columbia University in 1950, it was not the archival future he had imagined before the Great Depression. He could not rekindle the Gumby Book Studio, and we will never know which pieces of his original collection turned to "paper-mud."[6] In Chicago, Vivian Harsh retired in 1958 and watched as the Special Negro Collection—the object of her devotion for more than twenty-five years—received scant attention from her successor. The collection suffered from relative neglect before it was revived, after her death, during the Black Power era.[7] Dorothy Porter, meanwhile, enjoyed more funding for acquisitions during her brief stint at the National Library of Nigeria in the 1960s than she had for most of her career in the United States.[8] In Roanoke, Virginia Lee saved the Negro History collection at the Gainsboro Library, only to watch the neighborhoods around it razed during urban renewal—underscoring the fact that although many histories of Black branch libraries end with desegregation, that moment simply inaugurated another period of struggle over how blackness could exist in public space.

Back in Harlem, L. D. Reddick turned out to be more of an instigator than an archivist, always trailed by unfinished projects. When he left New York in 1948, he took the war letters he had solicited from Black soldiers and kept them through many moves—to Atlanta, Montgomery, Baltimore, Philadelphia, Boston, and New Orleans. As a result, the letters first gathered in 1944 did not become publicly available until roughly fifty years later, when the entirety of his personal papers came back to the Schomburg Center.[9] Reddick did, however, carry into his subsequent projects an enduring desire to preserve social movements at the moment of their unfolding. In 1955, on the eve of the Montgomery bus boycott, he accepted a teaching post at Alabama State College. Beginning with the first mass meeting to plan the boycott, Reddick served as what he called a "participant observer," saving clippings, keeping detailed notes on strategy sessions, and conducting interviews. He drew others into this documentation process, including the Montgomery Improvement Association's secretary, Maude Ballou, as well as his students at Alabama State, who gathered the movement's ephemera and wrote essays—now part of his papers at the Schomburg Center—about riding the buses in the boycott's aftermath.[10] "Apparently," Reddick remarked, "everybody wishe[d] to assist" in recording the daily labors that made a movement possible.[11]

In turn, Reddick found *himself* the object of data collection. Under watch by the Federal Bureau of Investigation (FBI), Reddick's activism spawned a second, shadow archive of intelligence reports and classified documents that tracked his activities through the 1960s. A small trace left in Reddick's wake at the New York Public Library serves as a reminder that mid-century Black archiving developed under the looming pressures and constrictions of the Cold War state. "September 24, 1962: Schomburg and Reddick correspondence 1939–1948 reviewed by Mr. Robert G. Ibbott, FBI agent": so reads a typewritten note attached to Reddick's personnel file at the library.[12] Not long before, FBI agents also paid a visit to Howard University's Negro Collection, not to monitor the curator, Dorothy Porter, but to use her collection as a space of surveillance.

As Porter chronicled in her annual reports, agents appeared more than once to peruse the university yearbooks she had preserved, presumably to investigate current or former students.[13] Porter's careful, bureaucratic prose broadcasts none of her feelings about this infiltration of the collection by federal authorities.

The scene of FBI agents showing up at the New York Public Library and the Moorland Foundation provides a snapshot of the evolving politics of Black recordkeeping and activism in the postwar era. The project of recovering Black history remained powerfully entwined with contemporary social justice movements, from curricula of the grassroots Freedom Schools to students' demands for the formal creation of Black Studies programs. Yet the questions Reddick raised in the 1940s—about where Black records should be preserved, and the relationship between Black history and the state—would mount in the wake of the civil rights movement and the enormous archive of text, image, sound, and data it generated. Struggles unfolded, for example, over whether southern civil rights records should remain in the region or go north for safekeeping in white liberal institutions. The location of Martin Luther King Jr.'s papers likewise prompted a decade of discord between Boston University, where the leader's pre-1964 papers remain housed, and the King Center, which wanted his papers in Atlanta, among the materials of the movement he had helped to build.[14] New, activist-oriented Black archives emerged and grew, but so, too, did government efforts to document Black protest, from files gathered by the Mississippi State Sovereignty Commission to the FBI's COINTELPRO regime. Seven decades after Reddick's work at the Schomburg Collection, declassified records of this surveillance have become paradoxical sources for writing Black history, raising questions about the ethics of researching social movements through the files of agencies that sought to suppress them.[15]

In the 1960s, a "Negro information explosion," as Porter termed it, recast the documentary apparatus she and her generation of Black librarians had created.[16] Across the United States and in newly independent African nations, university and public libraries scrambled to build collections that would keep pace with new curricula in Black and African studies. Bibliophile Charles Blockson characterized this moment as a "crash program to purchase Black literature." The correspondence of Walter Goldwater, a bookdealer who specialized in African American materials, bears out Blockson's quip; much of Goldwater's business at the University Place Book Shop during the 1960s and 1970s came from academic librarians seeking to expand their holdings as quickly as possible.[17] At Howard, Porter received requests from around the world for advice on how to rapidly replicate the work she had undertaken to build the Moorland-Spingarn collection for more than thirty years. Even the editor of the Dewey Decimal Classification asked for Porter's help to make its system "more serviceable abroad," especially in Africa. More than two decades after Dorcas Fellows, guardian of Dewey's decimals in the 1930s, refused to allow Porter even to mimeograph the classification system for Black materials she had developed, a subsequent Dewey editor wrote to inquire not only if Howard's librarians had "worked out [their] own expansions for specific parts of the classification system" but also if they would "be willing to share these with us, by gift, by loan with permission to copy, or otherwise."[18] Porter's reply—if she did reply—is unknown, but she could not have missed the irony of this request.

Reflecting on this transformation in the market for Black history, Fisk University curator Jessie Carney Smith worried that "many institutions—white as well as Black—are creating instant Black studies programs and establishing instant collections of Black literature—merely to say to themselves and to others who might listen to them, 'We have done our Black thing. Now, let's get on with the business of carrying on our *white* studies programs.'"[19] If Smith questioned the longevity of institutions' commitments to fundamentally change their collections and curricula, she and other curators knew that the economy of Black repositories had nevertheless shifted in enduring ways. Even as the Schomburg Center and the Moorland-Spingarn Research Center enjoyed overdue federal and foundation funding by the 1970s, the next generation of curators at Black archives—Smith and Ann Allen Shockley at Fisk, Donald F. Joyce at the Harsh Collection, and Thomas C. Battle at Moorland-Spingarn, among others—watched as the "instant" market for Black historical material rose beyond their means.[20]

Blockson described booksellers "cling[ing] to Black literature much the same way Americans once clung to gilt-edged stocks."[21] Just as Schomburg had once filled his letters with discussions of the rare books market, Porter and her colleagues tracked that market's postwar inflation, noting a price of fifty dollars in 1954 for Nancy Cunard's *Negro* anthology (a threefold increase since 1937), seventy-five dollars in 1965 for Paul Laurence Dunbar's *Oak and Ivy*, two thousand dollars in 1976 for a leather-bound Civil War ledger, and forty-five thousand dollars for a "Collection of Books on Africa."[22] Porter wondered what Schomburg "would have said if he had been present on April 28, 1970," when an autographed copy of Hughes's *Dear Lovely Death* sold for four hundred and fifty dollars at the Parke-Bernet Galleries in New York.[23] In the decades since Porter's retirement, prices have continued to climb, as evidenced by the auction of a two-page document by Phillis Wheatley in 2005 that yielded $253,000. While such a price might seem like the logical conclusion of Schomburg's project to recognize Black literature's worth—encapsulated in the celebrated sale of his library for ten thousand dollars in 1926—scholars of Black women's history have argued that these high-profile sales often conscript Black history into rhetorical economies that have little to do with Black ideas.[24] Moreover, this shift in economies of attention to and possession of Black historical material has led, in some cases, to Black collections getting priced out of the very market they inaugurated. A notable instance of such exclusion occurred in 1992, when some of Malcolm X's papers went up for sale at auction. The founding institutions for Black archives could afford little of what was offered.[25]

At the same time, much of the "Negro information explosion" leaned on the work of the founding era's collectors and curators.[26] As Hazel Carby has noted, the establishment of what became African American Studies required "the intellectual and political work of identifying intellectual ancestors" and "situating and classifying their texts."[27] Such work had taken shape for decades in research spaces devoted to Black study—before Black Studies—and it served as the scaffolding for an emerging field. In 1962, the publisher G. K. Hall reproduced the card catalog of the Schomburg Collection; it followed suit for the Moorland Foundation and Fisk University's Negro Collection in the next decade.[28] The Tuskegee Institute News Clippings File migrated to microfilm in 1976, making widely accessible the vast filing system for ephemera preserved in Monroe Work's Department of Records and Research since 1910. A proliferating number of "heritage presses," meanwhile, competed to produce facsimiles of out-of-print works by African American authors and meet the demands of a growing Black Studies marketplace. Librarians like Porter played a key role in this "reprint revolution" by recommending works for reproduction and loaning original copies of rare texts to publishers. In 1959, for example, Porter suggested to John Hope Franklin three "Negro classics" that should be reprinted: *Narrative of Sojourner Truth*; Elizabeth Keckley's *Thirty Years a Slave*; and Matthew Henson's *A Negro Explorer at the North Pole*.[29]

Together, transformations in the market and the rise of facsimile reprinting changed the nature of collections. As microfilming and reproduction projects made the published works and newspapers in Black collections more widely accessible, institutional prestige grew increasingly dependent on possession of the rare manuscripts and records that researchers valued for their uniqueness.[30] In addition, as prices climbed for Black historical items in the antiquarian print trade, construction of a general or comprehensive "Negro collection" became prohibitively expensive for many institutions (e.g., close to thirty thousand dollars for a "basic collection" of Afro-Americana in the 1970s). As a result, repositories became increasingly specialized, not attempting to acquire, as Porter had, "everything concerning the Negro."[31] At Delaware State College, for example, librarian Alice Jackson wrote to Porter seeking advice about "trends in Negro life and culture that need development and study" so that the library could make a "real contribution" rather than build "yet another Negro collection on the standard pattern."[32] In 1969, the Amistad Research Center emerged as the first archive specifically dedicated to preserving records of the modern civil rights movement, while in 1970, the Western Reserve Historical Society began a new Black History Archive Project that was among the first to focus exclusively on Black life in a single metropolitan area.[33] In other words, the very success of the founding generation of collectors made their efforts impossible to replicate, and new approaches to Black archives emerged as a result.

As sites for the study of revolution or as the object of new mobilizations, Black collections have both arisen from and been the subject of Black liberation movements. During widespread protests at Howard University in 1968, for example, one group of students threatened to burn down the library, seeing it as the symbol of a worn-out past, while another group of students demanded better access to the library's Negro Collection, seeing it as central to transforming the university's curriculum.[34] Likewise, ever since protests unfolded in the wake of Reddick's resignation in 1948, the Schomburg Collection—a place of symbolic importance to the Black radical tradition—has found itself at the center of controversy. In 1966, its curator, Jean Blackwell Hutson, warned that the city had underfunded Black history. Expected to say a few polite words at a municipal ceremony, she instead followed in the footsteps of Black women before her who took risks to defend their collections. "I am now like the Southern Negro who was brought to the microphone to testify how happy he was," she began, "and when he came to that position, he yelled 'Help, Help, Help!' The Schomburg Collection is less protected now than ever before. It seems that there is no responsible concern for its future."[35]

Following Hutson's remarks, *Ebony* magazine published an exposé questioning the city's commitment to Harlem's institutions and declaring that "despite the heightened interest in the Negro and Negro history, the famed Schomburg Collection is literally rotting away."[36] Journalists described the collection as physically and intellectually endangered, with poor climate protection, a backlog of unprocessed manuscripts, and insufficient funds to acquire coveted materials like the papers of Richard Wright (which ultimately went to Yale University). *Ebony*'s story marked the beginning of a fractious campaign to "Save Black Documents" that included a demand for community control of the collection, a protest that stopped trucks from taking materials out of Harlem for off-site microfilming, and a television documentary ominously titled "A Heritage in Peril."[37] Playwright Loften Mitchell described protests about the Schomburg Collection's future as tied to a broader fight for control over Harlem.[38] Once again, a Black collection sat at the center of a struggle over the right for blackness to exist and thrive in public space. Even as the centennial of Schomburg's collection at the New York Public Library approaches in 2026—a testament to the staying power of Black archives and their builders—this history of conflict serves as a reminder of the ongoing work required to keep Black records accessible to the communities that made them.

Ebony, which had sounded an alarm about the state of Black archives in 1967, became the subject of that same concern in 2015, when the Johnson Publishing Company announced that it would sell the magazine's vast photography archives, and those of *Jet*, to stave off financial peril.[39] The centrality of photography to these two magazines—and the way their iconic cover art turned them into readers' collectibles—made Johnson Publishing's image archive its most valuable financial asset *and* something the public felt was too sacred to be sold. *The Chicago Defender* captured the mood of public reaction after the announcement by vociferously objecting to the idea of "giving away our historical and iconic images" and selling seven decades worth of photographs to "a world that has capitalized off of telling our story."[40] Yet, in keeping with earlier moments when archival loss was entwined with invention, the *Ebony* crisis occasioned experimental acts of redress that would remake Black archival ideas anew. A consortium of cultural organizations ultimately stepped in to purchase the collection, but the most interesting responses to the sale came from local artists and archivists. The Johnson Publishing Company's collection of books and magazines now fill artist Theaster Gates's Stony Island Arts Bank which, like Gumby's Book Studio, is at once a library, art installation, and community lounge.[41] The Blackivists—a Chicago group whose name remixes the tradition of activism and archiving in Black life—inaugurated *Loss/Capture*, a curatorial project produced at a "dissonant crossroads" that reflects upon the uneven preservation of Black histories.[42]

Both responses belong to what Daphne A. Brooks has called "bold and exhilarating, experimental new work" grappling with "elusive histories that remain outside of our direct grasp."[43] Black archives—in their absence *and* abundance—continue to operate as a mode of thinking, an occasion for gathering and creating, and a site of ongoing struggle. In the tradition of Porter, who summoned Black data to her catalog, recent digital projects, such as the Black Women's Organizing Archive, are reimagining what an "archive" looks like when dispersed, promising to bring together "the scattered archives of nineteenth- and twentieth-century Black women's organizing."[44] Simultaneously, other initiatives have upheld Reddick's desire to capture the "mood and temper" of social movements not in the central files of their leaders but in the decentralized expressions of those in the streets. Archivists have worked closely with activists and artists to rethink what documentation can be saved—and what might need to remain fugitive.[45]

The stories told in *Scattered and Fugitive Things* remain relevant to the future of Black archives. As the founding repositories pass the centennial mark, Black history still faces threats—in book bans and legislation that exiles it from school curricula—even as the rarified market for Black papers continues to gentrify. In this bifurcated landscape of deflation and inflation—fear of Black history, on the one hand, and its hypervisibility, on the other—what is the "price of the ticket," to borrow James Baldwin's phrase, to care for Black collections? As someone who found a "connection to life" at the Schomburg Collection, Baldwin well knew that question to be both literal and ethical.[46] Who can afford to build Black collections? What is the cost of admission to the field? What kind of commitments do Black records require of their keepers? The history of Black collecting offers some possible answers to those questions.

Despite their heterogeneous tastes and styles, the collectors chronicled in this book converged around a set of principles that should continue to guide those who collect in their wake: to value Black records, order them capaciously, and take risks to make them accessible. Schomburg once prophesied that someday "the public will compel the libraries to have rooms devoted solely to Negro themes."[47] His prophecy has come true many times over, as repositories large and small have grown to understand, often belatedly, the value of objects once cast aside by historians and bookdealers. As exemplified by the work of the twentieth century's founding Black bibliophiles and librarians, however, Black collecting is not simply the accumulation of a certain set of objects. Rather, it is an intellectual tradition. The politics and ethics of that tradition endure not just in *what* they collected, but in *how* they built their collections and the risks—intellectual, material, and political—that work entailed. For institutions that have rushed to catch up with the collection of African American materials—especially those that can afford prices many of the founding repositories cannot—it is critical to think beyond the act of acquisition.

Contemporary collecting institutions might do well to follow the lead of Porter, who devoted herself not only to making one institution's collection the largest but also to building an entire field of collecting and study. On repeated occasions, she called for joint acquisition planning across institutions and a "program of co-operative relations with libraries containing Negro collections"—a vision that remains critical but unfinished.[48] Perhaps the cost of admission to Black archive-building today, then, should be a similar commitment to the field at large, directing resources to care for Black materials wherever they might be found—in repositories large and small, scattered or fugitive, under glass or under threat. Moreover, for Schomburg, Gumby, Lee, Harsh, Porter, and Reddick—as well as the other bibliophiles and librarians of their generation—the principles of Black archiving extended to readers as well as to resources. Each of these collectors modeled an imperative not only to value Black materials but also to transform public life. That commitment, still urgent today, took shape in the creation of collective spaces—such as Harsh's study hall for South Side thinkers—and like Reddick's incomplete wartime archive, the commitment developed in dynamic relationship to the unfinished work of Black liberation. By creating spaces for collective inquiry, the twentieth century's Black collectors changed the questions people could dream of asking, then and now.

ABBREVIATIONS

AAS Papers	Arthur A. Schomburg Papers
AUARC	Archives Research Center, Robert W. Woodruff Library, Atlanta University Center
BRBML	Beinecke Rare Book and Manuscript Library, Yale University
BRLF	Book Review and Lecture Forum
CPL	Chicago Public Library
CRBML	Rare Book and Manuscript Library, Columbia University Libraries
DPW OH	Oral History Interview of Dorothy Porter Wesley
DPW Papers	Dorothy Porter Wesley Papers
FUSCA	Special Collections and Archives, Fisk University
GLA	Gainsboro Library Archives, Roanoke Public Library
GLR	Gainsboro Library Records
GLVF	Gainsboro Library vertical files
HBLR	George Cleveland Hall Branch Library Archives
HUA	Hampton University Archives, Hampton University Museum
LDR Papers	Lawrence D. Reddick Papers
LDRWWII	Lawrence D. Reddick World War II Project Records

MARB	Manuscripts, Archives and Rare Books Division, Schomburg Center for Research in Black Culture, New York Public Library
MSRC	Moorland-Spingarn Research Center, Founders Library, Howard University
NABWH	National Archives for Black Women's History, Mary McLeod Bethune Council House Historic Site, National Parks Service
NYPL	New York Public Library
NYPLA	New York Public Library Archives, New York Public Library, Astor, Lenox and Tilden Foundations
RPL	Roanoke Public Library
SCCF	Schomburg Center Clipping File
SCRBC	Schomburg Center for Research in Black Culture, New York Public Library
SUSCRC	Special Collections Research Center, Syracuse University
UMSC	Special Collections and University Archives, University of Massachusetts at Amherst
VGHRC	Vivian G. Harsh Research Collection of Afro-American History and Literature, Carter G. Woodson Regional Library, Chicago Public Library

NOTES

INTRODUCTION

1. Claude McKay, [Circular letter for the creation of a Negro Writers Guild], October 23, 1937, in *The Passion of Claude McKay: Selected Poetry and Prose, 1912–1948*, ed. Wayne F. Cooper (New York: Schocken, 1973), 233. On the short-lived Negro Writers Guild, see Wayne F. Cooper, *Claude McKay: Rebel Sojourner in the Harlem Renaissance* (Baton Rouge: Louisiana State University, 1987), 326–28; Lawrence P. Jackson, *The Indignant Generation: A Narrative History of African American Writers and Critics, 1934–1960* (Princeton, NJ: Princeton University Press, 2011), 69–70; and Jean-Christophe Cloutier, *Shadow Archives: The Lifecycles of African American Literature* (New York: Columbia University Press, 2019), 108–9.
2. McKay elaborates on this idea in "Group Life and Literature," n.d., box 9, folder 287, Claude McKay Collection, BRBML. My thanks to Jean-Christophe Cloutier for drawing my attention to this essay.
3. Aubrey Bowser, "A Negro Documentarian," *New York Amsterdam News*, August 13, 1930; and Arthur A. Schomburg, "The Negro Digs Up His Past," *Survey Graphic* 6, no. 6 (March 1925): 672.
4. J. A. Rogers, "Arthur Schomburg, the Sherlock Holmes of Negro History," *Richmond Planet*, July 5, 1930; Claude McKay to Arthur Schomburg, March 1, 1924, and June 16, 1924, both in box 5, folder 34, Arthur A. Schomburg Papers (hereafter AAS Papers), Manuscripts, Archives and Rare Books Division (hereafter MARB), SCRBC.
5. McKay, [Circular letter]. McKay told Schomburg, "I have used your achievement and the Collection in my circular letter, to help promote the organization of the Group" (McKay to Schomburg, January 10, [1938], box 5, folder 34, AAS Papers).
6. Claude McKay, *Harlem: Negro Metropolis* (New York: Dutton, 1940), 140.
7. Eric D. Walrond, "Visit to Arthur Schomburg's Library Brings Out Wealth of Historical Information," *Negro World*, April 22, 1922, 6; "Rare Race Portraits and Prints to be Placed on Exhibit by New York Public Library," *Journal and Guide*, February 1, 1936, SCCF 004,447.
8. McKay, *Harlem*, 139, 142.
9. Booker T. Washington, *Future of the American Negro*, quoted in *Black Nationalism in America*, ed. John H. Bracey, August Meier, and Elliott Rudwick (Indianapolis, IN: Bobbs-Merrill, 1970), 233–34.
10. On the need to historicize "self-documentation in the African American community," see Rabia Gibbs, "The Heart of the Matter: The Developmental History of African American Archives," *American Archivist* 75 (Spring/Summer 2012): 201.

11. Elinor Des Verney Sinnette, W. Paul Coates, and Thomas C. Battle, eds., *Black Bibliophiles and Collectors: Preservers of Black History* (Washington, DC: Howard University Press, 1990), iv. The symposium featured librarians Dorothy Porter Wesley, Jean Blackwell Hutson, and Jessie Carney Smith; bibliophile Charles Blockson; theater collector Helen Armstead Johnson; and archivists Karen Jefferson and Clifford L. Muse Jr. See Roderick A. Ferguson, "Ode to the Black Bouquinistes: Bibliomaniacs of the Black Radical Tradition," *CLA Journal* 60, no. 4 (June 2017): 399–413.
12. Sinnette, Coates, and Battle, *Black Bibliophiles*, xix.
13. McKay, *Harlem*, 141.
14. Schomburg to John W. Cromwell, December 18, 1912, box 1, folder 14, Cromwell Family Papers (hereafter Cromwell Papers), Manuscript Division, MSRC.
15. Patricia Galloway, "Archives, Power, and History: Dunbar Rowland and the Beginning of the State Archives of Mississippi (1902–1936)," *American Archivist* 69, no. 1 (2006): 79–116; and Jay Reeves, "Alabama Archives Faces Its Legacy as Confederate 'Attic,'" *AP News*, September 21, 2020.
16. "Tells Concern at Howard U. Dedication," *Chicago Defender*, June 3, 1939.
17. Schomburg, "Negro Digs," 670 (emphasis added).
18. "People Talked About," *Negro World*, March 25, 1922.
19. Alice Dunbar Nelson, "Une Femme Dit," *Pittsburgh Courier*, June 12, 1926.
20. Black librarians frequently surveyed and noted the widespread distribution of Black historical materials across different types of repositories. See, for example, Mollie E. Dunlap, "Special Collections of Negro Literature in the United States," *Journal of Negro Education* 4, no. 4 (1935): 482–89; Dorothy Porter, "Library Sources for the Study of Negro Life and History," *Journal of Negro Education* 5, no. 2 (April 1936): 232–44; Arna Bontemps, "Special Collections of Negroana," *Library Quarterly* 14, no. 3 (July 1944): 187–206; and Jessie Carney Smith, *Black Academic Libraries and Research Collections: An Historical Survey* (Westport, CT: Greenwood, 1977).
21. Carl Van Vechten, "The J. W. Johnson Collection at Yale," *Crisis* 49, no. 7 (July 1942): 222.
22. Schomburg to Cromwell, February 23, 1915, box 1, folder 18, Cromwell Papers. Bruce may have first used this phrase in 1913 when conceptualizing the Loyal Order of the Sons of Africa; see William Seraile, *Bruce Grit: The Black Nationalist Writings of John Edward Bruce* (Knoxville: University of Tennessee Press, 2003), 119. It was also the title of a 1912 travel narrative by Daniel Crawford, *Thinking Black: 22 Years in the Long Grass of Central Africa*, which Schomburg owned and wrote about in "Story of the Word, Mulatto," n.d., box 1, folder 36, AAS Papers Additions, MARB, SCRBC.
23. Schomburg, "Negro Digs," 670. Bruce argued that those who "learned how to think black" would embrace the "movement to assemble historical data . . . for the use and benefit of the coming generation" (John E. Bruce to Alain Locke [emphasis in original], May 4, 1915, box 17, folder 40, Alain LeRoy Locke Papers [hereafter Locke Papers], Manuscript Division, MSRC).
24. David Scott, "On the Very Idea of a Black Radical Tradition," *Small Axe* 17, no. 1 (March 2013): 3; Kevin Young, *The Grey Album: On the Blackness of Blackness* (Minneapolis, MN: Graywolf, 2012), 51. Nikhil Pal Singh encapsulates Scott's idea of tradition as "commonness that we argue about" (quoted in Nijah Cunningham, "A Queer Pier: Roundtable on the Idea of a Black Radical Tradition," *Small Axe* 17, no. 1 [March 2013]: 95).
25. John Henrik Clarke, "The Influence of Arthur A. Schomburg on My Concept of Africana Studies," *Phylon* 49 (1992): 7 (emphasis added).
26. Anna-Sophie Springer and Etienne Turpin, "Dear Reader," in *Fantasies of the Library*, rev. ed. (Cambridge, MA: MIT Press, 2016), iii.
27. Bowser, "A Negro Documentarian."
28. "A Contribution from Arthur A. Schomburg," *New York Age*, January 19, 1935.
29. Schomburg, "Negro Digs," 672. Though composed of already-existing objects, a collection is itself a creative work that casts new meaning on the objects within it. Russell W. Belk, *Collecting in a Consumer Society* (London: Routledge, 1995), 55.

30. Schomburg, "Negro Digs," 671.
31. J. A. Rogers, "Schomburg Is the Detective of History," *New Journal and Guide*, July 5, 1930.
32. Bruce to Locke, June 5, 1912, box 98, folder 18, Locke Papers.
33. Ophelia Settle Egypt, *Unwritten History of Slavery* (Nashville: Social Science Institute, 1945); Tiffany Ruby Patterson, *Zora Neale Hurston and a History of Southern Life* (Philadelphia: Temple University Press, 2005), 50–63; Catherine A. Stewart, *Long Past Slavery: Representing Race in the Federal Writers' Project* (Chapel Hill: University of North Carolina Press, 2016), 62–90, 175–228. Assessments of what Schomburg did or did not collect are based on study of his correspondence, a circa 1914 list of his personal library holdings, and the work of the "Home to Harlem" initiative at the Schomburg Center for Research in Black Culture—all of which are discussed in chapter 1.
34. Daphne A. Brooks, *Liner Notes for the Revolution: The Intellectual Life of Black Feminist Sound* (Cambridge, MA: Harvard University Press, 2021), 380. On the collecting of "primitive" or "authentic" folk forms, see Marybeth Hamilton, *In Search of the Blues: Black Voices, White Visions* (London: Jonathan Cape, 2002); and Bryan Wagner, *Disturbing the Peace: Black Culture and the Police Power after Slavery* (Cambridge, MA: Harvard University Press, 2009), 25–57. On Black artists' embattled relationship with that framing, see Sonnet Retman, *Real Folks: Race and Genre in the Great Depression* (Durham, NC: Duke University Press, 2011); and Brooks, *Liner Notes*, 271–309.
35. Beyond print culture, other strains of Black memory work have taken shape through music, family narratives, celebrations, and commemorations. See Thavolia Glymph, "Liberty Dearly Bought: The Making of Civil War Memory in African American Communities in the South," in *Time Longer Than Rope: A Century of African American Activism, 1850–1950*, ed. Charles Payne and Adam Green (New York: New York University, 2003), 117. Black archives both incorporated and continued to exist alongside such nondiscursive practices of memory, as Geneviève Fabre and Robert O'Meally argue in their introduction to *History and Memory in African-American Culture* (New York: Oxford University Press, 1994), 3–17.
36. On collecting and reordering, see Springer and Turpin, "Dear Reader," iii; and Ellen Gruber Garvey, *Writing with Scissors: American Scrapbooks from the Civil War to the Harlem Renaissance* (New York: Oxford University Press, 2013), 28, 138–156. On collecting as a mode of theorizing diaspora, see Adalaine Holton, "Decolonizing History: Arthur Schomburg's Afrodiasporic Archive," *Journal of African American History* 92, no. 2 (Spring 2007): 218–238.
37. On the creative possibilities of fragmentation and obscurity, see Brent Hayes Edwards, "The Taste of the Archive," *Callaloo* 35, no. 4 (Fall 2012): 970; and Edouard Glissant, *Caribbean Discourse: Selected Essays* (Charlottesville: University of Virginia Press, 1989), 169–170.
38. Huey Copeland and Naomi Beckwith, "Black Collectivities: An Introduction," *Nka: Journal of Contemporary African Art* 34 (2014): 7; and Brent Hayes Edwards, Anna McCarthy, and Randy Martin, "Collective," *Social Text* 27, no. 3 (2009): 74.
39. See, e.g. Nicholas Basbanes, *A Gentle Madness: Bibliophiles, Bibliomanes, and the Eternal Passion for Books* (New York: Holt, 1995); and Thomas Richards, *The Imperial Archive: Knowledge and the Fantasy of Empire* (New York: Verso, 1993).
40. On understanding provenance in social terms, see Jennifer Douglas, "A Call to Rethink Archival Creation: Exploring Types of Creation in Personal Archives," *Archival Science* 18, no. 1 (March 2018): 29–49; and Tom Nesmith, "The Concept of Societal Provenance and Records of Nineteenth-Century Aboriginal-European Relations in Western Canada: Implications for Archival Theory and Practice," *Archival Science* 6 (2006): 351–360.
41. Basbanes, *A Gentle Madness*, 37.
42. Schomburg, "Negro Digs," 671. Donald Franklin Joyce has argued that movements, such as the Harlem Renaissance and the civil rights struggle, were "catalytic" to the creation of African American collections (Joyce, "Resources for Scholars: Four Major Collections of Afro-Americana," *Library Quarterly* 58, no. 1 [January 1988]: 66). See also Michael Flug, "Events and Issues That Motivated the

Evolution of African American Institutional Archival and Manuscripts Programs, 1919–1950," paper presented at the Collecting Our Past to Secure Our Future Conference, Jackson State University, November 30–December 2, 1995.

43. Schomburg to Cromwell, Labor Day 1912, box 1, folder 14, Cromwell Papers; Bontemps, "Special Collections of Negroana," 189.
44. Dorothy Porter Wesley and Constance Porter Uzelac, eds., Introduction to *William Cooper Nell: Nineteenth-Century African American Abolitionist, Historian, Integrationist, Selected Writings, 1832–1874* (Baltimore, MD: Black Classic Press, 2002), 51–52; and Frances Smith Foster, *Written by Herself: Literary Production by African American Women, 1746–1892* (Bloomington: Indiana University Press, 1992), 148. On Black historiography in the nineteenth century, see John Ernest, *Liberation Historiography: African American Writers and the Challenge of History* (Chapel Hill: University of North Carolina Press, 2004); Martha S. Jones, *All Bound Up Together: The Woman Question in African American Public Culture, 1830–1900* (Chapel Hill: University of North Carolina Press, 2007), 179–184; and Stephen G. Hall, *A Faithful Account of the Race: African American Historical Writing in Nineteenth-Century America* (Chapel Hill: University of North Carolina Press, 2009).
45. Dorothy Porter, speech at Symposium on Libraries for African and Afro-American Studies, ca. 1975, box 34, Dorothy Porter Wesley Papers (hereafter DPW Papers), BRBML. Note that at the time of research in 2013, this collection was minimally processed; box locations may have changed since processing. See also Elizabeth McHenry, *Forgotten Readers: Recovering the Lost History of African American Literary Societies* (Durham, NC: Duke University Press, 2002), 50–57.
46. Dorothy Porter Wesley, "Black Antiquarians and Bibliophiles Revisited, with a Glance at Today's Lovers of Books and Memorabilia," in Sinnette, Coates, and Battle, *Black Bibliophiles*, 5.
47. Excerpt from "National Council of the Colored People . . . 1853," in *Black Nationalism in America*, 64–65.
48. It is not clear whether the conventions' calls to archive were realized, and the collections of early Black literary societies were lost or repurposed. See Dorothy B. Porter, "The Organized Educational Activities of Negro Literary Societies, 1828–1846," *Journal of Negro Education* 5, no. 4 (October 1936): 575. By contrast, antislavery book collections built by prominent white abolitionists remained intact after the Civil War and found their way into northern libraries and historical societies. Richard Newman, "Books and Book Collectors," in *Encyclopedia of African-American Culture and History*, vol. 1, ed. Jack Salzman, David Lionel Smith, and Cornel West (New York: Macmillan, 1996), 399–400.
49. Nicholas Natanson, ed., *Index to the Hampton University Newspaper Clipping File* (Alexandria, VA: Chadwick-Healey, 1988); Smith, *Black Academic Libraries*, 173–74; "Library Bureaus," manuscript, n.d., and "Hampton Institute Library," typescript, ca. 1926, both in Library Correspondences, General Information (Letters), HUA.
50. F. G. Barbadoes quoted in Tony Martin, "Race Men, Bibliophiles, and Historians: The World of Robert M. Adger and the Negro Historical Society of Philadelphia," in *Rare Afro-Americana: A Reconstruction of the Adger Library*, ed. Wendy Ball and Tony Martin (Boston: Hall, 1981), 32.
51. On the ANHS, see Charles H. Wesley, "Creating and Maintaining an Historical Tradition," *Journal of Negro History* 49 (January 1964): 13–33; and James G. Spady, "The Afro-American Historical Society: The Nucleus of Black Bibliophiles (1897–1913)," *Negro History Bulletin* 37, no. 4 (June–July 1974): 254–257. On Philadelphia collectors, see Porter Wesley, "Black Antiquarians," 7; Martin, "Race Men, Bibliophiles, and Historians"; James G. Spady, "Robert Mara Adger," in *Africana: The Encyclopedia of the African and African American Experience*, vol. 1, ed. Kwame Anthony Appiah and Henry Louis Gates, Jr. (New York: Oxford University Press, 2005), 34–35; William C. Welburn, "To 'Keep the Past in Lively Memory': William Carl Bolivar's Efforts to Preserve African American Cultural Heritage," *Libraries & the Cultural Record* 42, no. 2 (2007): 165–79; and Aston Gonzalez,

"William Dorsey and the Construction of an African American History Archive," *Social Dynamics* 45, no. 1 (2019): 138–155.

52. Schomburg, "Negro Digs," 670.

53. Victoria Earle Matthews, "The Value of Race Literature: An Address Delivered at the First Congress of Colored Women of the United States at Boston, Mass., July 30, 1895," BRBML, brbl-dl.library.yale.edu.

54. W. E. Burghardt Du Bois, "The American Negro at Paris," *American Monthly Review of Books* 23, no. 5 (November 1900): 577. See also Mabel O. Wilson, *Negro Building: Black Americans in the World of Fairs and Museums* (Berkeley: University of California Press, 2012), 84–138; and Shawn Michelle Smith, *American Archives: Gender, Race, and Class in Visual Culture* (Princeton, NJ: Princeton University Press, 1999), 157–86.

55. Brent Hayes Edwards, *The Practice of Diaspora: Literature, Translation, and the Rise of Black Internationalism* (Cambridge, MA: Harvard University Press, 2003), 44. The "archival turn" usually references a recent efflorescence of writing that uses the term archive to reflect on how the construction of records makes certain stories possible or impossible to tell. But scholars have argued that Schomburg's writings anticipated this turn by nearly a century. See Margarita M. Castromán Soto, "Schomburg's Black Archival Turn: 'Racial Integrity' and 'The Negro Digs Up His Past,'" *African American Review* 54, nos. 1–2 (Spring/Summer 2021): 73–90; and Melanie Chambliss's forthcoming work on Schomburg's theorization of the fragment.

56. Arna Bontemps, "Buried Treasures of Negro Art," *Negro Digest* 9, no. 2 (December 1950): 17. On turn-of-the-century bibliophiles, see Elinor Des Verney Sinnette, *Arthur Alfonso Schomburg: Black Bibliophile and Collector* (New York: New York Public Library and Wayne State University, 1989), 73–89; Sinnette et al., *Black Bibliophiles*; and Melanie Chambliss, "A Library in Progress," in *The Unfinished Book*, ed. Alexandra Gillespie and Deidre Lynch (Oxford: Oxford University Press, 2021): 260–271.

57. L. D. Reddick, "Bibliographical Problems in Negro Research," *American Council of Learned Societies Bulletin* 32 (September 1941): 26–30; Doris E. Saunders to Dorothy Porter, April 14, 1960, Records of the MSRC, Record Group 1 (unprocessed), University Archives, MSRC (hereafter MSRC Record Group 1); and Mollie Dunlap, Review of *Rural America Reads: A Study of Rural Library Service*, by Marion Humble, *Journal of Negro Education* 8, no. 2 (April 1939): 217.

58. Linda O. McMurray, *Recorder of the Black Experience: A Biography of Monroe Nathan Work* (Baton Rouge: Louisiana State University Press, 1985).

59. Robert Hill, "On Collectors, Their Contributions to the Documentation of the Black Past," in Sinnette et al., *Black Bibliophiles*, 47–48.

60. Howard Dodson describes the efforts of the Negro Book Collectors Exchange as the beginning of "today's Africana archives eco-system" (Dodson, "Making Art at the Schomburg: Africana Archives as Sites of Art Making," *Callaloo* 38, no. 3 [Summer 2015]: 550).

61. "The First Biennial Meeting of the Association for the Study of Negro Life and History at Washington," *Journal of Negro History* 2, no. 4 (October 1917): 446. On Young, see "Rare Books for Negroes," unidentified newspaper clipping, November 1915, SCCF 005,931; and "Books left by Mr. Geo. Young," typescript, n.d., box 1, folder 4, SCRBC Records, MARB, SCRBC.

62. "The J. E. Moorland Foundation of the University Library," *Howard University Record* 10, no. 1 (1916): 14.

63. Sinnette, *Arthur Alfonso Schomburg*, 136–37; and Carter G. Woodson, "Ten Years of Collecting and Publishing the Records of the Negro," *Journal of Negro History* 10, no. 4 (October 1925): 598–607.

64. Catherine Allen Latimer, "Where Can I Get Material on the Negro," *Crisis* 41, no. 6 (June 1934): 164–65; and Dunlap, "Special Collections of Negro Literature."

65. Jessie Carney Smith, "Special Collections of Black Literature in the Traditionally Black College," *College and Research Libraries* 35, no. 5 (September 1974): 322–35.

66. Dorothy B. Porter noted that by the 1930s such efforts had reached a "high peak of production" (Porter, "Library Sources," 232).
67. "N.A.A.C.P. Presents Pen of Frederick Douglass to Harlem Library," typescript, n.d., Libraries scrapbook, L. S. Alexander Gumby Collection of Negroiana (hereafter Gumby Collection), CRBML; and Schomburg, [typescript fragment about "a small piece of wood"], n.d., box 14, folder 18, AAS Papers.
68. Barefield Gordon, "New Negro Libraries," *Crisis* 39, no. 9 (September 1932): 284.
69. Annual Report of the Moorland Foundation, 1947–48, Manuscript Division, MSRC; and Library Staff Bulletin, March 1941, MSRC Record Group 1.
70. "What Does the Schomburg Collection Need?," typescript, [1948], box 2, folder 5, SCRBC Records, MARB, SCRBC.
71. Schomburg to Cromwell, August 11, 1913, box 1, folder 16, Cromwell Papers.
72. Schomburg to Mrs. [Elizabeth H.] Forbes, November 2, 1934, George Washington Forbes Papers, Boston Public Library. It is especially interesting that Schomburg experimented with the term *archives* in the 1930s because it would be another two decades before the tradition of manuscript collecting, to which Schomburg belonged, fully merged with the American archives profession. See Terry Cook, "What Is Past Is Prologue: A History of Archival Ideas since 1898, and the Future Paradigm Shift," *Archivaria* 43 (Spring 1997): 21; and James O'Toole, *Understanding Archives and Manuscripts* (Chicago: Society of American Archivists, 1990), 31, 35, 42–43.
73. "The J. E. Moorland Foundation of The University Library," 12.
74. Stanley Cavell, "The World as Things: Collecting Thoughts on Collecting," in *Contemporary Collecting: Objects, Practices, and the Fate of Things*, ed. Kevin M. Moist and David Banash (Lanham, MD: Scarecrow, 2013), 99–130.
75. On the politics of the archival turn, see Marlene Manoff, "Theories of the Archive from Across the Disciplines," *Portal: Libraries and the Academy* 4, no. 1 (2004): 9–25; Gabrielle Dean, "Disciplinarity and Disorder," *Archive Journal* 1, no. 1 (Spring 2011): http://www.archivejournal.net/issue/1/archives-remixed/; and Laura E. Helton, "Archive," in *Information Keywords*, ed. Michele Kennerly, Samuel Frederick, and Jonathan Abel (New York: Columbia University Press, 2021), 44–56.
76. Laura Helton, Justin Leroy, Max A. Mishler, Samantha Seeley, and Shauna Sweeney, "The Question of Recovery: An Introduction," *Social Text* 33, no. 3 (December 2015): 1–18.
77. For examples of work that leverages the term *archive* to frame Black cultural production, see Wendy W. Walters, *Archives of the Black Atlantic: Reading Between Literature and History* (London: Routledge, 2013); Alexis Pauline Gumbs, *M Archive: After the End of the World* (Durham, NC: Duke University Press, 2018); Jenny Sharpe, *Immaterial Archives: An African Diaspora Poetics of Loss* (Chicago: Northwestern University Press, 2020); and Mark Anthony Neal, *Black Ephemera: The Crisis and Challenge of the Musical Archive* (New York: New York University Press, 2022).
78. Michele Caswell, "'The Archive' Is Not an Archives: On Acknowledging the Intellectual Contributions of Archival Science," *Reconstruction: Studies in Contemporary Culture* 16, no. 1 (2016): https://escholarship.org/uc/item/7bn4v1fk.
79. Ann Cvetkovich, *An Archive of Feelings: Trauma, Sexuality, and Lesbian Public Cultures* (Durham, NC: Duke University Press, 2003), 268.
80. Schomburg to Cromwell, August 19, 1913, box 1, folder 16, Cromwell Papers.
81. Glymph, "Liberty Dearly Bought," 114. For other meditations on the term *counterarchive*, see Castromán Soto, "Schomburg's Black Archival Turn," 74; and Deborah A. Thomas, *Political Life in the Wake of the Plantation: Sovereignty, Witnessing, Repair* (Durham, NC: Duke University Press, 2019), 6–7.
82. Schomburg, "Negro Digs," 670.
83. On the historical fluidity of the functions of archives, libraries, and museums, see Gabriella Giannachi, *Archive Everything: Mapping the Everyday* (Cambridge, MA: MIT Press, 2016), xv. I use the

term *library* to refer to book-oriented collections or to institutions designated as libraries. I use *archives* to refer to collections that contain not only books but also clippings, photographs, and manuscripts and that aim to preserve distinctive historical records for future use.

84. Antoinette Burton, "Archive Fever, Archive Stories," in *Archive Stories: Facts, Fictions, and the Writing of History*, ed. Burton (Durham, NC: Duke University Press, 2005), 7.
85. Kathy Peiss, *Information Hunters: When Librarians, Soldiers, and Spies Banded Together in World War II Europe* (New York: Oxford University Press, 2020), 6.
86. Ann Allen Shockley and E. J. Josey, "Black Librarians as Creative Writers," in *Handbook of Black Librarianship*, ed. Shockley and Josey (Littleton, CO: Libraries Unlimited, 1977): 160–66. On Du Bois as bibliographer, see Elizabeth McHenry, *To Make Negro Literature: Writing, Literary Practice, and African American Authorship* (Durham, NC: Duke University Press, 2021), 78–128. On Lorde's librarianship, see Keguro Macharia, *Frottage: Frictions of Intimacy Across the Black Diaspora* (New York: New York University Press, 2019), 54; and M. C. Kinniburgh, *Wild Intelligence: Poets' Libraries and the Politics of Knowledge in Postwar America* (Amherst: University of Massachusetts Press, 2022), 51–79. On authorship and librarianship as two "related critical experiences," see Karin Roffman, "Women Writers and Their Libraries in the 1920s," in *Institutions of Reading: The Social Life of Libraries in the United States*, ed. Thomas Augst and Kenneth Carpenter (Amherst: University of Massachusetts Press, 2007), 203–30.
87. Karin Roffman, "Nella Larsen, Librarian at 135th Street," *Modern Fiction Studies* 53, no. 4 (Winter 2007): 752–87; Jessie Carney Smith, "Black Women, Civil Rights, and Libraries," in *Untold Stories: Civil Rights, Libraries, and Black Librarianship*, ed. John Mack Turner (Champaign, IL: Graduate School of Library and Information Science, 1998), 141–50; Phillip Luke Sinitiere, "'An Impressive Basis for Research': Arna Bontemps' Co-Creation of the W. E. B. Du Bois Collection at Fisk University," *Black Scholar* 52, no. 2 (2022): 50–62; Alain Locke, *The Negro in America* (Chicago: American Library Association, 1933); Laura E. Helton, "Historical Form(s)," in *Elusive Archives: Material Culture in Formation*, ed. Martin Brückner and Sandy Isenstadt (Newark: University of Delaware Press, 2021): 49–63; Chicago Public Library, *The Chicago Afro-American Union Analytic Catalog: An Index to Materials on Afro-Americans in the Principal Libraries of Chicago* (Boston: Hall, 1972); Langston Hughes, "When I Worked for Dr. Woodson," *Negro History Bulletin* 30, no. 6 (October 1967): 17; Hubert H. Harrison Papers, Series IV, CRBML; Alice Dunbar-Nelson Papers, Series II, Special Collections, University of Delaware; Walrond, "Visit to Arthur Schomburg's Library"; Zora Neale Hurston, "Mr. Schomburg's Library," *Negro World*, April 22, 1922; Linda J. Henry, "Promoting Historical Consciousness: The Early Archives Committee of the National Council of Negro Women," *Signs* 7, no. 1 (October 1981): 251–59; "Harlem Leaders Back Negro[?]," *Pittsburgh Courier*, December 27, 1924, SCCF 004,447; and Jacqueline C. Jones, "The Unknown Patron: Harold Jackman and the Harlem Renaissance Archives," *Langston Hughes Review* 19 (2005): 55–66.
88. Young, *The Grey Album*, 53.
89. On methodologies for writing Black women's intellectual history that challenge the logic of such erasure, see Mia E. Bay, Farah J. Griffin, Martha S. Jones, and Barbara D. Savage, eds., *Toward an Intellectual History of Black Women* (Chapel Hill: University of North Carolina Press, 2015). In looking at classification schemes, reading lists, and catalogs as sites of intellectual work, I follow their call to study "how black women used a remarkable and unexpected array of vehicles . . . to set out, develop, and share their ideas" (5).
90. On the early history of women, gender, and librarianship, see Barbara A. Mitchell, "Boston Library Catalogues, 1850–1875: Female Labor and Technological Change," in *Institutions of Reading*, 120–47; and Mary Niles Maack, "Towards a History of Women in Librarianship: A Critical Analysis with Suggestions for Further Research," *Journal of Library History* 17 (Spring 1982): 165–85.
91. Robin D. G. Kelley, *Freedom Dreams: The Black Radical Imagination* (Boston: Beacon, 2002), 154.

92. The term *abundance* has a contested history in the field of archival theory, too. Although a presumption of "documentary abundance" undergirded prevailing postwar archival methods for managing the output of the modern office, some theorists countered that the uneven distribution of such abundance created "gaps in the documentary record." Brien Brothman, "Orders of Value: Probing the Theoretical Terms of Archival Practice," *Archivaria* 32 (Summer 1991): 97 n34; and Helen Willa Samuels, "Who Controls the Past," *American Archivist* 49, no. 2 (Spring 1986): 122. See also Gerald Ham, "Archival Choices: Managing the Historical Record in an Age of Abundance," *American Archivist* 47, no. 1 (Winter 1984): 11–22. Rather than try to resolve this conundrum, I take seriously the thinking of a generation of Black intellectuals who *aspired* to archival abundance.
93. Verne Harris, "The Archival Sliver: Power, Memory, and Archives in South Africa," *Archival Science* 2 (2002): 65.
94. Schomburg, "An Appreciation," in *Phillis Wheatley: Poems and Letters*, ed. Charles F. Heartman (New York: C. F. Heartman, 1915): 7–19.
95. Arthur B. Spingarn, "Collecting a Library of Negro Literature," *Journal of Negro Education* 7, no. 1 (1938): 15; and Derrick R. Spires, "African American Print Culture," in *American Literature in Transition, 1820–1860*, ed. Justine S. Murison (New York: Cambridge University Press, 2022), 222–23.
96. Tiya Miles, *All That She Carried: The Journey of Ashley's Sack, a Black Family Keepsake* (New York: Random House, 2021), 10.
97. Saidiya Hartman, "Venus in Two Acts," *Small Axe* 12, no. 2 (June 2008): 12. Michel-Rolph Trouillot's foundational meditation in *Silencing the Past: Power and the Production of History* (Boston: Beacon, 1995) underlines a robust body of work on the affective and methodological challenges of working within archival silences, including the following: Patricia Saunders, "Defending the Dead, Confronting the Archive: A Conversation with M. NourbeSe Philip," *Small Axe*, no. 26 (June 2008): 63–79; Ula Taylor, "Women in the Documents: Thoughts on Uncovering the Personal, Political, and Professional," *Journal of Women's History* 20, no. 1 (Spring 2008): 187–96; M. NourbeSe Philip, *Zong!* (Middletown, CT: Wesleyan University Press, 2008); Jennifer L. Morgan, "Archives and Histories of Racial Capitalism: An Afterword," *Social Text* 33, no. 4 (2015): 153–61; Simon Gikandi, "Rethinking the Archive of Enslavement," *Early American Literature* 50, no. 1 (2015): 81–102; Marisa J. Fuentes, *Dispossessed Lives: Enslaved Women, Violence, and the Archive* (Philadelphia: University of Pennsylvania Press, 2016); Tonia Sutherland, "Archival Amnesty: In Search of Black American Transitional and Restorative Justice," *Journal of Critical Library and Information Studies* 1, no. 2 (2017): https://doi.org/10.24242/jclis.v1i2.42; and Ashley Farmer, "In Search of the Black Women's History Archive," *Modern American History* 1, no. 2 (February 2018): 289–93.
98. Anjali Arondekar, Ann Cvetkovich, Christina B. Hanhardt, Regina Kunzel, Tavia Nyong'o, Juana María Rodríguez, and Susan Stryker, compiled by Daniel Marshall, Kevin P. Murphy, and Zeb Tortorici, "Queering Archives: A Roundtable Discussion," *Radical History Review* 122 (May 2015): 216.
99. Schomburg, "Negro Digs," 670.
100. Porter to Joseph H. Reason, June 17, 1957, Moorland Foundation Annual Reports, Manuscript Division, MSRC. Anjali Arondekar's work on archival surplus has shaped my rethinking of the terms scholars use to theorize Black archives. Her latest writing on this idea, *Abundance: Sexuality's History* (Durham, NC: Duke University Press, 2023), appeared while this book was in production.
101. Recent work attending to the heterogeneity of twentieth-century Black collecting includes Leah M. Kerr, "Collectors' Contributions to Archiving Early Black Film," *Black Camera* 5, no. 1 (2013): 274–84; Cheryl A. Wall, "On Collectors and Collecting: The Joanna Banks Collection," keynote address at the Black Women Writing Across Genres in the Late 20th Century Symposium, University of Pennsylvania, Philadelphia, PA, February 20, 2020; Melanie Chambliss, Brent Hayes Edwards, and Alexsandra Mitchell, "Archives from the Black Diaspora: A Roundtable Discussion," *African American Review* 54, nos. 1–2 (Spring/Summer 2021): 19–30; and Emily Lutenski, "Arna Bontemps and Black Literary Archives," in *African American Literature in Transition, 1930–1940*, ed. Eve Dunbar

and Ayesha K. Hardison (Cambridge: Cambridge University Press, 2022): 59–85. As Tina Campt notes, much of this work shifts from the "question of absence or presence" to an examination of the critical dynamics between archives and blackness (Campt, *Image Matters: Archive, Photography, and the African Diaspora* [Durham, NC: Duke University Press, 2012], 38).

102. Ann M. Blair, *Too Much to Know: Managing Scholarly Information Before the Modern Age* (New Haven, CT: Yale University Press, 2011).
103. Jacqueline D. Goldsby, "The Chicago Afro-American Analytic Union Catalog: The Meaning of 'Great' Events and the Making of Archives," paper presented at Modern Language Association meeting, Chicago, IL, January 8–11, 2014. In discussing the oscillation between "surfeit and scarcity" in Black Studies, Stephen Best argues that while the recovery imperative of 1970s social history rested on "the fiction of the archive [as] plentitude," the field has, since the 1990s, framed the archive as a site of erasure rather than repair (Best, *None Like Us: Blackness, Belonging, Aesthetic Life* [Durham, NC: Duke University Press, 2018], 84). I aim to understand how these two positions were entwined in early-twentieth-century Black intellectual history.
104. Schomburg, "Negro Digs," 672.
105. Alberto Manguel, *The Library at Night* (New Haven, CT: Yale University Press, 2006), 107. As Lisa Sánchez González argues, Schomburg's trust in the reparative capacity of archives can seem curiously wedded to the very sources that erased Black subjects from written history in the first place. Sánchez González, *Boricua Literature: A Literary History of the Puerto Rican Diaspora* (New York: New York University Press, 2010), 68–69. See also Jarrett Martin Drake, "Blood at the Root," *Journal of Contemporary Archival Studies* 8, article 6 (2021): 16.
106. Laura E. Helton, "Schomburg's Library and the Price of Black History," *African American Review* 54, nos. 1–2 (Spring/Summer 2021): 109–27.
107. Schomburg, "Negro Digs," 672. Evelyn Brooks Higginbotham has argued that the "quest for cultural identity" can superimpose "a 'natural' unity over a plethora of historical, socioeconomic, and ideological differences" (Higginbotham, "African-American Women's History and the Metalanguage of Race," *Signs* 17, no. 2 [Winter 1992]: 270). I am interested in how the practice of collecting lays bare the contested process of seeking that unity.
108. In identifying a core set of principles that define Black archiving, I take a cue from Jacqueline D. Goldsby and Meredith L. McGill, "What Is 'Black' About Black Bibliography?," *Papers of the Bibliographical Society of America* 116, no. 2 (June 2022): 161–89.
109. Schomburg to Locke, January 24, 1916, box 83, folder 31, Locke Papers.
110. L. D. Reddick, "The Miscellaneous Collection," n.d., box 2, folder 3, SCRBC Records; Porter, "The Role of the Negro Collection in Teaching and Research at Howard University," typescript, 1967, box 32, DPW Papers.
111. Eliza Atkins Gleason, *The Southern Negro and the Public Library* (Chicago: University of Chicago Press, 1941), 67.
112. Laura E. Helton, "On Decimals, Catalogs, and Racial Imaginaries of Reading," *PMLA* 134, no. 1 (January 2019): 99–120.
113. For a reflection on more recent iterations of this critical tradition, see Shannon Mattern, "Fugitive Libraries," *Places Journal* (October 2019), https://doi.org/10.22269/191022.
114. I draw on McHenry's formulation of the connection between "sociability and the acquisition of knowledge" (*Forgotten Readers*, 99). I am also indebted to Jeremy Braddock's argument that a collection is a provisional institution that proposes a "hitherto unimagined form of sociability and set of affiliations" in *Collecting as Modernist Practice* (Baltimore, MD: Johns Hopkins University Press, 2012), 3; and to Roger Chartier's argument that print can "transform forms of sociability" in *The Order of Books* (Cambridge, MA: Polity, 1994), 3.
115. Denise Gigante, *Book Madness: A Story of Book Collectors in America* (New Haven, CT: Yale University Press, 2022). The American Jewish Historical Society was founded in 1892; the American-Irish Historical Society and the American Negro Historical Society both began in 1897.

116. Schomburg quoted in Dorothy B. Porter, "Bibliography and Research in Afro-American Scholarship," *Journal of Academic Librarianship* 2, no. 2 (1976): 81.
117. Schomburg, "Negro Digs," 670.
118. Schomburg, "Negro Digs," 672.
119. Achille Mbembe, "The Power of the Archive and Its Limits," in *Refiguring the Archive*, ed. Carolyn Hamilton, Verne Harris, Michele Pickover, Graeme Reid, Razia Saleh, and Jane Taylor (Dordrecht, The Netherlands: Kluwer Academic, 2002), 22; and W. E. B. Du Bois, "A Portrait of Carter G. Woodson," *Masses and Mainstream* 3, no. 6 (June 1950): 20.
120. L. S. Alexander Gumby, [untitled notes on making scrapbooks], n.d., in "Mss of L.S.A. Gumby," Series I.1, Gumby Collection.
121. José Esteban Muñoz, "Ephemera as Evidence: Introductory Notes to Queer Acts," *Women and Performance: A Journal of Feminist Theory* 8, no. 2 (1996): 6.
122. Elise Johnson McDougald, "The Task of Negro Womanhood," in *The New Negro*, ed. Alain Locke (1925; repr., New York: Simon and Schuster, 1992), 376; and "Librarians Increasing," *New York Amsterdam News*, July 17, 1937.
123. Jennifer C. Nash, "Black Feminine Enigmas, or Notes on the Politics of Black Feminist Theory," *Signs: Journal of Women in Culture and Society* 45, no. 3 (2020): 521.
124. Dorothy Porter, [untitled speech beginning "The M.F. the library of Negro life"], ca. 1950, box 33, DPW Papers.
125. Patricia J. Williams, "Gathering the Ghosts," *The A-Line* 1, nos. 3–4 (2018): https://alinejournal.com/vol-1-no-3-4/gathering-the-ghosts/.
126. Adolph J. Slaughter, "Historian Who Never Wrote," *Chicago Daily Defender*, August 29, 1960.
127. Cheryl Clarke, remarks at Black Women Writing Across Genres in the Late 20th Century Symposium, University of Pennsylvania, Philadelphia, PA, February 21, 2020.
128. Stefano Harney and Fred Moten, *The Undercommons: Fugitive Planning and Black Study* (Wivenhoe, UK: Minor Compositions, 2013), 110–11.
129. L. D. Reddick, "Why I Left the North," typescript, ca. 1950, Lawrence D. Reddick Papers, MARB, SCRBC. Note that at the time of research, this collection was unprocessed and did not have permanent box/folder locations. On the tension between federal documentary projects and Black recordkeeping, see Michael Hanchard, "Black Memory versus State Memory," *Small Axe* 12, no. 2 (June 2008): 45–62.
130. Schomburg, "Negro Digs," 270.
131. Porter quoted in Elizabeth Stevens, "Howard Shows Nation's Finest Negro Works," *Washington Post*, December 25, 1965.
132. Van Vechten, "J. W. Johnson Collection," 222; Dorothy B. Porter, "Repositories of Materials on Negro Life and History: An Endless Quest" typescript speech, ca. 1965, box 34, DPW Papers.
133. Ernest Kaiser, "Library Holdings on Afro-Americans," in Josey and Shockley, *Handbook of Black Librarianship*, 230; and Arthur L Smith, "Review of the Johnson Reprint Series," *Journal of Black Studies* 1, no. 3 (March 1971): 374–76. Microfilm editions of the Tuskegee, Hampton, and Schomburg clipping files were published in the 1970s and 1980s.

1. THINKING BLACK, COLLECTING BLACK: SCHOMBURG'S DESIDERATA AND THE RADICAL WORLD OF BLACK BIBLIOPHILES

1. John E. Bruce to Alain Locke, June 5, 1912, box 98, folder 18, Alain LeRoy Locke Papers (hereafter Locke Papers), Manuscript Division, MSRC. I refer to Schomburg here as "Arthur" because he corresponded and published under that name (rather than "Arturo," as he was baptized in Puerto Rico) during the period discussed in this chapter.

2. Arthur A. Schomburg to John W. Cromwell, Labor Day 1912, box 1, folder 14, Cromwell Family Papers (hereafter Cromwell Papers), Manuscript Division, MSRC.
3. Schomburg to Locke, August 18, 1912, box 83, folder 31, Locke Papers.
4. "Schomburg Library Is Sold," *Pittsburgh Courier*, May 29, 1926.
5. Historical Records Survey of the Works Progress Administration of New York City, *Calendar of Manuscripts in the Schomburg Collection of Negro Literature* [1942] (New York: Andronicus, 1970).
6. Schomburg to Locke, August 18, 1912.
7. "Loyal Sons of Africa," *Cleveland Gazette*, October 25, 1913. On Schomburg's cultural migrations, see Jesse Hoffnung-Garskof, "The Migrations of Arturo Schomburg: On Being Antillano, Negro, and Puerto Rican in New York 1891–1938," *Journal of American Ethnic History* 21, no. 1 (Fall 2001): 3–49. On his diasporic biography, see Elinor Des Verney Sinnette, *Arthur Alfonso Schomburg; Black Bibliophile and Collector* (Detroit, MI: NYPL and Wayne State University Press, 1989); Winston James, *Holding Aloft the Banner of Ethiopia: Caribbean Radicalism in Early Twentieth-Century America* (London: Verso, 1998); Lisa Sánchez González, *Boricua Literature: A Literary History of the Puerto Rican Diaspora* (New York: New York University Press, 2010), 56–69; and Vanessa K. Valdés, *Diasporic Blackness: The Life and Times of Arturo Alfonso Schomburg* (Albany: SUNY Press, 2018). On Schomburg as an object of cross-disciplinary study, see Earl Lewis, "'To Turn as on a Pivot': Writing African Americans Into a History of Overlapping Diasporas," *American Historical Review* 100, no. 3 (June 1995): 765–87; José I. Fusté, "Schomburg's Blackness of a Different Matter: A Historiography of Refusal," *Small Axe* 24, no. 1 (March 2020): 120–31; and Laura E. Helton and Rafia Zafar, "Arturo Alfonso Schomburg in the Twenty-First Century: An Introduction," *African American Review* 54, nos. 1–2 (Spring/Summer 2021): 1–18.
8. Schomburg had at least six addresses in New York before 1912. From roughly 1897 to 1900, he lived in San Juan Hill. By 1902, he moved to Yorkville, and in 1906, he lived on the Upper West Side. By 1910, he had moved to Harlem. See Index to Birth Certificates, 1866–1909, certificate numbers 8690 and 38145, Ancestry.com. See John Hay to Schomburg, May 17, 1900, box 3, folder 20; Veronica Nickelson to Schomburg, December [4], 1911, box 5, folder 36; and F. C. Wieder to Schomburg, February 23, 1912, box 7, folder 57—all in Arthur A. Schomburg Papers (hereafter AAS Papers), Manuscripts, Archives and Rare Books Division (hereafter MARB), SCRBC. See also Sinnette, *Arthur Alfonso Schomburg*, 35.
9. On Ramon Rothschild, see "Notas," *La Correspondencia de Puerto-Rico* (San Juan), March 17, 1891; U.S. Bureau of the Census, Thirteenth Census of the United States: 1910—Population for Manhattan, New York, Ancestry.com; and Prince Hall Lodge No. 38, Free and Accepted Masons of the State of New York, "Past Masters, Our Pillars of Wisdom," http://princehall38ny.org/AboutUs.aspx#History.
10. Although various sources give 1914 as the year of his marriage to Elizabeth Green, their son Fernando was born on August 15, 1912, making the marriage likely to have taken place that year. See Fernando Alphonso Schomburg, Social Security Applications and Claims Index, 1936–2007, Ancestry.com. Elizabeth Green was Schomburg's third wife; he had been twice widowed.
11. New York State Census for 1915, Enumeration of the Inhabitants of the State of New York, Ancestry.com.
12. In his 1926 passport, Schomburg describes himself as a "clerk" by occupation. See Arthur Alfonso Schomburg Photograph Collection, box 1, Photographs and Prints Division, SCRBC.
13. Schomburg to Cromwell, Labor Day, 1912.
14. Schomburg to Locke, January 1, 1917, box 38, folder 31, Locke Papers; and Schomburg to Cromwell, Labor Day, 1912.
15. [Jack Thorne], "Arthur A. Schomburg," *Pioneer Press* (Martinsburg, WV), September 14, 1912.
16. "Library of Arthur A. Schomburg. Collection of books on the Negro race, slavery, emancipation, West Indies, South America, and Africa," n.d., box 13, folder 1, Robert Park Papers, FUSCA; and Arthur A. Schomburg, "Racial Integrity: A Plea for the Establishment of a Chair of Negro History

in Our Schools and Colleges, etc.," Negro Society for Historical Research Occasional Paper No. 3 (n.p.: August Valentine Bernier, 1913), 12.

17. "The Negro Society for Historical Research," *African Times and Orient Review*, Christmas Annual, 1912.

18. Negro Library Association, Program for Musical and Literary Evening, June 21, 1918, box 6, reel 3, John Edward Bruce Papers (hereafter Bruce Papers), MARB, SCRBC; and "Grand Concert for Negro Library," *New York Age*, May 31, 1917.

19. He proposed opening a "book agency" and stamped his stationary "Arthur A. Schomburg: Dealer in Rare and Old Books" (Schomburg to Cromwell, Labor Day, 1912).

20. Schomburg to Cromwell, June 18, 1912, box 1, folder 13, Cromwell Papers; and Schomburg to Cromwell, Labor Day, 1912.

21. An irony of Schomburg's story is that neither he nor the NYPL preserved a record of what his collection contained when purchased in 1926. In 2017, I came across an inventory of Schomburg's early library in the papers of sociologist Robert E. Park at Fisk University ("Library of Arthur A. Schomburg"). This list provides the most complete picture of his collection in the years before its sale. With this list and other tools, staff at SCRBC recataloged titles traceable to Schomburg's original collection. See Alice Adamczyk, Laura E. Helton, Miranda Mims, and Matthew J. Murphy, "Library Archaeology: Reconstructing a Catalog of the Arthur A. Schomburg Book and Pamphlet Collection," *African American Review* 54, nos. 1–2 (Spring/Summer 2021): 91–107; and NYPL, "Arturo (Arthur) Schomburg Research Guide: Schomburg's Library," https://libguides.nypl.org/arturoschomburg/library. A partial copy of this same list is preserved on the verso of manuscripts in the Bruce Papers.

22. "Library of Arthur A. Schomburg" adds texture to Hoffnung-Garskof's argument that the collection reflects his "preoccupations, his migrations, and his relationships" (Hoffnung-Garskof, "Migrations," 8). The list confirms that Schomburg had collecting priorities not well documented in his published writings. For example, he devoted a large portion of his library to works on Africa, a place he never visited and about which he wrote little. He also collected a significant number of works by Black women, although most of his writings depicted heroic male figures.

23. Walter Benjamin, "Unpacking My Library," in *Illuminations*, ed. Hannah Arendt, trans. Harry Zohn (New York: Schocken, 1968), 67.

24. *Figuras y Figuritas* is listed in "Library of Arthur A. Schomburg" among Schomburg's early holdings; for inscription information, see https://legacycatalog.nypl.org/record=b11721021~S67. All citations of inscriptions in Schomburg's books are thanks to the work of the "Home to Harlem" initiative at SCRBC. On the significance of *Figuras* as a work that contested the "impossibility of blackness as official history, memory, and archive," see Nancy Raquel Mirabal, *Suspect Freedoms: The Racial and Sexual Politics of Cubanidad in New York, 1823–1957* (New York: New York University Press, 2017), 136; and Susan D. Greenbaum, *More Than Black: Afro-Cubans in Tampa* (Gainesville: University Press of Florida, 2002), 70.

25. Schomburg to Cromwell, October 22, 1912, box 1, folder 14, Cromwell Papers.

26. Father John E. Burke appointed Schomburg "Librarian" of the lyceum at Saint Benedict the Moor parish in San Juan Hill (Thomas M. O'Keefe to Schomburg, May 14, 1918, box 5, folder 37, and Schomburg to Andrew C. Pedro, April 4, 1931, box 8, folder 16—both in AAS Papers). On Schomburg's organizational affiliations, see Sinnette, *Arthur Alfonso Schomburg*; Valdés, *Diasporic Blackness*; and Jeffrey B. Perry, *Hubert Harrison: The Voice of Harlem Radicalism, 1883–1918* (New York: Columbia University Press, 2009), 70–72.

27. Schomburg to Cromwell, July 5, 1912, box 1, folder 13, Cromwell Papers.

28. William C. Bolivar to Schomburg, n.d., box 1, folder 5, AAS Papers. Schomburg's friends belonged to the concentric circles of Black intellectuals Kevin K. Gaines has identified as nationalist, pan-African, and radical West Indian (Gaines, *Uplifting the Race: Black Leadership, Politics, and*

Culture in the Twentieth Century [Chapel Hill: University of North Carolina Press, 1996], 103–4, 239). They also belonged to a tradition of the "*working* man of letters" (Denise Gigante, *Book Madness: A Story of Book Collectors in America* [New Haven, CT: Yale University Press, 2022], 2).

29. Schomburg to Cromwell, February 23, 1915, box 1, folder 30, Cromwell Papers.
30. Arthur A. Schomburg, "The Negro Digs Up His Past," *Survey Graphic* 6, no. 6 (March 1925): 670–71.
31. Schomburg quoted in Dorothy B. Porter, "Bibliography and Research in Afro-American Scholarship," *Journal of Academic Librarianship* 2, no. 2 (1976): 81.
32. Andrew Ross, "Production," *Social Text* 27, no. 3 (2009): 199.
33. On the terms archive and collection, see Gabrielle Dean, "Disciplinarity and Disorder," *Archive Journal* 1, no. 1 (Spring 2011): http://www.archivejournal.net/issue/1/archives-remixed/.
34. Achille Mbembe, "The Power of the Archive and Its Limits," in *Refiguring the Archive*, ed. Carolyn Hamilton, Verne Harris, Michele Pickover, Graeme Reid, Razia Saleh, and Jane Taylor (Dordrecht, The Netherlands: Kluwer Academic, 2002): 19–26. (The phrase "instituting imaginary" is earlier used by philosopher Cornelius Castoriadis, but I draw here on Mbembe's use in an archival context.) On collecting as "a form of fiction through which imaginative constructions can be expressed," see Susan M. Pearce, *On Collecting: An Investigation Into Collecting in the European Tradition* (London: Routledge, 1999), 32.
35. Schomburg quoted in Porter, "Bibliography and Research," 81.
36. Advertisement for José González Font, Imprenta, Libreria y Encuaderna, *Boletin Mercantil de Puerto Rico*, May 28, 1884; and *Almanaque de Las Damas para 1885* (Puerto-Rico: Imprenta y Libreria de Jose González Font, 1884), http://biblioteca.galiciana.gal/pt/consulta/registro.cmd?id=7637. The *Almanaque* included writings by Salvador Brau, Lola Rodríguez de Tío, Luis Muñoz Rivera, Manuel Fernández Juncos, and José Gualberto Padilla. A copy of Font's *Escritos sobre Puerto Rico* was in Schomburg's library as of 1914 ("Library of Arthur A. Schomburg").
37. Schomburg to John H. Clarke, May 1, 1936, box 8, folder 3, AAS Papers; and Logogrifo Numérico [attributed to "Schumburg"], *La Correspondencia de Puerto Rico*, November 18, 1891. Schomburg often participated in *entretenimientos* with *El Club Triunvirato*, formed with typesetter Abelardo Prieto and Ramon Rothschild (who later joined him in New York). At least two of Schomburg's puzzles were printed in June 1891 after he left the island—a time lag explained by the fact, as the newspaper stated, that not all submissions received immediate publication ("Attención Aquí!!," *La correspondencia de Puerto Rico*, June 22, 1891).
38. Floyd J. Calvin, "Race Colleges Need Chair in Negro History," *Pittsburgh Courier*, March 5, 1927.
39. Alexander Joel Eastman, "Binding Consumption: Cuba's Early Black Press and the Struggle for Legitimacy, 1879–1886," *Siglo Diecinueve* 21 (2015): 29; and David Sartorius, *Ever Faithful: Race, Loyalty, and the Ends of Empire in Spanish Cuba* (Durham, NC: Duke University Press, 2014), 54–55, 80–82. At some point, Schomburg began to keep a log of his reading; in a 1912 letter to Locke, he mentions consulting "my note book" to confirm he had read a particular book in June 1903 (Schomburg to Locke, August 18, 1912).
40. Schomburg to Cromwell, December 18, 1912, box 1, folder 14, Cromwell Papers.
41. Quoted in Sinnette, *Arthur Alfonso Schomburg*, 42.
42. Hoffnung-Garskof, "Migrations," 7. His mother either emigrated with him or joined him soon after (Death notice for María Josefa, "madre del puertoriqueño Arturo A. Schumburg," *La correspondencia de Puerto Rico*, September 22, 1895). Rothschild is listed as a member of *Las Dos Antillas*, a New York–based club, in Las Dos Antillas Political Club minutes, MARB, SCRBC. On this period in Schomburg's life, see Jesse Hoffnung-Garskof, *Racial Migrations: New York City and the Revolutionary Politics of the Spanish Caribbean* (Princeton, NJ: Princeton University Press, 2019), 270–71.
43. Catalog record for José Pérez Moris, *Historia de la Insurrección de Lares* (Barcelona, Spain: Establecimiento Tipográfico de Narciso Ramirez y C., 1872), https://legacycatalog.nypl.org/record=b11732982~S67.

44. Catalog record for copy 2 of Rafael Serra, *Para Blancos y Negros: Ensayos Políticos, Sociales y Económicos* (Havana, Cuba: Imprenta El Score, 1907), https://legacycatalog.nypl.org/record=b11733850~S67. The inscription in his copy of Pachín reads, in part: "El autor y amigo querida hermana ha recitado la mayor parte durante su presencia en N.Y. y explicá los motivos a que dieron lugar, és poeta de corazón . . . buen amigo mío es, como pocos. Arturo" ["The author and friend dear sister recited most [of these poems] during his presence in New York and explained the motivations behind each one, he is a poet of the heart . . . a good friend of mine like few others. Arturo"]. Pachín wrote under the name F. Gonzalo Marín and was in New York as of January 1892; see "Fragmentos," *La democracia*, January 23, 1892. On Schomburg's admiration of Marín, see Hoffnung-Garskof, "Migrations," 18–19.
45. These titles are documented in "Library of Arthur A. Schomburg," which means he acquired them before 1914. Other titles on his list include *Poetas de Color*, published in Havana in 1887, and *Escritos sobre Puerto Rico* by José González Font. "Schomburg's Rare Negro Library Now at 135th Street Branch" (unidentified newspaper, January 19, 1927, SCCF 004,444) paraphrases Schomburg as saying his "first books collected were those of Negro authors of Spanish descent."
46. Harry A. Williamson, "Prince Hall Masons in the State of New York," *New York Age*, December 12, 1936. By 1894, Schomburg inscribed masonic symbols next to his name in the minutes of *Las Dos Antillas*. See Haydeé E. Reichard-De Cardona, *Arturo Alfonso Schomburg: Racial Identity and Afro-Caribbean Cultural Formation* (Aguadilla, Puerto Rico: printed by the author, 2023), 36.
47. Williamson, "Prince Hall Masons." Schomburg had possession of the lodge's "original ledger" and served as secretary because of his "knowledge of the Spanish language" (Schomburg to Harry Williamson, n.d., box 7, folder 57, AAS Papers). On Schomburg and masonry, see Jossianna Arroyo, "Technologies: Transculturations of Race, Gender, and Ethnicity in Arturo A. Schomburg's Masonic Writings," *CENTRO Journal* 17, no. 1 (2005): 5–25.
48. "The Masonic Craft," *New York Age*, December 26, 1907; and "Williamson—Alone and Supreme," *New York Age*, February 22, 1936.
49. Ralph L. Crowder, *John Edward Bruce: Politician, Journalist, and Self-Trained Historian of the African Diaspora* (New York: New York University Press, 2004), 95–98, 113, 115, 123, 127. Crowder states that Bruce was a Mason by 1897 (5), but it is not clear when Bruce joined Schomburg's lodge. They were certainly acquainted before 1905, when Schomburg hosted a testimonial dinner for Bruce on behalf of the Men's Sunday Club. Many of the club members, including Mojola Agbebi, F. J. Moultrie, and York Russell, became corresponding members of NSHR. See "Waller Memorial Exercises," *New York Age*, November 14, 1907.
50. Excerpt from "National Council of the Colored People . . . 1853," in *Black Nationalism in America*, ed. John H. Bracey, August Meier, and Elliott Rudwick (Indianapolis, IN: Bobbs-Merrill, 1970), 64–65. On Bolivar and Cromwell's ties to the conventions movement, see "Proceedings of the Civil Rights Mass-Meeting held at Lincoln Hall," October 22, 1883, coloredconventions.org; and William C. Welburn, "To 'Keep the Past in Lively Memory': William Carl Bolivar's Efforts to Preserve African American Cultural Heritage," *Libraries and the Cultural Record* 42, no. 2 (2007): 171–72.
51. Schomburg to Cromwell, n.d., box 2, folder 32, Cromwell Papers.
52. Bolivar quoted in Tony Martin, "Race Men, Bibliophiles, and Historians: The World of Robert M. Adger and the Negro Historical Society of Philadelphia," in *Rare Afro-Americana: A Reconstruction of the Adger Library*, ed. Wendy Ball and Tony Martin (Boston: Hall, 1981), 21.
53. "A Contribution from Arthur A. Schomburg," *New York Age*, January 19, 1935.
54. Schomburg to Bruce, November 18, [year unknown], box 7, reel 3, Bruce Papers. By "42 Broadway" Schomburg was referring to the bookstore A. R. Womrath, Inc. See "Books Wanted," *Publishers' Weekly*, December 9, 1922.
55. Schomburg to Bruce, April 22, 1913, box 2, reel 1, Bruce Papers. On Martin, see Irma Watkins-Owens, *Blood Relations: Caribbean Immigrants and the Harlem Community, 1900–1930* (Bloomington: Indiana University Press, 1996), 59–60. Martin's collection is now housed at North Carolina Central

University, purchased it in 1950. See "Special Collections," https://www.nccu.edu/james-e-shepard-memorial-library/special-collections#martin-collection.

56. "People Talked About," *Negro World*, March 25, 1922 (likely written by Bruce or William Ferris).
57. Many bibliophiles used the Abbé Grégoire's 1808 *De La Littérature des Nègres* to identify early works by Black authors, but there was no up-to-date checklist at the scale of their ambitions. See Daniel Murray, "Bibliographia-Africania," *Voice of the Negro* 4, no. 5 (May 1904): 186–91.
58. Schomburg to Cromwell, June 25, 1913, box 1, folder 15, Cromwell Papers.
59. Schomburg to Cromwell, August 6, 1913, box 1, folder 16, Cromwell Papers; and Derrick R. Spires, "African American Print Culture," in *American Literature in Transition, 1820–1860*, ed. Justine S. Murison (New York: Cambridge University Press, 2022), 222–23.
60. Bolivar to Schomburg, August 22, 1913, box 1, folder 5, AAS Papers.
61. Bolivar to Schomburg, July 14, 1914, box 1, folder 5, AAS Papers.
62. Schomburg to Locke, October 15, 1912, box 83, folder 31, Locke Papers.
63. Schomburg to Cromwell, n.d., box 2, folder 32, and August 26, 1913, box 1, folder 16—both in Cromwell Papers.
64. Thomas C. Battle, "Dorothy Porter Wesley," in *Dictionary of American Library Biography*, second supplement, ed. Donald G. Davis (Westport, CT: Libraries Unlimited, 2003), 220.
65. "Colored Collectors," *Times* (Philadelphia), June 8, 1890, box 3, folder 9, Thomas and William Henry Dorsey Collection, Manuscript Division, MSRC.
66. Schomburg to Locke, September 14, 1914, box 83, folder 31, Locke Papers.
67. Schomburg to Locke, August 18, 1912.
68. Anderson Galleries, Inc., *Catalog of Sales, 1916: Jan-Feb* (New York: Anderson Galleries, 1916).
69. Schomburg to Locke, January 24, 1916, box 83, folder 31, Locke Papers.
70. On the collection of Samuel Munson, who outbid Schomburg for Banneker's almanacs, see David Whitesell, Lauren B. Hewes, and Thomas Knoles, *In Pursuit of a Vision: Two Centuries of Collecting at the American Antiquarian Society* (Worcester, MA: American Antiquarian Society, 2012), 111–12; and John Allan Holden, *A List of Private Book Collectors in the United States and Canada* (New York: Bowker, 1922), 26.
71. Schomburg to Cromwell, June 29, 1916, box 1, folder 19, Cromwell Papers. Estimate of Schomburg's salary based on George Edmund Haynes, *The Negro at Work in New York City* (New York: Columbia University Press, 1912).
72. Schomburg to Cromwell, May 23, 1912, box 1, folder 13, Cromwell Papers.
73. *American Book-Prices Current: A Record of Books, Manuscripts, and Autographs Sold at Auction in New York, Boston, and Philadelphia, From September 1, 1910, to September 1, 1911, with the Prices Realized*, vol. 17 (New York: Dodd and Livingston, 1911), 740; and *American Book-Prices Current: A Record of Books, Manuscripts and Autographs Sold at Auction in New York, Boston, and Philadelphia, From September, 1919, to July, 1920*, vol. 26 (New York: Dutton, 1920), 924.
74. Anderson Galleries, Inc., *Catalog of Sales*, 47–48. In a 1931 letter about the process of determining the market value of a pamphlet or book, Schomburg notes that "books sold under five dollars are not listed" (Schomburg to Monroe N. Work, November 13, 1931, box 9, folder 23, AAS Papers).
75. The absence of information about Black-authored or Black-themed texts from such guides may be why these bibliophiles established in 1916 a Negro Book Collectors Exchange, a short-lived cooperative effort to pool bibliographic information about their holdings and those of other "collectors throughout the United States, Africa, the West Indies, South America and Europe" (Sinnette, *Arthur Alfonso Schomburg*, 73–74).
76. "Pullman Porter Now a Bookseller," *New York Evening Post*, October 12, 1921.
77. *American Book-Prices Current: A Record of Books, Manuscripts and Autographs Sold at Auction in New York, Boston, and Philadelphia, From September, 1917, to August, 1918*, vol. 24 (New York: Dutton, 1918); and Original Warrant of the Commonwealth of Virginia for the arrest of Douglass,

signed by Gov. Wise, Nov., 1859, with seal, in *American Book-Prices Current, A Record of Books, Manuscripts and Autographs Sold at Auction in New York, Boston, and Philadelphia, from September 1, 1914, to September 1, 1915, with Prices Realized*, vol. 21 (New York: Dodd, 1915), 767.

78. Antoinette Burton, "Archive Fever, Archive Stories," in *Archive Stories: Facts, Fictions, and the Writing of History*, ed. Burton (Durham, NC: Duke University Press, 2005), 10.
79. Anderson Galleries, Inc., *Catalog of Sales*; and *American Book-Prices Current: A Record of Books, Manuscripts and Autographs Sold at Auction in New York, Boston, and Philadelphia, From September 1, 1915, to September 1, 1916, With the Prices Realized*, vol. 22 (New York: Dodd, 1916).
80. Schomburg to Locke, January 27, 1916, box 83, folder 31, Locke Papers.
81. James M. Lindgren, "Joseph Bryan (1845–1908)," *Dictionary of Virginia Biography*, rev. ed. (Richmond: Library of Virginia, 2018): https://www.lva.virginia.gov/public/dvb/bio.php?b=Bryan_Joseph_1845-1908. Although the Bryan statue in Richmond was removed in 2020, there remains a "Joseph Bryan Reading Room" at the former Virginia Historical Society, where one can read another copy of Godwyn's 1680 text.
82. "The Bryan Family," *Encyclopedia of Virginia Biography*, vol. 4, ed. Lyon Gardiner Tyler (New York: Lewis Historical Publishing, 1915), 64; and Schomburg to Cromwell, July 5, 1912. On the Atlantic literary contexts in which seventeenth- and eighteenth-century works on slavery circulated, and on the ties of Anglo-American bibliophiles to the slave trade, see Sean D. Moore, *Slavery and the Making of Early American Libraries* (Oxford: Oxford University Press, 2019). Schomburg's list of historical heroes resembled Du Bois's idolization of male revolutionary figures as the "true" leaders of the race (Hazel V. Carby, *Race Men* [Cambridge, MA: Harvard University Press, 1998], 40).
83. Godwyn's argument in favor of educating enslaved Africans and admitting them to church membership made him, in Douglass's eyes, an "ethical wonder" and "the starting point" of antislavery (Frederick Douglass, "The United States Cannot Remain Half-Slave and Half-Free," April 16, 1883, https://teachingamericanhistory.org/library/document/the-united-states-cannot-remain-half-slave-and-half-free/).
84. Washington quoted in Henry Louis Gates Jr., "Harlem on Our Minds," *Critical Inquiry* 24, no. 1 (Autumn 1997): 3.
85. Works on the slave trade and scrapbooks on "Negro Problems" are documented in "Library of Arthur A. Schomburg." By 1916, Schomburg had collected fifty slave narratives. See Schomburg to Locke, December 31, 1916, box 83, folder 31, Locke Papers.
86. Laura E. Helton, "On Decimals, Catalogs, and Racial Imaginaries of Reading," *PMLA* 134, no. 1 (2019): 99–120.
87. Charles F. Heartman to Schomburg, [early November] 1935, box 8, folder 8, AAS Papers. Although books bound in human skin were not uncommon, Heartman's attempt to sell Wheatley's text in "negro skin" represents the "ghost values" of Black bodies commodified after death (Daina Ramey Berry, *The Price for Their Pound of Flesh: The Value of the Enslaved, from Womb to Grave, in the Building of a Nation* [New York: Beacon, 2017], 154).
88. Ann Laura Stoler, *Along the Archival Grain: Epistemic Anxieties and Colonial Common Sense* (Princeton, NJ: Princeton University Press, 2010), 35. A concept central to the book trade, rarity is measured by a combination of age, edition, size of print run, quality of binding, and authorial fame. In Black print culture, rarity is also the product of anti-blackness, because restrictions on literacy made Black writing relatively uncommon and some texts, such as David Walker's *Appeal*, were systematically destroyed.
89. Schomburg to Cromwell, January 18, 1913, box 1, folder 13, Cromwell Papers.
90. Schomburg to Cromwell, August 19, 1913, box 1, folder 16, Cromwell Papers. That framing in the future tense speaks to the nature of archives as "aspiration rather than a recollection" (Arjun Appadurai, "Archive and Aspiration," in *Information Is Alive: Art and Theory on Archiving and Retrieving Data*, ed. Joke Brouwer, Arjen Mulder, and Susan Charlton [Rotterdam: NAi, 2003], 16).

91. Alain Locke, "Arthur Schomburg: Race Patriot and Scholar," ca. 1939, box 1, folder 46, Arthur A. Schomburg Papers Additions (hereafter AAS Additions), MARB, SCRBC.
92. Nicholas Basbanes, *A Gentle Madness: Bibliophiles, Bibliomanes, and the Eternal Passion for Books* (New York: Holt, 1995), 37.
93. Schomburg to Cromwell, April 22, 1912, box 1, folder 13, Cromwell Papers.
94. Schomburg to Cromwell, August 11, 1913, box 1, folder 16, Cromwell Papers.
95. Schomburg to Cromwell, April 22, 1912.
96. Schomburg to Cromwell, August 19, 1913. Schomburg duplicated his catalog but did not publish it. Although only one complete copy has been located, there is evidence Schomburg sent versions to Cromwell, Locke, Bruce, Bolivar, and Monroe Work. See Schomburg to Locke, January 27, 1916; Bolivar to Schomburg, October 6, 1913, box 1, folder 5, AAS Papers; and Work to Schomburg, October 2, 1923, box 1, folder 35, AAS Additions.
97. Schomburg to Cromwell, August 11, 1913.
98. Bolivar to Schomburg, June 6, 1913, box 1, folder 5, AAS Papers.
99. "Library of Arthur A. Schomburg"; and *Library of William C. Bolivar* (Philadelphia: Watson, 1914) in Betty Kaplan Gubert, comp. *Early Black Bibliographies, 1863–1918* (New York: Garland, 1982), 297–328. Bolivar's catalog was prepared by his friends (including Schomburg) for his seventieth birthday; 250 copied were printed. See item description in Cowan's Auctions, *The Road West: The Steve Turner Collection of African Americana, Part I, February 20, 2020* (Chicago: Hindman, 2020), 143. A partial, handwritten list of ninety titles from Bolivar's holdings can be found in box 1, folder 4, AAS Additions.
100. Bolivar to Schomburg, August 22, 1913. Schomburg acquired Mungo Park between 1914 and 1926. See catalog record: https://legacycatalog.nypl.org/record=b19543677~S67
101. Bolivar to Schomburg, September 20, 1914, box 1, folder 5, AAS Papers.
102. Schomburg to Cromwell, July 2, 1916, box 1, folder 17, Cromwell Papers; and Bolivar to Schomburg, May 6, 1914, box 1, folder 5, AAS Papers.
103. I draw here on Brent Hayes Edwards, *The Practice of Diaspora: Literature, Translation, and the Rise of Black Internationalism* (Cambridge, MA: Harvard University Press, 2003), 13.
104. Bolivar to Schomburg, June 18, 1914.
105. Edmund Gibson, "The Life of Mr. Camden," *Camden's Britannia, Newly Translated Into English: With Large Additions and Improvements* (London: Collins, 1695), n.p. Early English Books Online Text Creation Partnership, 2011, http://name.umdl.umich.edu/B18452.0001.001; and Thomas Southey, *Chronological History of the West Indies*, vol. 1 (London: Longman, Rees, Orme, Brown, and Green, 1827). Thomas Southey's book is listed in "Library of Arthur A. Schomburg."
106. Southey, *Chronological History*, [preface n.p.].
107. On how Schomburg's collecting project represented "racial integrity" across difference, see Adalaine Holton, "Decolonizing History: Arthur Schomburg's Afrodiasporic Archive," *Journal of African American History* 92, no. 2 (Spring 2007): 233; and Lorgia García Peña, *Translating Blackness: Latinx Colonialities in Global Perspective* (Durham: Duke University Press, 2022), 88.
108. On bibliographies in Black intellectual practice, see Elizabeth McHenry, *To Make Negro Literature: Writing, Literary Practice, and African American Authorship* (Durham, NC: Duke University Press, 2021), 80; and Laura. E. Helton, "Black Bibliographers and the Category of Negro Authorship," in *African American Literature in Transition, 1900–1910*, ed. Shirley Moody-Turner (Cambridge: Cambridge University Press, 2021): 23–47. On lists as governed by the "principle of expandability," see Robert E. Belknap, *The List: The Uses and Pleasures of Cataloguing* (New Haven, CT: Yale University Press, 2004), 31.
109. The copy of Bolivar's catalog at Cornell University contains a typed slip "120 Titles To Be Added" as well as inked additions (https://hdl.handle.net/2027/coo.31924032838231).
110. "A Unique Negro," *Negro World*, September 3, 1921. According to a note in box 1, folder 37, AAS Additions, Hubert H. Harrison is the likely author of this article.

111. Bolivar to Schomburg, June 18, 1914. Julia F. Jones, a descendant of Absalom Jones, was a teacher in Philadelphia, as documented in Fanny Jackson-Coppin, *Reminiscences of School Life, and Hints on Teaching* (Philadelphia: A. M. E. Book Concern, 1913), 171.
112. See catalog records for Ali and Fulton: https://legacycatalog.nypl.org/record=b11722461~S1 and https://legacycatalog.nypl.org/record=b11747384~S67.
113. See catalog record for Clarke: https://legacycatalog.nypl.org/record=b11793257~S67. On Clarke, see Zita Nunes, *Cannibal Democracy: Race and Representation in the Literature of the Americas* (Minneapolis: University of Minnesota Press, 2008), xiii-xiv.
114. "Schomburg Should Shine," *Union* (Cincinnati), June 11, 1931; and "Plea for Negro History Alaine [sic] Le Roy Locke Addresses Negro Society for Historical Research," *Savannah Tribune*, January 13, 1912.
115. Schomburg to Cromwell, May 3, 1912, box 1, folder 13, Cromwell Papers (emphasis added). On Schomburg's investments in exhibition and display, see Frances Négron-Muntaner, "'Here Is the Evidence': Arturo Alfonso Schomburg's Black Countervisuality," *African American Review* 54, nos. 1–2 (Spring/Summer 2021): 49–71.
116. John E. Bruce, "Jan Curry's Work in German Army," *Indianapolis Recorder*, November 4, 1916; and "The Old Denmark Vesey Insurrection," *Indianapolis Recorder*, October 30, 1915.
117. Bruce to Locke, December 26, 1914, box 17, folder 40, Locke Papers.
118. Editorial, *Opportunity* 4, no. 42 (June 1926): 174–75.
119. Bruce to Locke, February 8, 1912, box 98, folder 18, Locke Papers; and Richard A. Ford, ed., *Washington Law Reporter*, vol. 31 (Washington, DC: Law Reporter, 1903), 351. On Bruce's friendship with Crummell, see Wilson Jeremiah Moses, *The Golden Age of Black Nationalism, 1850–1925* (New York: Oxford University Press, 1988), 76.
120. Bruce to Locke, December 26, 1914.
121. Bruce to Locke, December 26, 1914; and "Active Work of Society for Historical Research," *Indianapolis Recorder*, July 31, 1915.
122. Schomburg to Cromwell, n.d.; Bruce to Locke, April 27, 1914, box 98, folder 20, Locke Papers; and "Noted Visitor at Society for Historical Research," *Oakland Sunshine*, August 28, 1915.
123. "The Negro Society for Historical Research"; Rose Henderson, "The Schomburg Collection of Negro History and Literature," *Southern Workman* 63, no. 11 (November 1934): 329; Schomburg to Cromwell, October 22, 1912; and Bruce to Locke, May 4, 1915, box 17, folder 40, Locke Papers. Walter B. Hayson's nephew, Maxwell, spoke at an early NSHR meeting (listed as "Prof. Hayson"). It is not clear if he played a role in the gift of materials by his aunt, Julia Hayson. After coming into possession of the Crummell sermons, Schomburg gifted one to Cromwell and another to Bolivar. See Schomburg to Cromwell, October 22, 1912; and Alexander Crummell, "Greatness of Christ," manuscript sermon, January 1880, box 33, folder 7, Henry P. Slaughter Collection, AUARC.
124. Alice Moore Dunbar, preface to *Masterpieces of Negro Eloquence* (New York: Bookery, 1914).
125. Bruce to Cromwell, December 11, 1911, box 98, folder 17, Locke Papers. Sinnette states that Schomburg held the NSHR's collection at his apartment and that his "personal items were shelved among those of the society" (Sinnette, *Arthur Alfonso Schomburg*, 43–44).
126. "The Negro Society for Historical Research," *African Times and Orient Review*, Christmas Annual, 1912; and George W. Forbes, "Mr. A. A. Schomberg's [sic] Race Library," *A. M. E. Review* 31 (October 1914): 212–14. The 1912 profile, likely written by David B. Fulton, was reprinted in William H. Ferris, *The African Abroad or His Evolution in Western Civilization*, vol. 2 (New Haven, CT: Tuttle, Morehouse & Taylor, 1913), 863–66. The only discrepancy between Forbes' list of Schomburg's library and Fulton's list of the NSHR's holdings is that Forbes skips Josiah Henson, likely an oversight. The lists are otherwise identical, including mistakes in spelling. Many of the titles enumerated also appear in Schomburg's catalog, "Library of Arthur A. Schomburg."

127. D. B. Fulton to Schomberg [sic], October 24, 1910, box 3, folder 17, and Hubert H. Harrison to Schomburg, January 3, 1911, box 3, folder 20—both in AAS Papers.
128. "Arthur A. Schomburg," *The Pioneer Press*, September 14, 1912; and Schomburg to Cromwell, April 22, 1912.
129. Schomburg to Cromwell, July 8, 1916, box 1, folder 19, Cromwell Papers.
130. Schomburg to Locke, January 24, 1916.
131. These visits are documented in Schomburg to Cromwell, August 29, 1913, box 1, folder 15, Schomburg to Cromwell, December 11, 1918, box 1, folder 22, Schomburg to Cromwell, July 20, 1919, box 1, folder 23, Schomburg to Cromwell, August 27, 1919, box 1, folder 24, Schomburg to Cromwell, November 18, 1920, box 1, folder 25—all in Cromwell Papers. See also Arthur A. Schomburg, "Two Negro Missionaries to the American Indians, John Marrant and John Stewart," *Journal of Negro History* 21, no. 4 (October 1936): 394–405; "People Talked About"; and Sinnette, *Arthur Alfonso Schomburg*, 126.
132. Eric D. Walrond, "Visit to Arthur Schomburg's Library Brings Out Wealth of Historical Information," *Negro World*, April 22, 1922. On this visit, see James Davis, *Eric Walrond: A Life in the Harlem Renaissance and the Transatlantic Caribbean* (New York: Columbia University Press, 2015), 69.
133. On William J. Wilson's "Afric-American Picture Gallery" as "a visual archive wrought in textual form," see Leif Eckstrom and Britt Rusert, Introduction to "Afric-American Picture Gallery," Just Teach One: Early African American Print, no. 2 (Fall 2015), http://jtoaa.common-place.org/welcome-to-just-teach-one-african-american/introduction-afric-american-picture-gallery/. Schomburg owned the issues of *Anglo-African Magazine* in which Wilson's story appeared ("Library of Arthur A. Schomburg").
134. Elizabeth Alexander, *The Black Interior* (St. Paul, MN: Graywolf, 2004), 9–10.
135. Zora Neale Hurston, "Mr. Schomburg's Library," *Negro World*, April 22, 1922. On the symbolic role of home libraries as markers of literacy and class, see Michele Mitchell, *Righteous Propagation: African Americans and the Politics of Racial Destiny After Reconstruction* (Chapel Hill: University of North Carolina Press, 2004), 178. On Black libraries and interior design, see Tara Dudley, "Seeking the Ideal African-American Interior: The Walker Residences and Salon in New York," *Studies in the Decorative Arts* 14, no. 1 (Fall-Winter 2006–2007): 82, 97, 105.
136. "Ministers in Concert," *New York Age*, September 23, 1915.
137. Negro Library Association, Program for Musical and Literary Evening; Negro Library Association, *Exhibition Catalogue, First Annual Exhibition of Books, Manuscripts, Paintings, Engravings, Sculptures, Et cetera by The Negro Library Association*, August 7 to 16, 1918 (New York, The Pool Press Association Printers, 1918); and "Books, Etc., Wanted," *New York Age*, July 20, 1918.
138. Dorothy B. Porter, "The Organized Educational Activities of Negro Literary Societies, 1828–1846," *Journal of Negro Education* 5, no. 4 (October 1936): 555–76; and Victoria Earle Matthews, "The Value of Race Literature: An Address Delivered at the First Congress of Colored Women of the United States at Boston, Mass., July 30, 1895," https://collections.library.yale.edu/catalog/10171940.
139. Sarah A. Anderson, "'The Place to Go': The 135th Street Branch Library and the Harlem Renaissance," *Library Quarterly* 73, no. 4 (October 2003): 397.
140. *Catalog of The Negro Arts Exhibit*, August 1 to September 30, 1921, and *Catalog of the Exhibition by Negro Artists*, August 1 to October 1, 1922—both in box 2, folder 16, SCRBC Records.
141. Bruce to Locke, December 26, 1914; and Crowder, *John Edward Bruce*, 128. Sinnette states that because Schomburg "was not only the custodian of the collection but also its chief contributor, [he] retained the books and documents when the society disbanded and incorporated them into his personal collection" (Sinnette, *Arthur Alfonso Schomburg*, 44).
142. L. Hollingsworth Wood to Carnegie Corporation, December 6, 1925, folder 1, Schomburg Committee of the Trustees of New York Public Library Collection (hereafter Schomburg Committee Collection), MARB, SCRBC.
143. Wood to Mrs. A. A. Schomburg, June 13, 1938, Schomburg Committee Collection.

144. Kelly Miller to Schomburg, March 14, 1917, box 5, folder 33, AAS Papers; and NYPL Board of Directors minutes, May 7, 1926, box 21, James W. Henderson Papers, NYPLA.
145. Schomburg to Locke, May 4, 1915, box 83, folder 31, Locke Papers.
146. Schomburg to Cromwell, May 11, 1912. Schomburg was likely referring to Pierre Pinchinat's 1797 *Réponse de Pinchinat.*
147. Schomburg quoted in Sinnette, *Arthur Alfonso Schomburg*, 136.
148. Early announcements for this collection use different names: Department of Negro Literature and History; and Department of Negro History, Literature, and Art. By 1928, it was referred to as a Division. See Program for Opening of Department of Negro Literature and History, May 7, 1925, SCCF 004,447; Victoria Ortiz, *The Legacy of Arthur Alfonso Schomburg: A Celebration of the Past, a Vision for the Future* (New York: NYPL, 1986), 37; and NYPL, *Report of the New York Public Library for 1928* (New York: NYPL, 1929), 65.
149. "Editorials," *Survey Graphic* 6, no. 6 (March 1925): 699–700.
150. "List of early donors to Negro Division," box 1, folder 4, SCRBC Records.
151. On preliminary negotiations about the fate of Schomburg's library, see Wood to Charles S. Brown Jr., January 29, 1926, Wood to Carnegie Corporation, December 10, 1925 and December 8, 1925, and Wood to F. P. Keppel, March 22, 1926—all in Schomburg Committee Records. Wood seems to have imagined placing the collection on temporary deposit at the 135th Street branch rather than the NYPL owning it permanently.
152. "The Schomburg Negro Library Sold for $10,000," *Washington Eagle*, May 28, 1926; and "Public Library Gets Valuable Books on Negro," *Philadelphia Tribune*, May 29, 1926.
153. Arna Bontemps, "Buried Treasures of Negro Art," *Negro Digest* 9, no. 2 (December 1950): 19; J. A. Rogers, "Arthur Schomburg, the Sherlock Holmes of Negro History," *Richmond Planet*, July 5, 1930; and "People Talked About."
154. As quoted in Calvin, "Race Colleges Need Chair in Negro History." For a fuller discussion of the politics of the sale, see Laura E. Helton, "Schomburg's Library and the Price of Black History," *African American Review* 54, nos. 1–2 (Spring/Summer 2021): 109–27.
155. On acquisition as bestowing legitimacy on marginalized or avant-garde materials, see Libbie Rifkin, "Association/Value: Creative Collaborations in the Library," *RBM* 2, no. 2 (Fall 2001): 123–39.
156. "Historical Library, Schomburg Negro Library Sold," *Amsterdam News*, May 26, 1926.
157. Schomburg's collection included approximately 4,600 items when acquired by NYPL. See *Report of the New York Public Library for 1926* (New York: NYPL, 1927), 71.
158. Walrond, "Visit"; and Hurston, "Mr. Schomburg's Library."
159. Schomburg, "Negro Digs," 670; and Schomburg, "African Exploration," in *Arthur Alfonso Schomburg: A Puerto Rican's Quest for His Black Heritage*, ed. Flor Piñeiro de Rivera (San Juan: Centro de Estudios Avanzados de Puerto Rico y el Caribe, 1989), 189.
160. Schomburg to Cromwell, January 18, 1913; and Michel-Rolph Trouillot, *Silencing the Past: Power and the Production of History* (Boston: Beacon, 1995), 73. This list of terms is drawn from titles in Schomburg's collection. It reflects the fact that although Schomburg devoted careful attention to the oeuvre of Wheatley, wrote admiringly of Harriet Tubman and Sojourner Truth, and collected the major Black women writers of the nineteenth century, he nevertheless privileged heroic male revolutionary action in his framing of history.
161. Schomburg quoted in Porter, "Bibliography and Research," 81.
162. "Schomburg Collection to New Home," *Chicago Defender*, May 16, 1942, SCCF 004,447; and Porter, "Bibliography and Research," 81.
163. L. D. Reddick to Franklin Hopper, June 14, 1945, box 33, Lydenberg, Hopper, and Beals General Correspondence, NYPLA.
164. Schomburg, "Racial Integrity," 17.

165. From 1927 to 1929, Schomburg gifted more than thirteen hundred additional items to the collection. See Sinnette, *Arthur Alfonso Schomburg*, 146; Wood to Mrs. Charles S. Brown Jr., March 8, 1928, Schomburg Committee Records; Receipts of Purchases, Gifts, and Exchanges, vols. 12–13, Research Libraries Acquisitions Division Records, NYPLA; and [Franklin Hopper] to Frederick Keppel, March 2, 1932, box 1, folder 1, SCRBC Records.
166. Schomburg to Cromwell, November 18, 1920; and Schomburg to Mrs. [Elizabeth H.] Forbes, November 2, 1934, George Washington Forbes Papers, Boston Public Library.
167. Schomburg to Forbes, November 2, 1934; and Mollie E. Dunlap, "Special Collections of Negro Literature in the United States," *Journal of Negro Education* 4, no. 4 (October 1935): 486.
168. Mbembe, "The Power of the Archive," 21.

2. A "HISTORY OF THE NEGRO IN SCRAPBOOKS": THE GUMBY BOOK STUDIO'S EPHEMERAL ASSEMBLIES

1. Eric Walrond, "Visit to Arthur Schomburg's Library Brings Out Wealth of Historical Information," *Negro World*, April 22, 1922; and L. S. Alexander Gumby, [untitled notes on making scrapbooks], n.d., in "Mss of L.S.A. Gumby," Series I.1, L. S. Alexander Gumby Collection of Negroiana (hereafter Gumby Collection), CRBML.
2. Gumby was copying a line from E. W. Gurley, *Scrap-Books and How to Make Them* (New York: Authors' Publishing, 1880), 14. These notes are in "How I Made My Scrapbooks," ca. 1950, Gumby Collection accession file, CRMBL. In this and other quoted passages from Gumby's manuscripts, I have corrected his spelling—which, by his own admission, was terrible.
3. Gumby, "Why I Collect Negro Items," n.d., in "Mss of L.S.A. Gumby," Series I.1, Gumby Collection.
4. Richard Bruce Nugent, "On Alexander Gumby," in *Gay Rebel of the Harlem Renaissance: Selections from the Work of Richard Bruce Nugent*, ed. Thomas H. Wirth (Durham, NC: Duke University Press, 2002), 223; and Eleanor Hayden, "The Friendliest Place in New York," *New York Times Book Review*, March 27, 1921, "Greenwich Village" scrapbook, Series III, Gumby Collection. On George Walker's style of dandyism, which Gumby emulated, see Monica L. Miller, *Slaves to Fashion: Black Dandyism and the Styling of Black Diasporic Identity* (Durham, NC: Duke University Press, 2009), 176–218.
5. Aubrey Bowser, "A Negro Documentarian," *New York Amsterdam News*, August 13, 1930, "Gumby Book Studio" scrapbook, no. 1, Series III, Gumby Collection. Ethel Waters quoted in Jo Kadlecek, "Scrapbooks Help Preserve African Americans' Past," *Columbia University Record* 27, no. 10 (February 15, 2002): 5.
6. On the history of paper ephemera, see Todd S. Gernes, "Recasting the Culture of Ephemera," in *Popular Literacy: Studies in Cultural Practices and Poetics*, ed. John Trimbur (Pittsburgh: University of Pittsburgh Press, 2001), 107–27; Martin Andrews, "The Importance of Ephemera," in *A Companion to the History of the Book*, ed. Simon Eliot and Jonathan Rose (Malden, MA: Blackwell, 2007), 434–50; and Anne Garner, "Throwaway History: Towards a Historiography of Ephemera," *Book History* 24, no. 1 (Spring 2021): 244–63.
7. "New Calendar Moses to Skip Color Line," *Long Island Star*, February 25, 1934, box 1, folder 36, Arthur A. Schomburg Papers Additions (hereafter AAS Additions), Manuscripts, Archives and Rare Books Division (hereafter MARB), SCRBC; and Lisa Gitelman, *Paper Knowledge: Toward a Media History of Documents* (Durham, NC: Duke University Press, 2014), 54.
8. Ellen Gruber Garvey, "Scissoring and Scrapbooks: Nineteenth-Century Reading, Remaking, and Recirculating," in *New Media, 1740–1915*, ed. Lisa Gitelman and Geoffrey B. Pingree (Cambridge, MA: MIT Press, 2003), 209. On the rise of newspaper publishing in the late nineteenth century

and concomitant efforts to "extract, store, or digest" its contents, see Anke te Heesen "News, Paper, Scissors: Clippings in the Sciences and Arts Around 1920," in *Things That Talk: Object Lessons from Art and Science*, ed. Lorraine Daston (New York: Zone, 2004), 302. On the history of American scrapbooks, see Jessica Helfand, *Scrapbooks: An American History* (New Haven, CT: Yale University Press, 2008); and Susan Tucker, Katherine Ott, and Patricia P. Buckler, eds., *The Scrapbook in American Life* (Philadelphia: Temple University Press, 2006).

9. Ellen Gruber Garvey, *Writing with Scissors: American Scrapbooks from the Civil War to the Harlem Renaissance* (New York: Oxford University Press, 2013), 131–33.
10. Hubert H. Harrison, "The Negro and the Newspapers," ca. 1911, in *A Hubert Harrison Reader*, ed. Jeffrey B. Perry (Middletown, CT: Wesleyan University Press, 2001), 49.
11. Gumby, [untitled notes on making scrapbooks]. On the minstrelsy of American print culture at the turn of the century, see Martha S. Jones, *All Bound Up Together: The Woman Question in African American Public Culture, 1830–1900* (Chapel Hill, NC: University of North Carolina Press, 2007), 177–79.
12. Garvey, *Writing with Scissors*, 149, 155–56. See, for example, the Amos Gerry Beman Scrapbooks, volumes 1, 2, and 4, BRBML, https://archives.yale.edu/repositories/11/resources/954. On remixing, see Ivy G. Wilson, *Specters of Democracy: Blackness and the Aesthetics of Politics in the Antebellum U.S.* (New York: Oxford University Press, 2011), 9.
13. Gumby, [untitled notes on making scrapbooks].
14. Pocket labeled "A Silk Playbill of the Ziegfield Follies Frolic Ball of 1916," "Williams and Walker" scrapbook, Series III, Gumby Collection. Although silk playbills were designed to be sturdier mementoes than paper programs, in Gumby's scrapbook, it is the silk marked as fragile, rather than the paper around it. His note is performative: to produce a moment of reverence. "Silk Playbill," Victoria and Albert Museum, May 8, 2007, https://collections.vam.ac.uk/item/O134502/silk-playbill/.
15. John W. Douglas, "Unique Passion for Collecting Facts About Negroes," *Afro-American*, June 7, 1930, "Gumby Book Studio" scrapbook, no. 1, Series III, Gumby Collection; and Schomburg to James Weldon Johnson, August 3, 1931, box 17, folder 428, James Weldon Johnson Manuscripts 49, BRBML.
16. "Gumby's Studio Anniversary," *New York News*, March 1, 1930, "Gumby Book Studio" scrapbook, no. 1.
17. Gumby, [untitled notes on making scrapbooks].
18. Gumby describes his process of continuous rearrangement of scrapbook materials in L. S. Alexander Gumby, "The Gumby Scrapbook Collection of Negroana," *Columbia Library World* 5, no. 1 (January 1951): 4. On the newspaper clipping's "spatial maneuverability," see Anke te Heesen, *The Newspaper Clipping: A Modern Paper Object* (Manchester: Manchester University Press, 2014), 9.
19. This reading of Gumby's studio departs from characterizations of archives as spaces for solitary research. See, for example, "the archive is a place for the researcher to both to be alone and at home," in Mike Featherstone, "Archive," *Theory, Culture and Society* 23, nos. 2–3 (May 2006): 594. I would instead echo Gabrielle Dean's argument, which draws on Jerome McGann's work, that archives enact "social authorship long before the researcher enters the room" (Dean, "Disciplinarity and Disorder," *Archive Journal* 1, no. 1 [Spring 2011]: http://www.archivejournal.net/issue/1/archives-remixed/).
20. On Gumby, see Jani Scandura, *Down in the Dumps: Place, Modernity, American Depression* (Durham, NC: Duke University Press, 2008), 161–68; Garvey, *Writing with Scissors*, 159–66; Sharifa Rhodes-Pitts, *Harlem Is Nowhere: A Journey to the Mecca of Black America* (New York: Little, Brown, 2011), 121–22; and Nicholas Osborne, curator, "'The Unwritten History': Alexander Gumby's African America," Columbia University Libraries, 2012, https://exhibitions.library.columbia.edu/exhibits/show/gumby.

21. In his studio, Gumby embraced the "high arts" of painting and concert music as well as the "collectivities of sexual, racial, gender, and economic heterogeneity of the underworld" that Shane Vogel associates with the "Cabaret School" (Vogel, *The Scene of the Harlem Cabaret: Race, Sexuality, Performance* [Chicago: University of Chicago Press, 2009], 13).
22. José Esteban Muñoz, "Ephemera as Evidence: Introductory Notes to Queer Acts," *Women and Performance: A Journal of Feminist Theory* 8, no. 2 (1996): 6. On the often-fleeting nature of queer subcultures and their archives, see Jack Halberstam, *In a Queer Time and Place: Transgender Bodies, Subcultural Lives* (New York: New York University Press, 2005), 169–70. I describe Gumby's method as queer because he collected minor and ephemeral forms that challenged conventional approaches to race and sexuality in the field of "Negro History." Although Gumby's collection documents queer sexualities, he did not frame the collection as such, and thus it differs from the explicitly LGBTQ collections described in Alana Kumbier, *Ephemeral Material: Queering the Archive* (Sacramento, CA: Litwin, 2009).
23. Jean-Christophe Cloutier, *Shadow Archives: Lifecycles of African American Literature* (New York: Columbia University Press, 2019), 82. What we now call the Gumby Collection is, in fact, a second collection, partially remade after the 1930s and containing fragments of what the Gumby Group created in the 1920s. Rather than focus on the loss of the "original" collection, I follow Cloutier in emphasizing that all collections undergo revision across their life cycles. On another kind of Black shadow archive, see Laura E. Helton, "Historical Form(s)," in *Elusive Archives: Material Culture in Formation*, ed. Martin Brückner and Sandy Isenstadt (Newark: University of Delaware Press, 2021): 49–63.
24. See "Gumby's Autobiography" scrapbook, no. 4 [on Riverside Hospital] and no. 6 [on Triboro Hospital], Series III, Gumby Collection.
25. Eric Ketelaar, "Tacit Narratives: The Meanings of Archives," *Archival Science* 1 (2001): 131–41; and Sarah Wasserman, *The Death of Things: Ephemera and the American Novel* (Minneapolis: University of Minnesota Press, 2020), 3.
26. Gumby to Roland Baughman [corrected draft], ca. 1950, in "Mss of L.S.A. Gumby," Series I.1, Gumby Collection.
27. Gumby, "The Gumby Scrapbook Collection," 3; and Gumby to Baughman [corrected draft].
28. In 1925, Cheatham lived with or in the same building as Gumby at 2144 5th Avenue (New York State Census for 1915, Enumeration of the Inhabitants of New York City; and New York State Census for 1925, Enumeration of the Inhabitants of New York City, Ancestry.com). His initials are on some pieces of ephemera in Gumby's scrapbooks. Whipper's donations to Gumby's scrapbooks are documented in Leigh [Whipper] to Gumby, May 5, 1929, "Gumby Book Studio" scrapbook, no. 1.
29. In U.S. Bureau of the Census, Thirteenth Census of the United States: 1910—Population for Borough of the Bronx, New York, Ancestry.com, Gumby is listed as a butler in the Burghard Steiner household on Independence Avenue; sixteen-year-old Charles Newman's family, headed by Edgar B. Newman, lived across the street at W. 254th Street. See Plate 40 [Map bounded by Mosholu Ave., Broadway, W. 250th St., Hudson River], 1911, Lionel Pincus and Princess Firyal Map Division, New York Public Library Digital Collections, digitalcollections.nypl.org/items/a1e93824-8d50-50ee-e040-e00a18061 9ed. On their relationship, see Seth Clark Silberman, "Gumby Book Studio," in *Encyclopedia of the Harlem Renaissance*, ed. Cary D. Wintz and Paul Finkelman (New York: Routledge, 2004), 455.
30. Gumby, "The Gumby Scrapbook Collection," 5; and Gumby to "Wiseman," January 15, 1955, Subseries I.1 (reel 96–2041), Gumby Collection.
31. Gumby to Baughman [corrected draft]. "Wall Street friend" refers to Newman, who was a broker and partner in the firm Jewett, Newman & Co. (New York Stock Exchange Directory, January 1929, revised to April 2, 1929, https://archive.org/stream/newyorkstockexch1929newy/newyorkstockexch1929newy_djvu.txt).

32. Gumby, "The Gumby Scrapbook Collection," 5.
33. Arthur P. Davis, "Growing Up in the New Negro Renaissance," *Negro American Literature Forum* 2, no. 3 (Autumn 1968): 55. Davis was comparing the crowd at Gumby's studio to A'Lelia Walker's Dark Tower. Gumby's studio was one of many short-lived salons in New York in this period. Gumby's friend Glenn Carrington, for example, formed the Four to Seven literary club with librarian Roberta Bosley, author Dorothy West, and the white playwright Bernard Reines, hosting weekly symposia that attracted a crowd overlapping with Gumby's but with guest speakers of a higher profile than most of Gumby's friends. See " 'Green Pastures' Stars Guest 'Four to Seven,' " *New York Age*, April 5, 1930; and Carrington to Ophelia Settle, April 1, 1930, box 7, folder 20, C. Glenn Carrington Papers (hereafter Carrington Papers), Manuscript Division, MSRC.
34. "Book Studio Group Honors Cullen, Poet," *New York Amsterdam News*, September 17, 1930, Gumby Studio Guest Book, Series III, Gumby Collection.
35. "The Road Back: Alexander Gumby Plans Comeback with New Art Studio," *New York Amsterdam News*, December 8, 1934.
36. Gumby Studio Guestbook, Series III, Gumby Collection.
37. The Hobby Horse is identified as a gay club in George Chauncey, *Gay New York: Gender, Urban Culture, and the Making of the Gay Male World, 1890–1940* (New York: Basic Books, 1994), 252. Carrington mentions a raid there in Carrington to Ophelia Settle Egypt, June 28, 1929, box 7, folder 17, Carrington Papers. On queer New York, see Eric Garber, "A Spectacle in Color: The Lesbian and Gay Subculture of Jazz Age Harlem," in *Hidden from History: Reclaiming the Gay and Lesbian Past*, ed. Martin Duberman, Martha Vicinus, and George Chauncey (New York: New American Library, 1989), 318–31; Henry Louis Gates Jr., "The Black Man's Burden," in *Fear of a Queer Planet: Queer Politics and Social Theory*, ed. Michael Warner (Minneapolis: University of Minnesota Press, 1993), 230–38; and A. B. Christa Schwarz, *Gay Voices of the Harlem Renaissance* (Bloomington: Indiana University Press, 2003).
38. Floyd G. Snelson Jr., "Plan Big Benefit for Ill Harlem Book Collector," *Pittsburgh Courier*, November 14, 1931, "Gumby Book Studio" scrapbook, no. 2, Series III, Gumby Collection.
39. "Negro History in Scrapbooks," *New York Times*, December 27, 1929, "Gumby Book Studio" scrapbook, no. 1.
40. Theodore W. Hernandez, "Preface," *Gumby Book Studio Quarterly* [galley proofs], "Gumby Book Studio Quarterly" scrapbook, Series III, Gumby Collection.
41. Theodore Hernandez to Gumby, January 5, 1950, "Columbia University" scrapbook, Series III, Gumby Collection.
42. Gumby to Jack Johnson, May 31, 1928, "Jack Johnson" scrapbook, Series III, Gumby Collection.
43. Gumby, "The Gumby Scrapbook Collection," 8.
44. Gumby, "Making a scrap-book valuable," n.d., in "Mss of L.S.A. Gumby," Series I.1, Gumby Collection.
45. Gumby, "The Gumby Scrapbook Collection," 6.
46. Gumby, Chapter 6 of "Notes on How to Make a Scrap-Book," n.d., in "Mss of L.S.A. Gumby," Series I.1, Gumby Collection.
47. Gladys E. Flynn to Gumby, April 16, 1926, in "NAACP" scrapbook, no. 1, Series III, Gumby Collection. Flynn's initials GEF are on many of the carbon copies of Pickens's correspondence in the "William Pickens" scrapbook, Series III, Gumby Collection. The degree to which Gumby's scrapbooks were shaped by his friendships is evident in the fact that his documentation of Pickens and the NAACP decreased after 1927, when Flynn changed jobs. "TA Secretary Retires After 33 Yrs. Service," *N.Y. Amsterdam News*, September 17, 1960, in "Gumby's Autobiography" scrapbook, no. 1, Series III, Gumby Collection.
48. Leigh [Whipper] to Gumby, May 5, 1929. On Whipper as a collector, see Charles L. Blockson, *Damn Rare: The Memoirs of an African American Bibliophile* (Tracy, CA: Quantum Leap, 1998), 227–41.

49. See "Note" r.e. papers and letters of Hon. Henry P. Cheatham, 1935, "Negroes in Congress" scrapbook, Series III, Gumby Collection; and Program cover, Memorial to the Late Geo. W. Walker, Howard Theatre, 1911, "Williams and Walker" scrapbook, Series III, Gumby Collection.
50. Katherine Ott, "It's a Scrapbook Life: Using Ephemera to Reconstruct the Everyday of Medical Practice," *Watermark* 20, no. 1 (Winter 1996): 6.
51. Scandura, *Down in the Dumps*, 159.
52. Bowser, "A Negro Documentarian." My discussion of the relationship between sociality, collective literacy, and knowledge production draws on Elizabeth McHenry, *Forgotten Readers: Recovering the Lost History of African American Literary Societies* (Durham, NC: Duke University Press, 2002), 99.
53. Flap copy, dust jacket for Ferdinand Levy, *Flashes from the Dark* (Dublin: Sign of the Three Candles, 1941). On the need to study the Harlem Renaissance through an expanded set of genres and forms, see Rachel Farebrother and Miriam Thaggert, "Introduction: Revising and Renaissance," in *A History of the Harlem Renaissance*, ed. Farebrother and Thaggert (New York: Cambridge University Press, 2021), 11.
54. Robert Schlick to Gumby, September 8, 1930, Subseries I.1 (reel 96–2040), Gumby Collection.
55. Bowser, "A Negro Documentarian."
56. Label, "Negro Intellectuals Rendezvous" in "Autographs and Photographs" scrapbook, no. 3, Series II, Gumby Collection.
57. After Grayson's start as a playwright at Hunter College, she became ill and spent the rest of her life immobilized. González was a guitarist. Jenkins, who died in 1941, is identified elsewhere in the scrapbook as "associated with The Negro Art Theatre" and "a prominent member of the Harlem literati." Songer (sometimes spelled Sangre) is documented in "Gumby's Autobiography" scrapbook, no. 3, Series III, Gumby Collection. See "Westchester's Wonder Woman," *New York Age*, June 14, 1952; "Two Poets Read Verses at Gumby's Studios," *New York Amsterdam News*, December 4, 1929; and Mrs. Maggie Jenkins to Gumby, August 26, 1941, "Autographs and Photographs" scrapbook, no. 4, Series II, Gumby Collection. The sketch of Theodore Hernandez is by Hendrix.
58. Gumby, "The Gumby Scrapbook Collection," 5.
59. "The Road Back."
60. Stephen Best, *None Like Us: Blackness, Belonging, Aesthetic Life* (Durham, NC: Duke University Press, 2018), 22–23.
61. Invitation, February 23, 1930, "Gumby Book Studio" scrapbook, no. 2.
62. The James Weldon Johnson Memorial Collection of Negro Arts and Letters was founded by Carl Van Vechten in 1941.
63. Gumby felt slighted by the omission from *Black Manhattan*. See Gumby to Cornelius O'Connor, December 13, 1930, Subseries I.1 (reel 96–2041), Gumby Collection.
64. Siobhan B. Somerville, *Queering the Color Line: Race and the Invention of Homosexuality in American Culture* (Durham, NC: Duke University Press, 2000), 117–22.
65. Hernandez, "Preface."
66. Jack [Balmore?] to Gumby, n.d., Subseries I.1 (reel 96–2041), Gumby Collection.
67. Abby Ann Arthur Johnson and Ronald M. Johnson, "Forgotten Pages: Black Literary Magazines in the 1920s," *Journal of American Studies* 8, no. 3 (December 1974): 363; see also correspondence about *Black Bard* magazine in Arthur Spingarn Papers, box 3, folder 54, Manuscript Division, MSRC.
68. "Literary Folk Awaiting Gumby's Book Quarterly," *New York Amsterdam News*, October 22, 1930.
69. Snelson Jr., "Plan Big Benefit."
70. Galley proofs for Arthur A. Schomburg, "The African Origin of the Tango"; Theo. W. Hernandez, "Satanus Intervenes"; and [Richard] Bruce [Nugent], "The Tunic with a Thousand Pleats"—all in "Gumby Book Studio Quarterly" scrapbook. As will be discussed, the *Quarterly* never circulated. A run of five hundred copies was set to be issued on November 1, 1930, but none were distributed,

perhaps because Gumby could not pay the printer's bill after he fell ill. See Levi Hubert, "7th Ave.," *Afro-American*, November 29, 1930.

71. A. A. Schomburg, "Gumby Issues Magazine," *Afro-American*, October 25, 1930.
72. Hernandez, "Preface"; and Nugent, "On Alexander Gumby," 226.
73. Hernandez, "Preface."
74. Galley proofs for George S. Schuyler, "A Plea for Intolerance"; T. Thomas Fortune Fletcher, "Dr. Ward Is Embarrassed"; and Sydney Sanders, "Hollywood Discovers the Negro"—all in "Gumby Book Studio Quarterly" scrapbook.
75. Gumby, [untitled notes on making scrapbooks].
76. A. C. Sterling, "Adventure Into Scrapbooks," *Courier*, n.d., "Gumby's Autobiography" scrapbook, no. 5, Series III, Gumby Collection.
77. Finding aid for the L. S. Alexander Gumby Collection of Negroiana, 1800–1981, CRBML, https://findingaids.library.columbia.edu/ead/nnc-rb/ldpd_4078845.
78. Gumby to Roland Baughman [corrected draft]; and Gumby, "The Gumby Scrapbook Collection," 4.
79. Gumby, "The Gumby Scrapbook Collection," 4.
80. Gumby, "The Gumby Scrapbook Collection," 4.
81. Gumby, "The Gumby Scrapbook Collection," 4. Even when Gumby sent his scrapbooks to a binder, a seeming indication of their completion, he included blank leaves for "items I hope to get later" (Gumby, [untitled notes on making scrapbooks]).
82. John W. Douglas, typescript draft of "A Scrap Book Connoisseur," [1930], in "Gumby Book Studio" scrapbook, no. 1.
83. These volumes are in the Alice Dunbar Nelson Papers, Special Collections, University of Delaware; James Weldon and Grace Nail Johnson Papers, BRBML; Walter O. Evans Collection of Frederick Douglass and Douglass Family Papers, BRBML; and Ida B. Wells Papers, Hanna Holborn Gray Special Collections Research Center, University of Chicago Library. On Sarah Mapps Douglass and Ada H. Hinton, see Steven L. Jones, "A Keen Sense of the Artistic: African American Material Culture in the 19th Century," *International Review of African American Art* 12, no. 2 (1995): 4–30.
84. Dorothy Porter, Report on Cheyney State College Archives, typescript, October 23, 1976, box 9, Dorothy Porter Wesley Papers, BRBML. (At the time of research, Porter's papers at Yale were minimally processed; subsequent reprocessing may have changed box numbers.) See also W. C. Bolivar to W. H. Dorsey, [March?] 24, 1882, box 1, folder 10, Thomas and William Henry Dorsey Collection, Manuscript Division, MSRC. On Dorsey, see Garvey, *Writing with Scissors*, 137–157; Roger Lane, *William Dorsey's Philadelphia and Ours: On the Past and Future of the Black City in America* (New York: Oxford University Press, 1991); Aston Gonzalez, "William Dorsey and the Construction of an African American History Archive," *Social Dynamics* 45, no. 1 (2019): 138–55; and Cynthia Greenlee, "A Priceless Archive of Ordinary Life," *The Atlantic*, February 9, 2021, https://www.theatlantic.com/culture/archive/2021/02/race-save-black-history-archives/617932/.
85. Mossell quoted in Garvey, *Writing with Scissors*, 136–37.
86. Gumby, "Why I Collect Negro Items." Andrews argues that ephemera was often "the only record of great theatrical and dance performances, musical concerts, and art exhibitions . . . particularly for experimental or fringe events" ("The Importance of Ephemera," 448). Black newspapers also fostered discussions of sexuality absent elsewhere in print culture, underscoring why Gumby's interest in a queer history of blackness relied on ephemera as a medium. See Kim Gallon, *Pleasure in the News: African American Readership and Sexuality in the Black Press* (Urbana: University of Illinois Press, 2020).
87. Heesen, "News, Paper, Scissors," 304.
88. M. V. H., "The Clipping File," *Bulletin of the Art Institute of Chicago* 5, no. 2 (October 1911), 27. Library clipping projects were expanded by the Works Progress Administration (WPA) in the 1930s; see Harold E. Blinn, "W.P.A. Newspaper Clipping and Indexing Service," *Pacific Historical Review* 6, no. 3 (September 1937): 284–87; and Pat Henderson, "Clippings to Computers: The Great Newspaper Migration," *Library Mosaics* 12, no. 3 (May–June 2001): 17–18.

89. Nicholas Natanson, ed., *Index to the Hampton University Newspaper Clipping File* (Alexandria, VA: Chadwyck-Healey, 1988), 5–6; and Hampton Library Subject Headings, typescript, n.d., in Hampton Library School Records, HUA. For summaries of the Schomburg, Tuskegee, Hampton, and Gumby clipping files, see Albert J. Raboteau, David W. Wills, Randall K. Burkett, Will B. Gravely, and James Melvin Washington, "Retelling Carter Woodson's Story: Archival Sources for Afro-American Church History," *Journal of American History* 77, no. 1 (June 1990): 187–88.
90. Monroe N. Work, *Negro Year Book and Annual Encyclopedia of the Negro* (Tuskegee, AL: Tuskegee Normal and Industrial Institute, 1912); and Linda O. McMurray, *Recorder of the Black Experience: A Biography of Monroe Nathan Work* (Baton Rouge: Louisiana State University Press, 1985). On filing cabinets as a new storage medium, see JoAnne Yates, *Control Through Communication: The Rise of System in American Management* (Baltimore, MD: Johns Hopkins University Press, 1989), 56–63; and Craig Robertson, *The Filing Cabinet: A Vertical History of Information* (Minneapolis: University of Minnesota Press, 2021).
91. Benjamin Jacobowitz, "The Schomburg Collection of Negro Literature, History and Prints" [research paper], 1952, MARB, SCRBC; and Ernest Kaiser, "The Genesis of the Kaiser Index," in *The Kaiser Index to Black Resources, 1948–1986* (Brooklyn, NY: Carlson, 1992), xviii–xix. In the 1930s, Latimer turned the largest of these files into "bound volumes, resembling scrapbooks" with the aid of WPA workers. The clipping file was microfiched in 1985; the scrapbooks were microfilmed separately.
92. Garvey, *Writing with Scissors*, 254 n9.
93. Scott Herring, *Queering the Underworld: Slumming, Literature, and the Undoing of Lesbian and Gay History* (Chicago: University of Chicago Press, 2007), 140.
94. Schomburg Center for Research in Black Culture, *Index to the Schomburg Clipping File* (Cambridge: Chadwyck-Healey, 1986); and John W. Kitchens, *Guide to the Microfilm Edition of the Tuskegee Institute News Clippings File* (Tuskegee, AL: Tuskegee Institute, 1978).
95. Hernandez to Gumby, January 5, 1950.
96. Sam M. Steward to Gumby, Friday morning [September 1930], "Negro in Drama" scrapbook, no. 2, Series III, Gumby Collection; and Eric Garber, "T'Ain't Nobody's Bizness: Homosexuality in 1920s Harlem," in *Black Men—White Men: A Gay Anthology*, ed. Michael J. Smith (San Francisco, CA: Gay Sunshine, 1983), 13.
97. Vogel, *Scene of the Harlem Cabaret*, 130–31.
98. Douglas, "A Scrapbook Connoisseur"; Gumby to Jack Johnson, May 31, 1928; and Bessye J. Bearden, "Tid-Bits of New York Society," *Chicago Defender*, March 31, 1928, "Gumby Book Studio" scrapbook, no. 2. For an incomplete list made by Gumby of his Negro History scrapbooks around 1950, see Gumby Accession File.
99. Gumby, [untitled notes on making scrapbooks]; and Bowser, "A Negro Documentarian."
100. Arthur A. Schomburg to John W. Cromwell, February 23, 1915, box 1, folder 30 Cromwell Family Papers, Manuscript Division, MSRC.
101. Schomburg to Cromwell, August 26, 1913, box 1, folder 16, AAS Additions.
102. See Scrapbook 245 in William H. Dorsey Collection, Cheyney University; and "University Community Mourns Death of Dr. Jesse Moorland," *The Hilltop*, May 14, 1940.
103. L. E. Herron to Dr. James E. Gregg, [1924], Library School file, HUA.
104. Gene Andrew Jarrett, *Deans and Truants: Race and Realism in African American Literature* (Philadelphia: University of Pennsylvania Press, 2011). On Black artists' rejection of the expectation that they "are only qualified to . . . be consulted about race," see Farah Jasmine Griffin, "Langston Hughes and the Timeless Questions of Life and Death," *African American Review* 25, no. 1 (2019): 43.
105. I draw here on Gabeba Baderoon, "'I Compose Myself': Lesbian Muslim Autobiographies and the Craft of Self-Writing in South Africa," *Journal of the American Academy of Religion* 83, no. 4 (December 2015): 897–915.

106. Sketch of C. Carroll Clark by Haile Hendrix, ca. 1930, and other items, "Greenwich Village" scrapbook. This sketch has been misidentified as a drawing of Gumby, but it is autographed by and is a close likeness of Clark, who was the first recording artist for Black Swan records. On Clark, see Tim Brooks, *Lost Sounds: Blacks and the Birth of the Recording Industry, 1890–1919* (Urbana: University of Illinois Press, 2004), 159–72.
107. Gumby Book Studio Guestbook, Series III, Gumby Collection.
108. See, for example, Invitation to reception for Hubert Julian (hosted by Upshur), August 8, 1930, "Adventures" scrapbook, Series III, Gumby Collection.
109. David Levering Lewis, *When Harlem Was in Vogue* (1979; repr., New York: Penguin, 1997), 163–64; and Levi Hubert, "Whites Invade Harlem," December 12, 1938, in *A Renaissance in Harlem: Lost Essays of the WPA, by Ralph Ellison, Dorothy West, and Other Voices of a Generation*, ed. Lionel C. Bascom (New York: Amistad, 1999), 24–29.
110. Michel de Certeau and Luce Giard, "Ghosts in the City," in *The Practice of Everyday Life, Vol. 2, Living and Cooking*, ed. Certeau, Giard, and Pierre Mayol, trans. Timothy J. Tomasik (Minneapolis: University of Minnesota Press, 1998), 141. In this essay, de Certeau and Giard frame gestures as a type of archive.
111. Ralph Matthews, "Looking at the Stars," *Afro-American*, October 31, 1931; and Leigh Whipper collage, "Autographs and Photographs" scrapbook, no. 2. In a different volume, the "Leigh Whipper" scrapbook (Series III, Gumby Collection), Gumby likewise included a wide range of stage portraits and personal snapshots, but his layouts were less intricate.
112. Ed. Ballard, "[S]Trand Theatre Jacksonville, Florida," *Freeman*, April 8, 1916 (emphasis added). As scholars have argued, African American blackface performers like Whipper profited from racial caricatures while also using their profits to fund new forms of Black musical theater that eschewed these stereotypes. See Henry T. Sampson, *Blacks in Blackface: A Sourcebook* (Metuchen, NJ: Scarecrow, 1980), 19–45; Daphne A. Brooks, *Bodies in Dissent: Spectacular Performances of Race and Freedom, 1850–1910* (Durham, NC: Duke University Press, 2006), 215; and Dorothy Berry, "When Black Celebrities Wore Blackface," JSTOR Daily, August 12, 2020, https://daily.jstor.org/when-black-celebrities-wore-blackface/.
113. Elizabeth Freeman, *Time Binds: Queer Temporalities, Queer Histories* (Durham, NC: Duke University Press, 2010), 14.
114. Samuel Frederick, *The Redemption of Things: Collecting and Dispersal in German Realism and Modernism* (Ithaca, NY: Cornell University Press, 2021), 52–53.
115. R. B. N. [Richard Bruce Nugent], untitled typescript, 1939, Subseries I.1 (reel 96–2041), Gumby Collection. Next to this section of Nugent's typescript, Gumby wrote an annotation: "This is good and True."
116. Muñoz, "Ephemera as Evidence," 10–11.
117. "Green Pastures" scrapbook, 1930–1934, Schomburg Center Scrapbooks, MARB, SCRBC; and "Green Pastures" scrapbook, Series III, Gumby Collection.
118. Autographed photograph of Evelyn Burwell, 1930, "Autographs and Photographs" scrapbook, no. 3; and Autographed photograph signed Mr. Jarahal? (question mark included in original signature), n.d., "Autographs and Photographs" scrapbook, no. 2, Series II, Gumby Collection. Jarahal is mentioned in Langston Hughes, *The Big Sea* (1940; repr., New York: Hill and Wang, 1993), 176.
119. As Brent Hayes Edwards argues, a "queer practice of the archive" rejects the notion that archival enigmas might be clarified *if only* more documentation were available (Edwards, "The Taste of the Archive," *Callaloo* 35, no. 4 [Fall 2012]: 970).
120. Vogel, *Scene of the Harlem Cabaret*, 22.
121. Gumby to "Holloway," June 22, 1933, Subseries I.1 (reel 96–2041), Gumby Collection; and "Why I Collect Negro Items."

122. On bohemianism as defined, in part, by precisely the kinds of cross-racial and cross-class mobility Gumby enacted, see James Smethurst, *The African American Roots of Modernism: From Reconstruction to the Harlem Renaissance* (Chapel Hill: University of North Carolina Press, 2011), 123–54.
123. Of his excursions in Greenwich Village, Gumby noted that when he was with his white friends he was "treated with the greatest respect," but when alone, he knew not to enter certain venues. Gumby, Letter to the Editor, *Caricature* (October 1949), "Greenwich Village" scrapbook.
124. Gumby, Chapter 3 of "Notes on How to Make a Scrap-Book," n.d., in "Mss of L.S.A. Gumby," Series I.1, Gumby Collection.
125. de Certeau and Giard, "Ghosts in the City," 143. On opacity, see Édouard Glissant, *Poetics of Relation*, trans. Betsy Wing (Ann Arbor: University of Michigan Press, 1997), 193. On Black historical writing that grows out of small narratives grounded in the periodical press, see John Ernest, *Liberation Historiography: African American Writers and the Challenge of History* (Chapel Hill: University of North Carolina Press, 2004), 279.
126. Frank Byrd, "Backstage," *The Inter-State Tattler*, July 25, 1930, "Gumby Book Studio" scrapbook, no. 2.
127. See Schomburg to Hernandez, December 3, 1930, in "Autographs and Photographs" scrapbook, no. 3.
128. "Harlem Benefit for Gumby," *Afro-American*, November 14, 1931.
129. Gumby to Jas. H. Hubert, December 28, 1930, Subseries I.1 (reel 96–2041), Gumby Collection. Gumby wrote of Charles Newman: "I know of [no] greater [tragedy] than he being so indispose[d] at the time I needed him the most" (Gumby to John [Taylor], n.d., Subseries I.1 [reel 96-2041], Gumby Collection).
130. Gumby to Hubert.
131. Gumby to [Taylor]. Sharifa Rhodes-Pitts links the failure of the *Quarterly* to Gumby's disappearance (until recently) from accounts of the Harlem Renaissance: "Perhaps the open combination of white patronage and sex in Gumby's life accounts for the way his story has disappeared. Or maybe the silence also has to do with the fact that Gumby's story is, in part, a narrative of failure" (Rhodes-Pitts, *Harlem Is Nowhere*, 121–22).
132. Ernestine Rose, "Books and the Negro," *Library Journal* 52, November 1927, 1013.
133. [Unknown writer] to Rev. Wm. Lloyd Imes, July 12, 1933, "Autographs and Photographs" scrapbook, no. 4.
134. Schomburg to Hernandez; Schlick to Gumby; and Hernandez to Gumby, December 31, 1930, "Autographs and Photographs" scrapbook, no. 3.
135. The archival field, too, often devalued scrapbooks, which fell in the gap between published materials and personal papers. Archivists sometimes characterized scrapbooks as "notoriously difficult to catalog," a "preservation challenge," or even as "useless." See Wyman W. Parker, "How Can the Archivist Aid the Researcher?," *American Archivist* 16, no. 3 (July 1953): 239; Lucile M. Kane, "The Exhibition of Manuscripts at the Minnesota Historical Society," *American Archivist* 15, no. 1 (January 1952): 44; and Juliana Kuipers, Review of *The Scrapbook in American Life* by Susan Tucker, Katherine Ott, and Patricia P. Buckler, *American Archivist* 70, no. 1. (Spring-Summer 2007): 182.
136. "Dance Benefit to Help Gumby," *New York Amsterdam News*, November 4, 1931, and [untitled clipping], *Chicago Defender*, October 31, 1931—both in "Gumby Book Studio" scrapbook, no. 2. See also "The Arts Ball," *New York Amsterdam News*, November 25, 1931; and Geraldyn Dismond, "New York Society," *Afro-American*, October 31, 1931. On the idea of a collectivity that emerges—or becomes most visible—around a moment of loss, see Romi Crawford, "Yours in Blackness: Blocks, Corners, and Other Desire Settings," *Nka: Journal of Contemporary African Art* 34 (2014): 83.
137. Arts Committee to "Dear Friend," November 9, 1931, "Gumby Book Studio" scrapbook, no. 2.
138. Snelson, "Plan Big Benefit."

139. L. S. Alexander Gumby (per G. E. Flynn), "Letter to the Editor," *New York Amsterdam News*, December 16, 1931.
140. Carolyn Steedman, *Dust: The Archive and Cultural History* (New Brunswick, NJ: Rutgers University Press, 2002), 9.
141. Geoffrey C. Bowker, *Memory Practices in the Sciences* (Cambridge, MA: MIT Press, 2005), 39.
142. Gumby, "The Gumby Scrapbook Collection," 7.
143. Frank Byrd, "What's Happening in New York," *Pittsburgh Courier*, November 14, 1936.
144. Gumby, "The Gumby Scrapbook Collection," 7.
145. "Report on a Study of Scrapbooks," New York Public Library, June 1932, box 2, Keyes DeWitt Metcalf Records, NYPLA.
146. Gumby, "The Gumby Scrapbook Collection," 8.
147. Gumby to Mr. Shore, December 19, 1934, "Gumby's Autobiography" scrapbook, no. 3.
148. Postcard, [Alex?] Capers to Gumby, October 19, 1936, "Gumby's Autobiography" scrapbook, no. 3. The postcard bears Gumby's annotation: "To bring my collection from Brooklyn."
149. Susan Sontag, *Illness as Metaphor* (New York: Farrar, Straus and Giroux, 1978), 12, 21, 25, 33–34; and Katherine Ott, *Fevered Lives: Tuberculosis in American Culture Since 1870* (Cambridge, MA: Harvard University Press, 1996), 76–77, 145.
150. "Gumby's Autobiography" scrapbook, no. 4.
151. For a brief period in 1940, Gumby lived with Charles Newman, listed in the Census as his servant (U.S. Bureau of the Census, Sixteenth Census of the United States: 1940—Population Schedule for Borough of the Bronx, Ancestry.com). He then spent many years living at the Revella Hotel, as well as at Altora House near Columbia University.
152. "The Road Back."
153. Clifford Licorish to Gumby, July 16, 1934, "Gumby Book Studio" scrapbook, no. 2.
154. Polly J. Thistlethwaite, "Building 'A Home of Our Own': The Construction of the Lesbian Herstory Archives," in *Daring to Find Our Names: The Search for Lesbigay Library History*, ed. James V. Carmichael Jr. (Westport, CT: Greenwood Press, 1998), 153–74; and Huey Copeland and Naomi Beckwith, "Black Collectivities: An Introduction," *Nka: Journal of Contemporary African Art* 34 (2014): 4–7.
155. Farah Jasmine Griffin, "'Our Land That We Don't Own': A Review of Sharifa Rhodes-Pitts's *Harlem Is Nowhere: A Journey to the Mecca of Black America*," *Transition* 105 (2011): 151.
156. Gumby, [untitled notes on making scrapbooks].
157. Catherine A. Latimer, "Report of Reference Work, Schomburg Collection, 1946," box 2, folder 5, SCRBC Records, MARB, SCRBC.
158. Gumby to Arthur H. Fauset, Esq., February 3, 1928, Subseries I.1 (reel 96–2040), Gumby Collection.
159. Arthur A. Schomburg, "The Negro Digs Up His Past," *Survey Graphic* 6, no. 6 (March 1925): 672.
160. Roy Johnson, "A Man for a Man" [undated typescript], "Gumby's Autobiography" scrapbook, no. 1; and Inscription from Christopher Lazarre to Gumby on issue of *Blues: A Magazine of New Rhythms*, no. 8 (Spring 1930), "Gumby Book Studio" scrapbook, no. 1.
161. Tina Campt, *Other Germans: Black Germans and the Politics of Race, Gender and Memory in the Third Reich* (Ann Arbor: University of Michigan Press, 2004), 86–89. In documenting experimental sexualities that went unnamed in the scrapbook's formal categories, Gumby anticipated the "impressionistic" queer reading practices described in Shane Vogel, "The Sensuous Harlem Renaissance: Sexuality and Queer Culture," in *A Companion to the Harlem Renaissance*, ed. Cherene Sherrard-Johnson (Malden, MA: Wiley-Blackwell, 2015), 281.
162. Gumby to Porter, March 27, 1949, Records of the MSRC, Record Group 1, University Archives, MSRC.
163. Porter to Leigh Whipper, June 17, 1949, Records of the MSRC, Record Group 1, University Archives, MSRC. On the Moorland Foundation's holdings of ephemera, see descriptions in

Moorland Foundation Annual Reports for 1938–1939 and 1940–1941, Manuscript Division, MSRC. Porter told Whipper that Gumby's scrapbooks would "be more appreciated and better used here," at a Black institution, than at Columbia. In the 1960s, Gumby's scrapbooks constituted nearly the entirety of Columbia's "Negro" collection (Lorenzo J. Greene, "Manuscript Collections in Libraries," *Negro History Bulletin* 30, no. 3 [March 1967], 20). In recent years, however, Gumby's collection has become a cornerstone of Columbia's expanding African American collections.

164. It was not the first time that Columbia University acquired material Dorothy Porter wanted for Howard. See Ted O'Reilly, "Dorothy B. Porter, a Library Hero," New York Historical Society blog, April 8, 2021, https://www.nyhistory.org/blogs/dorothy-b-porter-a-library-hero. It is tempting to read Gumby's choice not to donate his collection to Howard as another instance of his truancy from the demands of racial representation, but he gave other parts of his collection to Delaware State College, a historically Black university. See Harold Jackman to Richard Bruce Nugent, March 18, 1961, box 7, James Weldon Johnson Memorial Collection MSS 92, BRBML; and E. J. Josey to Gumby, October 13, 1958, "Gumby's Autobiography" scrapbook, no. 1.
165. Memorandum, Reinhard H. Luthin to Roland Baughman, August 16, 1949, Gumby Accession File.
166. Gumby to Luthin, n.d., "Columbia University" scrapbook.
167. Memo, Baughman to Mr. Charles W. Mixer, May 21, 1952, Gumby Accession File.
168. Gumby, "The Gumby Scrapbook Collection," 8; and Penelope Papailias, *Genres of Recollection: Archival Poetics and Modern Greece* (New York: Palgrave Macmillan, 2005), 12.
169. Gumby's hesitation about relinquishing his material to a faraway repository, and his proposal to be in residence at Columbia to keep creating scrapbooks, foreshadowed recent conversations in the archives profession about changing notions of stewardship and postcustodial archiving. This archival literature is voluminous, but see, for example, Danielle Cooper, "House Proud: An Ethnography of the BC Gay and Lesbian Archives," *Archival Science* 16, no. 3 (2016): 261–88; Dorothy Berry, "The House Archives Built," up//root, June 22, 2021, https://www.uproot.space/features/the-house-archives-built; Jeannette A. Bastian, "Mine, Yours, Ours: Archival Custody from Transaction to Narrative," *Archival Science* 21, no. 1 (2021): 25–42; and on archival artist residences, ONE National Gay and Lesbian Archives, *Cruising the Archive: Queer Art and Culture in Los Angeles, 1945–1980* (Los Angeles: ONE National Gay and Lesbian Archives, 2011).

3. DEFIANT LIBRARIES: VIRGINIA LEE AND THE SECRETS KEPT BY GOOD BOOKLADIES

1. Except in states where the establishment of public libraries was tied to public schools, custom rather than law usually drove racial segregation in libraries. As L. D. Reddick argued, "library jimcrow has a flimsy basis in state law. Most of what is done in this regard must be accredited to the local and state library boards and to the librarians who run the libraries" (Reddick, "Where Can a Southern Negro Read a Book?," *New South* 9, no. 1 [January 1954]: 7–8). See also Eliza Atkins Gleason, *The Southern Negro and the Public Library* (Chicago: University of Chicago Press, 1941), 30–68.
2. Roanoke's Progressive-era projects consistently excluded African Americans. There was no hospital service for African Americans in Roanoke until 1915. A whites-only YMCA opened in 1914, and a colored branch in 1927. In 1942, after the City Council told the Black residents of Gainsboro that it could not afford land to expand Washington Park, it purchased acreage for additional whites-only park space. It also colocated the city dump at Washington Park in the 1940s. (Thanks to Darby Witek for research on this question.) See Petition to Central YMCA, 1927, Hunton YMCA Subject Files, GLA; "50 Year Anniversary of Burrell Memorial Hospital," *Roanoke Times*, March 14, 1965; Roanoke City Council Minutes, July 20, 1942, August 17, 1942, and September 21, 1942, Virginia

Room, RPL (hereafter City Council Minutes); "The Controversial Washington Park Dump in Roanoke Closes," May 31, 1963, WSLS-TV News Film Collection, 1951–1971, MSS 15988, Special Collections, University of Virginia, https://search.lib.virginia.edu/catalog/uva-lib:2396449; and Emily B. Harmon, "Shaping the City from Below: Urban Planning and Citizens' Battle for Control in Roanoke, Virginia, 1907–1928" (master's thesis, Virginia Polytechnic Institute and State University, 2018), 85–89.

3. Roanoke Public Library Board Minutes, October 9, 1920 and November 6, 1920, Virginia Room, RPL (hereafter Library Board Minutes). On Black print culture's rootedness in organizational life, see Frances Smith Foster, "A Narrative of the Interesting Origins and (Somewhat) Surprising Developments of African-American Print Culture," *American Literary History* 17, no. 4 (Winter 2005): 714–40. On James, Addison, and Downing, see A. B. Caldwell, ed., *History of the American Negro, Virginia Edition*, vol. 5 (Atlanta: Caldwell, 1921), 195–97, 263–66, and 294–97; "Rev. Arthur L. James, Our Present Minister, Has Served 19 Years," *Church News*, October 1938, First Baptist Church Subject Files, GLA; and Reginald Shareef, *The Roanoke Valley's African American Heritage: A Pictorial History* (Virginia Beach, VA: Donning, 1996), 12–14, 75, 88–89.

4. Isaac M. Warren, "Our Colored People," 1941, Gainsboro Library Vertical File 3, GLA; and National Register of Historic Places (NRHP) nomination for Gainsboro Library, 1996, Gainsboro Library Vertical File 1, GLA. Note that the Gainsboro Library vertical files (hereafter GLVF) were reorganized in 2019 and renamed the "Gainsboro Library Records"; because research was conducted before and after this reorganization, some locations cited herein may have changed.

5. Library Association quoted in NRHP nomination, section 8, page 9, GLVF 1. The Library Board later amended its bylaws, post hoc, to authorize establishment of a branch "for the use of colored people" (Library Board Minutes, October 7, 1920, November 6, 1920, and December 21, 1922).

6. Reddick, "Where Can a Southern Negro Read a Book?," 6. See also Louis Shores, "Library Service and the Negro," *Journal of Negro Education* 1, nos. 3/4 (October 1932): 374–80.

7. On the opening of the Gainsboro Library, see H. M. Miles, "The Gainsboro Colored Branch Library," 1924, Series I, folder 7, Gainsboro Library Records (hereafter GLR), GLA; Beth Macy, "Community by the Book," *Roanoke Times*, March 12, 2006, GLVF 1; and "No Ordinary Library," *Roanoke Times*, June 30, 2007, GLVF 1. On library access for African Americans, see Gleason, *The Southern Negro*, 90, 108; "Tells Concern at Howard U. Dedication," *Chicago Defender*, June 3, 1939; and Mollie Huston Lee, "Development of Negro Libraries in North Carolina," *North Carolina Libraries* 3, no. 2 (May 1944): 1–3, 7. The first separate public branch library for African Americans in the South was in Louisville, Kentucky.

8. Langston Hughes, "One-Way Ticket," *Collected Poems of Langston Hughes*, ed. Arnold Rampersad (New York: Vintage Classics, 1994), 361. For overviews of the Great Migration, see James R. Grossman, *Land of Hope: Chicago, Black Southerners, and the Great Migration* (Chicago: University of Chicago Press, 1989); and Isabel Wilkerson, *The Warmth of Other Suns: The Epic Story of America's Great Migration* (New York: Vintage, 2011).

9. On the daytime and nighttime strolls, see Davarian L. Baldwin, *Chicago's New Negroes: Modernity, The Great Migration, and Black Urban Life* (Chapel Hill: University of North Carolina Press, 2007), 45. On African American campaigns for library service, see Stephanie J. Shaw, *What a Woman Ought to Be and to Do: Black Professional Women Workers During the Jim Crow Era* (Chicago: University of Chicago Press, 1996), 172–74; and Wayne A. Wiegand and Shirley A. Wiegand, *The Desegregation of Public Libraries in the Jim Crow South: Civil Rights and Local Activism* (Baton Rouge: Louisiana State University, 2018), 18–43.

10. Nikhil Pal Singh, *Black Is a Country: Race and the Unfinished Struggle for Democracy* (Cambridge, MA: Harvard University Press, 2005), 50; and Thomas Augst, "Faith in Reading: Public Libraries, Liberalism, and the Civil Religion," in *Institutions of Reading: The Social Life of Libraries in the United States*, ed. Thomas Augst and Kenneth Carpenter (Amherst: University of Massachusetts Press, 2007), 169.

11. Hughes, "Café: 3 a.m.," *Collected Poems*, 406.
12. W. E. B. Du Bois, quoted in William F. Yust, "What of the Black and Yellow Races?," *Papers and Proceedings of the Thirty-Fifth Annual Meeting of the American Library Association Held at Katterskill, N.Y., June 23–28, 1913* (Chicago: American Library Association, 1913), 164; Hazel V. Carby, "Policing the Black Woman's Body in an Urban Context," *Critical Inquiry* 18, no. 4 (Summer 1992): 738–55; and Mollie Huston Lee to W. H. Carper, June 28, 1956, http://web.co.wake.nc.us/lee/mhlee/letters/mhlcorr560628.htm.
13. Some "colored libraries," while publicly funded, had autonomous governance, as in Charlotte, North Carolina; Savannah, Georgia; and Houston, Texas. See Ernestine Rose, "Work with Negroes Round Table," *Bulletin of the American Library Association* 16, no. 4 (July 1922): 363; and Michael Fultz, "Black Public Libraries in the South in the Era of De Jure Segregation," *Libraries and the Cultural Record* 41, no. 3 (Summer 2006): 341.
14. See Yust, "What of the Black and Yellow Races?," 162; Louis R. Wilson and Marion A. Milczewski, *Libraries of the Southeast, A Report of the Southeastern States Cooperative Library Survey, 1946–1947* (Chapel Hill: Southeastern Library Association, 1949), 261; Annie L. McPheeters, *Library Service in Black and White: Some Personal Recollections, 1921–1980* (Metuchen, NJ: Scarecrow, 1988), 77; and Wiegand and Wiegand, *Desegregation of Public Libraries*, 28.
15. Mollie E. Dunlap, Review of *Rural America Reads: A Study of Rural Library Service*, by Marion Humble, *Journal of Negro Education* 8, no. 2 (April 1939): 217; George T. Settle, "Work with Negroes Roundtable," *Bulletin of the American Library Association* 17, no. 4 (July 1923): 278; and Rose, "Work with Negroes Round Table" [1922], 363.
16. Herman Murphy [?] to Arna Bontemps, January 31, 1943, box 18, folder 33, Arna Bontemps Papers, SUSCRC. The field of book history has long treated "political and legal sanctions" as central to relations between books and readers; see Robert Darnton, "What Is the History of Books?," in *The Book History Reader*, ed. David Finkelstein and Alistair McCleery (London: Routledge, 2002): 9–26.
17. Catherine Latimer to Carter G. Woodson, November 17, 1931, Series 2, reel 1, Papers of Carter G. Woodson and the Association for the Study of Negro Life and History. This microfilmed material is now Part II, Correspondence, 1912–1950 of the Carter Godwin Woodson Papers, Manuscript Division, Library of Congress.
18. "J. Fauset Reading Club Nears End of 10th Year," *Norfolk Journal and Guide*, June 17, 1939. See also Cheryl Knott Malone, "African American Libraries," in *International Dictionary of Library Histories*, vol. 1, ed. David H. Stam (Chicago: Fitzroy Dearborn, 2001), 3.
19. While "colored branch libraries" often made a point to build collections of materials "by and about the Negro," they generally did not appear in surveys of special collections either because they were too small to generate notice or were not explicitly designated as special collections. See Dorothy B. Porter, "Library Sources for the Study of Negro Life and History," *Journal of Negro Education* 5, no. 2 (April 1936): 232–44; Mollie E. Dunlap, "Special Collections of Negro Literature in the United States," *Journal of Negro Education* 4, no. 4 (1935): 482–89; Naomi J. Rushing, "The Technical Organizing of Special Collections of Books By and About the Negro" (master's thesis, Columbia University, 1940), 8; and Arna Bontemps, "Special Collections of Negroana," *Library Quarterly* 14, no. 3 (July 1944): 187–206.
20. On the history of these southern branch libraries, see McPheeters, *Library Service in Black and White*; Patrick Valentine, "Mollie Huston Lee: Founder of Raleigh's Public Black Library," *North Carolina Libraries* 56, no. 1 (Spring 1998): 23–26; Jessica Harland-Jacobs, "The History of Public Library Service in Durham, 1897–1997" (Durham, NC: Durham County Library, 1999); Caitlin Reeves, "Red Brick and Stone: Atlanta's Pragmatic Civil Rights and the Auburn Avenue Library, 1899–1950" (master's thesis, Simmons College, 2016), 34; and Alex H. Poole, "'Could My Dark Hands Break Through the Dark Shadow?': Gender, Jim Crow, and Librarianship During the Long

Freedom Struggle, 1935–1955," *Library Quarterly* 88, no. 4 (October 2018): 348–74. Many of these collections are documented in Matthew Griffis, "Roots of Community: Segregated Carnegie Libraries as Spaces for Learning and Community-Making in Pre-Civil Rights America, 1900–65," https://aquila.usm.edu/rocprofiles/.

21. Mollie Huston Lee to Porter, January 17, 1939, box 5, Dorothy Porter Wesley Papers, BRBML (hereafter DPW Papers). Note that at the time of research, this collection was minimally processed. Subsequent reprocessing may have changed the box locations cited.
22. Dorothy Porter, Notecards for untitled speech upon receipt of Howard University Alumni Award, ca. 1973, box 34, DPW Papers.
23. Lillian Taylor Wright, "Thomas Fountain Blue, Pioneer Librarian, 1866–1935" (master's thesis, Atlanta University School of Library Service, 1955), 26–27, 39. On the Louisville model, see Fultz, "Black Public Libraries," 340–41; and Works Progress Administration in the State of Kentucky, *Libraries and Lotteries: A History of the Louisville Free Public Library* (Cynthiana, KY: Hobson, 1944), 123.
24. "Gainsboro Branch," typescript ca. 1941, in Series 1, folder 7, GLR; Wright, "Thomas Fountain Blue," 21, 24; and Cheryl Knott, *Not Free, Not for All: Public Libraries in the Age of Jim Crow* (Amherst: University of Massachusetts Press, 2015), 176–77.
25. Macy, "Community by the Book."
26. NRHP nomination, GLVF 1.
27. Miles, "The Gainsboro Colored Branch Library."
28. Program, Dedication of the Afro-American Collection, September 26, 1982, GLVF 2; and "Gainsboro Branch," typescript, ca. 1941.
29. Virginia Dare Young, Mercer County, West Virginia, 1910 United States Federal Census; Virginia Young, Roanoke, Virginia, 1920 United States Federal Census; World War I Draft Registration Card for Robert Daniel Young, 1918; William D. Young, Roanoke, Virginia, 1900 United States Federal Census; and *Roanoke City Directory 1922* (Richmond, VA: Hill Directory, 1922). All accessed via Ancestry.com.
30. The Harrison School, which opened in 1917, initially was accredited only through eighth grade. Lucy Addison added high school classes, eventually offering a full curriculum, and lobbied for its accreditation—another example of African Americans building infrastructure when the state refused to do so. The first class to finish with high school diplomas was 1924—the year of Virginia Young (Lee)'s graduation. Roanoke constructed its first high school building for African American students several years later. See John T. Kneebone, "Lucy Addison (1861–1937)," https://www.encyclopediavirginia.org/Addison_Lucy_1861-1937#start_entry.
31. Mary Bishop, "Gainsboro Honors a Librarian's Vision," *Roanoke Times*, November 20, 1992, GLVF 3.
32. George A. Kuyper, "Huntington Library Serves School and Public, Members of White and Negro Races," *Newport News Daily Press*, July 2, 1933, Hampton Library School file, HUA.
33. L. E. Herron, Library Report for 1913, in Library Reports 1899–1939, Collis P. Huntington Library Records, HUA.
34. Ann Trusler, "Literary Pioneer," *Roanoke Times*, August 30, 1970. HBCU (historically Black college or university) libraries, which began building Africana collections earlier than public libraries, played a key role in training librarians who went on to create many of the first "Negro Collections" in branch libraries. Mollie Huston Lee, for example, worked in the Negro Collection at Howard University, under E. C. Williams, before she built a similar collection at the Harrison Library in Raleigh, North Carolina. Ray Nichols Moore, "Mollie Huston Lee: A Profile," *Wilson Library Bulletin* 49, no. 6 (February 1975): 434.
35. Kuyper, "Huntington Library"; Report on Library, January 1, 1920–March 1, 1921, in Library Reports 1899–1939, Collis P. Huntington Library Records, HUA. Details of Lee's time at Hampton

are gleaned from Lucy B. Campbell, "Hampton Institute Library School," in *Handbook of Black Librarianship*, 2nd ed., ed. E. J. Josey and Marva L. DeLoach (Lanham, MD: Scarecrow, 2000): 35–48; Program, Dedication of the Afro-American Collection, September 26, 1982, GLVF 2; Joel Turner, "Black History Collection to Bear Librarian's Name," *Roanoke Times*, September 23, 1982, Virginia Lee Subject File, GLA; and "Twenty Thousand Dollar Library Open," *Roanoke Tribune*, May 15, 1942. (Copies of the *Roanoke Tribune* are rare; this copy is housed at GLA.)

36. Wallace Van Jackson, "Negro Library Workers," *Library Quarterly* 10, no. 1 (January 1940): 98.
37. "Library Problems Brought to Conference at Hampton," newspaper clipping, [1927], Collis P. Huntington Library Records, HUA.
38. David M. Battles, *The History of Public Library Access for African Americans in the South* (Lanham, MD: Scarecrow, 2009), 61; and "Historical Books About the Negro Race in Hampton Institute Library," typescript, February 1928, Library School files, HUA.
39. On Lee's hiring, see Library Board Minutes, May 16, 1928.
40. Warren, "Our Colored People." On similar clubs elsewhere, see Shawn Anthony Christian, *The Harlem Renaissance and the Idea of a New Negro Reader* (Amherst: University of Massachusetts Press, 2016), 3–4; and Christine Pawley, *Organizing Women: Home, Work, and the Infrastructure of Print in Twentieth-Century America* (Amherst: University of Massachusetts Press, 2022), 79–109.
41. Quoted in Brittney C. Cooper, *Beyond Respectability: The Intellectual Thought of Race Women* (Urbana: University of Illinois Press, 2017), 11. There is no membership list of the Fauset Reading Club in the GLA. I have compiled a list of fifty members from programs and newspaper articles and determined their family status and/or occupation through 1930 and 1940 U.S. Census records in Ancestry.com.
42. Program for Jessie Fauset Reading Club, [1930s], unprocessed box, GLR. This collection has been fully processed since the time of my research.
43. Fauset was active in New York literary circles and an occasional guest of Georgia Douglas Johnson's Saturday Nighters in Washington, DC. See Elizabeth McHenry, *Forgotten Readers: Recovering the Lost History of African American Literary Societies* (Durham, NC: Duke University Press, 2002), 383 n100; and "The Debut of the Younger School of Negro Writers," *Opportunity* 2, no. 17 (May 1924): 143.
44. Virginia D. Young Lee, "Clubs in the Public Library," *Negro Library Conference, Fisk University, Nashville Tennessee, Papers Presented, November 20–23, [1930]* (Nashville, TN: Fisk University, 1930), 46–49.
45. In the 1940s, teacher Sadye Lawson, who had been a speaker for the Fauset Club, offered a college extension course in "American Literature" at the Gainsboro branch ("Gainsboro Library News," *Roanoke Tribune*, January 8, 1943, GLVF 3).
46. Lee, "Clubs"; and Willmer Dillard, "Roanoke Writings," May 10, 1941, *New Journal and Guide*. Biographical information drawn from Electer Allred, Roanoke, Virginia, 1930 and 1940 United States Federal Censuses; *Hill's Roanoke Salem and Vinton (Virginia) City Directory, 1927* (Richmond, VA: Hill Directory, 1927); and *Hill's Roanoke (Roanoke County, Va.) City Directory 1941* (Richmond, VA: Hill Directory, 1941). All accessed through Ancestry.com.
47. Lee, "Clubs." Unlike the imagined publics that emerge among stranger-readers of a circulating text, the Fauset Club showed the importance of "physical space where social difference became visible" (Augst, "Faith in Reading," 172).
48. Abigail A. Van Slyck, *Free to All: Carnegie Libraries and American Culture, 1890–1920* (Chicago: University of Chicago Press, 1995), 76.
49. Nikhil Anand, Akhil Gupta, and Hannah Appel, "Introduction: Temporality, Politics, and the Promise of Infrastructure," in *The Promise of Infrastructure*, ed. Appel, Anand, and Gupta (Durham, NC: Duke University Press, 2018), 23.
50. Audio recording, "The Afro-American History Collection Honoring Mrs. Virginia Y. Lee," September 26, 1982, GLR.

51. After the Virginia Supreme Court's 1931 ruling in *Davis* v. *Allen* limited the power of local registrars to deny qualified registrants, Black voter leagues and NAACP chapters began spreading across the state. Conley L. Edwards, "A Political History of the Poll Tax in Virginia, 1900–1950" (master's thesis, University of Richmond, 1973), 87, 91–95.
52. "Things the Public Should Know," Dedication program, Gainsboro Library, May 10, 1942, GLVF 1. The Fauset Club helped build Gainsboro's collection, raised funds for its support, and put pressure on city officials to expand library service. Their work both inside and outside the library captures Michael Dawson's argument that post-Reconstruction African American communities worked to "reinsert themselves into the channels of public discourse" while also building an "active counter-public" (Dawson, "A Black Counterpublic?: Economic Earthquakes, Racial Agenda(s), and Black Politics," in *The Black Public Sphere: A Public Culture Book*, ed. Black Public Sphere Collective, [Chicago: University of Chicago Press, 1995], 204).
53. "Roanoke Citizens Seek New Library," August 14, 1937, *New Journal and Guide*; and "Civic Organizations Urged to Press for Bond Issue to Construct New Library," *Roanoke Times*, August 7, 1937.
54. J. L. Reid and J. H. Claytor, letter to "My dear ______," March 16, 1937, and Telegram, Florence R. Curtis to Virginia Lee, March 23, 1937, Series 1, folder 5, GLR; and Untitled typescript beginning "Gainsboro Branch Library, which has served . . .", ca. 1937, Series 1, folder 12, GLR.
55. Akhil Gupta, "Infrastructure in Ruins: Thoughts on the Temporality of Infrastructure," in *Promise of Infrastructure*, 63. Lee's "special library committee" took this list of demands to the Roanoke Woman's Club, the white civic improvement league spearheading the drive for a new main branch ("Roanoke Citizens Seek New Library").
56. In 1938, the Library Board failed to take any action on the needs of the Gainsboro branch. Lee convened a "special library committee," which dispatched attorney J. L. Reid and mortician C. C. Williams to appeal to the board, after which the city's proposed bond initiative was amended to include "improvement" of the existing Gainsboro branch but no new construction. That bond issue failed. See Library Board Minutes, June 30, 1938, and August 31, 1938; J. L. Reid and Virginia Y. Lee to Special Library Committee [carbon copy], July 27, 1938, Series 1, folder 10, GLR; and City Council Minutes, August 22, 1938 and October 3, 1938. After continued pressure from the "delegation of colored citizens," which stated that it "had waited 21 years for better library facilities," the bond proposal was amended again to fund a new building for the Gainsboro branch ("Council Allocates $20,000 of Proposed Bond Issue for Colored Library," *Roanoke Times*, October 1, 1940). See also City Council Minutes, September 9, 1940, September 23, 1940, November 12, 1940, and September 30, 1940; Library Board Minutes, September 17, 1940, and October 8, 1940; NRHP nomination, GLVF 1; and Pamphlet, "Vote for Bond Issues," 1940, Series 1, folder 1, GLR.
57. Paradoxically, the Gainsboro Library benefited from the city's failure to include it in the initial proposal to cofund library construction with Works Progress Administration (WPA) support. WPA funding slated for the main branch evaporated in the buildup to war in the early 1940s. Because the Gainsboro project was excluded from the WPA proposal, its funding was not contingent on federal support, and its construction moved ahead while the main branch did not (Library Board Minutes, July 29, 1941, and October 14, 1941). The bond issue was decided in an election of freeholders—those who held real estate in the city and had paid poll taxes. Black Roanoke had more sway in freeholder elections than general elections because 50 percent of Black qualified voters were also freeholders, versus 41 percent of whites. See "Bond Issue Ballot to Help Swell City Vote on Tuesday," *Roanoke Times*, November 3, 1940.
58. Audio recording, "The Afro-American History Collection Honoring Mrs. Virginia Y. Lee"; and "Gifts from Outstanding Negroes" typescript, ca. 1942, Series 1, folder 6, GLR.
59. "Twenty Thousand Dollar Library."
60. "Twenty Thousand Dollar Library." Evidence in the Gainsboro Library Archives suggests that Lee wrote the copy printed in this newspaper article.

61. Christmas pageant program, Golden Rule Bible Class; and Ella F. Dean, "Local Briefs," *Church News* (Roanoke, VA), May 1933—both in First Baptist Church Vertical File, GLA.
62. Gleason, *The Southern Negro*, 134.
63. "City 'Cop' Shoots to See Innocent Lad Run," *Roanoke Tribune*, May 15, 1942. This article names the officer as Mitchell; in 1942, there were two police officers in Roanoke with the last name Mitchell, both white (*Hill's Roanoke City Directory 1942* [Richmond, VA: Hill Directory, 1942], Ancestry .com).
64. Elizabeth Alexander, "'Can You Be BLACK and Look at This?': Reading the Rodney King Video(s)," in *Black Public Sphere*, 84.
65. "City 'Cop' Shoots."
66. Wilmer F. Dillard, "Roanoke in Review," *New Journal and Guide*, May 30, 1942. As Jarvis R. Givens argues, "In an antiblack world, achievement and criminality could be equivalent transgressions" (Givens, *Fugitive Pedagogy: Carter G. Woodson and the Art of Black Teaching* [Cambridge, MA: Harvard University Press, 2021], 73).
67. On L. A. Lee, see "Hunton Branch YMCA Purchases Former Odd Fellows Building," *Roanoke Times*, November 3, 1940, GLVF 3. L. A. Lee was one of several Black Roanoke residents who filed suit against the Roanoke police department after its officers attacked a crowd on Henry Street celebrating the Louis-Schmeling fight ("Police Toss Tear Gas in Roanoke, Va.," *New Journal and Guide*, 2 July 1938). This police crackdown on Black celebration in Roanoke echoed earlier incidents in other cities after Jack Johnson defeated James Jeffries in 1910 (Baldwin, *Chicago's New Negroes*, 2–5).
68. "Brief History of the William A. Hunton Young Men's Christian Association," Golden Anniversary Booklet, 1978, YMCA Subject File, GLA; "William A. Hunton Branch Y. M. C. A. Is Celebrating Tenth Year," *Roanoke Times*, July 3, 1938; and "City 'Cop' Shoots."
69. Richard Wright, "The Ethics of Living Jim Crow," in *Uncle Tom's Children: Five Long Stories* (New York: Harper, 1938), ix–xxx.
70. "Twenty Thousand Dollar Library."
71. Wiegand and Wiegand, *Desegregation of Public Libraries*, 28.
72. Harmon, "Shaping the City," 46–47.
73. "Police Toss Tear Gas in Roanoke, Va." Roanoke was one of a handful of municipalities that tried to codify residential segregation starting in 1911. One ordinance barred Black residents from moving onto majority-white blocks and vice versa, while another designated four "segregation districts" to confine the Black population. The U.S. Supreme Court ruled against these ordinances in 1917, but the city continued to mark a "Negro Residence" area on planning maps (Harmon, "Shaping the City," 62–89; and Matt Chittun, "When Segregation Ruled the Streets," *Roanoke Times*, August 13, 2005).
74. "Gainsboro Library Fills Need," *Roanoke World-News*, March 13, 1939, GLVF 3.
75. Eliza Atkins Gleason, "Facing the Dilemma of Public Library Service for Negroes," *Library Quarterly* 15, no. 4 (October 1945): 340; and "Suggested Needs of the Gainsboro Library," undated typescript, Series 1, folder 12, GLC.
76. Library Board Minutes, April 17, 1924, and April 2, 1921. It was typical in the South for African American citizens to participate in library governance "in an advisory capacity only" (Ernestine Rose, "Work with Negroes Round Table," *Bulletin of the American Library Association* 15, no. 4 [July 1921]: 201). By contrast, in Raleigh, the Richard B. Harrison Public Library operated with a county appropriation but independent of the main library; this arrangement meant that "Members of the community are given greater consideration in their requests for the purchase of desired books than if each requisition had to pass through the main library" (Mollie Huston Lee, "Securing a Branch Library," *Opportunity* 17, no. 9 [September 1939]: 261).
77. Library Board Minutes, April 22, 1936.
78. Trusler, "Literary Pioneer."

79. "Librarians to Invade Fisk Nov. 20," *Chicago Defender*, November 15, 1930.
80. "Significant Developments Are Noted in Library Service," *Norfolk Journal and Guide*, October 25, 1930; and Monroe Work, "Using a Collection of Materials on the Negro," *Negro Library Conference, Fisk University*, 63–66.
81. Henry Slaughter was slated to discuss "Negro History Collections," along with Work and Schomburg, but it is not clear from the press coverage whether he attended. [Tentative schedule for Negro Library Conference], typescript, ca. 1930, Thomas Elsa Jones Collection, FUA.
82. Macy, "Community by the Book"; and "Gifts from Outstanding Negroes."
83. "Twenty Thousand Dollar Library Opens."
84. Turner, "Black History Collection."
85. Macy, "Community by the Book"; NRHP nomination; and "The Virginia Y. Lee African-American History Collection," typescript, ca. 1983, unprocessed box, GLR.
86. The Virginia Y. Lee Collection, as it is now named, includes works acquired before, during, and after Lee's tenure. To determine what Lee acquired, I physically examined books now in the collection, looking for accession numbers, checkout dates, inscriptions, and bookplates, and I used the markings in books with known donation dates (such as those acquired for the 1942 opening) to determine an accession chronology. I have located approximately 135 of the books acquired by the Gainsboro Branch when Lee was librarian. My thanks to colleagues at SCRBC, whose bibliographic work reconstructing the library of Arthur Schomburg informed my approach to the Gainsboro books. See Alice Adamczyk, Laura E. Helton, Miranda Mims, and Matthew J. Murphy, "Library Archaeology: Reconstructing a Catalog of the Arthur A. Schomburg Book and Pamphlet Collection," *African American Review* 54, nos. 1–2 (Spring/Summer 2021): 1–18. Thanks also to Darby Witek for building the spreadsheet of bibliographic data.
87. "Books by and Relating to the Negro," ca. 1936, box 3, folder 13, George Cleveland Hall Branch Library Archives, VGHRC; "Making the Most of Idle Moments," *Chicago Defender*, January 25, 1936; and L. D. Reddick to Franklin F. Hopper, June 14, 1945, box 33, Lydenberg, Hopper, and Beals General Correspondence, NYPLA.
88. Although extant files of the branch in its early years are sparse, and most copies of *The Roanoke Tribune* were destroyed by a fire, other records from this period contain no mention of a special "collection" of books by and about the Negro—not in Library Board minutes or in news coverage. The first surviving list of the collection is from the mid-1950s (Gainsboro Branch of the Roanoke Public Library, "A List of Readable Books About Negro History," ca. 1955, Series 1, folder 14, GLR).
89. Trusler, "Literary Pioneer."
90. Trusler, "Literary Pioneer."
91. Rushing, "Technical Organizing," 42. Many books in the Virginia Y. Lee Collection are still shelved under the Dewey number 325.26 ("Negro Question") because of how they were cataloged from 1928 until the 1950s, when this Dewey class number was retired.
92. Quoted in NRHP nomination.
93. In national library histories, Roanoke is described as progressive because by the time the Southern Regional Council surveyed southern libraries in 1953, the city reported that its main branch was open to Black readers (see Fultz, "Black Public Libraries," 347). That reporting reflected a relatively recent change, however. In Gleason's 1941 study, Roanoke was *not* among the small number of cities that provided full or partial service to Black residents at the main branch (Gleason, *The Southern Negro*, 83).
94. Turner, "Black History Collection"; and Carla Pullen Lewis quoted in Macy, "Community by the Book."
95. In the 1930s, Roanoke's school superintendent proposed that the Gainsboro branch serve double duty as a school library to circumvent state regulations requiring library facilities in the recently constructed colored high school (Library Board Minutes, December 18, 1935).

96. Frank Taylor to Board of Estimate and Apportionment, February 18, 1937, box 1, folder 1c, SCRBC Records, SCRBC.
97. Macy, "Community by the Book"; and Bishop, "Gainsboro Honors."
98. Library Board Minutes, September 9, 1942, and October 14, 1941; and "Gifts Received by Library," [1942], Series 1, folder 6, GLR.
99. Turner, "Black History Collection"; and Dan Casey, "Roanoke Tour Brings Black History out of the Abstract," *Roanoke Times*, February 13, 2013.
100. Doug Stuber, "Recorded: Virginia Lee Gives Library Place in History," *Roanoke Times and World News*, February 28, 1987.
101. Casey, "Roanoke Tour."
102. Carla Pullen Lewis quoted in Macy, "Community by the Book." My thanks to Mrs. Carla Lewis for confirming the details of this story.
103. Quoted in Turner, "Black History Collection."
104. "Gainsboro Library News," *Roanoke Tribune*, January 3, 1943, GLVF 3. As Reddick quipped, to access research materials in southern repositories, Black readers sometimes had to enter "into conspiracy with the Negro janitor" (quoted in David A. Varel, *The Scholar and the Struggle: Lawrence Reddick's Crusade for Black History and Black Power* [Durham: University of North Carolina Press, 2021], 55).
105. Darlene Clark Hine, "Rape and the Inner Lives of Black Women in the Middle West: Preliminary Thoughts on the Culture of Dissemblance," *Signs: Journal of Women in Culture and Society* 14, no. 4 (1989): 912–20. On Black women librarians' engagement with the "culture of dissemblance," see Melanie Chambliss, "A Vital Factor in the Community: Recovering the Life and Legacy of Chicago Public Librarian Vivian G. Harsh," *Journal of African American History* 106, no. 3 (Summer 2021): 412–13.
106. Peter Galison, "Removing Knowledge," *Critical Inquiry* 31, no. 1 (Autumn 2004): 231, 229; Kevin Young, *The Grey Album: On the Blackness of Blackness* (Minneapolis, MN: Grey Wolf, 2012), 23; and Alexis Pauline Gumbs, *M Archive: After the End of the World* (Durham, NC: Duke University Press, 2018), 63. Verne Harris writes, in the context of South African apartheid, about countervailing motivations for secrecy: by anti-apartheid activists whose records were subject to confiscation by the state; and by apartheid bureaucrats who destroyed surveillance records on the eve of transition to democracy (Harris, "The Archival Sliver: Power, Memory, and Archives in South Africa," *Archival Science* 2 [2002]: 70).
107. Trusler, "Literary Pioneer."
108. Roanoke officials hoped to avoid the notoriety of Danville and Prince Edward County—both known as sites of massive white resistance in Virginia—by implementing token integration "quietly" and "completely without incident." To avoid "Birmingham-type" demonstrations, the city negotiated civil rights issues through a "secret commission" and the City Council aimed for a "minimum of publicity." These strategies are documented in a civil rights scrapbook in the Raymond R. Wilkinson Memorial Library at Hill Street Baptist Church: "2 Roanoke Schools Integrated Quietly," *Roanoke World News*, September 6, 1960; "Wilkinson Discloses Integration Progress," *Roanoke Times*, July 29, 1963; "Race-Accord Units Nothing New Here," [unidentified newspaper], ca. 1963; "Decision on Dump Believed to Lessen Danger of March," *Roanoke Times*, May 24, ca. 1963; "Negro Leader Declares," *Roanoke Star*, May 23, 1963; "Integration of Theater Supported," [unidentified newspaper], ca. 1963; and Arthur Hill, "Secret Group to Take Racial Lead," [unidentified newspaper], ca. 1963, https://drive.google.com/drive/folders/1N4RNZEunOnW4rvHbqK2deoGvCKofOR7t.
109. The phrase "basement exile" appears in Trusler, "Literary Pioneer."
110. Lara Langer Cohen, *Going Underground: Race, Space, and the Subterranean in the Nineteenth-Century United States* (Durham, NC: Duke University Press, 2023), 12. In 2023, Roanoke residents, led by former mayor Nelson Harris, successfully petitioned the Virginia Department of Historic Resources to place a marker in front of the Gainsboro Library honoring Lee's fight to save the collection.

See Lindsey Hull, "New Marker Will Share the History of Roanoke's Gainsboro Library—and of the Librarian Who Saved Its Collection," *Cardinal News*, September 13, 2023, https://cardinalnews.org/2023/09/13/new-marker-will-share-the-history-of-roanokes-gainsboro-library-and-of-the-librarian-who-saved-its-collection/.

111. Jennifer C. Nash, "Black Feminine Enigmas, or Notes on the Politics of Black Feminist Theory," *Signs: Journal of Women in Culture and Society* 45, no. 3 (2020): 521. See also Mia Bay, "The Battle for Womanhood Is the Battle for Race: Black Women and Nineteenth-Century Racial Thought," in *Toward an Intellectual History of Black Women*, ed. Mia Bay, Farah J. Griffin, Martha S. Jones, and Barbara D. Savage (Chapel Hill: University of North Carolina Press, 2015), 77.
112. "Lichtman Theatre Chain Proves Economic Factor: Unprecedented Growth Outcome of Unselfishness," *New Journal and Guide*, November 23, 1940; "Lichtman Theatre Gives Books," *New Journal and Guide*, August 15, 1942.
113. Lee often recorded the provenance of an acquisition near the book's inner hinge, and I found ten books in the current Virginia Y. Lee Afro-American History Collection with the note "Donated by A. E. Lichtman." I checked the accession numbers of these books to confirm the timing of their donation.
114. "Lichtman Theatre Gives Books."
115. Doxey A. Wilkerson, "The Negro School Movement in Virginia: From 'Equalization' to 'Integration,'" *Journal of Negro Education* 29, no. 1 (Winter 1960): 18–20.
116. "Lichtman Theatres Play Important Role in Amusement and Civic Life in Capital," *Baltimore Afro-American*, September 19, 1942; and "NAACP Gets Life Membership from A. E. Lichtman," *New Journal and* Guide, January 23, 1943. The same issue of the *Journal and Guide* (Virginia's largest African American weekly) that reported on the opening of the new Gainsboro Library also chronicled Lichtman's contributions to the NAACP: "Richmond NAACP Campaign Goal is 2,000 Members," *New Journal and Guide*, May 16, 1942; and "New Roanoke Library Is Dedicated," *New Journal and Guide*, May 16, 1942. White officials in Roanoke preferred to engage a handful of Black leaders in negotiations rather than confront organized efforts, such as the NAACP's campaigns; see Mary Bishop, "Black Movement Sparked," *Roanoke Times*, undated newspaper clipping, Urban Renewal Vertical File, GLA.
117. Willmer F. Dilard [Dillard], "Roanoke in Review," *New Journal and Guide*, July 4, 1942. Nabors chaired the NAACP membership drive in Roanoke in 1938 and spoke at mass meetings ("Bondage Charged to Whites," *New Journal and Guide*, November 5, 1938). When Ella Baker visited Virginia in 1942, she praised the financial contributions from Lichtman Theatres to the NAACP ("Richmond NAACP Campaign Goal Is 2,000 Members").
118. "Father and Son Programs Arranged by Roanoke YMCA," *New Journal and Guide*, November 13, 1943; "Congregation Regales Pastor on Birthday," *Chicago Defender*, August 16, 1952; and "Police Toss Tear Gas in Roanoke, Va."
119. Lee quoted in Trusler, "Literary Pioneer."
120. Lee quoted in Stuber, "Recorded"; and Audio recording, "The Afro-American History Collection Honoring Mrs. Virginia Y. Lee."
121. Michael Warner, "Publics and Counterpublics," *Public Culture* 14, no. 1 (Winter 2002): 81. Thomas C. Holt defines a counterpublic as "divorced from substantial control over how public power is deployed" (Holt, "Mapping the Black Public Sphere," in *Black Public Sphere*, 328).
122. Cohen, *Going Underground*, 2.
123. Anand, Gupta, and Appel, "Introduction," 11.
124. Evelyn Brooks Higginbotham, "African-American Women's History and the Metalanguage of Race," *Signs* 17, no. 2 (Winter 1992): 272. As Victoria W. Wolcott has argued, "southern norms of respectability" were often shared by the middle and working class and "sometimes masked resistance to the South's dominant power structure" (Wolcott, *Remaking Respectability: African American Women in Interwar Detroit* [Chapel Hill: University of North Carolina Press, 2001], 13).

125. "Facts About the Gainsboro Library," Series 1, folder 7, GLR; and Macy, "Community by the Book."
126. J. M. Gandy, president of Virginia Normal and Industrial Institute, quoted in "Roanoke Colored Library Started," *Roanoke Times*, December 14, 1921, GLVF 3.
127. Trusler, "Literary Pioneer."
128. Library Board Minutes, June 30, 1947.
129. "Gainsboro Branch Library Adult Books By and About Negroes," typescript fragment, 1947, Series 1, folder 17, GLR.
130. Estimated 1,282 books collected by Lee, based on pre-1971 titles in "The Virginia Y. Lee Afro-American History Collection Bibliography of Adult and Juvenile Book and Non-Book Materials," GLA.
131. Trusler, "Literary Pioneer."
132. At least two other branch library collections were also named for the Black women who founded them in the late 1920s and 1930s: the Mollie Huston Lee Collection of Black Literature, designated in 1972; and the Vivian G. Harsh Collection of Afro-American History and Literature, named in 1975.
133. In "Recorded," Stuber explicitly describes Lee's actions to add additional material to the audio recording of the dedication ceremony. He reports that in her formal speech, Lee "traced the history of the Gainsboro library and talked about why she felt black history is important." He then states that Lee "added other comments to the tape later," in which she "said that collecting black literature wasn't always embraced with open arms. In the 1940s members of the Roanoke City Council asked her to remove books about black history. She was told she would lose her job if she didn't abide by the request." In my research, however, I could not locate this second part of the recording. It may have been lost when the cassette tape (which was made from the reel-to-reel around 1987) was migrated to CDs.
134. Appel, "Infrastructural Time," in *Promise of Infrastructure*, 54–57.
135. Mindy Thompson Fullilove, *Root Shock: How Tearing Up City Neighborhoods Hurts America, and What We Can Do About It* (New York: Ballantine, 2004), 224. On urban renewal in Roanoke, see Mary Bishop, "Street by Street, Block by Block: How Urban Renewal Uprooted Black Roanoke," *Roanoke Times*, January 29, 1995; Fullilove, *Root Shock*, 71–107; Mason Adams, "Troubled Legacy," *Roanoke Times*, August 31, 2008; and Martha Park, "Even the Dead Could Not Stay," Citylab.com, January 19, 2018, Citylab.com/equity/2018/01/even-the-dead-could-not-stay/550838.
136. Young, *The Grey Album*, 11.
137. Without romanticizing it, Houston A. Baker Jr. argues for the existence of a "remarkable black public sphere" under segregation that "offered a sometimes radical critique of the dominant white society with which it coexisted" (Baker Jr., "Critical Memory and the Black Public Sphere," in *Black Public Sphere*, 23). The Gainsboro Library's struggle for survival in the post-desegregation era, when the City of Roanoke no longer saw it as necessary for the maintenance of segregation, is a reminder that the story of Black libraries does not end with desegregation, although that is how many histories of U.S. libraries are periodized.
138. Abdul Alkalimat, "African American Bibliography," paper presented to African American Expression in Print and Digital Culture Conference, University of Wisconsin at Madison, September 20, 2014.

4. UNAUTHORIZED INQUIRIES: DOROTHY PORTER'S WAYWARD CATALOG

1. Etta Belle Walker Northington to Dorothy Porter, December 1, 1938, Records of the Moorland-Spingarn Research Center, Record Group 1 (hereafter MSRC Record Group 1), University Archives,

MSRC. At the time of research, this collection was unprocessed, so materials did not have permanent box or folder numbers. I refer to Dorothy B. Porter, without the surname Wesley, because it was the name she used during the period referenced in this chapter, before her marriage to Charles Wesley in 1979. In the 1980s, she began publishing under the name Dorothy Porter Wesley. See Esme Bhan, "Dorothy Louise Burnett Porter Wesley, 1904–1995," *Washington History* 8 (Spring/Summer 1996): 88–89.

2. Gladys Brown Thompson to Porter, January 30, 1939, box 5, Dorothy Porter Wesley Papers (hereafter DPW Papers), BRBML. Note that at the time of research, this collection was minimally processed; subsequent reprocessing may have changed box locations of material cited.
3. Elizabeth Murphy Oliver to Mordecai Johnson, January 20, 1937, MSRC Record Group 1.
4. Richard Simmons to Mordecai Johnson, [March 1938], MSRC Record Group 1.
5. R. C. Owen to Porter, November 27, 1937, MSRC Record Group 1.
6. Porter to Bessie N. Hill, September 12, 1935, Alexine Tanner to Walter Daniels, November 4, 1935, and A. V. Powell to Librarian, March 26, 1938—all in MSRC Record Group 1.
7. "The J. E. Moorland Foundation of the University Library," *Howard University Record* 10, no. 1 (1916): 5. Kelly Miller, who persuaded Moorland to donate his library to Howard, proposed to make it the nucleus of a national museum. On that proposal, see Kelly Miller to Board of Trustees, September 20, 1922, box 32, folder 678, Jesse E. Moorland Papers (hereafter Moorland Papers), Manuscript Division, MSRC; and Ida E. Jones, *The Heart of the Race Problem: The Life of Kelly Miller* (Littleton, MA: Tapestry, 2011), 105–10. On the history of the Moorland Foundation, see E. C. Williams, "Negro Americana," *Howard University Record* 16, no. 6 (1922): 346–47; Dorothy B. Porter, "A Library on the Negro," *American Scholar* 7 (Winter 1938): 115–17; Michael R. Winston, "Moorland-Spingarn Research Center: A Past Revisited, A Present Reclaimed," *New Directions* (Summer 1974): 20–25; Thomas C. Battle, "Moorland-Spingarn Research Center, Howard University," *Library Quarterly* 58, no. 2 (April 1988): 143–51; and Melanie Chambliss, "A Library in Progress," in *The Unfinished Book*, ed. Alexandra Gillespie and Deidre Lynch (Oxford: Oxford University Press, 2021): 260–71. The Cathcart scrapbooks were deposited at Howard by John Wesley Cromwell circa 1900 but were removed by Otelia Cromwell around 1937; they returned to Howard in the 1960s. See Kelly Miller to S. M. Newman, November 4, 1914, box 1, folder 29, and Porter to Miller, June 1, 1938, box 1, folder 31—both in Kelly Miller Papers (hereafter Miller Papers), Manuscript Division, MSRC; Moorland Foundation Annual Reports for 1936–1937 and 1965–1966, Manuscript Division, MSRC (hereafter MSRC Annual Reports); and Porter to Miller, December 8, 1938, box 3, DPW Papers.
8. J. E. Moorland to S. M. Newman, December 18, 1914, box 1, folder 28, Miller Papers.
9. Porter was hired in 1930 as an assistant librarian and tasked with creating a reference collection from Moorland's donation and other relevant material in the library. She received a Julius Rosenwald Fund fellowship in 1931 to pursue additional studies in preparation for this work. She wrote a thesis titled "Afro-American Writings Published Before 1835" and earned her master's degree in library studies from Columbia University in 1932. The work of locating relevant material for the collection, developing a new classification scheme, and recataloging the books took more than two years. The Moorland Foundation officially opened as a reference collection on October 1, 1932. See Moorland to Porter, December 5, 1930, box 4, Porter to Moorland, December 17, 1931, box 4, Moorland to Porter, December 20, 1931, box 4, Edwin Embree to Porter, January 16, 1931, box 5—all in DPW Papers; and MSRC Annual Reports for June 6, 1932 and May 30, 1934.
10. MSRC Annual Report for 1937–1938.
11. Arna Bontemps, "Special Collections of Negroana," *Library Quarterly* 14, no. 3 (July 1944): 189.
12. Transcript, Oral History Interview of Dorothy Porter Wesley by Avril J. Madison, 1993 (hereafter DPW OH), Manuscript Division, MSRC, 29. See also Benjamin Quarles, "Black History Unbound," *Daedalus* 103, no. 2 (Spring 1974): 168: "All too often even in major research libraries, particularly those of state and local historical societies, Negro-related holdings have never been catalogued."

13. Moorland to Newman, December 18, 1914; DPW OH, 14. Upon the donation of Moorland's collection in 1914, librarians partially cataloged the books, marked them with an "M," and kept them with the general collection. Moorland hoped that the collection would have a separate catalog and reading room, but it was not until Porter's arrival that the collection's "formal organization" commenced. Moorland told Porter that he feared "valuable material had been lost" (Notes for an untitled speech, undated, box 34, DPW Papers; Moorland to Porter, March 5, 1930, box 4, DPW Papers; Dorothy Porter, "The Role of the Negro Collection in Teaching and Research at Howard University," typescript, 1967, box 32, DPW Papers; "Description of Project," typescript, ca. 1938, MSRC Record Group 1; and "The J. E. Moorland Foundation," 12).
14. In the 1930s, Hampton did not have adequate funds to keep the Peabody room open and staffed "with someone who knows the collection." Once it reopened in 1939 with National Youth Administration support, it was "well patronized" (Hampton Library Report, February 1, 1939–February 1, 1940, Collis P. Huntington Library Records, Library Reports 1899–1939, HUA; and "Hampton Institute Library," typescript, ca. 1926, Library Correspondences, HUA).
15. Moorland to Porter, December 20, 1931. A survey in the late 1930s found that while twenty HBCUs had special collections "by and about the Negro," only Howard's had a full-time librarian. The other library employing a full-time librarian for its collection was NYPL, where Catherine Latimer managed the Schomburg Collection (Naomi J. Rushing, "Technical Organizing of Special Collections of Books by and About the Negro" [master's thesis, Columbia University, 1940], 11–12).
16. DPW OH, 20. On Porter, see Maurice A. Lubin, "An Important Figure in Black Studies: Dr. Dorothy B. Porter," *CLA Journal* 16 (June 1973): 514–18; Harriet Jackson Scarupa, "The Energy-Charged Life of Dorothy Porter Wesley," *New Directions* (January 1990): 6–17; Arthur C. Gunn, "Dorothy Burnett Porter Wesley," in *Black Women in America*, ed. Darlene Clark Hine (Brooklyn, NY: Carlson, 1993), 1246–48; Esme Bhan, "Legacy of a Job Well Done," *Washington Post*, December 31, 1995; Julie Des Jardins, *Women and the Historical Enterprise in America: Gender, Race, and the Politics of Memory, 1880–1945* (Chapel Hill: University of North Carolina Press, 2003): 165–76; Thomas C. Battle, "Dorothy Porter Wesley," in *Dictionary of American Library Biography*, 2nd supplement, ed. Donald G. Davis (Westport, CT: Libraries Unlimited, 2003), 219–21; Janet Sims-Wood, *Dorothy Porter Wesley at Howard University: Building a Legacy of Black History* (Charleston, SC: History Press, 2014); Laura E. Helton, "On Decimals, Catalogs, and Racial Imaginaries of Reading," *PMLA* 134, no. 1 (2019): 99–120; and Derrick R. Spires, "Order and Access: Dorothy Porter and the Mission of Black Bibliography," *Papers of the Bibliographical Society of America* 116, no. 2 (June 2022): 255–75.
17. Porter quoted in Phil McCombs, "Touching History at Howard," *Washington Post*, December 16, 1989.
18. James Hatch and Camille Billops, *Interview of Dorothy Porter* (New York: Hatch Billops Collection, 1991), 138; DPW OH, 18; and "WPA Workers Make Howard University's New Library a Clearing House for Collection of Rare Books," press release, April 4, 1939, box 5, DPW Papers.
19. L. D. Reddick, "The State of the Schomburg Collection," typescript, August 1, 1940, box 2, folder 5, SCRBC Records, Manuscripts, Archives and Rare Books Division (hereafter MARB), SCRBC. In 1950, at Lincoln University, Horace Mann Bond "discovered an old cache of anti-slavery prints and portraits, donated to the school some years ago, which have since reposed in one of the basements on campus" (Horace M. Bond to Porter, June 7, 1950, MSRC Record Group 1).
20. Porter to Moorland, July 11, 1932, box 4, DPW Papers. For records of Moorland's additions to the collection between 1914 and 1930, see box 32, folder 678 of the Moorland Papers.
21. Porter to Moorland, December 8, 1932, box 4, DPW Papers.
22. Moorland to Porter, September 10, 1931, MSRC Record Group 1. Porter undertook what she called a "complete organization" of the *books* in Negro Collection; she continued working on manuscripts, ephemera, and pamphlets for many years (Porter to Mordecai W. Johnson, December 18, 1933, MSRC Record Group 1).

23. In 1927, two years after opening the Division of Negro History, Literature, and Prints, NYPL reported "constant requests for bibliographic work on the Negro. These requests come not only from New York but from all over the country" (NYPL, *Report of the New York Public Library for 1927* [New York: NYPL, 1928], 58).
24. L. D. Reddick, draft introduction to *What the Negro Thinks About Democracy*, typescript, n.d., Lawrence D. Reddick Papers (hereafter LDR Papers), MARB, SCRBC. Note that at the time of research, the LDR Papers were unprocessed.
25. Ann M. Blair, *Too Much to Know: Managing Scholarly Information Before the Modern Age* (New Haven, CT: Yale University Press, 2011).
26. "The J. E. Moorland Foundation of The University Library," 12. As early as 1906, librarians at Hampton noted the insufficiency of the Dewey Decimal Classification to catalog the George Foster Peabody collection. See Collis P. Huntington Library Records, Library Reports 1899–1939, HUA.
27. Porter, "Repositories of Materials on Negro Life and History: An Endless Quest," speech typescript, box 34, DPW Papers.
28. I draw here on Saidiya Hartman's use of the term "wayward" to frame the work of Black women inhabiting intellectual spaces "in ways inimical to those deemed proper," although Porter was far more likely to collect the papers of "uplifters" than of the women and girls chronicled by Hartman (Hartman, *Wayward Lives, Beautiful Experiments* [New York: Norton, 2019], 3, 227).
29. Dorothy Porter, "Tentative Plans for the Administration, Reclassification, and Cataloguing of the Moorland Foundation of Howard University," MSRC Annual Reports, 1932.
30. Paul Starr quoted in Ann Laura Stoler, "Colonial Archives and the Arts of Governance," *Archival Science* 2 (2002): 103.
31. David Scott, "On the Archaeologies of Black Memory," *Small Axe* 12, no. 2 (2008): xiv.
32. On early Black bibliographies, see Laura E. Helton, "Black Bibliographers and the Category of Negro Authorship," in *African American Literature in Transition, 1900–1910*, ed. Shirley Moody-Turner (New York: Cambridge University Press, 2021): 23–47; Elizabeth McHenry, *To Make Negro Literature: Writing, Literary Practice, and African American Authorship* (Durham, NC: Duke University Press, 2021); and Jacqueline Goldsby and Meredith M. McGill, "What Is 'Black' About Black Bibliography?," *Papers of the Bibliographical Society of America* 116, no. 2 (June 2022): 161–89.
33. DPW OH, 31, 37. Although Porter described her childhood as isolated from any Black community, it is clear she had exposure to a range of Black thought. In a letter on Marcus Garvey, she recalled that "Many years ago in my home town . . . I played the piano at a regular meeting his organization held there" (Porter to Eulalie Domingo, August 20, 1954, MSRC Record Group 1). Kelly Miller and Laura Eliza Wilkes, author of *Missing Pages in American History*, were occasional guests in her family's home. Her father took her to hear Booker T. Washington, and both parents were active members of the Montclair NAACP. See Program of the 50th Anniversary of Montclair NAACP, 1967, box 35, DPW Papers.
34. Hatch and Billops, *Interview*, 137.
35. Dorothy B. Porter, "Fifty Years of Collecting," in *Black Access: A Bibliography of Afro-American Bibliographies*, ed. Richard Newman (Westport, CT: Greenwood, 1984), xxi. Schomburg and Ernestine Rose encouraged Porter to work at the 135th Street Branch Library when she finished her studies at Columbia, but she was drawn back to Howard by E. C. Williams, the librarian, and by James Porter, a professor of art, whom she married in 1930. See DPW OH, 37.
36. Avril Johnson Madison and Dorothy Porter Wesley, "Dorothy Burnett Porter Wesley: Enterprising Steward of Black Culture," *Public Historian* 17, no. 1 (Winter 1995): 27.
37. Madison and Wesley, "Dorothy Burnett Porter Wesley," 17, 33. Lacking funds for his own collecting efforts, Woodson once sent Porter a bookdealer's catalog with a note: "It may interest you. You have money. I have none" (Carter G. Woodson to Porter, March 4, 1938, MSRC Record Group 1). See also Jacqueline Goggin, "Carter G. Woodson and the Collection of Source Materials for Afro-American

History," *American Archivist* 48 (Summer 1985): 263. On Slaughter, see Porter, "Fifty Years of Collecting," xxiii. On one occasion, dinner at Slaughter's house was three hours late, leaving the two dinner guests—Porter and Zora Neale Hurston—waiting together until 11 p.m. "I didn't believe any of the things she told me," Porter recalled of Hurston, but "I just sat and listened in awe of these marvelous things that she told" (Hatch and Billops, *Interview*, 145).

38. Dorothy Porter, [Untitled speech to announce Spingarn acquisition], ca. 1946, box 33, DPW Papers.
39. Alberto Manguel, *The Library at Night* (New Haven, CT: Yale University Press, 2006), 60.
40. Melvil Dewey, *Decimal Clasification and Relativ Index* [sic], ed. 12 (Essex Co., NY: Forest Pres [sic], 1927), 13. Dewey wrote in "Simpl Spelling," an early effort to reform English. I have modified his spellings for clarity.
41. Dewey, *Decimal Clasification* [sic], ed. 12, 14.
42. Although cast as universal, the Dewey Decimal Classification (DDC) was based on extant North American library holdings of the late nineteenth century, a structural reason for its Euro-American tilt. That initial constraint has had enduring repercussions. See Alex Wright, *Cataloging the World: Paul Otlet and the Birth of the Information Age* (New York: Oxford University Press, 2014), 39–40; and Hope A. Olson, "Mapping Beyond Dewey's Boundaries: Constructing Classificatory Space for Marginalized Knowledge Domains," *Library Trends* 47, no. 2 (1998): 233–54.
43. Dewey, *Decimal Clasification* [sic], ed. 12, n.p.
44. Similarly, Dewey placed works on Black servants at 647.24, the class for "Foreign employees Races and nationalities; orientals [sic], negroes [sic], etc." (Dewey *Decimal Clasification* [sic], ed. 12, n.p.). See Karin Roffman, *From the Modernist Annex: American Women Writers in Museums and Libraries* (Tuscaloosa: University of Alabama Press, 2010), 71–73.
45. In many places, because Black readers could not enter the main library, they also did not have access to its card catalog. See Wayne A. Wiegand and Shirley A. Wiegand, *The Desegregation of Public Libraries in the Jim Crow South* (Baton Rouge: Louisiana State University Press, 2018), 28.
46. Porter quoted in in Madison and Wesley, "Dorothy Burnett Porter Wesley," 25.
47. Porter, [fragment of speech for librarians' institute], ca. 1960s, box 34, DPW Papers.
48. DDC eliminated 325.26 in 1951, but its effect lingers in libraries that, due to legacy cataloging, still shelve together books like William Ferris's *The African Abroad*, E. Franklin Frazier's *The Free Negro Family*, J. A. Rogers's *100 Amazing Facts About the Negro*, and Harry Haywood's *Negro Liberation*. Evidence of what was classed at 325.26 is drawn from the OCLC Classify DeweyBrowser (now inoperable), but can still be found in Library of Congress, *The National Union Catalog, Pre-1956 Imprints*, vols. 1–685 (London: Mansell, 1968–1980). Because libraries purchased printed cards from the Library of Congress, its cataloging decisions informed shelving practices across the United States. Some smaller libraries followed the American Library Association's *Catalog* or *Booklist* instead, which in 1907 transformed 326 from "Slavery" to "Negroes." See Elva L. Bascom, ed., *A. L. A. Catalog, 1904–1911* (Chicago: American Library Association Publishing Board, 1912).
49. W. E. B. Du Bois, *The Souls of Black Folk: Essays and Sketches*, 4th ed. (Chicago: McClurg, 1904), 2.
50. MSRC Annual Report for 1935–36.
51. Sarah R. Line to Porter, May 10, 1935, MSRC Record Group 1.
52. Dewey, *Decimal Clasification* [sic], ed. 12, 35.
53. Jennie D. Fellows, "The Decimal Classification in the Tenth Edition," *Library Journal* 45 (February 15, 1920): 155–56; and Melvil Dewey, "Decimal Classification Beginning," *Library Journal* 45 (February 15, 1920): 152.
54. Dewey, "Decimal Classification Beginning," 152.
55. "Introduction," in *Decimal Classification*, devised by Melvil Dewey, Standard (15th) ed. (New York: Forest Press, Inc., 1951), xviii.
56. Manguel, *The Library at Night*, 47. See also Susan Stewart, *On Longing: Narratives of the Miniature, the Gigantic, the Souvenir, the Collection* (Durham, NC: Duke University Press, 1992), 162.

57. Manguel, *The Library at Night*, 46–49, 54; and Daniel Murray, "Bibliographia-Africania," *Voice of the Negro* 1, no. 5 (May 1904): 186–91.
58. Walter Benjamin, "Unpacking My Library," in *Illuminations: Essays and Reflections*, ed. Hannah Arendt, trans. Harry Zohn (New York: Schocken, 1968), 59.
59. Sharifa Rhodes-Pitts, *Harlem Is Nowhere: A Journey to the Mecca of Black America* (New York: Little, Brown, 2011), 55.
60. Transcription from Archibald MacLeish, *A Time to Speak* (New York: Houghton Mifflin, 1940) in [untitled manuscript notes], n.d., box 88, DPW Papers.
61. Naomi J. Rushing, Summary of thesis, 1941, in "Negro History Collection Policies," Tougaloo College Historical Files, Tougaloo College Archives; Jessie Carney Smith, "Special Collections of Black Literature in the Traditionally Black College," *College and Research Libraries* 35, no. 5 (September 1974): 322–35; and Karl Brown, comp., *American Library Directory 1942* (Camden, NJ: Bowker, 1942).
62. Rushing, "Technical Organizing," 42.
63. Alberto Manguel, *A History of Reading* (New York: Penguin, 2014), 199.
64. Porter quoted in Scarupa, "The Energy-Charged Life," 8; and Madison, "Dorothy Burnett Porter Wesley," 25. For Porter's class numbers for these books, see Moorland Foundation, *A Catalogue of Books in the Moorland Foundation, compiled by Workers on Projects 271 and 328 of the Works Progress Administration* (Washington, DC: Howard University, 1939).
65. The Schomburg Collection was cataloged in the 1920s by the NYPL Circulation department. In the 1940s, Latimer and Hill revisited this original cataloging and moved books that had been previously cataloged under 325.26 and 326. They did not change Dewey's numbers, but rather attempted to make the NYPL's classification of Black books "correct according to the Dewey decimal classification" (Kathleen Hill, Report of cataloging for the Schomburg Collection, December 12, 1946, box 2, folder 8, SCRBC Records).
66. Rushing, "Technical Organizing," 50.
67. Dewey, *Decimal Clasification* [sic], ed. 12.
68. See Nell Irvin Painter, *Exodusters: Black Migration to Kansas After Reconstruction* (New York: Norton, 1992); Michele Mitchell, *Righteous Propagation: African Americans and the Politics of Racial Destiny after Reconstruction* (Chapel Hill: University of North Carolina, 2004), 16–50; and Ousmane K. Power-Greene, *Against Wind and Tide: The African American Struggle Against the Colonization Movement* (New York: New York University Press, 2014).
69. Clarke quoted in Angela Ards, "Black Bibliophiles," *QBR: The Black Book Review* (May/June 1999): 2. Porter received another Julius Rosenwald Fund fellowship in 1944 to compile a bibliography on Afro-Latin American sources; this research resulted in a card file of four thousand entries, as well as multiple published articles and the publication of Dorothy B. Porter, *Afro-Braziliana: A Working Bibliography* (Boston: Hall, 1978). Porter developed a separate classification scheme for African materials. See Porter, "Tentative Supplementary Classification Used for the Books by and About the Negro in the Moorland Foundation, Howard University Library," ca. 1930s, MSRC Record Group 1.
70. See Porter, "Tentative Supplementary Classification"; Library of Congress, *Classification: Class H: Social Sciences*, 2nd ed. (Washington, DC: Government Printing Office, 1920); and Library of Congress, *Classification: Class E-F America*, 2nd ed. (Washington, DC: Government Printing Office, 1913).
71. "Free Masons," n.d., and "Classification AME Church," n.d.—both in MSRC Record Group 1.
72. Dewey, *Decimal Clasification* [sic], ed. 12; and Porter, "Tentative Supplementary Classification."
73. On Black list-making as a democratic gesture, and as a claim to Black knowledge, see Elizabeth Alexander, "Anna Julia Cooper: Turn-of-the-Century 'Aframerican' Intellectual," in *The Black Interior: Essays* (St. Paul, MN: Graywolf, 2004), 121.

74. Patricia J. Williams, "Gathering the Ghosts," *The A-Line* 1, nos. 3–4 (2018): https://alinejournal.com/vol-1-no-3-4/gathering-the-ghosts/.
75. Porter, "Tentative Supplementary Classification."
76. Porter, "Tentative Supplementary Classification"; Henry Pisciotta, "The Library in Art's Crosshairs," *Art Documentation* 35 (2016): 24 n51. See also Emily Drabinski, "Queering the Catalog: Queer Theory and the Politics of Correction," *Library Quarterly* 82, no. 3 (April 2013): 94–111; and Melissa Adler, *Cruising the Library: Perversities in the Organization of Knowledge* (New York: Fordham University Press, 2017).
77. Porter's work may be seen as an example of David Palumbo-Liu's call to "appropriate the 'universal' as an enabling fiction" (Palumbo-Liu, "Universalisms and Minority Culture," *Differences: A Journal of Feminist Cultural Studies* 7, no. 1 [Spring 1995]: 202).
78. Porter to Moorland May 9, 1933, box 4, DPW Papers. Requests came from Hampton, NYPL, Fisk, Atlanta University, and North Carolina College for Negroes, among others.
79. Edith M. Phelps to Porter, July 11 1934, and Phelps to Porter, December 11, 1934—both in box 5, DPW Papers; and Phelps to Porter, December 20, 1937, and Porter to Phelps, January 8, 1938—both in MSRC Record Group 1.
80. Emily V. D. Miller to Porter, July 12, 1934, box 5, DPW Papers. My thanks to Violet B. Fox for clarification of an earlier version of this argument.
81. Porter to Dorcas Fellows, December 5, 1934, and Dorkas Fellows to Porter, December 6, 1934—both in box 5, DPW Papers (Simpl Spelling modified). Fellows's prohibition contradicts the fact that other special collections shared their adaptations of Dewey, as documented in Isabel L. Towner, comp., *Classification Schemes and Subject Headings Lists: Loan Collection of Special Libraries Association*, rev. ed. (New York: Special Libraries Association, 1949). On related issues within Latin American collections, see Jose Guerrero, "Unpacking the Other's Library: Latin American Book Collectors and U.S. Research Libraries," in *The Collector and the Collected: Decolonizing Area Studies Librarianship*, eds. Megan Browndorf, Erin Pappas, and Anna Arays (Sacramento, CA: Library Juice Press, 2021), 153–54.
82. Gertrude Franklin to Porter, June 28, 1939, box 5, DPW Papers; and Franklin, Report of Cataloging for the Division of Negro Literature, August 1940, box 2, folder 8, SCRBC Records.
83. Rushing, "Technical Organizing," 59–67.
84. Moorland Foundation, *A Catalogue of Books*, preface.
85. Nathaniel Stewart to Porter, January 19, 1940, MSRC Record Group 1.
86. Elise Johnson McDougald, "The Task of Negro Womanhood," in *The New Negro*, ed. Alain Locke (1925; repr., New York: Simon and Schuster, 1992), 376.
87. Des Jardins, *Women and the Historical Enterprise*, 122. See also Bonnie G. Smith, *The Gender of History: Men, Women, and Historical Practice* (Cambridge, MA: Harvard University Press, 2000), 127, 160.
88. A. G. Sterling, "Lady Curator: Her Work Never Ends," unidentified clipping, n.d., SCCF 002,379. For recent work on Black women's librarianship, see Nicole A. Cooke, ed., special issue of *Libraries: Culture, History, and Society* 6, no. 1 (2022).
89. Kelly Miller, "Kelly Miller Revives Proposal of National Negro Museum at Howard U.," *Chicago Defender*, September 10, 1938; for Porter's corrections to one of these articles, see Porter to Miller, June 1, 1938, box 1, folder 31, Miller Papers.
90. Madison and Wesley, "Dorothy Burnett Porter Wesley," 27.
91. Porter, *Afro-Braziliana*, x.
92. Dorothy Porter Wesley, "Black Antiquarians and Bibliophiles Revisited, with a Glance at Today's Lovers of Books and Memorabilia," in *Black Bibliophiles and Collectors: Preservers of Black History*, ed. Elinor Des Verney Sinnette, W. Paul Coates, and Thomas C. Battle (Washington, DC: Howard University Press, 1990), 12.

93. Porter quoted in Scarupa, "The Energy-Charged Life," 8.
94. Dorothy Porter, "Documentation on the Afro-American: Familiar and Less Familiar Sources," *African Studies Bulletin* 12, no. 3 (December 1969): 295. On this diminutive strategy, see Deborah Gray White, "Private Lives, Public Personae: A Look at Early Twentieth-Century African American Clubwomen," in *Talking Gender: Public Images, Personal Journeys, and Political Critiques*, ed. Nancy Hewitt, Jean O'Barr, and Nancy Rosebaugh (Chapel Hill: University of North Carolina Press, 1996), 106–23.
95. "Librarian," *Washington Post*, January 16, 1992. On male historians' disdain for "library science," see Smith, *The Gender of History*, 187. On Merze Tate's related battles at Howard, see Barbara D. Savage, "Professor Merze Tate: Diplomatic Historian, Cosmopolitan Woman," in *Toward an Intellectual History of Black Women*, ed. Mia Bay, Farah Jasmine Griffin, Martha S. Jones, and Barbara D. Savage (Chapel Hill: University of North Carolina Press, 2015), 252–69.
96. Porter, "The Role of the Negro Collection." The term "Black Access" is from Newman, *Black Access*.
97. Librarian of Atlanta University to Miller, May 21, 1938, box 1, folder 34, Miller Papers.
98. Porter placed duplicate cards from the Moorland Foundation in the main library catalog, but otherwise kept the holdings separate. By contrast, most libraries with "Negro Collections" integrated their records into a single catalog (Rushing, "Technical Organizing"). Gammon Theological Seminary created a revised classification for the Dewey number 326 (normally used for works on slavery) to encompass all works on "Negro life" (Frank W. Clelland to Porter, March 8, 1940, MSRC Record Group 1).
99. Mary Wilson MacNair, ed. *Subject Headings Used in the Dictionary Catalogues of the Library of Congress*, 3rd ed. (Washington, DC: Government Printing Office, 1928).
100. Arthur A. Schomburg, *Racial Integrity: A Plea for the Establishment of a Chair of Negro History in Our Schools and Colleges, Etc.* (n.p.: August Valentine Bernier, 1913), 5.
101. MSRC Annual Reports for 1936–37 and 1940–41. Porter acquired donations for the Moorland Foundation from the Library of Congress and published her first bibliography with the Government Printing Office: Dorothy B. Porter, *A Selected List of Books by and About the Negro* (Washington, DC: Government Printing Office, 1936).
102. Elizabeth Alexander, "The Black Poet as Canon-Maker: Langston Hughes and the Road to *New Negro Poets: USA*," in *The Black Interior*, 41.
103. Dewey, *Decimal Clasification* [sic], ed. 12.
104. MSRC Annual Report for 1945–46. On the binding of pamphlets, see Meredith L. McGill, "Books on the Loose," in *The Unfinished Book*, 84–86. For contemporary commentary on this practice, see Dorothy Berry, "Introducing 'Archives Unbound,'" *JSTOR Daily*, February 24, 2022, https://daily.jstor.org/introducing-archives-unbound/.
105. "Anti-Slave[ry] Data for New Library," *Washington Star*, June 20, 1937; and Madison and Wesley, "Dorothy Burnett Porter Wesley," 23.
106. Battle, "Dorothy Porter Wesley," 220; and Frances L. Yocom, *A List of Subject Headings for Books By and About the Negro* (New York: Wilson, 1940), 6, 12. This work was continued by Doris H. Clack, "Investigation into the adequacy of Library of Congress Subject Headings for black studies" (PhD diss., University of Pittsburgh, 1973). The meaningful distinction between headings and subdivisions has faded with the availability of full-text search, but in a physical catalog, only "filing words" would be directly accessible to searchers.
107. Julia Pettee, *Subject Headings: The History and Theory of the Alphabetical Subject Approach to Books* (New York: Wilson, 1946). On the Cataloging Distribution Service, see Library of Congress, *The Card Catalog: Books, Cards, and Literary Treasures* (San Francisco: Chronicle, 2017), 146–48.
108. See Moorland Foundation, *Dictionary Catalog of the Jesse E. Moorland Collection of Negro Life and History* (Boston: Hall, 1970). On subject analytics, see Library of Congress, *Handbook of Card Distribution*, 6th ed. (Washington, DC: Government Printing Office, 1925), 16–17, 23–27. Porter's

project anticipated the work of Nicole Aljoe, whose digital humanities project "Embedded Slave Narratives" identifies narratives by enslaved persons that are submerged in "natural histories, travel narratives, colonial reports, and treatises" (http://hdl.handle.net/2047/D20265256).

109. MacNair, *Subject Headings*; Porter, "Brief Statement of Work Done Beginning October 1," December 20, 1932, MSRC Annual Reports; Porter, "Subject Headings Used in Moorland Foundation Catalog," MSRC Record Group 1; and Porter to Parepa R Watson, November 7, 1946, MSRC Record Group 1.

110. [Notes by Robert L. Harris Jr. on the American Council of Learned Societies' Conference on Negro Studies], n.d., LDR Papers. Cafeterias in federal agencies began to desegregate in the 1930s, so that by the time John Hope Franklin arrived to conduct research at the Library of Congress in 1939, he faced no restrictions on his use of any part of the building. See Charlynn Spencer Pyne, "Remembering Vintage Years: Historian Franklin Discusses Life and Career," *Library of Congress Information Bulletin* 60, no. 10 (October 2001): https://www.loc.gov/loc/lcib/0110/index.html.

111. Scarupa, "The Energy-Charged Life," 16; and Madison and Wesley, "Dorothy Burnett Porter Wesley," 33.

112. [E. C. Williams] to George F. Bowerman, June 10, 1929, box 1, folder 2, James A. Porter Papers, Stuart A. Rose Manuscript, Archives, and Rare Book Library, Emory University.

113. Dorothy B. Porter, "Library Sources for the Study of Negro Life and History," *Journal of Negro Education* 5, no. 2 (1936): 233.

114. Bontemps, "Special Collections of Negroana," 204.

115. Porter, "Fifty Years," xxv. The term "fugitive materials" has a specific meaning within library practice, but Porter certainly understood its echo with the history of fugitivity in Black life: "to elude capture by never settling" (Hartman, *Wayward Lives*, 227). For a longer discussion of fugitivity in Black librarianship, see Melanie Chambliss, *History in the Making: Black Archives, Black Liberation, and the Remaking of Modernity* (manuscript under production).

116. Paul E. Howard, "The Negro and His Library," introduction to *Books and Pamphlets By and About the Negro*, Bulletin no. 1, October 1939, box 3, DPW Papers. A 1942 survey found the largest holdings of Black-themed manuscript material at the University of North Carolina, Duke University, the Historical Society of Pennsylvania, and the Library of Congress. See Arnett G. Lindsay, "Manuscript Materials Bearing on the Negro in America," *Journal of Negro History* 27, no. 1 (1942): 94–101.

117. Dorothy B. Porter, "Padre Domingos Caldas Barbosa: Afro-Brazilian Poet," *Phylon* 12, no. 3 (Third Quarter, 1951), 269. On Washington's papers, see "Gives Negro Collection," *New York Times*, June 27, 1943. As part of her fieldwork for the Modern Archives Institute, Porter spent two weeks helping to process the Washington Papers. See [Notes by Esme Bahn], n.d., box 13, DPW Papers.

118. Porter to Carl Van Vechten, November 24, 1941, MSRC Record Group 1.

119. Van Vechten to Porter, November 29, 1941, MSRC Record Group 1.

120. Bernhard Knollenberg to Porter, July 23, 1942, MSRC Record Group 1.

121. Mollie Huston Lee to Porter, January 17, 1939, box 5, DPW Papers; MSRC Annual Report for 1945–1946; and Dorothy B. Porter, "The Librarian and the Scholar: A Working Partnership," *Proceedings of the Institute on Materials by and About the American Negro* (Atlanta, GA: Atlanta University School of Librarianship, 1967), 78–79.

122. Porter, "The Role of the Negro Collection"; MSRC Annual Reports for May 30, 1934, 1936–1937, and 1938–1939; "Description of Project," ca. 1938, MSRC Record Group 1; "Negro Materials Catalogued by WPA Project Workers," *The Hilltop*, April 13, 1939; John Templeton and Steven Nkrumah, "Dorothy Porter, Keeper of Our Heritage," *The Hilltop*, September 7, 1973; and "Title of Project: A Union of Books by and about the Negro," ca. 1938, box 32, folder 678, Moorland Papers.

123. Library of Congress, *Report of the Librarian of Congress for the Fiscal Year Ending June 30, 1937* (Washington, DC: Government Printing Office, 1937), 38; and Robert B. Downs, ed., *Union Catalogs in the United States* (Chicago: American Library Association, 1942). On the history of

union catalogs, see Jack Lynch, *You Could Look It Up: The Reference Shelf from Ancient Babylon to Wikipedia* (New York: Bloomsbury, 2016), 317–322.

124. Mentor A. Howe and Roscoe E. Lewis, comps., *A Classified Catalogue of the Negro Collection in the Collis P. Huntington Library, Hampton Institute* (Hampton, VA: Hampton Institute, 1940).

125. Chicago Public Library, *The Chicago Afro-American Union Analytic Catalog* (Boston: Hall, 1972); and Charlemae Rollins, "Library Work with Negroes," *Illinois Libraries* 25, no. 2 (February 1943): 92. Housed at the George Cleveland Hall Branch Library, this catalog resulted in more than seventy-five thousand cards representing citywide holdings. Because each title was filed by author, title, and sometimes subject, the number of individual works cataloged was likely around thirty thousand.

126. Miller proposed moving from the Recorder of Deeds office to Howard all records on the purchase, sale, or transfer of enslaved people in Washington, DC. Unsurprisingly, the Recorder of Deeds (an alumnus of Lincoln) responded that he could not transfer these papers to Howard but could provide photostatic copies. Miller, however, wanted possession of the original records rather than copies. See Miller to Oswald Garrison Villard, December 29, 1938, box 1, folder 35, Miller Papers; Miller, Letter to the editor, *Evening Star* (Washington, DC), March 10, 1939, MSRC Record Group 1; and William J. Thompkins to Miller, March 28, 1939, MSRC Record Group 1. By contrast, Porter's nonproprietary approach anticipated the late-twentieth-century "postcustodial" turn in archives. See Terry Cook, "What Is Past Is Prologue: A History of Archival Ideas Since 1898, and the Future Paradigm Shift," *Archivaria* 43 (Spring 1997): 39.

127. "A Union Catalog of Works By, On and Relating to the Negro," ca. 1937–38, box 5, DPW Papers; and "WPA Workers Make Howard University's New Library a Clearing House for Collection of Rare Books." Project A also encompassed the holdings in Henry Slaughter's private library. Other institutions that initially agreed to participate included the Schomburg Collection, Virginia Union University, Tougaloo College, Atlanta University, Kentucky State College, the University of Texas, and Virginia State College—but funding ended before they could join. See "Description of Project," (summer 1938), box 5, DPW Papers.

128. A comparison of the *Chicago Afro-American Union Analytic Catalog*, the *Dictionary Catalog* of the Schomburg Collection, and the *Dictionary Catalog* of the Moorland Foundation found surprisingly little overlap in their holdings. See Donald F. Joyce, "Publications," *Black World* 21, no. 3 (January 1972): 73.

129. Other HBCUs, such as Bennett College and Atlanta University, sent records of their "Negro holdings" to regional union catalogs housed at white institutions. Project A reversed this logic. See Downs, *Union Catalogs*.

130. Porter to Neil C. Van Deusen, September 21, 1939, box 5, DPW Papers; "WPA Workers Make Howard University's New Library a Clearing House for Collection of Rare Books"; and "Negro Materials Catalogued by WPA Project Workers."

131. Porter to Moorland, December 8, 1932, box 4, DPW Papers.

132. Porter to Ernestine Rose, May 26, 1938, and Catherine Latimer to Porter, July 13, 1938—both in box 33, DPW Papers. Project A was never published, but it anticipated successors such as Geraldine O. Matthews and the African-American Materials Project Staff, comps., *Black American Writers, 1773–1949: A Bibliography and Union List* (Boston: Hall, 1975). See also Quarles, "Black History Unbound," 168–69. In 1968, Porter was still arguing for the need to revive her Black union catalog and to create a Union Catalog of Manuscripts Relating to the African American (Porter, "A Report of the Need for a Union Catalog of Printed Works on the Afro-American," November 1968, box 33, DPW Papers).

133. Porter to Arthur Spingarn, May 27, 1938, box 33, DPW Papers; and State Department of Public Instruction, Division of Cooperation in Education and Race Relations, "Materials Relating to the Negro in Libraries at Duke University and the University of North Carolina," March 1937, box 10, DPW Papers.

134. Downs, *Union Catalogs*, 360.
135. State Department of Public Instruction, "Materials Relating to the Negro in Libraries at Duke University and the University of North Carolina"; W. C. Newbold to Mordecai W. Johnson, March 23, 1937, and Porter to Newbold, June 22, 1937—both in box 10, DPW Papers.
136. W. E. B. Du Bois to Virginia Lacy Jones, December 19, 1950, in *The Correspondence of W. E. B. Du Bois*, vol. 3, ed. Herbert Aptheker (Amherst: University of Massachusetts Press, 1997), 302.
137. W. E. B. Du Bois, "The Opening of the Library," *The Independent* (Atlanta, GA), April 3, 1902.
138. User numbers can be found in MSRC Annual reports; generally they rose each year and reached a crescendo in the mid-1960s.
139. MSRC Annual Report for 1952–53. These queries can be found in Pearl G. Richardson to Porter, October 18, 1938, Lena H. Watson to Porter, October 1, 1951, A. V. Powell to Librarian, March 26, 1938, Porter to Elizabeth Gardner, August 19, 1953, Porter to Florence Shreeve, July 1, 1938, Joanne Luedtke to Porter, August 27, 1958, and Castine Davis to Library of Congress [forwarded to Porter], June 18, 1951—all in MSRC Record Group 1.
140. DPW OH, 26.
141. I use "distant readers" both in its literal sense of "faraway" and to invoke "index reading": modes of apprehending a textual object via bibliographical intermediaries (Daniel Rosenberg, "Stop, Words," *Representations* 127 [2014], 91).
142. Glendora Johnson-Cooper, "African-American Historical Continuity: Jean Blackwell Hutson and the Schomburg Center for Research in Black Culture," in *Reclaiming the American Library Past: Writing the Women In*, ed. Suzanna Hildenbrand (Westport, CT: Greenwood, 1996), 32.
143. Schomburg quoted in Elinor Des Verney Sinnette, *Arthur Alfonso Schomburg: Black Bibliophile and Collector* (Detroit, MI: NYPL and Wayne State University Press, 1989), 82.
144. On the routinization of memory through paperwork, see Craig Robertson, "Learning to File: Reconfiguring Information and Information Work in the Early Twentieth Century," *Technology and Culture* 58, no. 4 (October 2017): 959–61, 967.
145. MSRC Annual Reports, "Projects—The Moorland Foundation," March 16, 1936.
146. MSRC Annual Report for May 30, 1934.
147. The bibliophile Henry Slaughter, whose private library Porter cataloged for Project A, felt her methods, which he called "schoolbook librarianship," did not capture his collection's richness (Bontemps, "Special Collections" 199). On sensuousness versus functionality in libraries, see Simon Gikandi, "The Fantasy of the Library," *PMLA* 128, no. 1 (January 2013): 15.
148. On Porter as "African America's national librarian," see Zachery R. Williams, *In Search of the Talented Tenth: Howard University Public Intellectuals and the Dilemmas of Race, 1926–1970* (Columbia: University of Missouri Press, 2009), 90.
149. George Murphy to Porter, April 7, 1938, box 10, DPW Papers.
150. Latimer, "Report of Reference Work, Schomburg Collection, 1946," box 2, folder 5, SCRBC Records.
151. Louise G. Caton to Porter, November 14, 1938, box 5, DPW Papers. For a similar encounter between James Abajian and the American Antiquarian Society, see Molly O'Hagan Hardy, "'Black Printers' on White Cards: Information Architecture in the Data Structures of the Early American Book Trades," *Debates in the Digital Humanities 2016*, ed. Matthew K. Gold and Lauren F. Klein (Minneapolis: University of Minnesota Press, 2017): 377–82. While the Library of Congress's named special collection on the "Negro" was smaller than the ones at most HBCUs, its wider holdings on Black subjects—scattered and not part of a special unit—were much larger. See Mollie E. Dunlap, "Special Collections of Negro Literature in the United States," *Journal of Negro Education* 4, no. 4 (1935): 485.
152. See, for example, Joanne Luedtke to Porter, August 27, 1958, MSRC Record Group 1.
153. MSRC Annual Report for 1939–40.

154. MSRC Annual Report for 1935–36.
155. MSRC Annual Report for 1937–38.
156. MSRC Annual Report for 1955–56.
157. Scott, "On the Archaeologies of Black Memory," ix. See also John Hope Franklin, "The New Negro History," *Journal of Negro History* 42, no. 2 (April 1957): 89–97.
158. MSRC Annual Report for 1939–40.
159. Quarles, "Black History Unbound." Margo Natalie Crawford's more recent use of the term "unbound" led me to consider Benjamin Quarles's work anew (Crawford, "Textual Productions of Black Aesthetics Unbound," in *Publishing Blackness*, ed. George Hutchinson and John K. Young [Ann Arbor: University of Michigan Press, 2013]: 188–210).
160. See, for example, MSRC Annual Reports for 1946–47 and 1953–54.
161. NYPL, press release, January 16, 1941, LDR Papers.
162. MSRC Annual Report for 1961–1962. Porter was secretary of the African Studies Association Libraries Committee, which operated American-run microfilming centers in Africa. On Howard's marginalization in African Studies, see Jerry Gershenhorn, "'Not an Academic Affair': African American Scholars and the Development of African Studies Program in the United States, 1942–1960," *Journal of African American History* 94, no. 1 (Winter 2009): 52.
163. Mimeographed flier, "The Negro in a Changing World," ca. 1940s; and Mordecai Johnson to Porter, October 15, 1952—both in MSRC Record Group 1. Porter also advised scores of other libraries on the development of their collections. See, for example, Nathaniel Stewart to Porter, January 19, 1940; Jane Watts to Porter, September 10, 1940; Beulah Davis to Porter, February 17, 1940; and Porter to Rufus Clement, January 16, 1945—all in MSRC Record Group 1.
164. Porter, "Repositories of Materials on Negro Life and History."
165. Porter quoted in Scarupa, "The Energy-Charged Life," 15.
166. Gikandi, "The Fantasy of the Library," 11.

5. A SPACE FOR BLACK STUDY: THE HALL BRANCH LIBRARY AND THE HISTORIANS WHO NEVER WROTE

1. "Negro Fellowship League," *The Broad Ax* (Chicago), August 7, 1915.
2. Jarvis R. Givens, *Fugitive Pedagogy: Carter G. Woodson and the Art of Black Teaching* (Cambridge, MA: Harvard University Press, 2021), 64–68.
3. Program, Annual Meeting and Celebration of the Twentieth Anniversary of ASNLH, September 9–11, 1935, box 5, folder 45, George Cleveland Hall Branch Library Archives (hereafter HBLR), VGHRC; and "Negro History Week Precedes Race Congress," *Chicago Defender*, January 1936, box 6, folder 22, HBLR.
4. "Crowd Jams Library on Opening Day," *Chicago Defender*, January 23, 1932; Barefield Gordon, "New Negro Libraries," *Crisis* 39, no. 9 (September 1932): 284; and Arna Bontemps, "G. C. Hall Library Does Worthy Job of Enlightening Knowledge Seekers," *Chicago Defender*, March 29, 1941.
5. Michael Flug, "Events and Issues That Motivated the Evolution of African American Institutional Archival and Manuscripts Programs, 1919–1950," paper presented at the Collecting Our Past to Secure Our Future Conference, Jackson State University, Jackson, MS, November 30–December 2, 1995, 7.
6. Hall Branch brochure, n.d., box 1, folder 23, HBLR; and Donald Franklin Joyce, "Vivian G. Harsh Collection of Afro-American History and Literature, Chicago Public Library," *Library Quarterly* 58, no. 1 (January 1988): 67–69.

7. As discussed in chapter 3, segregated southern branch libraries for Black readers also stocked their shelves with books "by and about the Negro," but did not always publicize these holdings as distinct "special collections." On Harsh's "Special Collection of Books By and About the Negro," see Christine Pawley, *Organizing Women: Home, Work, and the Institutional Infrastructure of Print in Twentieth-Century America* (Amherst: University of Massachusetts Press, 2022), 176–208.
8. Mabel O. Wilson, *Negro Building: Black Americans in the World of Fairs and Museums* (Berkeley: University of California Press, 2012), 241.
9. Adolph J. Slaughter, "The Historian Who Never Wrote," *Chicago Daily Defender*, August 29, 1960; and "Crowd Jams Library on Opening Day."
10. "Open George Cleveland Hall Library," *Chicago Defender*, January 23, 1932; U.S. Bureau of the Census, Fifteenth Census of the United States: 1930—Population Schedule for Chicago (for Charles C. Luck), Ancestry.com; and Hall Branch flyer, [pre-1950], box 1, folder 23, HBLR.
11. See, for example, Lawrence P. Jackson, *The Indignant Generation: A Narrative History of African American Writers and Critics, 1934–1960* (Princeton, NJ: Princeton University Press, 2011), 100; and Toru Kiuchi and Yoshinobu Hakutani, *Richard Wright: A Documented Chronology, 1908–1960* (New York: McFarland, 2013), 46. For cultural histories of Black Chicago in the 1930s and 1940s, see Bill V. Mullen, *Popular Fronts: Chicago and African-American Cultural Politics, 1935–1946* (Urbana: University of Illinois Press, 1999); Anne Meis Knupfer, *The Chicago Black Renaissance and Women's Activism* (Urbana: University of Illinois Press, 2006); Adam Green, *Selling the Race: Culture, Community, and Black Chicago, 1940–1955* (Chicago: University of Chicago Press, 2007); Christopher Robert Reed, *The Rise of Chicago's Black Metropolis, 1920–1929* (Urbana: University of Illinois Press, 2011); Robert Bone and Richard A. Courage, *The Muse in Bronzeville: African American Creative Expression in Chicago, 1932–1950* (New Brunswick, NJ: Rutgers University Press, 2011); and Liesl Olson, *Chicago Renaissance: Literature and Art in the Midwest Metropolis* (New Haven, CT: Yale University Press, 2017). On the vibrancy of Black public history in Chicago, see Ian Rocksborough-Smith, *Black Public History in Chicago: Civil Rights Activism from World War II into the Cold War* (Urbana: University of Illinois Press, 2018).
12. Charlemae Rollins, "Library Work with Negroes," *Illinois Libraries* 25, no. 2 (February 1943): 93; Annual report for 1961, box 2, folder 7, HBLR; and E. James West, *Ebony Magazine and Lerone Bennett Jr.: Popular Black History in Postwar America* (Urbana: University of Illinois Press, 2020), 20.
13. Liesl Olson, "Richard Wright's Chicago," in *Richard Wright in Context*, ed. Michael Nowlin (Cambridge: Cambridge University Press, 2021), 28; and Carolyn J. Brown, *Song of My Life: A Biography of Margaret Walker* (Jackson: University of Mississippi Press, 2014), 38.
14. Joyce, "Vivian G. Harsh Collection," 70.
15. Romi Crawford, "Yours in Blackness: Blocks, Corners, and Other Desire Settings," *Nka: Journal of Contemporary African Art* 34 (2014): 81.
16. Aubrey Bowser, "A Negro Documentarian," *New York Amsterdam News*, August 13, 1930; and Barbara Smith, "A Press of Our Own Kitchen Table: Women of Color Press," *Frontiers: A Journal of Women Studies* 10, no. 3 (1989): 11–13.
17. Slaughter, "The Historian Who Never Wrote"; and Claudia Tate, "Audre Lorde," in *Conversations with Audre Lorde*, ed. Joan Wylie Hall (Jackson: University of Mississippi Press, 2004), 94.
18. Pero Gaglo Dagbovie and Deborah Gray White have each invoked Earl Thorpe's concept of "historians without portfolio," extending it to understand the work of Black women historians. Pero Gaglo Dagbovie, "Black Women Historians from the Late 19th Century to the Dawning of the Civil Rights Movement," *Journal of African American History* 89, no. 3 (Summer 2004): 241–61; and Deborah Gray White, *Telling Histories: Black Women Historians in the Ivory Tower* (Chapel Hill: University of North Carolina Press, 2008), 24 n31. See also Abdul Alkalimat, *The History of Black Studies* (London: Pluto, 2021), 63–88.

19. L. D. Reddick, draft introduction to *What the Negro Thinks About Democracy*, typescript, n.d., Lawrence D. Reddick Papers, Manuscripts, Archives and Rare Books Division (hereafter MARB), SCRBC. Note that at the time of research, this collection was unprocessed and box locations were unavailable; the collection has since been processed.
20. "Schomburg Collection in New Home," *New Journal and Guide*, May 16, 1942.
21. Oral History with Miriam Matthews, interviewed by Robin D. G. Kelley, UCLA, 1985–1986, https://oralhistory.library.ucla.edu/catalog/21198-zz00179s7c, [164].
22. H. A. B. Jones-Quartey, "Africa Speaks," *Pittsburgh Courier*, June 1, 1946.
23. Harsh's papers were discarded by her sister-in-law shortly after her death, as revealed in Melanie Chambliss, "A Vital Factor in the Community: Recovering the Life and Legacy of Chicago Public Librarian Vivian G. Harsh," *Journal of African American History* 106, no. 4 (Summer 2021), 423 n44.
24. Achille Mbembe, "The Power of the Archive and Its Limits," in *Refiguring the Archive*, ed. Carolyn Hamilton, Verne Harris, Michele Pickover, Graeme Reid, Razia Saleh, and Jane Taylor (Dordrecht, The Netherlands: Kluwer Academic, 2002), 21.
25. Joyce, "Vivian G. Harsh Collection," 68; and Bontemps, "G. C. Hall Library Does Worthy Job."
26. Ann Cvetkovich, *An Archive of Feelings: Trauma, Sexuality, and Lesbian Public Cultures* (Durham, NC: Duke University Press, 2003), 245.
27. Stefano Harney and Fred Moten, *The Undercommons: Fugitive Planning and Black Study* (Wivenhoe, UK: Minor Compositions, 2013), 110–11.
28. Erik S. McDuffie, "Chicago, Garveyism, and the History of the Diasporic Midwest," *African and Black Diaspora* 8, no. 2 (2015): 129–45.
29. U.S. Federal Census records for Cook County, Illinois, East 44th Place: 1900 (Enumeration District 1016, Sheet 19), 1910 (Enumeration District 344, Sheet 7), 1920 (Enumeration District 170, Sheet 4), and 1930 (Enumeration District 16–90, Sheet 4B), Ancestry.com. On the neighborhood's development, see James R. Grossman, *Land of Hope: Chicago, Black Southerners, and the Great Migration* (Chicago: University of Chicago Press, 1989), 123–39.
30. U.S. Federal Census data for 1900, 1910, 1920, and 1930 for Vivian G. Harsh, Charlemae Rollins, Ellyn Askins, Consuelo Young, Edith Allman Gans, Dagmar Bell, and Arline Morrell, Ancestry.com. Unlike most of her colleagues, Rollins was a migrant to Chicago, born in Mississippi. See Beverly A. Cook, "Charlemae Hill Rollins," in *Women Building Chicago, 1790–1990*, ed. Rima Lunin Schultz and Adele Hast (Bloomington: Indiana University Press, 2001), 764–66.
31. St. Clair Drake and Horace Cayton, *Black Metropolis: A Study of Negro Life in a Northern City*, rev. edition, vol. 2 (1945; repr., New York: Harper and Row, 1962), 379–80; and Davarian Baldwin, *Chicago's New Negroes: Modernity, the Great Migration, and Black Urban Life* (Chapel Hill: University of North Carolina Press, 2007), 45.
32. Thomas P. Martin, "Sources of Negro History in the Manuscript Division of the Library of Congress," *Journal of Negro History* 19, no. 1 (January 1934): 74.
33. "Frederick Douglass Center," *Chicago Defender*, April 19, 1913; "City Churches," *Chicago Defender*, August 31, 1912; "Quinn Chapel," *Chicago Defender*, June 6, 1914; and "Want Reading Room Back," *Chicago Defender*, September 29, 1917. On adult education for migrants, see Marcia Chatelain, *South Side Girls: Growing Up in the Great Migration* (Durham, NC: Duke University Press, 2015), 8.
34. "The Hyde Park Settlement," *Chicago Defender*, September 6, 1913; "The Marquette Club's Beautiful Home," *Chicago Defender*, July 29, 1911; and "The Negro Fellowship League," *Chicago Defender*, June 11, 1910. On nineteenth-century literary societies in Chicago, see Richard A. Courage, "Chicago's Letters Group and the Emergence of the Black Chicago Renaissance," in *Roots of the Black Chicago Renaissance: New Negro Writers, Artists, and Intellectuals, 1893–1930*, ed. Richard A. Courage and Christopher Robert Reed (Urbana: University of Illinois Press, 2020), 222–43.
35. "2,000 Citizens Condemn U. S. Judges—Pass Strong Resolutions," *Chicago Defender*, November 23, 1912.

36. A Julius Rosenwald Fund fellowship supported Harsh's travels to other libraries. On contact between Porter and Harsh in the 1930s, see Chambliss, "A Vital Factor," 424; and Vivian G. Harsh to Mrs. Porter, July 13 [1930s], Records of the Moorland-Spingarn Research Center, Record Group 1, University Archives, MSRC. On Harsh's visit with Latimer, see "Society," *New York Amsterdam News*, September 16, 1931. In New York, Harsh stayed at the home of Latimer's mother, Mrs. M. B. Trotman.
37. Catherine Latimer to Carter G. Woodson, November 17, 1931, reel 1, series 2, Papers of Carter G. Woodson and the Association for the Study of Negro Life and History, University Publications of America; *Report of the New York Public Library for 1926* (New York: NYPL, 1927), 109; and *Report of the New York Public Library for 1927* (New York: NYPL, 1928), 115.
38. Catherine Allen Latimer, "Where Can I Get Material on the Negro," *Crisis* 41, no. 6 (June 1934): 165.
39. On the public library movement and crime prevention, see Sidney Ditzion, "Social Reform, Education, and the Library, 1850–1900," *Library Quarterly* 9, no. 2 (April 1939): 156–84.
40. Christopher Robert Reed, *The Depression Comes to the South Side: Protest and Politics in the Black Metropolis, 1930–1933* (Bloomington: Indiana University Press, 2011), 67, 77, 87; and Drake and Cayton, *Black Metropolis*, vol. 1, 84–87.
41. Carl Roden to Andrew J. Kolar, October 3, 1931, box 4, folder 36, HBLR. On Roden's compromises when faced with challenges to the library's holdings, see Eric Novotny, "From Inferno to Freedom: Censorship in the Chicago Public Library, 1910–1936," *Library Trends* 63, no. 1 (2014): 27–41.
42. Langston Hughes, "Twelve Millions," *The Book League Monthly* 2 (June 1929): 174–75; Reed, *Depression Comes to the South Side*, 66–93; and Roden to Kolar, October 30, 1931, box 4, folder 36, HBLR.
43. Arthur A. Schomburg to John W. Cromwell, August 19, 1913, box 1, folder 16, Cromwell Family Papers, Manuscript Division, MSRC.
44. Oral history of Nannie Pinkney, December 16, 1994, box 1, Nannie Pinkney Papers, VGHRC (hereafter Pinkney OH).
45. In 1931, before the Hall Branch opened, the Chicago Public Library announced the curtailment of all new book purchases because of budget shortages. See "Halts Purchase of New Books," *Chicago Daily Tribune*, June 18, 1931.
46. Pinkney OH.
47. Pinkney suggests that the bookstore owner might have been Doris Saunders, a librarian at the Hall Branch who opened The Studio bookstore with Eloise Boone. See Pinkney OH; "Windy City Sophisticates," *Chicago Bee*, January 14, 1945; and Mary Unger, "Selling the Black Chicago Renaissance: Bronzeville's Black-Owned Bookstores," *Chicago Review of Books*, April 14, 2021, https://chireviewofbooks.com/2021/04/14/selling-the-black-chicago-renaissance-bronzevilles-black-owned-bookstores/.
48. Annual Report for 1933, box 1, folder 2, HBLR; Bessie S. King and Madeline R. Morgan, Supplementary Units for the course of Study in Social Studies, box 2, folder 2, Madeline Stratton Morris Papers, VGHRC; and Virginia Lacy Jones, "A Tribute to Charlemae Hill Rollins," box 10, Charlemae Hill Rollins Papers, VGHRC. At the time of research, the Rollins Papers were partially processed; box locations may have changed since processing.
49. Pinkney OH; "Negro Culture Collection," [unidentified newspaper], November 1, 1936, box 9, folder 22, HBLR; and Annual Report for 1943, box 1, folder 13, HBLR.
50. Vivian Harsh, "George Cleveland Hall Branch Library and Its Social Environment," typescript, 1957, box 3, folder 20, HBLR; and Rollins, "Library Work with Negroes," 92–93.
51. Annual Report for 1941, box 1, folder 11, HBLR.
52. "Club Names Old Settlers' Day," *Chicago Defender*, 1950, box 6, folder 37, HBLR; "Hall Branch Activities," typescript, 1947, box 5, folder 15, HBLR; and Harsh, "George Cleveland Hall Branch Library and Its Social Environment."

53. Janet Peck, "Hall Library Noted for Its Negro Works," *Chicago Tribune*, [October?] 2, 1945, box 6, folder 32, HBLR; Arna Bontemps to Jack Conroy, September 14, 1943, box 5, folder 21, Arna Bontemps Papers (hereafter Bontemps Papers), SUSCRC; Brian Dolinar, "Editor's Introduction," *The Negro in Illinois: The WPA Papers* (Urbana: University of Illinois Press, 2013), xxxv; and Illinois Writers Project, "Negro in Illinois" Papers, Finding Aid, VGHRC, https://www.chipublib.org/fa-illinois-writers-project-2/.
54. Michael Flug, "Vivian Gordon Harsh," in *Women Building Chicago*, 360; Peck, "Hall Library Noted for Its Negro Works"; and Langston Hughes Papers, Finding Aid, VGHRC, www.chipublib.org/fa-langston-hughes-papers. Harsh's collection-building strategy prefigured the approach of the field now called "community archives"; see, for example, Michelle Caswell, Joyce Gabiola, Jimmy Zavala, Marika Cifor, and Gracen Brilmyer, "Imagining Transformative Spaces: The Personal-Political Sites of Community Archives," *Archival Science* 18 (2018): 73–93.
55. Final Narrative Report, Bibliography by and about the Negro in the United States, [1940], box 1, Chicago Afro-American Union Analytic Catalog Records, VGHRC.
56. Annual report for 1933, box 1, folder 2, HBLR; Richard Durham, "Biggest Text Book Buyer Never Got to College," *Chicago Defender*, July 22, 1944; and Bontemps, "G. C. Hall Library Does Worthy Job."
57. George Coleman Moore, "Books Are Live Things," *Chicago Bee*, [1945], box 5, folder 32, HBLR.
58. Pinkney OH; Malcolm B. Smith, "People in Chicago," *Pittsburgh Courier*, October 24, 1936.
59. Program, Book Review and Lecture Forum (hereafter BRLF), November 29, 1944, box 5, folder 12, HBLR; and Program, BRLF, March 16, 1938, box 5, folder 6, HBLR.
60. These names are drawn from BRLF programs, box 5, folders 5–22, HBLR. Biographical information is drawn from "Praises Editorials," *Chicago Defender*, February 5, 1938; "Congratulating a Star," *Afro-American*, May 16, 1942; and 1930 and 1940 U.S. Federal Census records for Cook County, Illinois, Ancestry.com.
61. Chambliss argues that the library was a "safe place where inflammatory perspectives could still be heard" (Chambliss, "A Vital Factor," 428–29).
62. Harsh to Joseph Rollins Jr., May 18, 1945, box 4, folder 24, HBLR.
63. BRLF program, May 14, 1945, box 5, folder 13, HBLR. Laura Burt has argued that Harsh was politically savvy in her reports to CPL, eliding details about the discussions that took place in the branch's programs to avoid scrutiny by white library administrators. Burt, "Vivian Harsh, Adult Education, and the Library's Role as Community Center," *Libraries and the Cultural Record* 44, no. 2 (2009): 243–44.
64. "What's Going on at Hall Branch Library," *Chicago Bee*, April 15, 1945.
65. U.S. Congress, House of Representatives, Special Committee on Un-American Activities, *Investigation of Un-American Propaganda Activities in the United States, Appendix—Part IX Communist Front Organizations* (Washington, DC: Government Printing Office, 1944), 294, 567, 968, 978.
66. Conroy to Bontemps, June 4, 1945, box 5, folder 22, Bontemps Papers, SUSCRC; "What's Going on at Hall Branch Library"; and Douglas Wixson, *Worker-Writer in America: Jack Conroy and the Tradition of Midwestern Literary Radicalism, 1898–1990* (Urbana: University of Illinois Press, 1994), 455. On Conroy's relationship to South Side artists, see Mary Helen Washington, *The Other Blacklist: The African American Literary and Cultural Left of the 1950s* (New York: Columbia University Press, 2015), 193–96.
67. Keith Gilyard, *John Oliver Killens: A Life of Black Literary Activism* (Athens: University of Georgia Press, 2010), 114–15.
68. BRLF Program, March 20, 1940, box 5, folder 8, HBLR.
69. Cait McKinney, "'Finding the Lines to My People': Media History and Queer Bibliographic Encounter," *GLQ: A Journal of Lesbian and Gay Studies* 24, no. 1 (January 2018): 69.
70. "The Book Shelf," *Bags and Baggage*, November 1, 1942, 4.

71. "George Hall Library News," *Chicago Bee*, April 11, 1943.
72. BRLF program, October 5, 1938, box 5, folder 6, HBLR.
73. Lisa Gitelman, *Paper Knowledge: Toward a Media History of Documents* (Durham, NC: Duke University Press, 2014), 11, 30–31. On Harsh's reading lists, see Laura E. Helton, "Making Lists, Keeping Time: Infrastructures of Black Inquiry, 1900–1950," in *Against a Sharp White Background: Infrastructures of African American Print*, ed. Brigitte Fielder and Jonathan Senchyne (Madison: University of Wisconsin Press, 2019), 88.
74. W. E. B. Du Bois, "Progress by Poverty," typed speech draft, February 12, 1939, W. E. B. Du Bois Papers (hereafter Du Bois Papers), UMSC, https://credo.library.umass.edu/view/full/mums312-b198-i003; and Harsh to Du Bois, March 14, 1939, Du Bois Papers, https://credo.library.umass.edu/view/full/mums312-b087-i488.
75. "Interest in Race History Increases," *Chicago Defender*, March 2, 1940; and "Hall Library," *Chicago Bee*, February 1939, box 6, folder 25, HBLR.
76. Photographs of "Original Manuscripts by Contemporary Negro Writers" exhibit at Hall Branch Library, 1943, box 12, folders 179, 180 and 183, HBLR; and [typescript about manuscript donations], n.d., box 3, folder 4, HBLR. Also included were manuscripts sent by Monroe Work, Carter G. Woodson, and Charles S. Johnson.
77. [Clipping on Negro History Week], *Chicago Bee*, February 1939, box 6, folder 25, HBLR; and Du Bois to Harsh, February 24, 1936, Du Bois Papers, https://credo.library.umass.edu/view/full/mums312-b077-i299
78. Harsh to Du Bois, March 14, 1939; Harsh to Du Bois, January 12, 1939, Du Bois Papers, https://credo.library.umass.edu/view/full/mums312-b087-i486; and Du Bois to Harsh, January 14, 1939, Du Bois Papers, https://credo.library.umass.edu/view/pageturn/mums312-b087-i487. During a visit to Chicago, Du Bois used the *Selected Bibliography, Illinois, Chicago and Its Environs* (Chicago: Federal Writers' Project Illinois, 1937), which Richard Wright had worked on and was held at the Hall Branch. See Michel Fabre, *The Unfinished Quest of Richard Wright* (Urbana: University of Illinois Press, 1973), 546 n8.
79. Carl Van Vechten, "The J. W. Johnson Collection at Yale," *Crisis* 49, no. 7 (July 1942): 222; and "Booker T.'s Papers Presented to Library," *Afro-American*, July 3, 1943.
80. Dagmar Bell to Bontemps, box 2, folder 11, October 18, 1943, Bontemps Papers.
81. BRLF programs, November 1, 1939 and November 15, 1939, box 5, folder 7, HBLR; and Harsh, "George Cleveland Hall Branch Library and Its Social Environment."
82. Annual report for 1942, box 1, folder 12, HBLR; "When George Cleveland Hall Branch Library Held 'Open House,'" *Chicago Bee*, June 6, 1943; and "Hall Library Cites Importance of Books in War-Time Activities," *Chicago Bee*, May 16, 1943.
83. "Author," *Chicago Defender*, January 18, 1947; "Hall Library Exhibits Manuscripts," *Chicago Bee*, January 19, 1947.
84. "Talk of the Town," *Chicago Heights Star*, September 18, 1951; [Photograph in unidentified clipping shows Aldridge exhibit], 1954, box 7, folder 2, HBLR; Roi Ottley, "Library to Fete History Week," [unidentified clipping], 1955, box 7, folder 3, HBLR; "Praise Robb for Bringing Easterners to Pageant," *Chicago Defender*, September 8, 1934; and "Scholar Tells Why Ethiopia Will Triumph," *Chicago Defender*, January 11, 1936.
85. Elizabeth Alexander, *The Black Interior* (St. Paul, MN: Graywolf, 2004).
86. "Rear Adm. Evers Is Speaker at Library Forum," *Chicago Daily Times*, February 1, 1942. On the South Chicago branch, see Joyce M. Latham, "Memorial Day to Memorial Library: The South Chicago Branch Library as Cultural Terrain, 1937–1947," *Libraries and the Cultural Record* 46, no. 3 (2011): 337–39; and Eric Gelman, "Chicago's Native Son: Charles White and the Laboring of the Black Renaissance," in *The Black Chicago Renaissance*, ed. Darlene Clark Hine and John McCluskey Jr. (Urbana: University of Illinois Press, 2012), 157–58.

87. Untitled typescript [begins "A branch library is an auxiliary unit . . ."], n.d., box 3, folder 2, HBLR.
88. Yearly Report, Hall Branch Library, 1938, box 5, folder 7, HBLR; and " 'Negro History' to Hold Spotlight Here Next Week: Programs Will Touch All Phases of Race Progress in U.S.," *Chicago Defender*, February 10, 1934, box 6, folder 20, HBLR.
89. "Ralph Korngold at Parkway Community House," *Chicago Bee*, December 10, 1944.
90. Flier, Reception in honor of Arna Bontemps, April 26, 1936, box 21, folder 5, Bontemps Papers; Annual report for 1942, box 1, folder 12, HBLR; and Margaret Reynolds Hurton to L. D. Reddick, September 28, 1944, SCRBC Records, MARB, SCRBC. (At the time of research, this letter was among unprocessed material from the Reddick papers slated for incorporation into the SCRBC Records.)
91. "So. Parkway YWCA Nite Owl Parties," *Chicago Bee*, November 21, 1943.
92. Annual Report for 1933, box 1, folder 2, HBLR.
93. Edwin Rosskam, photograph captioned "Books on display in show [sic] store window, 47th Street, Chicago, Illinois," April 1941, Farm Security Administration Office of War Information photograph collection, Library of Congress Prints and Photographs Division, https://www.loc.gov/pictures/item/2017729445/. On James Knight, the shoe store owner and "Mayor of Bronzeville," see Elizabeth Schroeder Schlabach, *Along the Streets of Bronzeville: Black Chicago's Literary Landscape* (Urbana: University of Illinois Press, 2013), 20.
94. "Hall Library to Give Labor Exhibit," *Chicago Bee*, September 10, 1944. Other branch librarians used similar strategies to attract readers through newspaper columns and shop window displays. See Annie L. McPheeters, *Library Service in Black and White: Some Personal Recollections, 1921–1980* (Metuchen, NJ: Scarecrow, 1988), 95.
95. Hazel V. Carby, "Policing the Black Woman's Body in an Urban Context," *Critical Inquiry* 18, no. 4 (Summer 1992): 754.
96. Michael Flug, "Vivian Gordon Harsh," in *Black Women in America: An Historical Encyclopedia*, ed. Darlene Clark Hine (Brooklyn, NY: Carlson, 1993), 542–43.
97. Richard Wright, *Lawd Today* (New York: Walker, 1963), 62.
98. Chambliss, "A Vital Factor," 426; and Burt, "Vivian Harsh," 250.
99. As Jessica Pressman argues in *Bookishness: Loving Books in a Digital* Age (New York: Columbia University Press, 2020), " 'bookishness' suggests an identity derived from a physical nearness to books, not just from the 'reading' of them" (10). As Karla F. C. Holloway underscores, "bookish" was an identity often denied to African Americans (Holloway, *BookMarks: Reading in Black and White* (Rutgers: Rutgers University Press, 2006), 31.
100. Langston Hughes, "Things I Like About Chicago I Like, and What I Don't, I Don't," *Chicago Defender*, June 18, 1949.
101. Houston A. Baker Jr., "Critical Memory and the Black Public Sphere," in *The Black Public Sphere: A Public Culture Book* (Chicago: University of Chicago Press, 1995), 17.
102. Hughes, "Things I Like About Chicago"; Baldwin, *Chicago's New Negroes*, 22; and Drake and Cayton, *Black Metropolis*, vol. 2, 382.
103. Hughes, "Things I Like About Chicago."
104. Bontemps, "G. C. Hall Library Does Worthy Job."
105. Langston Hughes, "From the International House, Bronzeville Seems Far Away," *Chicago Defender*, June 11, 1949. On Black readers' use of the CPL main branch, see Zita Louise Baker, "Who Reads the Books?," *Chicago Defender*, August 24, 1929.
106. For a comparison of holdings, see CPL, *The Chicago Afro-American Union Analytic Catalog: An Index to Materials on Afro-Americans in the Principal Libraries of Chicago* (Boston: Hall, 1972).
107. Hughes, "Things I Like About Chicago."
108. "University of Chicago Is Target of Race Citizens," *New Journal and Guide*, November 13, 1937.
109. Hughes, "From the International House."

110. Gwendolyn Brooks, "kitchenette building," in *The Essential Gwendolyn Brooks*, ed. Elizabeth Alexander (New York: Library of America, 2005).
111. Drake and Cayton, *Black Metropolis*, vol. 1, 81.
112. Hughes, "From the International House."
113. Benjamin F. Smith, "Readers in an All-Negro Community," *Negro Educational Review*, October 1, 1952, 179, in box 3, folder 31, HBLR.
114. Rollins, "Library Work with Negroes," 92.
115. New borrowers survey, ca. 1930s, box 2, folder 28, HBLR.
116. George Coleman Moore, "Book Club All Set for New Season" [unidentified clipping], 1943, box 6, folder 30, HBLR.
117. Annual report for 1954, box 1, folder 24, HBLR.
118. Bontemps, "G. C. Hall Library Does Worthy Job."
119. Rollins, "Library Work with Negroes," 93.
120. Alexander, *The Black Interior*, 16.
121. Horace Cayton, "Reflections on Richard Wright," quoted in Bone and Courage, *The Muse in Bronzeville*, 117. When the WPA-sponsored research study of Bronzeville displayed its "maps, charts, graphs and tables" at the Good Shepherd Community Center, five hundred people attended. See "Community in Charts, Maps Seen by 500," *Chicago Defender*, January 21, 1939, 24; and Bone and Courage, *The Muse in Bronzeville*, 130.
122. "Things You Should Know About the Chicago Public Library," *Chicago Bee*, May 7, 1944.
123. Annual report for 1954, box 1, folder 24, HBLR.
124. Madeline R. Stratton, "Chicago Public School Project, 1942," paper presented at National Convention of Association for the Study of Afro-American Life and History, October 15–19, 1975, box 2, folder 12, Madeline Stratton Morris Papers, VGHRC.
125. "DuSable History Club Continues Lectures," *Chicago Defender*, January 18, 1941, box 6, folder 28, HBLR.
126. [Clipping on Negro History Week], *Chicago Bee*, February 1939, box 6, folder 25, HBLR; and Yearly report for 1938, box 1, folder 7, HBLR.
127. "George C. Hall Library Notes," *Chicago Defender*, February 6, 1937, box 6, folder 23, HBLR; and Knupfer, *The Chicago Black Renaissance*, 63.
128. Flier, DuSable History Club of Hall Branch Library Celebrates Chicago Day, October 9, 1954, box 5, folder 50, HBLR. The DuSable History Club emerged from, but is not the same as, the De Saible Memorial Society, which organized an exhibition about du Sable at the 1933 Century of Progress Exposition. Annie E. Oliver founded the Memorial Society around 1928, and it was described as an "organization of colored women." Oliver also founded the DuSable History Club around 1934. See "14th Reception Held," *Chicago Defender*, January 10, 1942; "De Saible Day Celebrated at the World's Fair," *Plaindealer*, July 28, 1933; "Three States Have Negro Representation at World's Fair," *Negro Star*, July 7, 1933; "National DuSable Memorial Society Mrs. Annie Oliver Tea," *Chicago Bee*, June 13, 1943; "Nat'l DuSable Society Holds 18th Open House," *Chicago Bee*, January 12, 1947; "Society to Salute Annie E. Oliver," *Chicago Daily Defender*, November 22, 1960; and "Annie Oliver Interviewed on Radio Show," *Chicago Defender*, February 1, 1952, box 6, folder 39, HBLR.
129. "DuSable History Club," typescript, 1954–1955, box 5, folder 50, HBLR. Biographical information on Oliver drawn from U.S. Bureau of the Census, Fourteenth Census of the United States: 1920—Population Schedule for Chicago, Ancestry.com; "A Scrap Book for Women in Public Life," *Chicago Defender*, October 5, 1929; "DuSable Society Founder, Mrs. Annie Oliver, Dies," *Chicago Daily Defender*, November 14, 1962; and Rocksborough-Smith, *Black Public History*, 45–46.
130. I estimate that the DuSable History Club moved to the Hall Branch in 1938 based on a statement in "History Class to Visit Grave of Sojourner Truth," *Chicago Sunday Bee*, June 29, 1941. Other accounts give the date as 1940; see "DuSable History Club at Hall Branch" index card, n.d., box 3, folder 7, HBLR.

131. Biographical sketch of S. Stratton, n.d., box 12, folder 2, Madeline Stratton Morris Papers, VGHRC.
132. Harsh designed a curriculum for the Flying Squadron, a women's auxiliary of the NAACP, and supported a book group for the South Side's Camp Fire Girls. See Chambliss, "A Vital Factor," 417, 422; Chatelain, *South Side Girls*, 140; "Flying Squadron," *Chicago Defender*, November 16, 1929; and "Benefit Given by Flying Squadron Huge Success," *Chicago Defender*, June 8, 1929.
133. "DuSable History Club Sponsors New Program," *Chicago Defender*, March 15, 1941, box 6, folder 28, HBLR. On Hilliard, see Knupfer, *The Chicago Black Renaissance*, 28, 67; John F. Lyons, *Teachers and Reform: Chicago Public Education, 1929–1970* (Urbana: University of Illinois Press, 2008), 161; "Campbell, Esquire Cartoonist, Life Member of Art Center," *Chicago Bee*, May 23, 1943; and [Photo caption], *Chicago Bee*, March 21, 1943.
134. "DuSable History Club Plans Historical Lectures," *Chicago Defender*, January 11, 1941, box 6, folder 28, HBLR.
135. "Flyer Continues Lectures on Ethiopia," *Chicago Defender*, April 12, 1941, box 6, folder 28, HBLR.
136. "DuSable History Club Tours U.C. Egyptian Shrine," *Chicago World*, May 4, 1941.
137. In the early 1950s, the Hall Branch also hosted an "Africa Today Study Club." See CPL Calendar of Events, January 1953, box 5, folder 24, HBLR. On other study curricula and history clubs of this period, see the *Negro History Bulletin's* feature on "The Negro in Foreign Lands" (vol. 4, no. 1, October 1940); and Clare Corbould, *Becoming African Americans: Black Public Life in Harlem, 1919–1939* (Cambridge, MA: Harvard University Press, 2009), 95–97.
138. Gloria Chuku, "African Intellectuals as Cultural Nationalists: A Comparative Analysis of Edward Wilmot Bylden and Mbonu Ojike," *Journal of African American History*, vol. 99, no. 4 (Fall 2014): 362–63.
139. "At Our Libraries," *Chicago Bee*, April 15, 1945.
140. Jones-Quartey, "Africa Speaks"; "High School Notes," *Chicago Defender*, June 16, 1928.
141. DuSable History Club programs, 1947, box 5, folder 15, HBLR; DuSable History Club invitations, 1953–1957, box 5, folder 50, HBLR; "History Club to Hear Vets' Pacific Story" [unidentified clipping], 1946, box 6, folder 33, HBLR; "History Club to Stress 'The Value of Voting,'" *Chicago Defender*, March 8, 1947, box 6, folder 33, HBLR; "Flyer Continues Lectures on Ethiopia," *Chicago Defender*, April 12, 1941, box 6, folder 28, HBLR; and "History Club Announces Afro-American Lecture," *Chicago Defender*, January 25, 1941, box 6, folder 28, HBLR.
142. "Overflow Crowd Sees 'On Freedom Road,'" *Sunday Chicago Bee*, February 18, 1945; Gelman, "Chicago's Native Son," 157–158; and Rocksborough-Smith, *Black Public History*, 43–44 and 55–61.
143. "Headliners in Fifth Annual Artists Model Ball," *Chicago Defender*, October 31, 1942; "Testimonial Luncheon to Laud Atty. Edith Sampson," *Chicago Defender*, December 13, 1958; "Plan Discussion of John Jones," *Chicago Defender*, June 9, 1951; Mavis Mixon, "The Development of the Study of Negro History in Chicago," *Chicago Defender*, February 7, 1942; "N.A.A.C.P. Auxiliary Launches Drive," *Chicago Defender*, October 4, 1941; and Polly Harris, "Book Chats," *Chicago Defender*, June 15, 1935.
144. "Chaplain's Wife Is Top Theological Student," *Pittsburgh Courier*, August 21, 1943; and "High School Notes."
145. In the late 1920s, Robb edited two volumes of *The Wonder Book* under the name Frederic H. Robb. By 1932, he was publishing as "Ras Hammurabi" (Hammurabi, "The Traveler," *Philadelphia Tribune*, April 14, 1932). On Hammurabi, see Adam Green, "The Rising Tide of Youth: Chicago's Wonder Books and the 'New' Black Middle Class," in *The Middling Sorts: Explorations in the History of the American Middle Class*, ed. Burton J. Bledstein and Robert D. Johnston (New York: Routledge, 2001), 253–54. Alkalimat calls him the "Chicago equivalent of New York's J. A. Rogers" (Alkalimat, *The History of Black Studies*, 75).
146. William Sites, *Sun Ra's Chicago: Afrofuturism and the City* (Chicago: University of Chicago Press, 2020), 101; and St. Clair Drake, *Churches and Voluntary Associations in the Chicago Negro Community* (Chicago: WPA District 3, December 1940), 3. The term "street scholar" comes from Ralph

Crowder, "The Historical Context and Political Significance of Harlem's Street Scholar Community," *Afro-Americans in New York Life and History* 34, no. 1 (2010): 34–71. Hammurabi Robb was connected to overlapping religious and nationalist circles shaped by Garveyism. In 1936, for example, two readers from Detroit wrote to the *Chicago Defender* in praise of Robb's writings on Africa, using the language of "original man" characteristic of both Noble Drew Ali and Elijah Muhammad's followers (Mamie and Ruth Hajjie, "Likes African Article," *Chicago Defender*, March 14, 1936). He cited Garvey's call to "Organize!" in "Robb Writes on Changing Africa as Europe Prepares to Commit Suicide with War," *Chicago Defender*, September 12, 1936.

147. F. Hammurabi Robb, "Whites Attempt to Crush Black World," *Chicago Defender*, April 3, 1937.

148. Raymond Whittaker, "Scores Robb on College Article," *Pittsburgh Courier*, July 22, 1933; Gerald Horne, *Facing the Rising Sun: African Americans, Japan, and the Rise of Afro-Asian Solidarity* (New York: New York University Press, 2018), 105, 197 n49; "FBI Announces Apprehension of Chicagoans," *Atlanta Daily World*, September 22, 1942; "FBI Accuses 80 in Chicago of Part in Seditious Activities," *Baltimore Afro-American*, September 26, 1942; "Grand Jury Is Probing Three Chicago Cults," *Atlanta Daily World*, September 28, 1942; David H. Orro, "Seek Indictments of Sedition Suspects," *Chicago Defender*, October 3, 1942; "Cultists Remain Undaunted," *Chicago Defender*, October 24, 1942; and "Sedition, Draft Evasion Cases Up in Three Cities," *Chicago Defender*, December 5, 1942.

149. "5 Lectures on Africa Slated," *Chicago Defender*, March 5, 1948, box 6, folder 35, HBLR; and "History Club to Conduct Book Reviews," *Chicago Defender*, March 1947, box 6, folder 34, HBLR. The Hall branch was one of five sites on the South Side that displayed Hammurabi's Black history calendars. See "Calendar Tells Negro History," [unidentified clipping], n.d., box 7, folder 21, HBLR.

150. "History Class to Visit Grave of Sojourner Truth"; and "History Club Visits Tomb of S. Truth," *Chicago Defender*, July 19, 1941.

151. Annual report for 1951, box 1, folder 21, HBLR; and [clipping about DuSable wreath laying], *Daily Defender*, October 9, 1956, box 6, folder 4, HBLR.

152. "History Club to Hear Vets' Pacific Story"; and "Club Names Old Settlers' Day," *Chicago Defender*, [1950], box 6, folder 37, HBLR.

153. "Negro History Group to Meet Tuesday Night," *Chicago Daily Tribune*, March 16, 1947, box 5, folder 50, HBLR.

154. Brochure, "Hall Branch Activities, April 1947," box 5, folder 50, HBLR.

155. Du Bois to Harsh, October 15, 1952, Du Bois Papers, https://credo.library.umass.edu/view/full/mums312-b137-i030.

156. See location information in CPL, *The Negro and His Achievements in America: A List of Books Compiled for the American Negro Exposition*, 1940, box 3, folder 13, HBLR. The fact that many of the items in the Hall branch collection were "not obtainable at other local libraries" is also noted in [Unidentified newspaper clipping], *Chicago Daily News*, [early 1930s], box 7, folder 21, HBLR. By 1975, a Hall Branch annual report noted that answering reference queries had become easier because "most of the desired information could be obtained from any local branch carrying a Black collection"—a shift that indicates how in previous decades the holdings of the Hall Branch had been unique among the city's libraries (Annual Report for 1975, box 2, folder 17, HBLR).

157. Typescript announcement for DuSable History Club, 1951, box 5, folder 50, HBLR.

158. On the age of participants, see Annual report for 1940, box 1, folder 9, HBLR. At one point there was also a "Young People's Unit" of the club ("Negro History Symposium," *Chicago Bee*, April 8, 1945).

159. Although the ASNLH helped seed the Black history movement in Chicago, local activists were ideologically heterogeneous and sometimes clashed with ASNLH leadership (Rocksborough-Smith, *Black Public History*, 65–68). There was, however, some overlap between the ASNLH and DuSable History Club. See, for example, a cosponsored panel discussion moderated by Horace Cayton: Flier, "What Is the Negro Up Against," [February 14, 1944], box 5, folder 50, HBLR.

160. "DuSable History Club Continues Lectures," *Chicago Defender*, January 18, 1941, box 6, folder 28, HBLR; and "History Club Announces Afro-American Lecture," *Chicago Defender*, January 25, 1941, box 6, folder 28, HBLR.
161. Rollins, "Library Work with Negroes," 92.
162. "DuSable History Club Continues Lectures."
163. "History Club to Conduct Book Reviews," *Chicago Defender*, n.d., box 6, folder 34, HBLR; and "5 Lectures on Africa Slated," *Chicago Defender*, March 5, 1938, box 6, folder 35, HBLR.
164. Untitled typescript [begins "A branch library is an auxiliary unit . . ."], n.d., box 3, folder 2, HBLR; and "History Class to Visit Grave of Sojourner Truth."
165. Moten and Harney, *The Undercommons*, 110–11. The club's practice also embodies Barbara Christian's argument that theory is a "collective endeavor" (Christian, "The Race for Theory," *Cultural Critique* 6 (Spring 1987): 53.
166. "Hall Library Program Set for Oct. 10," *Chicago Globe*, October 7, 1950, box 6, folder 37, HBLR. Building on Moten and Harney, Joshua Myers defines "Black Study" as "that tradition of refusal of the knowledge of the world as it was given to us by those committed to colonial and racial order" (Myers, *Of Black Study* [London: Pluto, 2023], 8).
167. These repositories for Black study include, for example, the basement library of Sterling A. Brown and the circulating photocopies of Julius S. Scott's *Common Wind*. See Joanne V. Gabbin, "Sterling Brown's Poetic Voice: A Living Legacy," *African American Review* 31, no. 3 (Autumn 1997), 427; and Vincent Brown, Laurent Dubois, and Jennifer L. Morgan, "In Memoriam: Julius S. Scott (1955–2021), Historian of the Black Atlantic," *Perspectives on History* (March 2022), https://www.historians.org/research-and-publications/perspectives-on-history/march-2022/julius-s-scott-(1955–2021).
168. Many accounts of Chicago's Black intellectual history tend to focus either on university-based academics (the famed Chicago sociologists) or popular culture of the South Side. Compare, for example, Baldwin, *Chicago's New Negroes*, to Francille Rusan Wilson, *The Segregated Scholars: Black Social Scientists and the Creation of Black Labor Studies, 1890–1950* (Charlottesville: University of Virginia Press, 2006).
169. Annual report for 1957, box 2, folder 6, HBLR.
170. Hammurabi ran the Century Service Exchange (later named House of Knowledge) at 3806 Michigan Boulevard, where he sold books and printed custom fans and calendars featuring "Beautiful Afro-American Subjects." The space had affinities with Charles Seifert's Ethiopian Research Library in Harlem. See Advertisement, *Chicago Defender*, December 16, 1944; Advertisement, *Chicago Defender*, March 31, 1945; Rocksborough-Smith, *Black Public History*, 49–73; and Wilson, *Negro Building*, 234–47 and 289–90.
171. This club was named in memory of the novelist and union organizer Frank London Brown. See "U. Of C. Unit to Offer Negro History Course," *Chicago Daily Defender*, January 25, 1962; Melvin S. Smith, "Negro History," *Chicago Daily Defender*, June 11, 1962; "Black History Exhibition Slated At Library," *Chicago Daily Defender*, December 4, 1968; and "Seminar Slated by New Negro History Club," *Chicago Daily Defender*, June 18, 1964. The Frank London Brown History Club raised funds to purchase a Negro History Library for the Mississippi Freedom Schools; Gwendolyn Brooks was the club's honorary chair at the time. See "Freedom Schools to Benefit from Dinner," *Chicago Defender*, February 20, 1965.
172. "Negro History Exhibit," *Chicago Daily Defender*, January 16, 1968; "Community Events Calendar," *Chicago Daily Defender*, February 20, 1968; "Highlights of the Frank London Brown Memorial Society, Ten Years, 1963–1973," booklet, box 35, folder 3, HBLR; and Frank Petty, "Why Negro History: A Lecture," n.d., box 35, folder 6, HBLR.
173. Bontemps, "G. C. Hall Library Does Worthy Job"; and "George Cleveland Hall Branch Library," [typescript], ca. 1940, box 3, folder 12, HBLR.
174. Cheryl Clarke, remarks at Black Women Writing Across Genres in the Late 20th Century symposium, University of Pennsylvania, February 21, 2020.

6. MOBILIZING MANUSCRIPTS: L. D. REDDICK AND BLACK ARCHIVAL POLITICS

1. "War Letters Wanted," typescript, n.d., box 1, folder 1, Lawrence D. Reddick World War II Project Records (hereafter LDRWWII), Manuscripts, Archives and Rare Books Division (hereafter MARB), SCRBC. These examples are drawn from [Wilbert Solard?] to Curator, August 17, 1946, box 5, folder 24, LDRWWII; E. M. Jones to L. D. Reddick, December 16, 1945, box 1, folder 8, LDRWWII; and Hoyt W. Fuller to Reddick, June 22, 1945, box 1, folder 8, LDRWWII.
2. N. L. Whittico to Reddick, July 19, 1945, box 1, folder 7, LDRWWII.
3. Josie Shorter to Reddick, July 10, 1945, box 1, folder 7, LDRWWII.
4. Emmitt Quarles to Reddick, June 4, 1946, box 1, folder 7, LDRWWII.
5. "War Letters Wanted."
6. L. D. Reddick, draft materials for *What the Negro Thinks About Democracy* [unfinished manuscript], n.d., Lawrence D. Reddick Papers (hereafter LDR Papers), MARB, SCRBC. Note that at the time of this research, the Reddick Papers were unprocessed, so material is cited without box locations. The papers were processed by Allison Hughes in 2021.
7. In a letter written three months before his death, Schomburg remarked to Reddick, "it has been many years since we used to see each other in the cloisters of Fisk University, and I am very proud of the progress that you have made since then" (Arthur A. Schomburg to Lawrence D. Reddick, March 1, 1938, box 8, folder 18, Arthur A. Schomburg Papers [hereafter AAS Papers], MARB, SCRBC).
8. Reddick, draft materials for *What the Negro Thinks About Democracy*.
9. David A. Varel, *The Scholar and the Struggle: Lawrence Reddick's Crusade for Black History and Black Power* (Durham, NC: University of North Carolina Press, 2021), 47–49. Although the FBI considered Reddick a "concealed member" of the Communist Party, Herbert Hill described him as belonging to an "independent black radical tradition" (Hill quoted in Varel, *Scholar and the Struggle*, 11; Federal Bureau of Investigation file for Lawrence Dunbar Reddick, obtained through Freedom of Information Act request, July 2019). Nevertheless, in 1960, after supporting a student sit-in movement, he was dismissed from a position at Alabama State College on charges of Communist affiliation. See Reddick to Horace Mann Bond, May 16, 1947, Horace Mann Bond Papers (hereafter Bond Papers), UMSC, http://credo.library.umass.edu/view/full/mums411-b062-f020); "Negro Teacher Linked to Reds, Ordered Fired," *Montgomery Advertiser*, June 15, 1960, SCCF 004,226; and Joy-Ann Williamson-Lott, "The Battle Over Power, Control, and Academic Freedom at Southern Institutions of Higher Education, 1955–1965," *Journal of Southern History* 79, no. 4 (November 2013): 879–920.
10. L. D. Reddick, "A New Interpretation for Negro History," *Journal of Negro History* 22, no. 1 (January 1937): 26–27. Reddick's approach anticipated the later social history turn. See August Meier and Elliott Rudwick, *Black History and the Historical Profession, 1915–1980* (Urbana: University of Illinois Press, 1986), 233–34, 240.
11. Reddick, draft materials for *What the Negro Thinks About Democracy*.
12. L. D. Reddick, "The Relative Status of the Negro in the American Armed Forces," *Journal of Negro Education* 22, no. 3 (Summer 1953): 380.
13. L. D. Reddick, "Africa Speaks," *Opportunity* 20, no. 7 (July 1942): 206.
14. A compilation of these demands is found in *What the Negro Wants*, ed. Rayford W. Logan (Chapel Hill: University of North Carolina Press, 1944). The historiography on African American activism during World War II is voluminous. Recent scholarship includes Penny Von Eschen, *Race Against Empire: Black Americans and Anticolonialism, 1937–1957* (Ithaca, NY: Cornell University Press, 1997); Kimberly L. Phillips, *War! What Is It Good For? Black Freedom Struggles and the U.S. Military from World War II to Iraq* (Chapel Hill: University of North Carolina Press, 2012); Thomas A. Guglielmo, "A Martial Freedom Movement: Black G.I.s' Political Struggles during World War II,"

Journal of American History 104, no. 4 (March 2018): 879–903; Christine Knauer, *Let Us Fight as Free Men: Black Soldiers and Civil Rights* (Philadelphia: University of Pennsylvania Press, 2014); and Chris Dixon, *African Americans and the Pacific War, 1941–1945: Race, Nationality, and the Fight for Freedom* (Cambridge, MA: Cambridge University Press, 2018).

15. L. D. Reddick, "Frederick Douglass—The First Great Voice," *The People's Voice*, February 14, 1942; and L. D. Reddick, "The Negro Soldier Writes Home," typescript, box 4, folder 10, LDRWWII. Reddick built on earlier historians' view of war as a potential turning point in Black freedom struggles: George W. Williams, *A History of the Negro Troops in the War of the Rebellion, 1861–1865* (New York: Bergman, 1888); Emmett J. Scott, *The American Negro In the World War* (1919); Kelly Miller, *Authentic History of the Negro in the World War* (1920); Carter G. Woodson, *The Negro in Our History* (1922); and W. E. B. Du Bois, *The Gift of Black Folk* (1924).
16. Reddick, draft materials for *What the Negro Thinks About Democracy*. On 1940s Black radicalism, see Erik S. McDuffie, *Sojourning for Freedom: Black Women, American Communism, and the Making of Black Left Feminism* (Durham, NC: Duke University Press, 2011); and Erik S. Gellman, *Death Blow to Jim Crow: The National Negro Congress and the Rise of Militant Civil Rights* (Chapel Hill: University of North Carolina Press, 2012).
17. Farah J. Griffin, "Ann Petry's Harlem," in *Toward an Intellectual History of Black Women*, ed. Mia Bay, Farah J. Griffin, Martha S. Jones, and Barbara D. Savage (Chapel Hill: University of North Carolina Press, 2015), 138.
18. Reddick, draft materials for *What the Negro Thinks About Democracy*.
19. Sarah A. Anderson, "'The Place to Go': The 135th Street Branch Library and the Harlem Renaissance," *Library Quarterly* 73, no. 4 (October 2003): 383–421; Ethelene Whitmire, *Regina Anderson Andrews: Harlem Renaissance Librarian* (Urbana: University of Illinois Press, 2014); Celeste Tibbets, "Ernestine Rose and the Origins of the Schomburg Center," Schomburg Center Occasional Papers no. 2 (New York: NYPL, 1989); Betty L. Jenkins, "A White Librarian in Black Harlem," *Library Quarterly* 60, no. 3 (July 1990): 216–31; and Rhonda Evans, "Catherine A. Latimer: Librarian of the Harlem Renaissance," *Libraries: Culture, History, and Society* 6, no. 1 (2022): 21–41.
20. Reddick, draft materials for *What the Negro Thinks About Democracy*; and "A Record of Achievement," typescript, ca. 1947, box 62, folder 21, Bond Papers, http://credo.library.umass.edu/view/full/mums411-b062-f021.
21. L. D. Reddick, "The Honor Roll in Race Relations," *Bulletin of the New York Public Library* 47, no. 12 (December 1943): 872–73. Reddick saw the library as a site of mass communication akin to radio, film, and the press. See L. D. Reddick, "Educational Programs for the Improvement of Race Relations: Motion Pictures Radio, The Press, and Libraries," *Journal of Negro Education* 13, no. 3 (Summer 1944): 367–80. On the ways Black thought was embedded in specific transformations of media and information networks in the 1930s and 1940s, see Barbara Dianne Savage, *Broadcasting Freedom: Radio, War, and the Politics of Race, 1938–1948* (Chapel Hill: University of North Carolina Press, 1999); and Nikhil Pal Singh, *Black Is a Country: Race and the Unfinished Struggle for Democracy* (Cambridge, MA: Harvard University Press, 2005), 69, 19.
22. "Says Negro Must Write Own Story of World War," *New Jersey Record*, December [no year], box 2, folder 10, SCRBC Records, MARB, SCRBC.
23. Michael Carter, "Preview of Film, *The Negro Soldier*," *Afro-American*, March 4, 1944.
24. L. D. Reddick, "Letters from the Jim-Crow Army," corrected typescript, n.d., box 1, folder 8, LDRWWII. See Reddick's transcriptions of archival material, including a 1920 War Department memorandum, "Use to be made of negroes [sic] in the U.S. Military Service," box 4, folder 1, LDRWWII. Reddick struggled to gain access to information on Black troops from the War Department; the Army in particular rebuffed Reddick's repeated requests for information. See Reddick to James C. Evans, June 20, 1946, RG 107, Records of the Secretary of War, Records of the Office of the Assistant Secretary of War, Entry188: Civilian Aide to the Secretary—Subject File

[General Correspondence (Hastie), 1940–1948], National Archives and Records Administration, accessed via ProQuest.

25. Reddick to Charles S. Johnson, October 1, 1945, box 549, folder 9, Rosenwald Fund Records, FUSCA. Reddick invoked a modern understanding of archives as a requisite component of democratic government, one that had failed in the case of Black America. See Terry Cook, "What Is Past Is Prologue: A History of Archival Ideas Since 1898, and the Future Paradigm Shift," *Archivaria* 43 (Spring 1997): 39; and Jennifer S. Milligan, "'What Is an Archive?' in the History of Modern France," in *Archive Stories: Facts, Fictions, and the Writing of History*, ed. Antoinette Burton (Durham, NC: Duke University Press, 2005), 169.
26. Reddick, draft materials for *What the Negro Thinks About Democracy*. The title of Reddick's manuscript riffed on R. R. Moton's 1929 *What the Negro Thinks* and indirectly critiqued Gunnar Myrdal's *An American Dilemma*, which Reddick described as "more about America than it is about the Negro" (L. D. Reddick, "Scholarship and Candor," *Journal of Negro Education* 13, no. 2 [Spring 1944]: 191).
27. Wright quoted in Constance Webb, *Richard Wright: A Biography* (New York: Putnam, 1968), 227.
28. Reddick, "Letters from the Jim-Crow Army"; and Reddick, draft materials for *What the Negro Thinks About Democracy*.
29. Barbara Foley, "Questionnaire Responses," *Modernism/modernity* 20, no. 3 (September 2013): 441.
30. Lawrence P. Jackson, *The Indignant Generation: A Narrative History of African American Writers and Critics, 1934–1960* (Princeton, NJ: Princeton University Press, 2011), 8.
31. Carl Van Vechten, "The J. W. Johnson Collection at Yale," *Crisis* 49, no. 7 (July 1942): 222.
32. Dorothy Porter to Henry O. Tanner, January 28, 1936, Records of the Moorland-Spingarn Research Center, Record Group 1 (hereafter MSRC Record Group 1), University Archives, MSRC; Dorothy Porter, *Afro-Braziliana: A Working Bibliography* (Boston: Beacon, 1978); and African American Museum and Library at Oakland History, accessed October 9, 2023, https://oaklandlibrary.org/aamlo/about-aamlo/.
33. Gertrude P. McBrown, "The Countee Cullen Memorial Collection of Atlanta University," *Negro History Bulletin* 17 (October 1953): 11–13; Jacqueline C. Jones, "The Unknown Patron: Harold Jackman and the Harlem Renaissance Archives," *Langston Hughes Review* 19 (2004): 55–66; and Romie Minor, "Preserving the Black Performance for Posterity," *Michigan History Magazine* 99, no. 3 (2015): 50–55.
34. Florence K. Norman and Mary McLeod Bethune to "President," February 1941, Series 4, box 1, folder 16, National Council of Negro Women Records (hereafter NCNW Records), NABWH.
35. Quoted in Jarvis R. Givens, *Fugitive Pedagogy: Carter G. Woodson and the Art of Black Teaching* (Cambridge, MA: Harvard University Press, 2021), 67. See also Jacqueline Goggin, "Carter G. Woodson and the Collection of Source Materials for Afro-American History," *American Archivist* 48 (Summer 1985): 261–71.
36. "Material for Race History Being Sought," *Chicago Defender*, September 14, 1929.
37. "Five Ways to Help This Cause," *Journal of Negro History* 11, no. 1 (January 1926): ii. Woodson made the "Historical Collection" a formal part of the ASNLH's work in 1926.
38. "Material for Race History Being Sought."
39. Carter G. Woodson, "Annual Report of the Director," *Journal of Negro History* 12, no. 4 (October 1927): 576; and Typescripts, "Letters from Negro Migrants of 1923 Addressed to John T. Clark of Pittsburgh Urban League. 2nd Migration," and "Manuscripts Recently Turned Over to the Library of Congress," n.d., reel 9, Carter G. Woodson Collection of Negro Papers and Related Documents, Manuscript Division, Library of Congress.
40. Herbert Putman to Carter G. Woodson, December 5, 1928, series 2, reel 1, Papers of Carter G. Woodson and the Association for the Study of Negro Life and History, University Publications of America. Known as the Carter G. Woodson Collection of Negro Papers, and sometimes just

as the "Negro papers," these materials were used for exhibitions but remained unprocessed until 1968. See Library of Congress, *Report of the Librarian of Congress for the Fiscal Year Ending June 30 1946* (Washington, DC: Government Printing Office, 1947), 377; "American Blacks Collection Cataloged and Indexed," *Library of Congress Information Bulletin*, January 18, 1974, 13–15; and Avril Johnson Madison and Dorothy Porter Wesley, "Dorothy Burnett Porter Wesley: Enterprising Steward of Black Culture," *Public Historian* 17, no. 1 (Winter 1995): 26.

41. Solon Buck quoted by Kathy Peiss, *Information Hunters: When Librarians, Soldiers, and Spies Banded Together in World War II Europe* (Oxford: Oxford University Press, 2020), 20.
42. Moorland Foundation Annual Report for 1945–1946, Manuscript Division, MSRC. There were 240 manuscripts in Schomburg's collection at the time of its purchase in 1926; a decade later there were nearly two thousand—an illustration of the uptick in manuscript collecting in the 1930s. See *Report of the New York Public Library for 1926* (New York: NYPL, 1927), 71; and [A. A. Schomburg Report to Ernestine Rose], ca. 1936, box 2, folder 5, SCRBC Records. On Reddick's subsequent manuscript collecting efforts, which built on Schomburg's, see Stanton F. Biddle, "The Schomburg Collection: Documenting the Black Experience," paper delivered to Society of American Archivists Conference, Washington, DC, October 1, 1970, 8–9.
43. Dorothy Porter, untitled notes, n.d., box 32, Dorothy Porter Wesley Papers (hereafter DPW Papers), BRBML. At the time of research, the DPW Papers were minimally processed; box information may have changed since reprocessing.
44. Dorothy Porter, untitled speech typescript, ca. 1968, box 34, DPW Papers.
45. L. D. Reddick, "Final Report: The Schomburg Collection," January 1, 1948–February 29, 1948, box 2, folder 5, SCRBC Records; and "Material at the Schomburg Collection to be cataloged," typescript, ca. 1948, box 2, folder 8, SCRBC Records. Such acquisitions were encouraged by the Modern Archives Institute, established in 1945, which encouraged librarians to collect *fonds* rather than single manuscripts. See Bruce Ambacher, "The Modern Archives Institute: A History and Profile of Recent Students," *Archival Issues* 18, no. 2 (1993): 109–19. Porter attended the institute in the 1950s, as documented in Report of the Moorland Foundation for 1955, Manuscript Division, MSRC.
46. Moorland Foundation Annual reports for 1955–56 and 1957–58, Manuscript Division, MSRC; and Edwin R. Embree and Julia Waxman, *Investment in People: The Story of the Julius Rosenwald Fund* (New York: Harper, 1947), 208. Librarians' mid-century reports describe inadequate staffing levels to describe and catalog this deluge of incoming material. See, for example, Annual Report of the Moorland Foundation for 1957, Manuscript Division, MSRC. In this case, then, archival silences resulted not only from the scarcity of records but also from their preponderance. On the paperwork explosion of twentieth-century offices, see Gerald Ham, "Archival Choices: Managing the Historical Record in an Age of Abundance," *American Archivist* 47, no. 1 (Winter 1984): 11–22.
47. Jean-Christophe Cloutier, *Shadow Archives: The Lifecycles of African American Literature* (New York: Columbia University Press, 2019), 54.
48. Saidiya Hartman, "On Working with Archives," Interview with Thora Siemsen, April 18, 2018, *The Creative Independent*, https://thecreativeindependent.com/people/saidiya-hartman-on-working-with-archives/; and Dorothy Porter to Sue Bailey Thurman, March 27, 1940, series 4, box 1, folder 1, NCNW Records. The NCNW's archival work began as part of Mary Beard's World Center for Women's Archives project, which dissolved at the onset of World War II. See Linda J. Henry, "Promoting Historical Consciousness: The Early Archives Committee of the National Council of Negro Women," *Signs* 7, no. 1 (October 1981): 251–59; and Deborah Gray White, *Too Heavy a Load: Black Women in Defense of Themselves, 1894–1994* (New York: Norton, 1999), 148–75.
49. "The National Archives of The National Council of Negro Women," n.d., reel 16, Mary McLeod Bethune Papers, NABWH. Though indebted to Thurman's commitment to saving women's everyday artifacts, the NCNW ultimately solicited documents primarily from leaders and "firsts." See Susan E. Davis, "Collection Development and the Special Subject Repository," *The Bookmark* 39, no. 2 (Winter 1981): 102.

50. Van Vechten, "J. W. Johnson Collection," 222. On the James Weldon Johnson Collection, see Kirsten MacLeod, "The 'Librarian's Dream-Prince': Carl Van Vechten and America's Modernist Cultural Archives Industry," *Libraries and the Cultural Record* 46, no. 4 (2011): 360–87; Jeremy Braddock, *Collecting as Modernist Practice* (Baltimore, MD: Johns Hopkins University Press, 2012), 218–30; and Cloutier, *Shadow Archives*, 42–45.
51. Carl Van Vechten to Arna Bontemps (emphasis in original), November 22, 1945, box 28, folder 3, Arna Bontemps Papers (hereafter Bontemps Papers) SUSCRC; and James Weldon Johnson, ed., *The Book of American Negro Poetry*, revised ed. (New York: Harcourt, Brace, 1931), 9.
52. Van Vechten to Hughes, April 5, 1941, in *Remember Me to Harlem: The Letters of Langston Hughes and Carl Van Vechten*, ed. Emily Bernard (New York: Vintage, 2001), 187; and Van Vechten, "J. W. Johnson Collection," 222.
53. Arna Bontemps, "The James Weldon Johnson Memorial Collection of Negro Arts and Letters," *Yale University Library Gazette* 18, no. 2 (October 1943): 22; and Cloutier, *Shadow Archives*, 44.
54. "The National Archives of The National Council of Negro Women."
55. "War Letters Wanted for Schomburg Group," *Atlanta Daily World*, December 1, 1944.
56. "War Letters Wanted for Schomburg Group."
57. Margaret Taylor Goss [Burroughs], "Schomburg Collection Asks for Letters From Soldiers," *Atlanta Daily World*, September 11, 1945; "WANTED: Make Appeal for Letters from Servicemen and Women for the Schomburg Collection," *Pittsburgh Courier*, December 9, 1944; "GI Letters Being Collected," *New York Amsterdam News*, December 16, 1944; and "War Letters Needed by N.Y. Library for History of This War," *Afro-American*, December 9, 1944.
58. "Says Negro Must Write Own Story of World War."
59. "War Letters Wanted."
60. Reddick, "Letters from the Jim-Crow Army."
61. "Need for War Letters Cited," *Atlanta Daily World*, November 3, 1945; and W. E. B. Du Bois, "The League of Nations," *Crisis* 18, no. 1 (May 1919): 11.
62. Peiss, *Information Hunters*, 29–31. At the end of the war, the Western Historical Manuscript Collection at the University of Missouri began acquiring the letters of soldiers, mostly white. These can be found in the World War II Letters Collection, 1940–1946, State Historical Society of Missouri. A later project compiling Black soldiers' letters is Phillip McGuire, ed., *Taps for a Jim Crow Army: Letters from Black Soldiers in World War II* (Lexington: University Press of Kentucky, 1983).
63. Moorland Foundation Annual Report, 1943–1944, Manuscript Division, MSRC. At Howard University, Porter gathered letters that enlisted students wrote to faculty, including almost two hundred donated by history professor Merze Tate. See Porter to Merze Tate, April 10, 1946, MSRC Record Group 1; and Moorland Foundation Annual Reports for 1943–1944 and 1945–1946, Manuscript Division, MSRC.
64. Reddick, "The Negro Soldier Writes Home."
65. Hughes, "Here to Yonder," *Chicago Defender*, December 4, 1943.
66. George S. Schuyler, "Views and Reviews," *Pittsburgh Courier*, December 4, 1943; and McKenzie, "Pursuit of Democracy."
67. W. E. B. Du Bois, "Returning Soldiers," *Crisis* 18, no. 1 (May 1919): 14; and L. D. Reddick, "To Fight or Not To Fight!" *New York Amsterdam News*, February 19, 1944. After World War I, Du Bois solicited photographs and other materials documenting Black soldiers to prepare a manuscript, "The Black Man in the Wounded World," which was never published. The materials for this project are in the Du Bois papers at Fisk. See W. E. B. Du Bois, "Documents of the War," *Crisis* 18, no. 1 (May 1919): 21; Jennifer D. Keene, "W. E. B. Du Bois and the Wounded World: Seeking Meaning in the First World War for African-Americans," *Peace and Change* 26, no. 2 (April 2001): 135–52; and Pero Gaglo Dagbovie, *The Early Black History Movement, Carter G. Woodson, and Lorenzo Johnston Greene* (Urbana: University of Illinois Press, 2007), 24.

68. Du Bois, "Returning Soldiers," 14 (emphasis in original); and "Documents of the War," 21. According to the *Chicago Defender*, this issue of *The Crisis* so alarmed federal officials that they "made an effort to keep it out of the mails" ("Dr. Du Bois in Lecture Here," *Chicago Defender*, May 17, 1919).
69. Ada Ferrer, "Talk About Haiti: The Archive and the Atlantic's Haitian Revolution," in *Tree of Liberty: Cultural Legacies of the Haitian Revolution in the Atlantic World*, ed. Doris L. Garraway (Charlottesville: University of Virginia Press, 2008), 36.
70. L. D. Reddick, Memorial Anniversary Program at the Society for Ethical Culture, typescript, April 9, 1945, box 2, folder 5, SCRBC Records.
71. Reddick, "Letters from the Jim-Crow Army."
72. Reddick, "Letters from the Jim-Crow Army"; and L. D. Reddick, "What the Northern Negro Thinks About Democracy," *Journal of Educational Sociology* 17, no. 5 (January 1944): 305.
73. Du Bois, "Returning Soldiers," 13–14; and W. E. B. Du Bois, "My Mission," *Crisis* 18, no. 1 (May 1919): 9.
74. Reddick to Johnson, October 1, 1945.
75. Reddick, "New Interpretation," 27.
76. Reddick, "The Negro Soldier Writes Home."
77. Reddick, "Letters from the Jim-Crow Army" (emphasis added); and "Wanted," *Pittsburgh Courier*, December 9, 1944. Reddick also conducted interviews as part of his collecting project, several of which were with Women's Army Corps members. Transcripts or notes from these interviews are located in LDRWWII.
78. See Julie Des Jardins, *Women and the Historical Enterprise in America: Gender, Race, and the Politics of Memory* (Chapel Hill: University of North Carolina Press, 2003), 122.
79. Malcolm A. Davis to Reddick, April 24, 1945, box 2, folder 6, LDRWWII.
80. Reddick, "Letters from the Jim-Crow Army."
81. Goss, "Schomburg Collection Asks."
82. George D. Clements to Reddick, June 22, 1946, box 1, folder 6, LDRWWII.
83. Whittico to Reddick. Carter G. Woodson's call to preserve Black family records in the 1910s was also answered primarily by women. See Des Jardins, *Women and the Historical Enterprise*, 156.
84. Goss, "Schomburg Collection Asks."
85. "Need for War Letters Cited." Although there are currently less than six hundred letters in the LDRWWII collection at the Schomburg Center, evidence suggests that Reddick may once have been in possession of additional material, including letters collected by Horace Mann Bond, Marjorie McKenzie, and Margaret Taylor Goss. See Reddick to Bond, October 11, 1945, Bond Papers, http://credo.library.umass.edu/view/pageturn/mums411-b062-f019/#page/42/mode/1up; McKenzie, "Pursuit of Democracy"; and Margaret Goss to Reddick, February 19, 1946, box 1, folder 8, LDRWWII. Reddick kept the letters in his possession for decades; they returned to the Schomburg Center in the 1990s with the rest of his personal papers.
86. "Schomburg Collection in New Home," *New Journal and Guide*, May 16, 1942; and L. D. Reddick, "The Miscellaneous Collection," typescript, n.d., box 2, folder 3, SCRBC Records.
87. Van Vechten, "J. W. Johnson Collection," 226. See list of recipients of letters from Dorothy Porter, sent on behalf of the NCNW Archives Committee to solicit records for the American Negro Exposition, June 21, 1940, series 4, box 1, folder 1, NCNW Records.
88. Dorothy Porter, untitled speech, ca. 1968, box 34, DPW Papers. On Black women's reluctance to place their papers in an institutional repository, see Deborah Gray White, "Mining the Forgotten: Manuscript Sources for Black Women's History," *Journal of American History* 74, no. 1 (June 1987): 238. At the University of Buffalo, curator Charles Abbott faced similar challenges, under different circumstances, when he launched a collection of contemporary poetry manuscripts. See Charles D. Abbott, "Poetry in the Making," *Poetry: A Magazine of Verse* 55 (February 1940): 259; and Braddock, *Collecting as Modernist Practice*, 214–28.

89. Draft transcript of forum sponsored by the Lynn Committee and The Schomburg Collection, October 26, 1945, Box 6, folder 4, LDRWWII.
90. As many archival theorists have argued, collectors do not simply acquire "records of value"; rather, the act of collecting creates and bestows value on the collected object (Brien Brothman, "Orders of Value: Probing the Theoretical Terms of Archival Practice," *Archivaria* 32 [Summer 1991]: 82).
91. "War Letters Wanted."
92. Achille Mbembe, "The Power of the Archive and Its Limits," in *Refiguring the Archive*, ed. Carolyn Hamilton, Verne Harris, Michele Pickover, Graeme Reid, Razia Saleh, and Jane Taylor (Dordrecht, The Netherlands: Kluwer Academic, 2022), 20. Libbie Rifkin calls the value that accrues to authors' work when collected by an archive "authorization by association" (Rifkin, "Association/Value: Creative Collaborations in the Library," *RBM: A Journal of Rare Books, Manuscripts, and Cultural Heritage* 2, no. 2 [Fall 2001]: 129). On questions of archival valuation and prestige in literary culture, see Amy Hildreth Chen, *Placing Papers: The American Literary Archives Market* (Amherst: University of Massachusetts Press, 2020).
93. "War Letters Wanted."
94. Goss, "Schomburg Collection Asks."
95. Hannibal E. Moore to Reddick, January 16, 1946, box 1, folder 8, LDRWWII.
96. Joseph Jameson to Evelyna Forney Marable, April 25, 1945, box 2, folder 2, LDRWWII.
97. Fuller to Reddick.
98. Reddick, "Letters from the Jim-Crow Army."
99. Clifford R. Moore to George Schuyler, February 25, 1944, box 3, folder 5, LDRWWII.
100. Stirling W. [Peters?] to Fredi Washington, August 21, 1944, box 3, folder 14, LDRWWII.
101. Liston O. Nicholson and Alfred E. Craig to George S. Schuyler, February 21, 1944, box 3, folder 5, LDRWWII.
102. "Military Camp Gets Modern City at Fry," *Pittsburgh Courier*, November 14, 1942; and "In the Camps: Fort Huachuca," *Chicago Defender*, October 2, 1943.
103. Buck Private [pseudonym], "The Low-Down," typescript, n.d., box 3, folder 5, LDRWWII; and Edward T. Mayfield to Schuyler, January 18, 1944, box 3, folder 5, LDRWWII.
104. Mayfield to Schuyler.
105. See box 3, folder 5, LDRWWII.
106. Reddick, "Letters from the Jim-Crow Army." On representations of the Black male soldier as "would-be citizen," see Maurice O. Wallace, "Framing the Black Soldier: Image, Uplift, and the Duplicity of Pictures," in *Pictures and Progress: Early Photography and the Making of African American Identity*, ed. Maurice O. Wallace and Shawn Michelle Smith (Durham, NC: Duke University Press, 2012), 247.
107. Reddick, "Letters from the Jim-Crow Army."
108. H. G. Kelly to Gloria Kelly, October 24, 1944, box 1, folder 2, LDRWWII.
109. Dorothy Porter, "Of Men and Records," speech notes, n.d., box 32, DPW Papers.
110. Ralph E. Jones to Kenneth Smith, July 19, 1943, box 1, folder 3, LDRWWII.
111. Clements to Reddick; and Mayfield to Schuyler.
112. Jones to Smith.
113. Letter from Alfonso McGready et al. reprinted in Fredi Washington, "Excerpts from Letters from Men in Uniform, *People's Voice*, April 8, 1944, accessed via Reanimate Collective, Fredi Washington: A Reader in Black Feminist Media Criticism, http://editions.reanimatepublishing.org/projects/fredi-washington.
114. Raymond Cojoe to Fredi Washington, October 13, 1944, box 3, folder 10, LDRWWII.
115. Edward Campbell to Washington, [November 1944], box 3, folder 10, LDRWWII; and Oliver Fullard to Washington, [July 1945], box 3, folder 6, LDRWWII.
116. [C. S. Gibbons] to Reddick, June 5, 1944, box 1, folder 7, LDRWWII; and Frank L. Bonitto to Washington, July 2, 1944, box 3, folder 16, LDRWWII. The imbrication of pleasure and protest in

Washington's correspondence with soldiers was emblematic of the *Pittsburgh Courier*'s style in this period. See Kim Gallon, *Pleasure in the News: African American Readership and Sexuality in the Black Press* (Urbana: University of Illinois Press, 2020), 23.

117. Van Vechten, "J. W. Johnson Collection," 222; and Hughes to Van Vechten, October 30, 1941, in *Remember Me to Harlem*, 193. On how Hughes and Van Vechten's correspondence becomes explicitly archival, see Michele Birnbaum, *Race, Work, and Desire in American Literature, 1860–1930* (Cambridge: Cambridge University Press 2003), 128–30.
118. Reddick, "What the Northern Negro Thinks About Democracy," 305; and "National Archives Celebration," typescript, n.d., reel 16, Mary McLeod Bethune Papers, NABWH.
119. Reddick, "A New Interpretation," 23–24; and Reddick, "Letters from the Jim-Crow Army."
120. [Name illegible] to Josie, May 19, 1945, box 1, folder 7, LDRWWII.
121. Clyde G. Atwell to Reddick, May 15, 1944, box 1, folder 7, LDRWWII; and Du Bois, "Returning Soldiers," 14 (emphasis in original).
122. Buck Private, "The Lowdown."
123. Willie Edwards to Reddick, November 3, 1945, box 1, folder 6, LDRWWII (spelling corrected); and Jones to Reddick.
124. Clements to Reddick.
125. Eric Ketelaar, "Tacit Narratives: The Meanings of Archives," *Archival Science* 1 (2001): 137.
126. Jones to Smith.
127. Reddick, draft introduction to *What the Negro Thinks About Democracy*; and draft transcript of forum sponsored by the Lynn Committee. Wartime speakers included Ollie Harrington, Enoch Waters, Roi Ottley, and Ruth Wilson.
128. "'First Lady' to give F.D.R. Manuscript to N.Y. Library," *Pittsburgh Courier*, September 26, 1942.
129. Horne quoted in Varel, *Scholar and the Struggle*, 80–81. On Reddick's anti-imperialist thought, see Von Eschen, *Race Against Empire*, 28, 35, 62; and James L. Roark, "American Black Leaders: The Response to Colonialism and the Cold War, 1943–1953," *African Historical Studies* 4, no. 2 (1971): 256.
130. L. D. Reddick, "The Negro in the United States Navy During World War II," *Journal of Negro History* 32, no. 2 (April 1947): 218. Reddick's phrasing of a "rising wind" echoed the title of Walter White's account of Black thought during World War II, *A Rising Wind* (Garden City, NY: Doubleday, 1945). See Brenda Gayle Plummer, *Rising Wind: Black Americans and U.S. Foreign Affairs, 1935–1960* (Chapel Hill: University of North Carolina Press, 1996).
131. L. D. Reddick, "Why I Left the North," typescript, ca. 1950, LDR Papers.
132. Press accounts quoted in "A Record of Achievement."
133. Reddick, "Why I Left the North."
134. Franklin F. Hopper to Schomburg, January 15, 1930, box 3, folder 21, AAS Papers; and Hopper to Ernestine Rose and Catherine Latimer, November 4, 1938, box 2, folder 3, SCRBC Records.
135. Reddick, "Why I Left the North."
136. Reddick, "Why I Left the North."
137. George S. Schuyler, "Views and Reviews," *Pittsburgh Courier*, January 31, 1948, SCCF 004,448.
138. F. [Freddie] Forest [Raya Dunayevskaya], "Maintain the Schomburg Collection!" *Militant* 12, no. 10 (March 8, 1948): 4. On her use of the Schomburg Collection, see Raya Dunayevskaya, "Volume XII: Retrospective and Perspective—The Raya Dunayevskaya Collection, 1924–1986," 1986, 59.
139. "Library Is Picketed After False Report," unidentified newspaper, March 16, 1948, SCCF 004,448; "Harlem Aroused Over Fate of Schomburg Unit," *Atlanta Daily World*, February 3, 1948; and Brian Dolinar, *The Black Cultural Front: Black Writers and Artists of the Depression Generation* (Jackson: University Press of Mississippi, 2012), 64–65.
140. Michael Flug, "Events and Issues That Motivated the Evolution of African American Institutional Archival and Manuscripts Programs, 1919–1950," paper presented at the Collecting Our Past to

Secure Our Future Conference, Jackson State University, November 30–December 2, 1995, 6. Reddick's name appears in proceedings of the Committee on Un-American Activities as early as 1947; he was investigated by the FBI in the 1950s and 1960s. See U.S. House of Representatives, Hearings Before the Committee on Un-American Activities, *Testimony of Walter S. Steele Regarding Communist Activities in the United States*, July 21, 1947, 39, 41, 96, 115; Federal Bureau of Investigation file on Lawrence Dunbar Reddick; and Varel, *Scholar and the Struggle*, 107, 151.

141. On the Hackley Collection, see Minor, "Preserving the Black Performance for Posterity," 50–55. Efforts to establish the collection began in 1942, before the riots, but its opening at the Detroit Public Library in December 1943 pointedly claimed civic space for Black culture at a moment when the city's racial boundary lines were heavily policed.
142. Reddick secured support from the Julius Rosenwald Fund to hire St. Clair Drake to work with him on two books, one a social history of the Negro in World War II and the other compiling the letters Reddick collected. Bernice G. Jones and Esther Watson also assisted Reddick on the project, which was headquartered at the Schomburg Collection. See Reddick to Johnson, October 1, 1945, November 2, 1945, and June 7, 1946, box 549, folder 9, Rosenwald Fund Records, FUSCA. Reddick published some of this research in the *Journal of Negro History* in 1947 and 1949, but never completed either book.
143. Goss to Reddick.
144. Chief of Circulation Department to Lucille C. Naddy, August 31, 1948, and Dorothy G. Williams to Mrs. Busby, Book Order Office, August 25, 1948, box 1, folder 1c, SCRBC Records.
145. Allison Hughes, "Witness to History: Lawrence Reddick's Crusade to Document the Black 20th Century," September 16, 2021, https://www.nypl.org/blog/2021/09/16/lawrence-reddick-crusade-document-black-experience.
146. On the Cold War's effects on libraries, see M. C. Kinniburgh, *Wild Intelligence: Poets' Libraries and the Politics of Knowledge in Postwar America* (Amherst: University of Massachusetts Press, 2022), 59.
147. "Schomburg's Ailing Collection," *Ebony* 12, no. 12 (October 1967): 55; and "Harlem Heats Up Over Schomburg Collection Controversy," *New York Times*, July 17, 1982. This history of contention is discussed at greater length in the Epilogue.
148. "Hymn to Schomburg," typescript, n.d., box 3a, folder 20, SCRBC Records.
149. The hymn bears Reddick's annotations. Reddick penned rousing if gauche sonnets on occasion, though Horace Mann Bond suggested he abandon poetry. See Bond to Reddick, June 30, 1937, Bond Papers, http://credo.library.umass.edu/view/full/mums411-b062-f016. A later poem by L. D. Reddick, "The City of Man," n.d., is in SCCF 004,226.
150. Robert Hayden, *Collected Prose*, ed. Frederick Glaysher (Ann Arbor: University of Michigan Press, 1984), 170–71.
151. John Henrik Clarke, "The Influence of Arthur A. Schomburg on My Concept of Africana Studies," *Phylon* 49 (1992): 7.
152. Annual Report of the Moorland Foundation, 1953–1954, Manuscript Division, MSRBC; and "The New Schomburg Center for Research in Black Culture," *Crisis* 90, no. 2 (February 1983): 29.
153. A. A. Schomburg to J. W. Cromwell, August 19, 1913, box 1, folder 16, Cromwell Family Papers, Manuscript Division, MSRC.

EPILOGUE

1. Claude McKay, [Circular letter for the creation of a Negro Writers' Guild], October 23, 1937, in *The Passion of Claude McKay: Selected Poetry and Prose, 1912–1948*, ed. Wayne F. Cooper (New York: Schocken, 1973), 233.

2. Until the 1970s, the Schomburg Collection was part of a neighborhood branch library with a circulating collection. In 1972, these functions were divided. The Schomburg Center was designated a research facility, while the Countee Cullen Branch Library on 136th Street continued to serve general readers. Still, the Schomburg Collection has always been a site of heterogeneous encounters and uses, as evocatively captured in Sharifa Rhodes-Pitts, *Harlem Is Nowhere: A Journey to the Mecca of Black America* (New York: Little, Brown, 2011), 72–81.
3. Langston Hughes, "My Early Days in Harlem," *Freedomways* 3 (1963): 312; reprinted in John Henrik Clarke, ed., *Harlem: U.S.A.* (New York: Collier, 1971), 76. On the trope of journey narratives that end at a library, see Thomas Augst, "Faith in Reading: Public Libraries, Liberalism, and the Civil Religion," in *Institutions of Reading: The Social Life of Libraries in the United States*, ed. Thomas Augst and Kenneth Carpenter (Amherst: University of Massachusetts Press, 2007), 154–55, 168.
4. Schomburg's collection arrived in Harlem in 1926, two years *after* the *Opportunity* dinner that has become a shorthand for the Harlem Renaissance's inaugural moment.
5. Jeffrey C. Stewart and Fath Davis Ruffins argue that the Schomburg Collection was "an early model of what African American museums would become in the 1960s—a community institution where people from different groups and classes could interact, exchange ideas, and redefine their collective mission" (Stewart and Ruffins, "A Faithful Witness: Afro-American Public History in Historical Perspective, 1828–1984," in *Presenting the Past: Essays on History and the Public*, ed. Susan Porter Benson, Stephen Brier, and Roy Rosenzweig [Philadelphia: Temple University Press, 1986], 315).
6. L. S. Alexander Gumby, "The Gumby Scrapbook Collection of Negroana," *Columbia Library World* 5, no. 1 (January 1951): 8.
7. Melanie Chambliss, "A Vital Factor in the Community: Recovering the Life and Legacy of Chicago Public Librarian Vivian G. Harsh," *Journal of African American History* 106, no. 3 (Summer 2021): 437.
8. Avril Johnson Madison and Dorothy Porter Wesley, "Dorothy Burnett Porter Wesley: Enterprising Steward of Black Culture," *Public Historian* 17, no. 1 (Winter 1995): 36.
9. See Lawrence D. Reddick Papers accession file and Lawrence D. Reddick World War II Project Collection finding aid, Manuscripts, Archives and Rare Books Division (hereafter MARB), SCRBC, https://archives.nypl.org/scm/24667.
10. The students' writings are in the Lawrence D. Reddick Papers (hereafter LDR Papers), MARB, SCRBC. This story is told more fully in David A. Varel, *The Scholar and the Struggle: Lawrence Reddick's Crusade for Black History and Black Power* (Durham, NC: University of North Carolina Press, 2021).
11. L. D. Reddick, *Crusader Without Violence: A Biography of Martin Luther King, Jr.* (New York: Harper, 1959), 235.
12. Filing note, September 24, 1962, box 53, Lydenberg, Hopper, and Beals General Correspondence, NYPLA; and Memorandum, September 20, 1962, box 42, Edward Geier Freehafer Records, NYPLA.
13. See, for example, Report of the Use of Materials in Moorland Foundation, Summer Session 1954, Manuscript Division, MSRC. On the pervasiveness of state surveillance of Black writers and cultural spaces, see William J. Maxwell, *F.B. Eyes: How J. Edgar Hoover's Ghostreaders Framed African American Literature* (Princeton, NJ: Princeton University Press, 2015); and Lisa K. Speer, "Mississippi's 'Spy Files': The State Sovereignty Commission Records Controversy, 1977–1999," *Provenance* 17 (1999): 101–17.
14. Lotus Norton-Wisla, "Freedom Summer Digital Collection at Wisconsin Historical Society," *Primary Source* 33, no. 1 (Summer 2014): 1–6; "Tapes on Dr. King Ordered Sealed for Next 50 Years," *Atlanta Daily World*, February 3, 1977; "King Family Files Suit Against Boston U.," *Afro-American*, January 16, 1988; "King Estate Battles Boston U Over Papers," *Afro-American*, February 6, 1988; and "Coretta Scott King Sues for Husband's Papers," *New Journal and Guide*, December 16, 1987.

15. Athan G. Theoharis, "The FBI and the FOIA: Problems of Access and Destruction," *Midwestern Archivist* 5, no. 2 (1981): 61–74; and Sarah Rowe-Sims, Sandra Boyd, and H. T. Holmes, "Balancing Privacy and Access: Opening the Mississippi State Sovereignty Commission Records," in *Privacy and Confidentiality Perspectives: Archivists and Archival Records*, ed. Peter J. Wosh (Chicago: Society of American Archivists, 2005): 159–74.
16. Porter quoted in Elizabeth Stevens, "Howard Shows Nation's Finest Negro Works," *Washington Post*, December 25, 1965.
17. Charles L. Blockson, "Black Giants in Bindings," in *Black Bibliophiles and Collectors: Preservers of Black History*, ed. Elinor Des Verney Sinnette, W. Paul Coates, and Thomas C. Battle (Washington, DC: Howard University Press, 1990), 118; and University Book Shop Records, Tamiment Library and Robert F. Wagner Labor Archives, Elmer Holmes Bobst Library, New York University.
18. Benjamin A. Custer to Joseph H. Reason, December 7, 1959, Records of the Moorland-Spingarn Research Center, Record Group 1, University Archives, MSRC (hereafter MSRC Record Group 1).
19. Jessie Carney Smith, "Developing Collections of Black Literature," *Black World* 20, no. 8 (June 1971): 23. For a more recent take on Smith's critique, see Chaitra Powell, Holly Smith, Shanee' Murrain, and Skyla Hearn, "This [Black] Woman's Work: Exploring Archival Projects That Embrace the Identity of the Memory Worker," *KULA: Knowledge Creation, Dissemination, and Preservation Studies* 2, no. 1 (2018): 3.
20. The Negro Collection at Howard became known as the Moorland-Spingarn Research Center in 1973. It received a major Ford Foundation grant in 1971 to process backlogged collections. The Schomburg Center for Research in Black Culture, as it was named in 1973, received its first major National Endowment for the Humanities (NEH) award in 1972. The Fisk University Library received its first NEH award in 1971 for the Black Oral History Program. See Moorland-Spingarn Collection Annual Report for 1971, Manuscript Division, MSRC; and National Endowment for the Humanities, Funded Project Query Form, https://apps.neh.gov/publicquery/main.aspx.
21. Blockson, "Black Giants in Bindings," 119.
22. Postcard, Walter Goldwater to Dorothy Porter, [1954], and Advertisement for University Place Book Shop, ca. 1970s, MSRC Record Group 1; Moorland Foundation Annual Report for 1964–1965, Manuscript Division, MSRC; and Dorothy B. Porter, "Bibliography and Research in Afro-American Scholarship," *Journal of Academic Librarianship* 2, no. 2 (1976): 80.
23. Dorothy B. Porter, [Talk on collectors], n.d., box 33, Dorothy Porter Wesley Papers, BRBML. Note that at the time of research, these papers were minimally processed; box locations have likely changed since reprocessing was completed.
24. "Introduction: Toward an Intellectual History of Black Women," in *Toward an Intellectual History of Black Women*, ed. Mia E. Bay, Farah J. Griffin, Martha S. Jones, and Barbara D. Savage (Chapel Hill: University of North Carolina Press, 2015), 10.
25. "Pulitzer for 'Roots' Goes for $50,000 at Haley Sale," *New York Times*, October 4, 1992; and Detine L. Bowers, "Uprooting of Black Heritage: Lessons from an African-American Collection," in *Untold Stories: Civil Rights, Libraries, and Black Librarianship*, ed. John Mack Turner (Champaign, IL: Graduate School of Library and Information Science, 1998), 182–99. In spite of such prohibitive costs, a new slate of private collectors emerged—not only Blockson but also John Henrik Clarke, Clarence L. Holte, Middleton A. "Spike" Harris, and Camille Billops. See Angela Ards, "Black Bibliophiles," *QBR: The Black Book Review* (May/June 1999): 1–2, 29; and Blockson, "Black Giants in Bindings," 126.
26. See, for example, the acknowledgement of Porter in Library Company of Philadelphia, *Afro-Americana 1553–1906: A Catalog of the Holdings of the Library Company of Philadelphia and the Historical Society of Pennsylvania* (Boston: Hall, 1973), v.
27. Hazel V. Carby, *Race Men* (Cambridge, MA: Harvard University Press, 2000), 14.

28. *Dictionary Catalog of the Schomburg Collection of Negro Literature and History*, 9 vols. (Boston: Hall, 1962); *Dictionary Catalog of the Jesse E. Moorland Collection of Negro Life and History*, 9 vols. (Boston: Hall, 1970); and *Dictionary Catalog of the Negro Collection of the Fisk University Library*, 6 vols. (Boston: Hall, 1974).
29. Dorothy Porter to John Hope Franklin, November 25, 1959, MSRC Record Group 1. See also Autumn Womack, "Reprinting the Past/Re-Ordering Black Social Life," *American Literary History* 32, no. 4 (Winter 2020): 755–80. Abdul Alkalimat has argued that the reprint revolution ultimately undermined Black repositories because only wealthy institutions had the resources to buy all the competing sets of reprints and because the availability of reproductions lessened the value of repositories that held the originals (Alkalimat, "African American Bibliography," paper presented to African American Expression in Print and Digital Culture Conference, University of Wisconsin at Madison, September 20, 2014).
30. Annual Report of the Negro Collection, 1960–1961, Manuscript Division, MSRC.
31. Porter to Henry O. Tanner, January 28, 1936, and Advertisement for University Place Book Shop, ca. 1970s, MSRC Record Group 1.
32. Alice Jackson to Porter, October 11, 1960, MSRC Record Group 1.
33. Press Release, Western Reserve Historical Society, September 1970, MSRC Record Group 1. On new kinds of Black repositories that emerged in the 1960s and 1970s, see Vivian D. DeWitt, "Black Special Libraries," in *Handbook of Black Librarianship*, ed. E. J. Josey and Ann Allen Shockley (Littleton, CO: Libraries Unlimited, 1977), 222–28.
34. Interview of Dorothy Porter by James Hatch and Camille Billops (New York: Hatch Billops Collection, 1991), 147; and Michael R. Winston, "The Howard University Department of History, 1913–1973," *Negro History Bulletin* 61, nos. 3–4 (1998): 25.
35. Jean Blackwell Hutson notes, February 2, 1966, SCRBC Records.
36. "Schomburg's Ailing Collection," *Ebony* 12, no. 12 (October 1967): 55.
37. Henry Walter to Edward G. Freehafer, May 2, 1968, and Memo, Mr. Cory to Mr. Freehafer and Mrs. Godfrey, June 10, 1968, box 42, Edward Geier Freehafer Records, NYPLA; "$80,000 To Be Used to Save Black Documents," *Chicago Defender*, June 22, 1968; Cathy Aldridge, "Schomburg Collection Stays There," *New York Amsterdam News*, May 4, 1968; and "Save the Schomburg Collection," *Black Scholar* 2, no. 5 (January 1971): n.p.
38. Loften Mitchell, "The Fear of Losing Harlem Behind the Rage and Anger," *Amsterdam News*, May 4, 1968.
39. Robert Channick, "For Sale: Images of a Pivotal Era," *Chicago Tribune*, January 26, 2015.
40. "Ebony, Jet to Sell Historic Photo Archive," *Chicago Defender*, January 28–February 3, 2015. Eventually, an institutional consortium—led by the Getty Foundation, in cooperation with the Ford Foundation, the Catherine T. MacArthur Foundation, and the Andrew W. Mellon Foundation—purchased the Johnson Publishing Company Photo Archives, of more than four million negatives and prints, in July 2019 for 28.5 million dollars, with a pledge to donate the collection to the National Museum of African American History and Culture and the Getty Research Institute. See Ford Foundation, "Foundation Consortium Acquires Historic African American Photographic Archive," press release, July 25, 2019, https://www.prnewswire.com/news-releases/foundation-consortium-acquires-historic-african-american-photographic-archive-300891246.html.
41. Theaster Gates, *Black Archive*, ed. Thomas D. Trummer (Bregenz, Austria: Kunsthaus Bregenz, 2017); and "A Johnson Publishing Story," exhibition at Stony Island Arts Bank, Chicago, IL, June 28–September 30, 2018.
42. Stacie Williams and Steven D. Booth, "Letter from the Editors," *Loss/Capture* 1 (2020): https://losscaptureproject.cargo.site/Letter-from-the-Editors.
43. Daphne A. Brooks, *Liner Notes for the Revolution: The Intellectual Life of Black Feminist Sound* (Cambridge, MA: Harvard University Press, 2021), 314.

44. Black Women's Organizing Archive, bwoaproject.org.
45. L. D. Reddick, draft materials for *What the Negro Thinks About Democracy* [unfinished manuscript], n.d., LDR Papers; Tracy S. Drake, Aisha Conner-Gaten, and Steven D. Booth, "Archiving Black Movements: Shifting Power and Exploring a Community-Centered Approach," *Journal of Critical Library and Information Studies* 4, no. 1 (2022): 7–8, 19; and Zakiya Collier, "Call to Action: Archiving State-Sanctioned Violence Against Black People," June 6, 2020, https://medium.com/community-archives/call-to-action-archiving-state-sanctioned-violence-against-black-people-d629c956689a. For model projects, see Documenting the Now, Documenting Ferguson, and Project STAND.
46. Baldwin paraphrased by Jean Blackwell Hutson in Norman Wilson, "Schomburg Collection Needs Much More Room," *Amsterdam News*, February 13, 1971. The phrase "price of the ticket" is from James Baldwin, *The Price of the Ticket: Collected Nonfiction, 1948–1985* (New York: St. Martin's, 1985).
47. Schomburg quoted in Porter, "Bibliography and Research," 81.
48. Moorland Foundation Annual Report for 1945–46, Manuscript Division, MSRC.

BIBLIOGRAPHY

ARCHIVAL COLLECTIONS

Archives Research Center, Robert W. Woodruff Library, Atlanta University Center
    Henry P. Slaughter Collection
Beinecke Rare Book and Manuscript Library, Yale University
    James Weldon Johnson Manuscripts
    Dorothy Porter Wesley Papers
Gainsboro Library, Roanoke Public Library
    Gainsboro Library Archives
    Virginia Y. Lee African-American History Collection
Manuscript Division, Moorland-Spingarn Research Center, Howard University
    C. Glenn Carrington Papers
    Cromwell Family Papers
    Thomas and William Henry Dorsey Collection
    Alain LeRoy Locke Papers
    Kelly Miller Papers
    Jesse E. Moorland Papers
    Moorland Foundation Annual Reports
    Oral History Interview of Dorothy Porter Wesley by Avril J. Madison
    Arthur B. Spingarn Papers
Manuscripts, Archives and Rare Books Division, Schomburg Center for Research in Black Culture, New York Public Library
    John Edward Bruce Papers
    Las Dos Antillas Political Club Minutes
    Arthur A. Schomburg Papers
    Arthur A. Schomburg Papers Additions
    Schomburg Committee of the Trustees of New York Public Library Collection
    Lawrence D. Reddick Papers
    Lawrence D. Reddick World War II Project Collection
    Schomburg Center for Research in Black Culture Records
National Archives for Black Women's History, Mary McLeond Bethune Council House National Historic Site
    Mary McLeod Bethune Papers
    National Council of Negro Women Records

New York Public Library Archives, New York Public Library, Astor, Lenox and Tilden Foundations
Edward Geier Freehafer Records
James W. Henderson Papers
Lydenberg, Hopper, and Beals General Correspondence
Keyes DeWitt Metcalf Records
Research Libraries Acquisitions Division Records
Rare Book and Manuscript Library, Columbia University
L. S. Alexander Gumby Collection of Negroiana
Photographs and Prints Division, Schomburg Center for Research in Black Culture, New York Public Library
Arthur Alfonso Schomburg Photograph Collection
Special Collections, Boston Public Library
George Washington Forbes Papers
Special Collections and Archives, John Hope and Aurelia E. Franklin Library, Fisk University
Charles S. Johnson Papers
Thomas Elsa Jones Collection
Robert Park Papers
Rosenwald Fund Records
Special Collections Research Center, Syracuse University Library
Arna Bontemps Papers
Stuart A. Rose Manuscript, Archives, and Rare Book Library, Emory University
James A. Porter Papers
Tamiment Library and Robert F. Wagner Labor Archives, Elmer Holmes Bobst Library, New York University
University Book Shop Records
Tougaloo College Archives, Touglaoo College
Tougaloo College Historical Files
University Archives, Hampton University Museum, Hampton University
Hampton Library School Records
Collis P. Huntington Library Records
University Archives, Moorland-Spingarn Research Center, Howard University
Records of the Moorland-Spingarn Research Center, Record Group 1
Virginia Room, Roanoke Public Library
Roanoke City Council Minutes
Roanoke Public Library Board Minutes
Vivian G. Harsh Research Collection of Afro-American History and Literature, Carter G. Woodson Regional Library, Chicago Public Library
Chicago Afro-American Union Analytic Catalog Records
George Cleveland Hall Branch Archives
Madeline Stratton Morris Papers
Nannie Pinkey Papers
Charlemae Hill Rollins Papers

ONLINE COLLECTIONS

Ancestry.com
Horace Mann Bond Papers, Special Collections and University Archives, University of Massachusetts Amherst
Coloredconventions.org

W. E. B. Du Bois Papers, Special Collections and University Archives, University of Massachusetts Amherst Libraries
Encyclopedia Virginia
Farm Security Administration Office of War Information Photograph Collection, Library of Congress Prints and Photographs Division
ProQuest History Vault
WSLS-TV News Film Collection, 1951–1971, Special Collections, University of Virginia
Raymond R. Wilkinson Memorial Library, Hill Street Baptist Church Digital Collection

COLLECTIONS ON MICROFILM

Carter G. Woodson Collection of Negro Papers and Related Documents, Manuscript Division, Library of Congress
Papers of Carter G. Woodson and the Association for the Study of Negro Life and History, University Publications of America
Schomburg Center Clipping File, Schomburg Center for Research in Black Culture, New York Public Library

SELECTED NEWSPAPERS

Afro-American (Baltimore, MD)
Atlanta Daily World
Bags and Baggage (Chicago, IL)
Boletin Mercantil de Puerto Rico (San Juan, PR)
Broad Ax (Chicago, IL)
Chicago Bee
Chicago Defender
Cleveland Gazette
La Correspondencia de Puerto-Rico (San Juan, PR)
La Democracia (Ponce, PR)
The Hilltop (Washington, DC)
Indianapolis Recorder
Montgomery Advertiser
New York Age
New York Amsterdam News
Negro World (New York, NY)
Norfolk Journal and Guide
Oakland Sunshine
People's Voice (New York, NY)
Philadelphia Tribune
Pittsburgh Courier
Pioneer Press (Martinsburg, WV)
Richmond Planet
Roanoke Times
Roanoke Tribune
Savannah Tribune
Washington Eagle

BOOKS, ARTICLES, ESSAYS, AND THESES

Abbott, Charles D. "Poetry in the Making." *Poetry: A Magazine of Verse* 55 (February 1940): 258–66.

Adamczyk, Alice, Laura E. Helton, Miranda Mims, and Matthew J. Murphy. "Library Archaeology: Reconstructing a Catalog of the Arthur A. Schomburg Book and Pamphlet Collection." *African American Review* 54, nos. 1–2 (Spring/Summer 2021): 91–107.

Adler, Melissa. *Cruising the Library: Perversities in the Organization of Knowledge*. New York: Fordham University Press, 2017.

Alexander, Elizabeth. *The Black Interior: Essays*. St. Paul, MN: Graywolf, 2004.

Alkalimat, Abdul. "African American Bibliography." Paper presented at African American Expression in Print and Digital Culture Conference, University of Wisconsin at Madison, September 20, 2014.

——. *The History of Black Studies*. London: Pluto, 2021.

Ambacher, Bruce. "The Modern Archives Institute: A History and Profile of Recent Students." *Archival Issues* 18, no. 2 (1993): 109–19.

"American Blacks Collection Cataloged and Indexed." *Library of Congress Information Bulletin*. January 18, 1974, 13–15.

American Book-Prices Current: A Record of Books, Manuscripts, and Autographs Sold at Auction in New York, Boston, and Philadelphia, From September 1, 1910 to September 1, 1911, with the Prices Realized. Vol. 17. New York: Dodd and Livingston, 1911.

American Book-Prices Current: A Record of Books, Manuscripts and Autographs Sold at Auction in New York, Boston, and Philadelphia, from September 1, 1914, to September 1, 1915, with Prices Realized. Vol. 21. New York: Robert H. Dodd, 1915.

American Book-Prices Current: A Record of Books, Manuscripts and Autographs Sold at Auction in New York, Boston, and Philadelphia, From September 1, 1915, to September 1, 1916, with the Prices Realized. Vol. 22. New York: Robert H. Dodd, 1916.

American Book-Prices Current: A Record of Books, Manuscripts and Autographs Sold at Auction in New York, Boston, and Philadelphia, From September, 1917, to August, 1918. Vol. 24. New York: Dutton, 1918.

American Book-Price Current: A Record of Books, Manuscripts and Autographs Sold at Auction in New York, Boston, and Philadelphia, From September, 1919, to July, 1920. Vol. 26. New York: Dutton, 1920.

Anderson Galleries. *Catalog of Sales, 1916: Jan–Feb*. New York: Anderson Galleries, 1916.

Anderson, Sarah A. "'The Place to Go': The 135th Street Branch Library and the Harlem Renaissance." *Library Quarterly* 73, no. 4 (October 2003): 383–421.

Andrews, Martin. "The Importance of Ephemera." In *A Companion to the History of the Book*, ed. Simon Eliot and Jonathan Rose, 434–50. Malden, MA: Blackwell, 2007.

Appadurai, Arjun. "Archive and Aspiration." In *Information Is Alive: Art and Theory on Archiving and Retrieving Data*, ed. Joke Brouwer, Arjen Mulder, and Susan Charlton, 14–25. Rotterdam, The Netherlands: NAi, 2003.

Appel, Hannah, Nikhil Anand, and Akhil Gupta, eds. *The Promise of Infrastructure*. Durham, NC: Duke University Press, 2018.

Appiah, Kwame Anthony, and Henry Louis Gates Jr. *Africana: The Encyclopedia of the African and African American Experience*. Vol. 1. New York: Oxford University Press, 2005.

Ards, Angela. "Black Bibliophiles." *QBR: The Black Book Review*, May/June 1999, 1–3.

Arondekar, Anjali, Ann Cvetkovich, Christina B. Hanhardt, Regina Kunzel, Tavia Nyong'o, Juana Maria Rodríguez, and Susan Stryker. "Queering Archives: A Roundtable Discussion." Ed. Daniel Marshall, Kevin P. Murphy, and Zeb Tortorici. *Radical History Review* 122 (May 2015): 29–53.

Arroyo, Jossianna. "Technologies: Transculturations of Race, Gender, and Ethnicity in Arturo A. Schomburg's Masonic Writings." *CENTRO Journal* 17, no. 1 (2005): 5–25.

Augst, Thomas, and Kenneth Carpenter, eds. *Institutions of Reading: The Social Life of Libraries in the United States*. Amherst: University of Massachusetts Press, 2007.

Baderoon, Gabeba. "'I Compose Myself': Lesbian Muslim Autobiographies and the Craft of Self-Writing in South Africa." *Journal of the American Academy of Religion* 83, no. 4 (December 2015): 897–915.

Baldwin, Davarian L. *Chicago's New Negroes: Modernity, the Great Migration, and Black Urban Life*. Chapel Hill: University of North Carolina Press, 2007.

Ball, Wendy, and Tony Martin, eds. *Rare Afro-Americana: A Reconstruction of the Adger Library*. Boston: Hall, 1981.

Basbanes, Nicholas A. *A Gentle Madness: Bibliophiles, Bibliomanes, and the Eternal Passion for Books*. New York: Holt, 1995.

Bascom, Elva L., ed. *A. L. A. Catalog, 1904–1911*. Chicago: American Library Association Publishing Board, 1912.

Bascom, Lionel C., ed. *A Renaissance in Harlem: Lost Essays of the WPA, by Ralph Ellison, Dorothy West, and Other Works of a Generation*. New York: Amistad, 1999.

Bastian, Jeannette A. "Mine, Yours, Ours: Archival Custody from Transaction to Narrative." *Archival Science* 21 (2021): 25–42.

Battle, Thomas C. "Dorothy Porter Wesley." In *Dictionary of American Library Biography, Second Supplement*, ed. Donald G. Davis, 219–21. Westport, CT: Libraries Unlimited, 2003.

——. "Moorland-Spingarn Research Center, Howard University." *Library Quarterly* 58, no. 2 (April 1988): 143–51.

Battles, David M. *The History of Public Library Access for African Americans in the South*. Lanham, MD: Scarecrow, 2009.

Bay, Mia, Farah J. Griffin, Martha S. Jones, and Barbara D. Savage, eds. *Toward an Intellectual History of Black Women*. Chapel Hill: University of North Carolina Press, 2015.

Belk, Russell W. *Collecting in a Consumer Society*. London: Routledge, 1995.

Belknap, Robert E. *The List: The Uses and Pleasures of Cataloguing*. New Haven, CT: Yale University Press, 2004.

Benjamin, Walter. *Illuminations: Essays and Reflections*. Ed. Hannah Arendt. Trans. Harry Zohn. New York: Schocken, 1968.

Berry, Daina Ramey. *The Price for Their Pound of Flesh: The Value of the Enslaved, from Womb to Grave, in the Building of a Nation*. New York: Beacon, 2017.

Berry, Dorothy. "The House Archives Built." up//root, June 22, 2021, https://www.uproot.space/features/the-house-archives-built.

——. "Introducing 'Archives Unbound.'" JSTOR Daily, February 24, 2022. https://daily.jstor.org/introducing-archives-unbound/.

——. "When Black Celebrities Wore Blackface." JSTOR Daily, August 12, 2020. https://daily.jstor.org/when-black-celebrities-wore-blackface/.

Best, Stephen M. *None Like Us: Blackness, Belonging, Aesthetic Life*. Durham, NC: Duke University Press, 2018.

Bhan, Esme. "Dorothy Louise Burnett Porter Wesley, 1904–1995." *Washington History* 8 (Spring/Summer 1996): 88–89.

——. "Legacy of a Job Well Done." *Washington Post*, December 31, 1995.

Biddle, Stanton F. "The Schomburg Collection: Documenting the Black Experience." Paper presented to the Society of American Archivists, Washington, DC, October 1, 1970.

Birnbaum, Michele. *Race, Work, and Desire in American Literature, 1860–1930*. Cambridge: Cambridge University Press, 2003.

Bishop, Mary. "Street by Street, Block by Block: How Urban Renewal Uprooted Black Roanoke." *Roanoke Times*, January 29, 1995.

Black Public Sphere Collective, ed. *The Black Public Sphere: A Public Culture Book*. Chicago: University of Chicago Press, 1995.

Blair, Ann M. *Too Much to Know: Managing Scholarly Information Before the Modern Age*. New Haven, CT: Yale University Press, 2011.

Blinn, Harold E. "W.P.A. Newspaper Clipping and Indexing Service." *Pacific Historical Review* 6, no. 3 (September 1937): 284–87.

Blockson, Charles L. *Damn Rare: The Memoirs of an African American Bibliophile*. Tracy, CA: Quantum Leap, 1998.

Bolivar, William C. *Library of William C. Bolivar*. Philadelphia: Watson, 1914.

Bone, Robert, and Richard A. Courage. *The Muse in Bronzeville: African American Creative Expression in Chicago, 1932–1950*. New Brunswick, NJ: Rutgers University Press, 2011.

Bontemps, Arna. "Buried Treasures of Negro Art." *Negro Digest* 9, no. 2 (December 1950): 17–21.

——. "The James Weldon Johnson Memorial Collection of Negro Arts and Letters." *Yale University Library Gazette* 18, no. 2 (October 1943): 21–26.

——. "Special Collections of Negroana." *Library Quarterly* 14, no. 3 (July 1944): 187–206.

Bowker, Geoffrey C. *Memory Practices in the Sciences*. Cambridge, MA: MIT Press, 2005.

Bracey, John H., Jr., August Meier, and Elliott Rudwick, eds. *Black Nationalism in America*. Indianapolis, IN: Bobbs-Merrill, 1970.

Braddock, Jeremy. *Collecting as Modernist Practice*. Baltimore, MD: Johns Hopkins University Press, 2012.

Brooks, Daphne A. *Bodies in Dissent: Spectacular Performances of Race and Freedom, 1850–1910*. Durham, NC: Duke University Press, 2006.

——. *Liner Notes for the Revolution: The Intellectual Life of Black Feminist Sound*. Cambridge, MA: Harvard University Press, 2021.

Brooks, Gwendolyn. *The Essential Gwendolyn Brooks*. Ed. Elizabeth Alexander. New York: Library of America, 2005.

Brooks, Tim. *Lost Sounds: Blacks and the Birth of the Recording Industry, 1890–1919*. Urbana: University of Illinois Press, 2004.

Brothman, Brien. "Orders of Value: Probing the Theoretical Terms of Archival Practice." *Archivaria* 32 (Summer 1991): 78–100.

Brown, Carolyn J. *Song of My Life: A Biography of Margaret Walker*. Jackson: University of Mississippi Press, 2014.

Brown, Karl, comp. *American Library Directory 1942*. Camden, NJ: Bowker, 1942.

Brown, Vincent, Laurent Dubois, and Jennifer L. Morgan. "In Memoriam: Julius S. Scott (1955–2021), Historian of the Black Atlantic." *Perspectives on History*, March 2022. https://www.historians.org/research-and-publications/perspectives-on-history/march-2022/julius-s-scott-(1955–2021).

Burt, Laura. "Vivian Harsh, Adult Education, and the Library's Role as Community Center." *Libraries and the Cultural Record* 44, no. 2 (2009): 234–55.

Burton, Antoinette, ed. *Archive Stories: Facts, Fictions, and the Writing of History*. Durham, NC: Duke University Press, 2005.

Caldwell, A. B., ed. *History of the American Negro, Virginia Edition*. Vol. 5. Atlanta, GA: Caldwell, 1921.

Campt, Tina. *Image Matters: Archive, Photography, and the African Diaspora*. Durham, NC: Duke University Press, 2012.

——. *Other Germans: Black Germans and the Politics of Race, Gender, and Memory in the Third Reich*. Ann Arbor: University of Michigan Press, 2004.

Carby, Hazel V. "Policing the Black Woman's Body in an Urban Context." *Critical Inquiry* 18, no. 4 (Summer 1992): 738–55.

——. *Race Men*. Cambridge, MA: Harvard University Press, 2000.

Castromán Soto, Margarita M. "Schomburg's Black Archival Turn: 'Racial Integrity' and 'The Negro Digs Up His Past.'" *African American Review* 54, nos. 1–2 (Spring/Summer 2021): 73–90.

Caswell, Michele. "'The Archive' Is Not an Archives: On Acknowledging the Intellectual Contributions of Archival Science." *Reconstruction: Studies in Contemporary Culture* 16, no. 1 (2016). https://escholarship.org/uc/item/7bn4v1fk.

Caswell, Michelle, Joyce Gabiola, Jimmy Zavala, Grace Brilmyer, and Marika Cifor. "Imagining Transformative Spaces: The Personal-Political Sites of Community Archives." *Archival Science* 18 (2018): 73–93.

Cavell, Stanley. "The World as Things: Collecting Thoughts on Collecting." In *Contemporary Collecting: Objects, Practices, and the Fate of Things*, ed. Kevin M. Moist and David Banash, 99–130. Lanham, MD: Scarecrow, 2013.

Certeau, Michel de, Luce Giard, and Pierre Mayol. *The Practice of Everyday Life*. Vol. 2, *Living and Cooking*. Trans. Timothy J. Tomasik. Minneapolis: University of Minnesota Press, 1998.

Chambliss, Melanie. "A Library in Progress." In *The Unfinished Book*, ed. Alexandra Gillespie and Deidre Lynch, 260–71. Oxford: Oxford University Press, 2021.

——. "A Vital Factor in the Community: Recovering the Life and Legacy of Chicago Public Librarian Vivian G. Harsh." *Journal of African American History* 106, no. 3 (Summer 2021): 411–38.

Chambliss, Melanie, Brent Hayes Edwards, and Alexsandra Mitchell. "Archives from the Black Diaspora: A Roundtable Discussion." *African American Review* 54, nos. 1–2 (Spring/Summer 2021): 19–303.

Chartier, Roger. *The Order of Books*. Cambridge, MA: Polity, 1994.

Chatelain, Marcia. *South Side Girls: Growing Up in the Great Migration*. Durham, NC: Duke University Press, 2015.

Chauncey, George. *Gay New York: Gender, Urban Culture, and the Making of the Gay Male World, 1890–1940*. New York: Basic Books, 1994.

Chen, Amy Hildreth. *Placing Papers: The American Literary Archives Market*. Amherst: University of Massachusetts Press, 2020.

Chicago Public Library. *The Chicago Afro-American Union Analytic Catalog*. Boston: Hall, 1972.

Christian, Barbara. "The Race for Theory." *Cultural Critique* 6 (Spring 1987): 51–63.

Christian, Shawn Anthony. *The Harlem Renaissance and the Idea of a New Negro Reader*. Amherst: University of Massachusetts Press, 2016.

Chuku, Gloria. "African Intellectuals as Cultural Natioanlists: A Comparative Analysis of Edward Wilmot Bylden and Mbonu Ojike." *Journal of African American History* 99, no. 4 (Fall 2014): 350–78.

Clack, Doris H. "Investigation into the Adequacy of Library of Congress Subject Headings for Black Studies." PhD diss., University of Pittsburgh, 1973.

Clarke, Cheryl. Remarks at the Black Women Writing Across Genres in the Late 20th Century Symposium, University of Pennsylvania, Philadelphia, PA, February 21, 2020.

Clarke, John Henrik, ed. *Harlem: U.S.A.* New York: Collier Books, 1971.

——. "The Influence of Arthur A. Schomburg on My Concept of Africana Studies." *Phylon* 49 (1992): 4–9.

Cloutier, Jean-Christope. *Shadow Archives: The Lifecycles of African American Literature*. New York: Columbia University Press, 2019.

Cohen, Lara Langer. *Going Underground: Race, Space, and the Subterranean in the Nineteenth-Century United States*. Durham, NC: Duke University Press, 2023.

Collier, Zakiya. "Call to Action: Archiving State-Sanctioned Violence Against Black People." June 6, 2020. https://medium.com/community-archives/call-to-action-archiving-state-sanctioned-violence-against-black-people-d629c956689a.

Cook, Terry. "What Is Past Is Prologue: A History of Archival Ideas Since 1898, and the Future Paradigm Shift." *Archivaria* 43 (Spring 1997): 17–63.

Cooper, Brittney C. *Beyond Respectability: The Intellectual Thought of Race Women*. Urbana: University of Illinois Press, 2017.

Cooper, Danielle. "House Proud: An Ethnography of the BC Gay and Lesbian Archives." *Archival Science* 16 (2016): 261–88.

Cooper, Wayne F. *Claude McKay: Rebel Sojourner in the Harlem Renaissance*. Baton Rouge: Louisiana State University Press, 1987.

Copeland, Huey, and Naomi Beckwith. "Black Collectivities: An Introduction." *Nka: Journal of Contemporary African Art* 34 (2014): 4–7.

Corbould, Clare. *Becoming African Americans: Black Public Life in Harlem, 1919–1939*. Cambridge, MA: Harvard University Press, 2009.

Courage, Richard A., and Christopher Robert Reed, eds. *Roots of the Black Chicago Renaissance: New Negro Writers, Artists, and Intellectuals, 1893–1930*. Urbana: University of Illinois Press, 2020.

Cowan's Auctions. *The Road West: The Steve Turner Collection of African Americana, Part I, February 20, 2020*. Chicago: Hindman, 2020.

Crawford, Margo Natalie. "Textual Productions of Black Aesthetics Unbound." In *Publishing Blackness*, ed. George Hutchinson and John K. Young, 188–210. Ann Arbor: University of Michigan Press, 2013.

Crawford, Romi. "Yours in Blackness: Blocks, Corners, and Other Desire Settings." *Nka: Journal of Contemporary African Art* 34 (2014): 80–89.

Crowder, Ralph L. "The Historical Context and Political Significance of Harlem's Street Scholar Community." *Afro-Americans in New York Life and History* 34, no. 1 (2010): 34–71.

——. *John Edward Bruce: Politician, Journalist, and Self-Trained Historian of the African Diaspora*. New York: New York University Press, 2004.

Cunningham, Nijah. "A Queer Pier: Roundtable on the Idea of a Black Radical Tradition." *Small Axe* 17, no. 1 (March 2013): 84–95.

Cvetkovich, Ann. *An Archive of Feelings: Trauma, Sexuality, and Lesbian Public Cultures*. Durham, NC: Duke University Press, 2003.

Cvetkovich, Ann, David Frantz, and Mia Locks. *Cruising the Archive: Queer Art and Culture in Los Angeles, 1945–1980*. Los Angeles: ONE National Gay and Lesbian Archives, 2011.

Dagbovie, Pero Gaglo. "Black Women Historians from the Late 19th Century to the Dawning of the Civil Rights Movement." *Journal of African American History* 89, no. 3 (Summer 2004): 241–61.

——. *The Early Black History Movement, Carter G. Woodson, and Lorenzo Johnston Greene*. Urbana: University of Illinois Press, 2007.

Darnton, Robert. "What Is the History of Books?" In *The Book History Reader*, ed. David Finkelstein and Alistair McCleery, 9–26. London: Routledge, 2002.

Davis, Arthur P. "Growing Up in the New Negro Renaissance." *Negro American Literature Forum* 2, no. 3 (Autumn 1968): 53–59.

Davis, James. *Eric Walrond: A Life in the Harlem Renaissance and the Transatlantic Caribbean*. New York: Columbia University Press, 2015.

Davis, Susan E. "Collection Development and the Special Subject Repository." *The Bookmark* 39, no. 2 (Winter 1981): 100–104.

Dean, Gabrielle. "Disciplinarity and Disorder." *Archive Journal* 1, no. 1 (Spring 2011). http://www.archivejournal.net/issue/1/archives-remixed/.

"The Debut of the Younger School of Negro Writers." *Opportunity* 2, no. 17 (May 1924): 143–44.

Des Jardins, Julie. *Women and the Historical Enterprise in America: Gender, Race, and the Politics of Memory, 1880–1945*. Chapel Hill: University of North Carolina Press, 2003.

Dewey, Melvil. *Decimal Clasification and Relative Index*. 12th ed. Lake Placid, NY: Forest, 1927.

——. *Decimal Classification*. Standard. 15th ed. Lake Placid, NY: Forest, 1951.

——. "Decimal Classification Beginning." *Library Journal* 45 (February 15, 1920): 151–54.

Ditzion, Sidney. "Social Reform, Education, and the Library, 1850–1900." *Library Quarterly* 9, no. 2 (April 1939): 156–84.

Dixon, Chris. *African Americans and the Pacific War, 1941–1945: Race, Nationality, and the Fight for Freedom*. Cambridge: Cambridge University Press, 2018.

Dodson, Howard. "Making Art at the Schomburg: Africana Archives as Sites of Art Making." *Callaloo* 38, no. 3 (Summer 2015): 549–58.

Dolinar, Brian. *The Black Cultural Front: Black Writers and Artists of the Depression Generation*. Jackson: University Press of Mississippi, 2012.

——, ed. *The Negro in Illinois: The WPA Papers*. Urbana: University of Illinois Press, 2013.

Douglas, Jennifer. "A Call to Rethink Archival Creation: Exploring Types of Creation in Personal Archives." *Archival Science* 18, no. 1 (March 2018): 29–49.

Douglass, Frederick. "The United States Cannot Remain Half-Slave and Half-Free." April 16, 1883. https://teachingamericanhistory.org/library/document/the-united-states-cannot-remain-half-slave-and-half-free.

Downs, Robert B., ed. *Union Catalogs in the United States*. Chicago: American Library Association, 1942.

Drabinski, Emily. "Queering the Catalog: Queer Theory and the Politics of Correction." *Library Quarterly* 82, no. 3 (April 2013): 94–111.

Drake, Jarrett Martin. "Blood at the Root." *Journal of Contemporary Archival Studies* 8 (2021): article 6. https://elischolar.library.yale.edu/jcas/vol8/iss1/6.

Drake, St. Clair. *Churches and Voluntary Associations in the Chicago Negro Community*. Chicago: WPA District 3, 1940.

Drake, St. Clair, and Horace R. Cayton. *Black Metropolis: A Study of Negro Life in a Northern City*. Revised. Vols. 1–2. 1945. Reprint, Chicago: University of Chicago Press, 1962.

Drake, Tracy S., Aisha Conner-Gaten, and Steven D. Booth. "Archiving Black Movements: Shifting Power and Exploring a Community-Centered Approach." *Journal of Critical Library and Information Studies* 4, no. 1 (2022): https://doi.org/10.24242/jclis.v4i1.170.

Du Bois, W. E. B. "The American Negro at Paris." *American Monthly Review of Books* 22 (1900): 575–77.

——. *The Correspondence of W. E. B. Du Bois*. Vol. 3. Ed. Herbert Aptheker. Amherst: University of Massachusetts Press, 1997.

——. "Documents of the War." *Crisis* 18, no. 1 (May 1919): 16–21.

——. "The League of Nations." *Crisis* 18, no. 1 (May 1919): 10–11.

——. "My Mission." *Crisis* 18, no. 1 (May 1919): 7–9.

——. "The Opening of the Library." *The Independent* (Atlanta, GA), April 3, 1902.

——. "A Portrait of Carter G. Woodson." *Masses and Mainstream* 3, no. 6 (June 1950): 19–25.

——. "Returning Soldiers." *Crisis* 18, no. 1 (May 1919): 13–14.

——. *The Souls of Black Folk: Essays and Sketches*. 4th ed. Chicago: McClurg, 1904.

Dudley, Tara. "Seeking the Ideal African-American Interior: The Walker Residences and Salon in New York." *Studies in the Decorative Arts* 14, no. 1 (Fall–Winter 2006–2007): 80–112.

Dunayevskaya, Raya. "Volume XII: Retrospective and Perspective, Introduction to Finding Aid for the Raya Dunayevskaya Collection, 1924–1986." Walter P. Reuther Library, Wayne State University, Detroit, Michigan, 1986.

Dunayevskaya, Raya [Freddie Forest]. "Maintain the Schomburg Collection!" *Militant*, March 8, 1948.

Dunbar, Alice Moore. *Masterpieces of Negro Eloquence*. New York: Bookery, 1914.

Dunbar Nelson, Alice. "Une Femme Dit." *Pittsburgh Courier*, June 12, 1926.

Dunlap, Mollie E. Review of *Rural America Reads: A Study of Rural Library Service* by Marion Humble. *Journal of Negro Education* 8, no. 2 (April 1939): 216–17.

——. "Special Collections of Negro Literature in the United States." *Journal of Negro Education* 4, no. 4 (October 1935): 482–89.

Eastman, Alexander Joel. "Binding Consumption: Cuba's Early Black Press and the Struggle for Legitimacy, 1879–1886." *Siglo Diecinueve* 21 (2015): 29–46.

Eckstrom, Leif, and Britt Rusert. "Introduction to 'Afric-American Picture Gallery.'" *Just Teach One: Early African American Print*, no. 2 (Fall 2015). http://jtoaa.common-place.org/welcome-to-just-teach-one-african-american/introduction-afric-american-picture-gallery/.

Edwards, Brent Hayes. *The Practice of Diaspora: Literature, Translation, and the Rise of Black Internationalism*. Cambridge, MA: Harvard University Press, 2003.

——. "The Taste of the Archive." *Callaloo* 34, no. 4 (Fall 2012): 943–72.

Edwards, Brent Hayes, Anna McCarthy, and Randy Martin. "Collective." *Social Text* 27, no. 3 (2009): 74–77.

Edwards, Conley L. "A Political History of the Poll Tax in Virginia, 1900–1950." Master's thesis, University of Richmond, 1973.

Egypt, Ophelia Settle. *Unwritten History of Slavery*. Nashville, TN: Social Science Institute, 1945.

Embree, Edwin R., and Julia Waxman. *Investment in People: The Story of the Julius Rosenwald Fund*. New York: Harper, 1947.

Ernest, John. *Liberation Historiography: African American Writers and the Challenge of History, 1794–1861*. Chapel Hill: University of North Carolina Press, 2004.

Evans, Rhonda. "Catherine A. Latimer: Librarian of the Harlem Renaissance." *Libraries: Culture, History, and Society* 6, no. 1 (2022): 21–41.

Fabre, Geneviève, and Robert O'Meally, eds. *History and Memory in African-American Culture*. New York: Oxford University Press, 1994.

Fabre, Michel. *The Unfinished Quest of Richard Wright*. Urbana: University of Illinois Press, 1973.

Farebrother, Rachel, and Miriam Thaggert, eds. *A History of the Harlem Renaissance*. New York: Cambridge University Press, 2021.

Farmer, Ashley. "In Search of the Black Women's History Archive." *Modern American History* 1, no. 2 (February 2018): 289–93.

Featherstone, Mike. "Archive." *Theory, Culture and Society* 23, nos. 2–3 (May 2006): 591–96.

Fellows, Jennie D. "The Decimal Classification in the Tenth Edition." *Library Journal* 45 (February 15, 1920): 154–56.

Ferrer, Ada. "Talk About Haiti: The Archive and the Atlantic's Haitian Revolution." In *Tree of Liberty: Cultural Legacies of the Haitian Revolution in the Atlantic World*, ed. Doris L. Garraway, 21–40. Charlottesville: University of Virginia Press, 2008.

Ferris, William H. *The African Abroad or His Evolution in Western Civilization*. Vol. 2. New Haven, CT: Tuttle, Morehouse and Taylor, 1913.

"The First Biennial Meeting of the Association for the Study of Negro Life and History." *Journal of Negro History* 2, no. 4 (October 1917): 442–48.

Fisk University. *Dictionary Catalog of the Negro Collection of the Fisk University Library*. 6 vols. Boston: Hall, 1974.

——. *Negro Library Conference, Fisk University, Nashville Tennessee, Papers Presented, November 20–23, [1930]*. Nashville: Fisk University, 1930.

"Five Ways to Help This Cause." *Journal of Negro History* 12, no. 1 (January 1927): n.p.

Flug, Michael. "Events and Issues That Motivated the Evolution of African American Institutional Archival and Manuscripts Programs, 1919–1950." Paper delivered at Collecting Our Past to Secure Our Future Conference, Jackson State University, Jackson, MS, 1995.

Foley, Barbara. "Questionnaire Responses." *Modernism/modernity* 20, no. 3 (September 2013): 439–41.

Forbes, George W. "Mr. A. A. Schomberg's [sic] Race Library." *A. M. E. Review* 31 (October 1914): 212–14.

Ford Foundation. "Foundation Consortium Acquires Historic African American Photographic Archive." July 25, 2019. https://www.prnewswire.com/news-releases/foundation-consortium-acquires-historic-african-american-photographic-archive-300891246.html.

Ford, Richard A., ed. *Washington Law Reporter*. Vol. 31. Washington, DC: Law Reporter, 1903.

Foster, Frances Smith. "A Narrative of the Interesting Origins and (Somewhat) Surprising Developments of African-American Print Culture." *American Literary History* 17, no. 4 (Winter 2005): 714–40.

——. *Written by Herself: Literary Production by African American Women, 1746–1892*. Bloomington: Indiana University Press, 1992.

Franklin, John Hope. "The New Negro History." *Journal of Negro History* 42, no. 2 (April 1957): 89–97.

Frederick, Samuel. *The Redemption of Things: Collecting and Dispersal in German Realism and Modernism*. Ithaca, NY: Cornell University Press, 2021.

Freeman, Elizabeth. *Time Binds: Queer Temporalities, Queer Histories*. Durham, NC: Duke University Press, 2010.

Fuentes, Marisa J. *Dispossessed Lives: Enslaved Women, Violence, and the Archive*. Philadelphia: University of Pennsylvania Press, 2016.

Fullilove, Mindy Thompson. *Root Shock: How Tearing Up City Neighborhoods Hurts America, and What We Can Do About It.* New York: Ballantine, 2004.

Fultz, Michael. "Black Public Libraries in the South in the Era of De Jure Segregation." *Libraries and the Cultural Record* 41, no. 3 (Summer 2006): 337–59.

Fusté, José I. "Schomburg's Blackness of a Different Matter: A Historiography of Refusal." *Small Axe* 24, no. 1 (March 2020): 120–31.

Gabbin, Joanne V. "Sterling Brown's Poetic Voice: A Living Legacy." *African American Review* 31, no. 3 (Autumn 1997): 423–31.

Gaines, Kevin K. *Uplifting the Race: Black Leadership, Politics, and Culture in the Twentieth Century.* Chapel Hill: University of North Carolina Press, 1996.

Galison, Peter. "Removing Knowledge." *Critical Inquiry* 31, no. 1 (Autumn 2004): 229–43.

Gallon, Kim. *Pleasure in the News: African American Readership and Sexuality in the Black Press.* Urbana: University of Illinois Press, 2020.

Galloway, Patricia. "Archives, Power, and History: Dunbar Rowland and the Beginning of the State Archives of Mississippi (1902–1936)." *American Archivist* 69, no. 1 (2006): 79–116.

Garber, Eric. "A Spectacle in Color: The Lesbian Past." In *Hidden from History: Reclaiming the Gay and Lesbian Past*, ed. Martin Duberman, Martha Vicinus, and George Chauncey, 227–67. New York: New American Library, 1989.

——. "T'Aint Nobody's Bizness: Homosexuality in 1920s Harlem." In *Black Men—White Men: A Gay Anthology*, ed. Michael J. Smith, 7–16. San Francisco, CA: Gay Sunshine, 1983.

Garner, Anne. "Throwaway History: Towards a Historiography of Ephemera." *Book History* 24, no. 1 (Spring 2021): 244–63.

Garvey, Ellen Gruber. "Scissoring and Scrapbooks: Nineteenth-Century Reading, Remaking, and Recirculating." In *New Media, 1740–1915*, ed. Lisa Gitelman and Geoffrey B. Pingree, 207–27. Cambridge, MA: MIT Press, 2003.

——. *Writing with Scissors: American Scrapbooks from the Civil War to the Harlem Renaissance.* New York: Oxford University Press, 2012.

Gates, Henry Louis, Jr. "The Black Man's Burden." In *Fear of a Queer Planet: Queer Politics and Social Theory*, ed. Michael Warner, 230–38. Minneapolis: University of Minnesota Press, 1993.

——. "Harlem on Our Minds." *Critical Inquiry* 24, no. 1 (Autumn 1997): 1–12.

Gates, Theaster, and Kunsthaus Bregenz. *Black Archive.* Ed. Thomas D. Trummer. Bregenz, Austria: Kunsthaus Bregenz, 2017.

Gellman, Erik S. *Death Blow to Jim Crow: The National Negro Congress and the Rise of Militant Civil Rights.* Chapel Hill: University of North Carolina Press, 2012.

Gernes, Todd S. "Recasting the Culture of Ephemera." In *Popular Literacy: Studies in Cultural Practices and Poetics*, ed. John Trimbur, 107–27. Pittsburgh: University of Pittsburgh Press, 2001.

Gershenhorn, Jerry. "'Not an Academic Affair': African American Scholars and the Development of African Studies Programs in the United States, 1942–1960." *Journal of African American History* 94, no. 1 (Winter 2009): 44–68.

Gigante, Denise. *Book Madness: A Story of Book Collectors in America.* New Haven, CT: Yale University Press, 2022.

Giannachi, Gabriella. *Archive Everything: Mapping the Everyday.* Cambridge, MA: MIT Press, 2016.

Gibbs, Rabia. "The Heart of the Matter: The Developmental History of African American Archives." *American Archivist* 75, no. 1 (Spring/Summer 2012): 195–204.

Gibson, Edmund. "The Life of Mr. Camden." In *Camden's Britannia, Newly Translated into English: With Large Additions and Improvements.* London: Collins, 1695. Early English Books Online, 2011, http://name.umdl.umich.edu/B18452.0001.001.

Gikandi, Simon. "The Fantasy of the Library." *PMLA* 128, no. 1 (January 2013): 9–20.

——. "Rethinking the Archive of Enslavement." *Early American Literature* 50, no. 1 (2015): 81–102.

Gillespie, Alexandra, and Deidre Lynch, eds. *The Unfinished Book.* Oxford: Oxford University Press, 2021.

Gilyard, Keith. *John Oliver Killens: A Life of Black Literary Activism*. Athens: University of Georgia Press, 2010.

Gitelman, Lisa. *Paper Knowledge: Toward a Media History of Documents*. Durham, NC: Duke University Press, 2014.

Givens, Jarvis R. *Fugitive Pedagogy: Carter G. Woodson and the Art of Black Teaching*. Cambridge, MA: Harvard University Press, 2021.

Gleason, Eliza Atkins. "Facing the Dilemma of Public Library Service for Negroes." *Library Quarterly* 15, no. 4 (October 1945): 339–44.

——. *The Southern Negro and the Public Library*. Chicago: University of Chicago Press, 1941.

Glissant, Édouard. *Poetics of Relation*. Trans. Betsy Wing. Ann Arbor: University of Michigan Press, 1997.

Goggin, Jacqueline. "Carter G. Woodson and the Collection of Source Materials for Afro-American History." *American Archivist* 48, no. 3 (Summer 1985): 261–71.

Goldsby, Jacqueline. "The Chicago Afro-American Analytic Union Catalog: The Meaning of 'Great' Events and the Making of Archives." Paper presented to the Modern Language Association, Chicago, IL, January 8–11, 2014.

Goldsby, Jacqueline, and Meredith L. McGill. "What Is 'Black' About Black Bibliography?" *Papers of the Bibliographical Society of America* 116, no. 2 (June 2022): 161–89.

Gonzalez, Aston. "William Dorsey and the Construction of an African American History Archive." *Social Dynamics* 45, no. 1 (2019): 138–55.

Gordon, Barefield. "New Negro Libraries." *Crisis* 39, no. 9 (September 1932): 284–85.

Green, Adam. "The Rising Tide of Youth: Chicago's Wonder Books and the 'New' Black Middle Class." In *The Middling Sorts: Explorations in the History of the American Middle Class*, ed. Burton J. Bledstein and Robert D. Johnston, 239–55. New York: Routledge, 2001.

——. *Selling the Race: Culture, Community, and Black Chicago, 1940–1955*. Chicago: University of Chicago Press, 2007.

Greenbaum, Susan D. *More Than Black: Afro-Cubans in Tampa*. Gainesville: University Press of Florida, 2002.

Greene, Lorenzo J. "Manuscript Collections in Libraries." *Negro History Bulletin* 30, no. 3 (March 1967): 20.

Greenlee, Cynthia. "A Priceless Archive of Ordinary Life." *The Atlantic*, February 9, 2021.

Griffin, Farah Jasmine. "Langston Hughes and the Timeless Questions of Life and Death." *African American Review* 25, no. 1 (2019): 41–47.

——. " 'Our Land That We Don't Own': A Review of Sharifa Rhodes-Pitts's Harlem Is Nowhere: A Journey to the Mecca of Black America." *Transition* 105 (2011): 146–55.

Griffis, Matthew. "Roots of Community: Segregated Carnegie Libraries as Spaces for Learning and Community-Making in Pre-Civil Rights America, 1900–65." https://aquila.usm.edu/rocprofiles/.

Grossman, James R. *Land of Hope: Chicago, Black Southerners, and the Great Migration*. Chicago: University of Chicago Press, 1989.

Gubert, Betty Kaplan, comp. *Early Black Bibliographies, 1863–1918*. New York: Garland, 1982.

Guerrero, Jose. "Unpacking the Other's Library: Latin American Book Collectors and U.S. Research Libraries." In *The Collector and the Collected: Decolonizing Area Studies Librarianship*, ed. Megan Browndorf, Erin Pappas, and Anna Arays, 141–64. Sacramento, CA: Library Juice Press, 2021.

Guglielmo, Thomas A. "A Martial Freedom Movement: Black G.I.s' Political Struggles During World War II." *Journal of American History* 104, no. 4 (March 2018): 879–903.

Gumby, L. S. Alexander. "The Gumby Scrapbook Collection of Negroana." *Columbia Library World* 5, no. 1 (January 1951): 1–8.

Gumbs, Alexis Pauline. *M Archive: After the End of the World*. Durham, NC: Duke University Press, 2018.

Gurley, E. W. *Scrap-Books and How to Make Them*. New York: Authors' Publishing, 1880.

Halberstam, Jack. *In a Queer Time and Place: Transgender Bodies, Subcultural Lives*. New York: New York University Press, 2005.

Hall, Stephen G. *A Faithful Account of the Race: African American Historical Writing in Nineteenth-Century America*. Chapel Hill: University of North Carolina Press, 2009.

Ham, Gerald. "Archival Choices: Managing the Historical Record in an Age of Abundance." *American Archivist* 47, no. 1 (Winter 1984): 11–22.

Hamilton, Carolyn, Verne Harris, Jane Taylor, Michele Pickover, Graeme Reid, and Razia Saleh, eds. *Refiguring the Archive*. Dordrecht, The Netherlands: Kluwer Academic, 2002.

Hamilton, Marybeth. *In Search of the Blues: Black Voices, White Visions*. London: Jonathan Cape, 2002.

Hanchard, Michael. "Black Memory versus State Memory." *Small Axe* 12, no. 2 (June 2008): 45–62.

Hardy, Molly O'Hagan. "'Black Printers' on White Cards: Information Architecture in the Data Structure of the Early American Book Trades." In *Debates in the Digital Humanities 2016*, ed. Matthew K. Gold and Lauren F. Klein, 377–82. Minneapolis: University of Minnesota Press, 2017.

Harland-Jacobs, Jessica. *The History of Public Library Service in Durham, 1897–1997*. Durham, NC: Durham County Library, 1999. https://durhamcountylibrary.org/exhibits/dclhistory/.

Harmon, Emily B. "Shaping the City from Below: Urban Planning and Citizens' Battle for Control in Roanoke, Virginia, 1907–1928." Master's thesis, Virginia Polytechnic Institute and State University, 2018.

Harris, Verne. "The Archival Sliver: Power, Memory, and Archives in South Africa." *Archival Science* 2 (2002): 63–86.

Harrison, Hubert H. *A Hubert Harrison Reader*. Ed. Jeffrey B. Perry. Middletown, CT: Wesleyan University Press, 2001.

Hartman, Saidiya. "On Working with Archives." Interview by Thora Siemsen. *The Creative Independent*, April 18, 2018. https://thecreativeindependent.com/people/saidiya-hartman-on-working-with-archives/.

——. "Venus in Two Acts." *Small Axe* 12, no. 2 (June 2008): 1–14.

——. *Wayward Lives, Beautiful Experiments: Intimate Histories of Social Upheaval*. New York: Norton, 2019.

Hatch, James, and Camille Billops. *Interview of Dorothy Porter, May 20, 1990*. New York: Hatch Billops Collection, 1991.

Hayden, Robert. *Collected Prose*. Ed. Frederick Glaysher. Ann Arbor: University of Michigan Press, 1984.

Haynes, George Edmund. *The Negro at Work in New York City*. New York: Columbia University, 1912.

Heesen, Anke te. "News, Paper, Scissors: Clippings in the Sciences and Arts Around 1920." In *Things That Talk: Object Lessons from Art and Science*, ed. Lorraine Daston, 297–328. New York: Zone Books, 2004.

——. *The Newspaper Clipping: A Modern Paper Object*. Manchester, UK: Manchester University Press, 2014.

Helfand, Jessica. *Scrapbooks: An American History*. New Haven, CT: Yale University Press, 2008.

Helton, Laura E. "Archive." In *Information Keywords*, ed. Michele Kennerly, Samuel Frederick, and Jonathan Abel, 44–56. New York: Columbia University Press, 2021.

——. "Black Bibliographers and the Category of Negro Authorship." In *African American Literature in Transition, 1900–1910*, ed. Shirley Moody-Turner, 23–47. New York: Cambridge University Press, 2021.

——. "Historical Form(s)." In *Elusive Archives: Material Culture in Formation*, ed. Martin Brückner and Sandy Isenstadt, 49–63. Newark: University of Delaware Press, 2021.

——. "Making Lists, Keeping Time: Infrastructures of Black Inquiry, 1900–1950." In *Against a Sharp White Background: Infrastructures of African American Print*, ed. Brigitte Fielder and Jonathan Senchyne, 82–108. Madison: University of Wisconsin Press, 2019.

——. "On Decimals, Catalogs, and Racial Imaginaries of Reading." *PMLA* 134, no. 1 (2019): 99–120.

——. "Schomburg's Library and the Price of Black History." *African American Review* 54, nos. 1–2 (Spring/Summer 2021): 109–27.

Helton, Laura, Justin Leroy, Max A. Mishler, Samantha Seeley, and Shauna Sweeney. "The Question of Recovery: An Introduction." *Social Text* 33, no. 3 (December 2015): 1–18.

Helton, Laura E., and Rafia Zafar. "Arturo Alfonso Schomburg in the Twenty-First Century: An Introduction." *African American Review* 54, nos. 1–2 (Spring/Summer 2021): 1–18.

Henderson, Pat. "Clippings to Computers: The Great Newspaper Migration." *Library Mosaics* 12, no. 3 (June 2001): 17–18.

Henderson, Rose. "The Schomburg Collection of Negro History and Literature." *Southern Workman* 63, no. 11 (November 1934): 328–34.

Henry, Linda J. "Promoting Historical Consciousness: The Early Archives Committee of the National Council of Negro Women." *Signs: Journal of Women in Culture and Society* 7, no. 1 (October 1981): 251–59.

Herring, Scott. *Queering the Underworld: Slumming, Literature, and the Undoing of Lesbian and Gay History*. Chicago: University of Chicago Press, 2007.

Higginbotham, Evelyn Brooks. "African-American Women's History and the Metalanguage of Race." *Signs: Journal of Women in Culture and Society* 17, no. 2 (Winter 1992): 251–74.

Hine, Darlene Clark, ed. *Black Women in America: An Historical Encyclopedia*. Brooklyn, NY: Carlson, 1993.

——. "Rape and the Inner Lives of Black Women in the Middle West: Preliminary Thoughts on the Culture of Dissemblance." *Sings: Journal of Women in Culture and Society* 14, no. 4 (1989): 912–20.

Hine, Darlene Clark, and John McCluskey Jr., eds. *The Black Chicago Renaissance*. Urbana: University of Illinois Press, 2012.

Historical Records Survey of the Works Progress Administration of New York City. *Calendar of Manuscripts in the Schomburg Collection of Negro Literature* [1942]. New York: Andronicus, 1970.

Hoffnung-Garskof, Jesse. "The Migrations of Arturo Schomburg: On Being Antillano, Negro, and Puerto Rican in New York 1891–1938." *Journal of American Ethnic History* 21, no. 1 (Fall 2001): 3–49.

——. *Racial Migrations: New York City and the Revolutionary Politics of the Spanish Caribbean*. Princeton, NJ: Princeton University Press, 2019.

Holden, John Allan. *A List of Private Book Collectors in the United States and Canada*. New York: Bowker, 1922.

Holloway, Karla F. C. *BookMarks: Reading in Black and White*. New Brunswick, NJ: Rutgers University Press, 2006.

Holton, Adalaine. "Decolonizing History: Arthur Schomburg's Afrodiasporic Archive." *Journal of African American History* 92, no. 2 (Spring 2007): 218–38.

Horne, Gerald. *Facing the Rising Sun: African Americans, Japan, and the Rise of Afro-Asian Solidarity*. New York: New York University Press, 2018.

Howe, Mentor A., and Roscoe E. Lewis, comps. *A Classified Catalogue of the Negro Collection in the Collis P. Huntington Library, Hampton Institute*. Hampton, VA: Hampton Institute, 1940.

Hughes, Allison. "Witness to History: Lawrence Reddick's Crusade to Document the Black 20th Century." *New York Public Library* (blog), September 16, 2021. https://www.nypl.org/blog/2021/09/16/lawrence-reddick-crusade-document-black-experience.

Hughes, Langston. *The Big Sea*. 1940. Reprint, New York: Hill and Wang, 1993.

——. *Collected Poems of Langston Hughes*. Ed. Arnold Rampersad. New York: Vintage Classics, 1994.

——. "My Early Days in Harlem." *Freedomways* 3 (1963): 312–14.

——. "Twelve Millions." *The Book League Monthly* 2 (June 1929): 174–75.

——. "When I Worked for Dr. Woodson." *Negro History Bulletin* 30, no. 6 (October 1967): 17.

Hughes, Langston, and Carl Van Vechten. *Remember Me to Harlem: The Letters of Langston Hughes and Carl Van Vechten, 1925–1964*. Ed. Emily Bernard. New York: Knopf, 2001.

Hurston, Zora Neale. "Mr. Schomburg's Library." *Negro World*, April 22, 1922.

"The J. E. Moorland Foundation of the University Library." *Howard University Record* 10, no. 1 (1916).

Jackson, Lawrence P. *The Indignant Generation: A Narrative History of African American Writers and Critics, 1934–1960*. Princeton, NJ: Princeton University Press, 2011.

Jackson-Coppin, Fanny. *Reminiscences of School Life, and Hints on Teaching*. Philadelphia: A. M. E. Book Concern, 1913.

James, Winston. *Holding Aloft the Banner of Ethiopia: Caribbean Radicalism in Early Twentieth-Century America*. London: Verso, 1998.

Jarrett, Gene Andrew. *Deans and Truants: Race and Realism in African American Literature*. Philadelphia: University of Pennsylvania Press, 2011.

Jenkins, Betty L. "A White Librarian in Black Harlem." *Library Quarterly* 60, no. 3 (July 1990): 216–31.

Johnson, Abby Ann Arthur, and Ronald M. Johnson. "Forgotten Pages: Black Literary Magazines in the 1920s." *Journal of American Studies* 8, no. 2 (December 1974): 363–82.

Johnson, James Weldon, ed. *The Book of American Negro Poetry*. Revised ed. New York: Harcourt, Brace, 1931.

Johnson-Cooper, Glendora. "African-American Historical Continuity: Jean Blackwell Hutson and the Schomburg Center for Research in Black Culture." In *Reclaiming the American Library Past: Writing the Women In*, ed. Suzanna Hildenbrand, 27–51. Westport, CT: Greenwood, 1996.

Jones, Ida E. *The Heart of the Race Problem: The Life of Kelly Miller*. Littleton, MA: Tapestry, 2011.

Jones, Jacqueline C. "The Unknown Patron: Harold Jackman and the Harlem Renaissance Archives." *Langston Hughes Review* 19 (Fall 2004): 55–66.

Jones, Martha S. *All Bound Up Together: The Woman Question in African American Public Culture, 1830–1900*. Chapel Hill: University of North Carolina Press, 2007.

Jones, Steven L. "A Keen Sense of the Artistic: African American Material Culture in the 19th Century." *International Review of African American Art* 12, no. 2 (1995): 4–30.

Josey, E. J., and Marva L. DeLoach, eds. *Handbook of Black Librarianship*. 2nd ed. Lanham, MD: Scarecrow, 2000.

Josey, E. J., and Ann Allen Shockley, eds. *Handbook of Black Librarianship*. Littleton, CO: Libraries Unlimited, 1977.

Joyce, Donald Franklin. "Publications." *Black World* 21, no. 2 (January 1972): 71–73.

——. "Resources for Scholars: Four Major Collections of Afro-Americana, Part 1: Two Public Library Collections [Introduction]." *Library Quarterly* 58, no. 1 (January 1988): 66.

——. "Vivian G. Harsh Collection of Afro-American History and Literature, Chicago Public Library." *Library Quarterly* 58, no. 1 (January 1988): 67–74.

Kadlecek, Jo. "Scrapbooks Help Preserve African Americans' Past." *Columbia University Record* 27, no. 10 (February 15, 2002): 1, 5.

Kane, Lucile M. "The Exhibition of Manuscripts at the Minnesota Historical Society." *American Archivist* 15, no. 1 (January 1952): 39–45.

Keene, Jennifer D. "W. E. B. Du Bois and the Wounded World: Seeking Meaning in the First World War for African-Americans." *Peace and Change* 26, no. 2 (April 2001): 135–52.

Kelley, Robin D. G. *Freedom Dreams: The Black Radical Imagination*. Boston: Beacon, 2002.

Kerr, Leah M. "Collectors' Contributions to Archiving Early Black Film." *Black Camera* 5, no. 1 (2013): 274–84.

Ketelaar, Eric. "Tacit Narratives: The Meanings of Archives." *Archival Science* 1 (2001): 131–41.

Kinniburgh, M. C. *Wild Intelligence: Poets' Libraries and the Politics of Knowledge in Postwar America*. Amherst: University of Massachusetts Press, 2022.

Kitchens, John W., ed. *Guide to the Microfilm Edition of the Tuskegee Institute News Clippings File*. Tuskegee, AL: Division of Behavioral Science Research, 1978.

Kiuchi, Toru, and Yoshinobu Hakutani. *Richard Wright: A Documented Chronology, 1908–1960*. Jefferson, NC: McFarland, 2013.

Knauer, Christine. *Let Us Fight as Free Men: Black Soldiers and Civil Rights*. Philadelphia: University of Pennsylvania Press, 2014.

Knott, Cheryl. *Not Free, Not for All: Public Libraries in the Age of Jim Crow*. Amherst: University of Massachusetts Press, 2015.

Knupfer, Anne Meis. *The Chicago Black Renaissance and Women's Activism*. Urbana: University of Illinois Press, 2006.

Kuipers, Juliana. Review of *The Scrapbook in American Life* by Susan Tucker, Katherine Ott, and Patricia P. Buckler. *American Archivist* 70, no. 1 (2007): 182–84.

Kumbier, Alana. *Ephemeral Material: Queering the Archive*. Sacramento, CA: Litwin, 2009.

Lane, Roger. *William Dorsey's Philadelphia and Ours: On the Past and Future of the Black City in America*. New York: Oxford University Press, 1991.

Latham, Joyce M. "Memorial Day to Memorial Library: The South Chicago Branch Library as Cultural Terrain, 1937–1947." *Libraries and the Cultural Record* 46, no. 3 (2011): 321–42.

Latimer, Catherine Allen. "Where Can I Get Material on the Negro." *The Crisis* 41, no. 6 (June 1934): 164–65.

Lee, Mollie Huston. "Development of Negro Libraries in North Carolina." *North Carolina Libraries* 3, no. 2 (May 1944): 1–3, 7.

——. "Securing a Branch Library." *Opportunity* 17, no. 9 (September 1939): 260–61.

Levy, Ferdinand. *Flashes from the Dark*. Dublin: Sign of the Three Candles, 1941.

Lewis, David Levering. *When Harlem Was in Vogue*. 1981. Reprint, New York: Penguin, 1997.

Lewis, Earl. " 'To Turn as on a Pivot': Writing African Americans into a History of Overlapping Diasporas." *American Historical Review* 100, no. 3 (June 1995): 765–87.

Library Company of Philadelphia. *Afro-Americana 1553–1906: A Catalog of the Holdings of the Library Company of Philadelphia and the Historical Society of Pennsylvania*. Boston: Hall, 1973.

Library of Congress. *The Card Catalog: Books, Cards, and Literary Treasures*. San Francisco, CA: Chronicle Books, 2017.

——. *Classification: Class E–F America*. 2nd ed. Washington, DC: Government Printing Office, 1913.

——. *Classification: Class H: Social Sciences*. 2nd ed. Washington, DC: Government Printing Office, 1920.

——. *Handbook of Card Distribution*. 6th ed. Washington, DC: Government Printing Office, 1925.

——. *The National Union Catalog, Pre-1956 Imprints*. 685 vols. London: Mansell, 1968–1980.

——. *Report of the Librarian of Congress for the Fiscal Year Ending June 30, 1937*. Washington, DC: Government Printing Office, 1937.

——. *Report of the Librarian of Congress for the Fiscal Year Ending June 30, 1946*. Washington, DC: Government Printing Office, 1947.

Lindgren, James M. "Joseph Bryan (1845–1908)." *Dictionary of Virginia Biography*. Rev. ed. Richmond: Library of Virginia, 2018. https://www.lva.virginia.gov/public/dvb/bio.asp?b=Bryan_Joseph_1845-1908.

Lindsay, Arnett G. "Manuscript Materials Bearing on the Negro in America." *Journal of Negro History* 27, no. 1 (1942): 94–101.

Locke, Alain. *The Negro in America*. Chicago: American Library Association, 1933.

——, ed. *The New Negro: An Interpretation*. 1925. Reprint, New York: Simon and Schuster, 1992.

Logan, Rayford W., ed. *What the Negro Wants*. Chapel Hill: University of North Carolina Press, 1944.

Lubin, Maurice A. "An Important Figure in Black Studies: Dr. Dorothy B. Porter." *CLA Journal* 16 (June 1973): 514–18.

Lutenski, Emily. "Arna Bontemps and Black Literary Archives." In *African American Literature in Transition, 1930–1940*, ed. Eve Dunbar and Ayesha K. Hardison, 59–85. Cambridge: Cambridge University Press, 2022.

Lynch, Jack. *You Could Look It Up: The Reference Shelf from Ancient Babylon to Wikipedia*. New York: Bloomsbury, 2016.

Lyons, John F. *Teachers and Reform: Chicago Public Education, 1929–1970*. Urbana: University of Illinois Press, 2008.

M. V. H. "The Clipping File." *Bulletin of the Art Institute of Chicago* 5, no. 2 (October 1911): 27–29.

Maack, Mary Niles. "Towards a History of Women in Librarianship: A Critical Analysis with Suggestions for Further Research." *Journal of Library History* 17 (Spring 1982): 165–85.

Macharia, Keguro. *Frottage: Frictions of Intimacy Across the Black Diaspora*. New York: New York University Press, 2019.

MacLeish, Archibald. *A Time to Speak*. New York: Houghton Mifflin, 1940.

MacLeod, Kirsten. "The 'Librarian's Dream-Prince': Carl Van Vechten and America's Modernist Cultural Archives Industry." *Libraries and the Cultural Record* 46, no. 4 (2011): 360–87.

MacNair, Mary Wilson, ed. *Subject Headings Used in the Dictionary Catalogues of the Library of Congress*. 3rd ed. Washington, DC: Government Printing Office, 1928.

Madison, Avril Johnson, and Dorothy Porter Wesley. "Dorothy Burnett Porter Wesley: Enterprising Steward of Black Culture." *Public Historian* 17, no. 1 (Winter 1995): 15–40.

Manguel, Alberto. *A History of Reading*. New York: Penguin, 2014.

——. *The Library at Night*. New Haven, CT: Yale University Press, 2006.

Manoff, Marlene. "Theories of the Archive from Across the Disciplines." *Portal: Libraries and the Academy* 4, no. 1 (2004): 9–25.

Martin, Thomas P. "Sources of Negro History in the Manuscript Division of the Library of Congress." *Journal of Negro History* 19, no. 1 (January 1934): 72–76.

Mattern, Shannon. "Fugitive Libraries." *Places Journal* (October 2019). https://doi.org/10.22269/191022.

Matthews, Geraldine O., and the African-American Materials Project Staff. *Black American Writers, 1773–1939: A Bibliography and Union List*. Boston: Hall, 1975.

Matthews, Miriam. "Oral History with Miriam Matthews." Interviewed by Robin D. G. Kelley. University of California at Los Angeles, 1985–86. https://oralhistory.library.ucla.edu/catalog/21198-zz00179s7c.

Matthews, Victoria Earle. "The Value of Race Literature: An Address Delivered at the First Congress of Colored Women of the United States at Boston, Mass., July 30, 1895." https://collections.library.yale.edu/catalog/10171940.

Maxwell, William J. *F.B. Eyes: How J. Edgar Hoover's Ghostreaders Framed African American Literature*. Princeton, NJ: Princeton University Press, 2015.

McBrown, Gertrude P. "The Countee Cullen Memorial Collection of Atlanta University." *Negro History Bulletin* 17 (October 1953): 11–13.

McDuffie, Erik S. "Chicago, Garveyism, and the History of the Diasporic Midwest." *African and Black Diaspora* 8, no. 2 (2015): 129–45.

——. *Sojourning for Freedom: Black Women, American Communism, and the Making of Black Left Feminism*. Durham, NC: Duke University Press, 2011.

McGuire, Phillip, ed. *Taps for a Jim Crow Army: Letters from Black Soldiers in World War II*. Lexington: University Press of Kentucky, 1983.

McHenry, Elizabeth. *Forgotten Readers: Recovering the Lost History of African American Literary Societies*. Durham, NC: Duke University Press, 2002.

——. *To Make Negro Literature: Writing, Literary Practice, and African American Authorship*. Durham, NC: Duke University Press, 2021.

McKay, Claude. *Harlem: Negro Metropolis*. New York: Dutton, 1940.

——. *The Passion of Claude McKay: Selected Poetry and Prose, 1912–1948*. Ed. Wayne F. Cooper. New York: Schocken, n.d.

McKinney, Cait. "'Finding the Lines to My People': Media History and Queer Bibliographic Encounter." *GLQ: A Journal of Lesbian and Gay Studies* 24, no. 1 (January 2018): 55–83.

McMurray, Linda O. *Recorder of the Black Experience: A Biography of Monroe Nathan Work*. Baton Rouge: Louisiana State University Press, 1985.

McPheeters, Annie L. *Library Service in Black and White: Some Personal Recollections, 1921–1980*. Metuchen, NJ: Scarecrow, 1988.

Meier, August, and Elliott Rudwick. *Black History and the Historical Profession, 1915–1980*. Urbana: University of Illinois Press, 1986.

Miles, Tiya. *All That She Carried: The Journey of Ashley's Sack, a Black Family Keepsake*. New York: Random House, 2021.

Miller, Monica L. *Slaves to Fashion: Black Dandyism and the Styling of Black Diasporic Identity*. Durham, NC: Duke University Press, 2009.

Minor, Romie. "Preserving the Black Performance for Posterity." *Michigan History Magazine* 99, no. 3 (2015): 50–55.

Mirabal, Nancy Raquel. *Suspect Freedoms: The Racial and Sexual Politics of Cubanidad in New York, 1823–1957*. New York: New York University Press, 2017.

Mitchell, Michele. *Righteous Propagation: African Americans and the Politics of Racial Destiny After Reconstruction*. Chapel Hill: University of North Carolina Press, 2004.

Moore, Ray Nichols. "Mollie Huston Lee: A Profile." *Wilson Library Bulletin* 49, no. 6 (February 1975): 432–39.

Moore, Sean D. *Slavery and the Making of Early American Libraries*. Oxford: Oxford University Press, 2019.

Moorland Foundation. *A Catalogue of Books in the Moorland Foundation, Compiled by Workers on Projects 271 and 328 of the Works Progress Administration*. Washington, DC: Howard University, 1939.

——. *Dictionary Catalog of the Jesse E. Moorland Collection of Negro Life and History, Howard University Library, Washington, D.C.* Boston: Hall, 1970.

Morgan, Jennifer L. "Archives and Histories of Racial Capitalism: An Afterword." *Social Text* 33, no. 4 (2015): 153–61.

Moses, Wilson Jeremiah. *The Golden Age of Black Nationalism, 1850–1925*. New York: Oxford University Press, 1988.

Moten, Fred, and Stefano Harney. *The Undercommons: Fugitive Planning and Black Study*. Wivenhoe, UK: Minor Compositions, 2013.

Mullen, Bill V. *Popular Fronts: Chicago and African-American Cultural Politics, 1935–1946*. Urbana: University of Illinois Press, 1999.

Muñoz, José Esteban. "Ephemera as Evidence: Introductory Notes to Queer Acts." *Women and Performance: A Journal of Feminist Theory* 8, no. 2 (1996): 5–16.

Murray, Daniel. "Bibliographia-Africania." *The Voice of the Negro* 1, no. 5 (May 1904): 186–91.

Myers, Joshua. *Of Black Study*. London: Pluto, 2023.

Nash, Jennifer C. "Black Feminine Enigmas, or Notes on the Politics of Black Feminist Theory." *Signs: Journal of Women in Culture and Society* 45, no. 3 (2020): 519–23.

Natanson, Nicholas, ed. *Index to the Hampton University Newspaper Clipping File*. Alexandria, VA: Chadwyck-Healey, 1988.

Neal, Mark Anthony. *Black Ephemera: The Crisis and Challenge of the Musical Archive*. New York: New York University Press, 2022.

Negro Library Association. *Exhibition Catalogue, First Annual Exhibition of Books, Manuscripts, Paintings, Engravings, Sculptures, Et Cetera by The Negro Library Association*. New York: Pool Press Association, 1918.

"The Negro Society for Historical Research." *African Times and Orient Review*, Christmas Annual, 1912.

Négron-Muntaner, Frances. "'Here Is the Evidence': Arturo Alfonso Schomburg's Black Countervisuality." *African American Review* 54, nos. 1–2 (Spring/Summer 2021): 49–71.

Nell, William Cooper. *William Cooper Nell: Nineteenth-Century African American Abolitionist, Historian, Integrationist, Selected Writings, 1832–1874*. Ed. Dorothy Porter Wesley and Constance Porter Uzelac. Baltimore, MD: Black Classic Press, 2002.

Nesmith, Tom. "The Concept of Societal Provenance and Records of Nineteenth-Century Aboriginal-European Relations in Western Canada: Implications for Archival Theory and Practice." *Archival Science* 6 (2006): 351–60.

"The New Schomburg Center for Research in Black Culture." *Crisis* 90, no. 2 (February 1983): 28–9.

New York Public Library. "Arturo (Arthur) Schomburg Research Guide: Schomburg's Library." https://libguides.nypl.org/arturoschomburg/library.

——. *Report of the New York Public Library for 1926*. New York: New York Public Library, 1927.

——. *Report of the New York Public Library for 1927*. New York: New York Public Library, 1928.

——. *Report of the New York Public Library for 1928*. New York: New York Public Library, 1929.

Newman, Richard. *Black Access: A Bibliography of Afro-American Bibliographies*. Westport, CT: Greenwood, 1984.

Norton-Wisla, Lotus. "Freedom Summer Digital Collection at Wisconsin Historical Society." *Primary Source* 33, no. 1 (Summer 2014): 1–6.

Novotny, Eric. "From Inferno to Freedom: Censorship in the Chicago Public Library, 1910–1936." *Library Trends* 63, no. 1 (2014): 27–41.

Nugent, Richard Bruce. *Gay Rebel of the Harlem Renaissance: Selections from the Work of Richard Bruce Nugent*. Ed. Thomas H. Wirth. Durham, NC: Duke University Press, 2002.

Nunes, Zita. *Cannibal Democracy: Race and Representation in the Literature of the Americas*. Minneapolis: University of Minnesota Press, 2008.

Olson, Hope A. "Mapping Beyond Dewey's Boundaries: Constructing Classificatory Space for Marginalized Knowledge Domains." *Library Trends* 47, no. 2 (1998): 233–54.

Olson, Liesl. *Chicago Renaissance: Literature and Art in the Midwest Metropolis*. New Haven, CT: Yale University Press, 2017.

——. "Richard Wright's Chicago." In *Richard Wright in Context*, ed. Michael Nowlin, 22–33. Cambridge: Cambridge University Press, 2021.

O'Reilly, Ted. "Dorothy B. Porter, a Library Hero." New York Historical Society, April 8, 2021. https://www.nyhistory.org/blogs/dorothy-b-porter-a-library-hero.

Ortiz, Victoria, ed. *The Legacy of Arthur Schomburg: A Celebration of the Past, a Vision for the Future*. New York: New York Public Library, 1986.

Osborne, Nicholas. "'The Unwritten History': Alexander Gumby's African America." Columbia University Libraries exhibition, 2012. https://exhibitions.library.columbia.edu/exhibits/show/gumby.

O'Toole, James. *Understanding Archives and Manuscripts*. Chicago: Society of American Archivists, 1990.

Ott, Katherine. *Fevered Lives: Tuberculosis in American Culture Since 1870*. Cambridge, MA: Harvard University Press, 1996.

——. "It's a Scrapbook Life: Using Ephemera to Reconstruct the Everyday of Medical Practice." *Watermark* 20, no. 1 (Winter 1996): 1–7.

Painter, Nell Irvin. *Exodusters: Black Migration to Kansas After Reconstruction*. New York: Norton, 1992.

Palumbo-Liu, David. "Universalisms and Minority Culture." *Differences: A Journal of Feminist Cultural Studies* 7, no. 1 (Spring 1995): 188–208.

Papailias, Penelope. *Genres of Recollection: Archival Poetics and Modern Greece*. New York: Palgrave Macmillan, 2005.

Park, Martha. "Even the Dead Could Not Stay." Citylab.com, January 19, 2018. citylab.com/equity/2018/01/even-the-dead-could-not-stay/550838.

Parker, Wyman W. "How Can the Archivist Aid the Researcher?" *American Archivist* 16, no. 3 (July 1953): 233–40.

Patterson, Tiffany Ruby. *Zora Neale Hurston and a History of Southern Life*. Philadelphia: Temple University Press, 2005.

Pawley, Christine. *Organizing Women: Home, Work, and the Institutional Infrastructure of Print in Twentieth-Century America*. Amherst: University of Massachusetts Press, 2022.

Payne, Charles, and Adam Green, eds. *Time Longer Than Rope: A Century of African American Activism, 1850–1950*. New York: New York University, 2003.

Pearce, Susan M. *On Collecting: An Investigation into Collecting in the European Tradition*. London: Routledge, 1999.

Peiss, Kathy. *Information Hunters: When Librarians, Soldiers, and Spies Banded Together in World War II Europe*. New York: Oxford University Press, 2020.

Peña, Lorgia García. *Translating Blackness: Latinx Colonialities in Global Perspective*. Durham: Duke University Press, 2022.

Perry, Jeffrey B. *Hubert Harrison: The Voice of Harlem Radicalism, 1883–1918*. New York: Columbia University Press, 2009.

Pettee, Julia. *Subject Headings: The History and Theory of the Alphabetical Subject Approach to Books*. New York: Wilson, 1946.

Philip, M. NourbeSe. *Zong!* Middletown, CT: Wesleyan University Press, 2008.

Phillips, Kimberly L. *War! What Is It Good For? Black Freedom Struggles and the U.S. Military from World War II to Iraq*. Chapel Hill: University of North Carolina Press, 2012.

Piñeiro de Rivera, Flor, ed. *Arthur Alfonso Schomburg: A Puerto Rican's Quest for His Black Heritage*. San Juan: Centro de Estudios Avanzados de Puerto Rico y el Caribe, 1989.

Pisciotta, Henry. "The Library in Art's Crosshairs." *Art Documentation* 35 (2016): 2–26.

Plummer, Brenda Gayle. *Rising Wind: Black Americans and U.S. Foreign Affairs, 1935–1960*. Chapel Hill: University of North Carolina Press, 1996.

Poole, Alex H. "'Could My Dark Hands Break Through the Dark Shadow?': Gender, Jim Crow, and Librarianship During the Long Freedom Struggle, 1935–1955." *Library Quarterly* 88, no. 4 (October 2018): 348–74.

Porter, Dorothy B. *Afro-Braziliana: A Working Bibliography*. Boston: Hall, 1978.

——. "Bibliography and Research in Afro-American Scholarship." *Journal of Academic Librarianship* 2, no. 2 (1976): 77–81.

——. "Documentation on the Afro-American: Familiar and Less Familiar Sources." *African Studies Bulletin* 12, no. 3 (December 1969): 293–303.

——. "The Librarian and the Scholar: A Working Partnership." In *Proceedings of the Institute on Materials By and About the American Negro*, 71–80. Atlanta: Atlanta University School of Librarianship, 1967.

——. "A Library on the Negro." *American Scholar* 7 (Winter 1938): 115–17.

——. "Library Sources for the Study of Negro Life and History." *Journal of Negro Education* 5, no. 2 (April 1936): 232–44.

——. "The Organized Educational Activities of Negro Literary Societies, 1828–1846." *Journal of Negro Education* 5, no. 4 (October 1936): 555–76.

——. "Padre Domingos Caldas Barbosa: Afro-Brazilian Poet." *Phylon* 12, no. 3 (Third Quarter 1951): 264–71.

——. *A Selected List of Books By and About the Negro*. Washington, DC: Government Printing Office, 1936.

Powell, Chaitra, Holly Smith, Shanee' Murrain, and Skyla Hearn. "This [Black] Woman's Work: Exploring Archival Projects That Embrace the Identity of the Memory Worker." *KULA: Knowledge Creation, Dissemination, and Preservation Studies* 2, no. 1 (2018): 1–8.

Power-Greene, Ousmane K. *Against Wind and Tide: The African American Struggle Against the Colonization Movement*. New York: New York University Press, 2014.

Pressman, Jessica. *Bookishness: Loving Books in a Digital Age*. New York: Columbia University Press, 2020.

Pyne, Charlynn Spencer. "Remembering Vintage Years: Historian Franklin Discusses Life and Career." *Library of Congress Information Bulletin* 60, no. 10 (October 2001). https://www.loc.gov/loc/lcib/0110/index.html.

Quarles, Benjamin. "Black History Unbound." *Daedalus* 103, no. 2 (Spring 1974): 163–78.

Raboteau, Albert J., David W. Wills, Randall K. Burkett, Will B. Gravely, and James Melvin Washington. "Retelling Carter Woodson's Story: Archival Sources for Afro-American Church History." *Journal of American History* 77, no. 1 (June 1990): 183–99.

Reanimate Collective. "Fredi Washington: A Reader in Black Feminist Media Criticism," 2022. http://editions.reanimatepublishing.org/projects/fredi-washington.

Reddick, L. D. "Africa Speaks." *Opportunity* 20, no. 7 (July 1942): 205–6.

——. "Bibliographical Problems in Negro Research." *American Council of Learned Societies Bulletin* 32 (September 1941): 26–30.

——. *Crusader Without Violence: A Biography of Martin Luther King, Jr.* New York: Harper, 1959.

——. "Educational Programs for the Improvement of Race Relations: Motion Pictures, Radio, The Press, and Libraries." *Journal of Negro Education* 13, no. 3 (Summer 1944): 367–89.

——. "The Honor Roll in Race Relations." *Bulletin of the New York Public Library* 47, no. 12 (December 1943). 872–73.

——. "The Negro in the United States Navy During World War II." *Journal of Negro History* 32, no. 2 (April 1947): 201–19.

——. "A New Interpretation for Negro History." *Journal of Negro History* 22, no. 1 (January 1937): 17–28.

——. "The Relative Status of the Negro in the American Armed Forces." *Journal of Negro Education* 22, no. 3 (Summer 1953): 380–87.

——. "Scholarship and Candor." *Journal of Negro Education* 13, no. 2 (Spring 1944): 191–94.

——. "What the Northern Negro Thinks About Democracy." *Journal of Educational Sociology* 17, no. 5 (January 1944): 296–306.

——. "Where Can a Southern Negro Read a Book." *New South* 9, no. 1 (January 1954): 5–11.

Reed, Christopher Robert. *The Depression Comes to the South Side: Protest and Politics in the Black Metropolis, 1930–1933*. Bloomington: Indiana University Press, 2011.

——. *The Rise of Chicago's Black Metropolis, 1920–1929*. Urbana: University of Illinois Press, 2011.

Reeves, Caitlin. "Red Brick and Stone: Atlanta's Pragmatic Civil Rights and the Auburn Avenue Library, 1899–1950." Master's thesis, Simmons College, 2016.

Reeves, Jay. "Alabama Archives Faces Its Legacy as Confederate 'Attic.'" *AP News*, September 21, 2020.

Reichard-De Cardona, Haydée E. *Arturo Alfonso Schomburg: Racial Identity and Afro-Caribbean Cultural Formation*. Aguadilla, PR: printed by the author, 2023.

Retman, Sonnet. *Real Folks: Race and Genre in the Great Depression*. Durham, NC: Duke University Press, 2011.

Rhodes-Pitts, Sharifa. *Harlem Is Nowhere: A Journey to the Mecca of Black America*. New York: Little, Brown, 2011.

Richards, Thomas. *The Imperial Archive: Knowledge and the Fantasy of Empire*. New York: Verso, 1993.

Rifkin, Libbie. "Association/Value: Creative Collaborations in the Library." *RBM: A Journal of Rare Books, Manuscripts, and Cultural Heritage* 2, no. 2 (Fall 2001): 123–39.

Roark, James L. "American Black Leaders: The Response to Colonialism and the Cold War, 1943–1953." *African Historical Studies* 4, no. 2 (1971): 253–70.

Robertson, Craig. *The Filing Cabinet: A Vertical History of Information*. Minneapolis: University of Minnesota Press, 2021.

——. "Learning to File: Reconfiguring Information and Information Work in the Early Twentieth Century." *Technology and Culture* 58, no. 4 (October 2017): 955–81.

Rocksborough-Smith, Ian. *Black Public History in Chicago: Civil Rights Activism from World War II Into the Cold War*. Urbana: University of Illinois Press, 2018.

Roffman, Karin. *From the Modernist Annex: American Women Writers in Museums and Libraries*. Tuscaloosa: University of Alabama Press, 2010.

——. "Nella Larsen, Librarian at 135th Street." *Modern Fiction Studies* 53, no. 4 (Winter 2007): 752–87.

Rogers, J. A. "Arthur Schomburg, The Sherlock Holmes of Negro History." *Richmond Planet*, July 5, 1930.

Rollins, Charlemae. "Library Work with Negroes." *Illinois Libraries* 25, no. 2 (February 1943): 92–94.

Rose, Ernestine. "Books and the Negro." *Library Journal* 52 (November 1927): 1012–14.

——. "Work with Negroes Round Table." *Bulletin of the American Library Association* 16, no. 4 (July 1922): 361–66.

Rosenberg, Daniel. "Stop, Words." *Representations* 127 (2014): 83–92.

Ross, Andrew. "Production." *Social Text* 27, no. 3 (2009): 199–202.

Rowe-Sims, Sarah, Sandra Boyd, and H. T. Holmes. "Balancing Privacy and Access: Opening the Mississippi State Sovereignty Commission Records." In *Privacy and Confidentiality Perspectives: Archivists and Archival Records*, ed. Peter J. Wosh, 159–74. Chicago: Society of American Archivists, 2005.

Rushing, Naomi J. "The Technical Organizing of Special Collections of Books By and About the Negro." Master's thesis, Columbia University, 1940.

Salzman, Jack, David Lionel Smith, and Cornel West, eds. *Encyclopedia of African-American Culture and History*. Vol. 1. New York: Macmillan, 1996.

Sampson, Henry T. *Blacks in Blackface: A Sourcebook*. Metuchen, NJ: Scarecrow, 1980.

Samuels, Helen Willa. "Who Controls the Past." *American Archivist* 49, no. 2 (Spring 1986): 109–124.

Sánchez González, Lisa. *Boricua Literature: A Literary History of the Puerto Rican Diaspora*. New York: New York University Press, 2010.

Sartorius, David. *Ever Faithful: Race, Loyalty, and the Ends of Empire in Spanish Cuba*. Durham, NC: Duke University Press, 2014.

Saunders, Patricia. "Defending the Dead, Confronting the Archive: A Conversation with M. NourbeSe Philip." *Small Axe* 12, no. 2 (June 2008): 63–79.

Savage, Barbara Dianne. *Broadcasting Freedom: Radio, War, and the Politics of Race, 1938–1948*. Chapel Hill: University of North Carolina Press, 1999.

Scandura, Jani. *Down in the Dumps: Place, Modernity, American Depression*. Durham, NC: Duke University Press, 2008.

Scarupa, Harriet Jackson. "The Energy-Charged Life of Dorothy Porter Wesley." *New Directions*, January 1990, 6–17.

Schlabach, Elizabeth Schroeder. *Along the Streets of Bronzeville: Black Chicago's Literary Landscape*. Urbana: University of Illinois Press, 2013.

Schomburg, Arthur A. "An Appreciation." In *Phillis Wheatley: Poems and Letters*, ed. Charles F. Heartman, 7–19. New York: Heartman, 1915.

——. "The Negro Digs Up His Past." *Survey Graphic* 6, no. 6 (March 1925): 670–72.

——. "Racial Integrity: A Plea for the Establishment of a Chair of Negro History in Our Schools and Colleges, Etc.," Negro Society for Historical Research Occasional Paper No. 3. August Valentine Bernier, 1913.

——. "Two Negro Missionaries to the American Indians, John Marrant and John Stewart." *Journal of Negro History* 21, no. 4 (October 1936): 394–405.

Schomburg Center for Research in Black Culture. *Index to the Schomburg Clipping File*. Alexandria, VA: Chadwyck-Healey, 1986.

——. *The Kaiser Index to Black Resources, 1948–1986*. Brooklyn, NY: Carlson, 1992.

Schomburg Collection of Negro Literature and History. *Dictionary Catalog of the Schomburg Collection of Negro Literature and History*. 9 vols. Boston: Hall, 1962.

"Schomburg's Ailing Collection." *Ebony*, October 1967.

Schultz, Rima Lunin, and Adele Hast, eds. *Women Building Chicago, 1790–1990: A Biographical Dictionary*. Bloomington: Indiana University Press, 2001.

Schwarz, A. B. Christa. *Gay Voices of the Harlem Renaissance*. Bloomington: Indiana University Press, 2003.

Scott, David. "Introduction: On the Archaeologies of Black Memory." *Small Axe* 12, no. 2 (June 2008): v–xvi.

——. "On the Very Idea of a Black Radical Tradition." *Small Axe* 17, no. 1 (March 2013): 1–6.

Writers' Program of the Works Progress Administration in the State of Illinois. *Selected Bibliography, Illinois, Chicago and Its Environs*. Chicago: Federal Writers' Project Illinois, Works Progress Administration, 1937.

Seraile, William. *Bruce Grit: The Black Nationalist Writings of John Edward Bruce*. Knoxville: University of Tennessee Press, 2003.

Settle, George T. "Work with Negroes Roundtable." *Bulletin of the American Library Association* 17, no. 4 (1923): 274–79.

Shareef, Reginald. *The Roanoke Valley's African American Heritage: A Pictorial History*. Virginia Beach: Donning, 1996.

Sharpe, Jenny. *Immaterial Archives: An African Diaspora Poetics of Loss.* Chicago: Northwestern University Press, 2020.

Shaw, Stephanie J. *What a Woman Ought to Be and to Do: Black Professional Women Workers During the Jim Crow Era.* Chicago: University of Chicago Press, 1996.

Shockley, Ann Allen. "Special Collections, Fisk University Library," *Library Quarterly* 58, no. 2 (April 1988): 151–63.

Shores, Louis. "Library Service and the Negro." *Journal of Negro Education* 1, nos. 3/4 (October 1932): 374–80.

"Silk Playbill." Victoria and Albert Museum, May 8, 2007. https://collections.vam.ac.uk/item/O134502/silk-playbill/.

Sims-Wood, Janet. *Dorothy Porter Wesley at Howard University: Building a Legacy of Black History.* Charleston, SC: History Press, 2014.

Singh, Nikhil Pal. *Black Is a Country: Race and the Unfinished Struggle for Democracy.* Cambridge, MA: Harvard University Press, 2005.

Sinitiere, Phillip Luke. "'An Impressive Basis for Research': Arna Bontemps' Co-Creation of the W. E. B. Du Bois Collection at Fisk University." *Black Scholar* 52, no. 2 (2022): 50–62.

Sinnette, Elinor Des Verney. *Arthur Alfonso Schomburg: Black Bibliophile and Collector.* New York: New York Public Library and Wayne State University Press, 1989.

Sinnette, Elinor Des Verney, W. Paul Coates, and Thomas C. Battle, eds. *Black Bibliophiles and Collectors: Preservers of Black History.* Washington, DC: Howard University Press, 1990.

Sites, William. *Sun Ra's Chicago: Afrofuturism and the City.* Chicago: University of Chicago Press, 2020.

Slaughter, Adolph J. "The Historian Who Never Wrote." *Chicago Daily Defender*, August 29, 1960.

Smethurst, James. *The African American Roots of Modernism: From Reconstruction to the Harlem Renaissance.* Chapel Hill: University of North Carolina Press, 2011.

Smith, Arthur L. "Review of the Johnson Reprint Series." *Journal of Black Studies* 1, no. 3 (March 1971): 374–76.

Smith, Barbara. "A Press of Our Own Kitchen Table: Women of Color Press." *Frontiers: A Journal of Women Studies* 10, no. 3 (1989): 11–13.

Smith, Bonnie G. *The Gender of History: Men, Women, and Historical Practice.* Cambridge, MA: Harvard University Press, 2000.

Smith, Jessie Carney. *Black Academic Libraries and Research Collections: An Historical Survey.* Westport, CT: Greenwood, 1977.

——. "Developing Collections of Black Literature." *Black World* 20, no. 8 (June 1971): 18–29.

——. "Special Collections of Black Literature in the Traditionally Black College." *College and Research Libraries* 35, no. 5 (September 1974): 322–35.

Smith, Shawn Michelle. *American Archives: Gender, Race, and Class in Visual Culture.* Princeton, NJ: Princeton University Press, 1999.

Somerville, Siobhan B. *Queering the Color Line: Race and the Invention of Homosexuality in American Culture.* Durham, NC: Duke University Press, 2000.

Sontag, Susan. *Illness as Metaphor.* New York: Farrar, Straus and Giroux, 1978.

Southey, Thomas. *Chronological History of the West Indies.* Vol. 1. London: Longman, Rees, Orme, Brown, and Green, 1827.

Spady, James G. "The Afro-American Historical Society: The Nucleus of Black Bibliophiles, (1897–1913)." *Negro History Bulletin* 37, no. 4 (July 1974): 254–57.

Speer, Lisa K. "Mississippi's 'Spy Files': The State Sovereignty Commission Records Controversy, 1977–1999." *Provenance* 17 (1999): 101–16.

Spingarn, Arthur B. "Collecting a Library of Negro Literature." *Journal of Negro Education* 17, no. 1 (January 1938): 12–18.

Spires, Derrick S. "African American Print Culture." In *American Literature in Transition, 1820–1860*, ed. Justine S. Murison, 211–34. New York: Cambridge University Press, 2022.

——. "Order and Access: Dorothy Porter and the Mission of Black Bibliography." *Papers of the Bibliographical Society of America* 116, no. 2 (June 2022): 255–75.

Springer, Anna-Sophie and Etienne Turpin, eds. *Fantasies of the Library*. Rev. ed. Cambridge, MA: MIT Press, 2016.

Stam, David H., ed. *International Dictionary of Library Histories*. Vol. 1. Chicago: Fitzroy Dearborn, 2001.

Steedman, Carolyn. *Dust: The Archive and Cultural History*. New Brunswick, NJ: Rutgers University Press, 2002.

Stewart, Catherine A. *Long Past Slavery: Representing Race in the Federal Writers' Project*. Chapel Hill: University of North Carolina Press, 2016.

Stewart, Jeffrey C., and Fath Davis Ruffins. "A Faithful Witness: Afro-American Public History in Historical Perspective, 1828–1984." In *Presenting the Past: Essays on History and the Public*, ed. Susan Porter Benson, Stephen Brier, and Roy Rosenzweig, 307–36. Philadelphia: Temple University Press, 1986.

Stewart, Susan. *On Longing: Narratives of the Miniature, the Gigantic, the Souvenir, the Collection*. Durham, NC: Duke University Press, 1993.

Stoler, Ann Laura. *Along the Archival Grain: Epistemic Anxieties and Colonial Common Sense*. Princeton, NJ: Princeton University Press, 2010.

——. "Colonial Archives and the Arts of Governance." *Archival Science* 2 (2002): 87–109.

Sutherland, Tonia. "Archival Amnesty: In Search of Black American Transitional and Restorative Justice." *Journal of Critical Library and Information Studies* 1, no. 2 (2017): 1–23. https://doi.org/10.24242/jclis.v1i2.42.

Tate, Claudia. "Audre Lorde." In *Conversations with Audre Lorde*, ed. Joan Wylie Hall. Jackson: University of Mississippi Press, 2004.

Taylor, Ula. "Women in the Documents: Thoughts on Uncovering the Personal, Political, and Professional." *Journal of Women's History* 20, no. 1 (Spring 2008): 187–96.

Theoharis, Athan G. "The FBI and the FOIA: Problems of Access and Destruction." *Midwestern Archivist* 5, no. 2 (1981): 61–74.

Thistlethwaite, Polly J. "Building 'A Home of Our Own': The Construction of the Lesbian Herstory Archives." In *Daring to Find Our Names: The Search for Lesbigay Library History*, ed. James V. Carmichael Jr., 153–74. Westport, CT: Greenwood, 1998.

Thomas, Deborah A. *Political Life in the Wake of the Plantation: Sovereignty, Witnessing, Repair*. Durham, NC: Duke University Press, 2019.

Tibbets, Celeste. "Ernestine Rose and the Origins of the Schomburg Center." Schomburg Center Occasional Papers Series, no. 2. New York: New York Public Library, 1989.

Towner, Isabel L., comp. *Classification Schemes and Subject Headings Lists: Loan Collection of Special Libraries Association*. Rev. ed. New York: Special Libraries Association, 1949.

Trouillot, Michel-Rolph. *Silencing the Past: Power and the Production of History*. Boston: Beacon, 1995.

Tucker, Susan, Katherine Ott, and Patricia P. Buckler, eds. *The Scrapbook in American Life*. Philadelphia: Temple University Press, 2006.

Turner, John Mack, ed. *Untold Stories: Civil Rights, Libraries, and Black Librarianship*. Champaign, IL: Graduate School of Library and Information Science, 1998.

Tyler, Lyon Gardiner, ed. *Encyclopedia of Virginia Biography*. Vol. 4. New York: Lewis Historical Publishing, 1915.

Unger, Mary I. "Selling the Black Chicago Renaissance: Bronzeville's Black-Owned Bookstores." *Chicago Review of Books*, April 14, 2021.

U.S. Congress, House of Representatives, Special Committee on Un-American Activities. *Investigation of Un-American Propaganda Activities in the United States, Appendix—Part IX Communist Front Organizations*. Washington, DC: Government Printing Office, 1944.

U.S. House of Representatives, Hearings Before the Committee on Un-American Activities. *Testimony of Walter S. Steele Regarding Communist Activities in the United States*. Washington, DC: Government Printing Office, 1947.

Valdés, Vanessa K. *Diasporic Blackness: The Life and Times of Arturo Alfonso Schomburg*. Albany, NY: SUNY University Press, 2018.

Valentine, Patrick. "Mollie Huston Lee: Founder of Raleigh's Public Black Library." *North Carolina Libraries* 56, no. 1 (Spring 1998): 23–26.

Van Jackson, Wallace. "Negro Library Workers." *Library Quarterly* 10, no. 1 (January 1940): 95–108.

Van Slyck, Abigail A. *Free to All: Carnegie Libraries and American Culture, 1890–1920*. Chicago: University of Chicago Press, 1995.

Van Vechten, Carl. "The J. W. Johnson Collection at Yale." *The Crisis* 49, no. 7 (July 1942): 222–26.

Varel, David A. *The Scholar and the Struggle: Lawrence Reddick's Crusade for Black History and Black Power*. Durham, NC: University of North Carolina Press, 2021.

Vogel, Shane. *The Scene of the Harlem Cabaret: Race, Sexuality, Performance*. Chicago: University of Chicago Press, 2009.

——. "The Sensuous Harlem Renaissance: Sexuality and Queer Culture." In *A Companion to the Harlem Renaissance*, ed. Cherene Sherrard-Johnson, 267–83. Malden, MA: Wiley-Blackwell, 2015.

Von Eschen, Penny. *Race Against Empire: Black Americans and Anticolonialism, 1937–1957*. Ithaca, NY: Cornell University Press, 1997.

Wagner, Bryan. *Disturbing the Peace: Black Culture and the Police Power After Slavery*. Cambridge, MA: Harvard University Press, 2009.

Wall, Cheryl A. "On Collectors and Collecting: The Joanna Banks Collection." Keynote address at the Black Women Writing Across Genres in the Late 20th Century Symposium, University of Pennsylvania, Philadelphia, PA, February 20, 2020.

Wallace, Maurice O. "Framing the Black Soldier: Image, Uplift, and the Duplicity of Pictures." In *Pictures and Progress: Early Photography and the Making of African American Identity*, ed. Maurice O. Wallace and Shawn Michelle Smith, 244–66. Durham, NC: Duke University Press, 2012.

Walrond, Eric D. "Visit to Arthur Schomburg's Library Brings Out Wealth of Historical Information." *Negro World*, April 22, 1922.

Walters, Wendy W. *Archives of the Black Atlantic: Reading Between Literature and History*. London: Routledge, 2013.

Warner, Michael. "Publics and Counterpublics." *Public Culture* 14, no. 1 (Winter 2002): 49–90.

Washington, Mary Helen. *The Other Blacklist: The African American Literary and Cultural Left of the 1950s*. New York: Columbia University Press, 2015.

Wasserman, Sarah. *The Death of Things: Ephemera and the American Novel*. Minneapolis: University of Minnesota Press, 2020.

Watkins-Owens, Irma. *Blood Relations: Caribbean Immigrants and the Harlem Community, 1900–1930*. Bloomington: Indiana University Press, 1996.

Webb, Constance. *Richard Wright: A Biography*. New York: Putnam's, 1968.

Welburn, William C. "To 'Keep the Past in Lively Memory': William Carl Bolivar's Efforts to Preserve African American Cultural Heritage." *Libraries and the Cultural Record* 42, no. 2 (2007): 165–79.

Wesley, Charles H. "Creating and Maintaining an Historical Tradition." *Journal of Negro History* 49 (January 1964): 13–33.

West, E. James. *Ebony Magazine and Lerone Bennett Jr.: Popular Black History in Postwar America*. Urbana: University of Illinois Press, 2020.

White, Deborah Gray. "Mining the Forgotten: Manuscript Sources for Black Women's History." *Journal of American History* 74, no. 1 (June 1987): 237.

——. "Private Lives, Public Personae: A Look at Early Twentieth-Century African American Clubwomen." In *Talking Gender: Public Images, Personal Journeys, and Political Critiques*, ed. Nancy Hewitt, Jean O'Barr, and Nancy Rosebaugh, 106–23. Chapel Hill: University of North Carolina Press, 1996.

——. *Telling Histories: Black Women Historians in the Ivory Tower*. Chapel Hill: University of North Carolina Press, 2008.

——. *Too Heavy a Load: Black Women in Defense of Themselves, 1894–1994*. New York: Norton, 1999.

White, Walter. *A Rising Wind*. Garden City, NY: Doubleday, 1945.

Whitesell, David, Lauren B. Hewes, and Thomas Knoles. *In Pursuit of a Vision: Two Centuries of Collecting at the American Antiquarian Society*. Worcester, MA: American Antiquarian Society, 2012.

Whitmire, Ethelene. *Regina Anderson Andrews: Harlem Renaissance Librarian*. Urbana: University of Illinois Press, 2014.

Wiegand, Wayne A., and Shirley A. Wiegand. *The Desegregation of Public Libraries in the Jim Crow South: Civil Rights and Local Activism*. Baton Rouge: Louisiana State University Press, 2018.

Wilkerson, Doxey A. "The Negro School Movement in Virginia: From 'Equalization' to 'Integration.'" *Journal of Negro Education* 29, no. 1 (Winter 1960): 17–29.

Wilkerson, Isabel. *The Warmth of Other Suns: The Epic Story of America's Great Migration*. New York: Vintage, 2011.

Williams, E. C. "Negro Americana." *Howard University Record* 16, no. 6 (1922): 346–47.

Williams, George W. *A History of the Negro Troops in the War of the Rebellion, 1861–1865*. New York: Bergman, 1888.

Williams, Patricia J. "Gathering the Ghosts." *A-Line* 1, nos. 3–4 (2018). https://alinejournal.com/vol-1-no-3-4/gathering-the-ghosts/.

Williams, Stacie, and Steven D. Booth. "Letter from the Editors." Loss/Capture 1 (2020). https://losscaptureproject.cargo.site/Letter-from-the-Editors.

Williams, Zachery R. *In Search of the Talented Tenth: Howard University Public Intellectuals and the Dilemmas of Race, 1926–1970*. Columbia: University of Missouri Press, 2009.

Williamson-Lott, Joy-Ann. "The Battle Over Power, Control, and Academic Freedom at Southern Institutions of Higher Education, 1955–1965." *Journal of Southern History* 79, no. 4 (November 2013): 879–920.

Wilson, Francille Rusan. *The Segregated Scholars: Black Social Scientists and the Creation of Black Labor Studies, 1890–1950*. Charlottesville: University of Virginia Press, 2006.

Wilson, Ivy G. *Specters of Democracy: Blackness and the Aesthetics of Politics in the Antebellum U.S.* New York: Oxford University Press, 2011.

Wilson, Louis R., and Marion A. Milczewski. *Libraries of the Southeast, A Report of the Southeastern States Cooperative Library Survey, 1946–1947*. Chapel Hill: Southeastern Library Association, 1949.

Wilson, Mabel O. *Negro Building: Black Americans in the World of Fairs and Museums*. Berkeley: University of California Press, 2012.

Winston, Michael R. "The Howard University Department of History, 1913–1973." *Negro History Bulletin* 61, nos. 3–4 (1998): 5–31.

——. "Moorland-Spingarn Research Center: A Past Revisited, A Present Reclaimed." *New Directions*, Summer 1974, 20–25.

Wintz, Cary D., and Paul Finkelman, eds. *Encyclopedia of the Harlem Renaissance*. New York: Routledge, 2004.

Wixson, Douglas. *Worker-Writer in America: Jack Conroy and the Tradition of Midwestern Literary Radicalism, 1898–1990*. Urbana: University of Illinois Press, 1994.

Wolcott, Victoria W. *Remaking Respectability: African American Women in Interwar Detroit*. Chapel Hill: University of North Carolina Press, 2001.

Womack, Autumn. "Reprinting the Past/Re-Ordering Black Social Life." *American Literary History* 32, no. 4 (Winter 2020): 775–80.

Woodson, Carter G. "Annual Report of the Director." *Journal of Negro History* 12, no. 4 (October 1927): 567–76.

——. "Ten Years of Collecting and Publishing the Records of the Negro." *Journal of Negro History* 10, no. 4 (October 1925): 598–607.

Work, Monroe N. *Negro Year Book and Annual Encyclopedia of the Negro*. Tuskegee, AL: Tuskegee Normal and Industrial Institute, 1912.

Works Progress Administration in the State of Kentucky. *Libraries and Lotteries: A History of the Louisville Free Public Library*. Cynthiana, KY: Hobson Book, 1944.

Wright, Alex. *Cataloging the World: Paul Otlet and the Birth of the Information Age*. New York: Oxford University Press, 2014.

Wright, Lillian Taylor. "Thomas Fountain Blue, Pioneer Librarian, 1866–1935." Master's thesis, Atlanta University School of Library Service, 1955.

Wright, Richard. *Lawd Today*. New York: Walker, 1963.

——. *Uncle Tom's Children: Five Long Stories*. New York: Harper, 1938.

Yates, JoAnne. *Control Through Communication: The Rise of System in American Management*. Baltimore, MD: Johns Hopkins University Press, 1989.

Yocom, Frances L. *A List of Subject Headings for Books By and About the Negro*. New York: Wilson, 1940.

Young, Kevin. *The Grey Album: On the Blackness of Blackness*. Minneapolis, MN: Graywolf, 2012.

Yust, William F. "What of the Black and Yellow Races?" In *Papers and Proceedings of the Thirty-Fifth Annual Meeting of the American Library Association Held at Katterskill, N.Y., June 23–28, 1913*, 159–67. Chicago: American Library Association, 1913.

INDEX

Italicized page numbers refer to figures

Printed in the USA
CPSIA information can be obtained
at www.ICGtesting.com
LVHW040137071224
798548LV00001B/70

* 9 7 8 0 2 3 1 2 1 2 7 5 5 *